AAT

TECHNICIAN

NVQ Level 4

Unit 10
Drafting Financial Statements
(Accounting practice, industry and commerce)

TEXTBOOK

0939/A99

British Library Cataloguing-in-Publication Data

A catalogue record for this book is available from the British Library.

Published by AT Foulks Lynch Ltd
Number 4
The Griffin Centre
Staines Road
Feltham
Middlesex
TW14 0HS

ISBN 0 7483 4093 9

© AT Foulks Lynch Ltd, 1999

Acknowledgements

CONTENTS

PREFACE - USING THIS TEXTBOOK

This is the new edition of the AAT NVQ textbook for the Revised Standards for Unit 10 – Drafting Financial Statements (Accounting practice, industry and commerce).

The text has been written to cover the Revised Standards in great detail and adopts a brick-building style, building up the knowledge or practical skills required in a carefully constructed manner. Thus at the start of each chapter we identify the underpinning knowledge and understanding or performance criteria covered in that chapter and then list the main topics covered to show how the subject matter is built up.

Our texts are, however, very different from a more traditional style text book. The texts are written in a way that will help you assimilate the information easily and give you plenty of practice at the various techniques involved. The Units require a very practical approach to the various topics and these texts use many simulations and practical examples to illustrate precisely how the various techniques work.

Particular attention has been paid to producing an interactive text that will maintain your interest with a series of carefully designed features.

- **Pathfinder introduction.** Each chapter starts with the relevant part of the Teaching Guide that the chapter specifically addresses. We then show you how the chapter coverage builds on the content of earlier chapters if appropriate, and also outline in some detail how the chapter is structured and what key learning areas are covered.

- **Definitions.** The text clearly defines key words or concepts. The purpose of including these definitions is not that you should learn them - rote learning is not required and is positively harmful. The definitions are included to focus your attention on the point being covered.

- **Brick-building approach.** Each topic is developed slowly and carefully, with clear explanations and illustrations to build your understanding of each technique.

- **Activities.** This text involves you in the learning process with a series of activities designed to arrest your attention and make you concentrate and respond.

- **Step-by-step illustrations.** Where appropriate, we illustrate topics using a step-by-step technique that explains how each part of an operation or answer is performed in a logical way.

- **Conclusions.** Where helpful, the text includes conclusions that summarise important points as you read through the chapter rather than leaving the conclusion to the chapter end. The purpose of this is to summarise concisely the key material that has just been covered so that you can constantly monitor your understanding of the material as you read it.

- **Self test questions.** At the end of each chapter there is a series of self test questions. The purpose of these is to help you revise some of the key elements of the chapter. The answer to each is a paragraph reference, encouraging you to go back and re-read and revise that point.

Complementary workbook

There is a complementary workbook that is designed to be used with this textbook which contains numerous practice questions and simulations which reflect and simulate the workplace environment. These workbooks also contain practice central assessments which will prepare you for the assessment procedures that are part of your course.

UNIT 10: DRAFTING FINANCIAL STATEMENTS (ACCOUNTING PRACTICE, INDUSTRY AND COMMERCE)

UNIT COMMENTARY

What is the unit about?

This unit is concerned with being able to interpret and understand the structure and purpose of financial statements from various organisations. It requires individuals to have a sound understanding of the elements of financial statements and the relationship between them. Individuals must be able to interpret the relationships between the elements of limited company financial statements by using ratio analysis. It also focuses on the drafting of limited company, sole trader and partnership year end financial statements from a trial balance. The job holder has responsibility for ensuring the accounts comply with any relevant domestic standards and legislation and that confidentiality procedures are followed.

Elements contained within this unit are:

ELEMENT: 10.1   INTERPRET FINANCIAL STATEMENTS

ELEMENT: 10.2   DRAFT LIMITED COMPANY, SOLE TRADER AND PARTNERSHIP YEAR END
FINANCIAL STATEMENTS

Content

Chapter where covered in this text

KNOWLEDGE AND UNDERSTANDING

The Business Environment

• An awareness of the elements and purposes of financial statements of different types of organisations (Element 10.1)	1, 2
• The requirements of the legislative and regulatory framework (Elements 10.1 & 10.2)	Throughout
• General legal framework of limited companies, partnerships and sole traders: types of limited companies, obligations of Directors, Partners and Sole Traders in respect of the accounts (Element 10.2)	1, 8
• Forms of equity and loan capital (Element 10.2)	1, 8
• Main requirements of relevant SSAPs, FRSs and other relevant pronouncements and their application to this element (Element 10.2)	10 – 17
• Statutory form of accounting statements: disclosure requirements (Element 10.2)	9
• The presentation of Corporation Tax in financial statements (Element 10.2)	10
• The need to prepare accounts and statements in proper form (Element 10.2)	Throughout

Accounting Techniques

• Form and method of preparation of financial statements (Element 10.2)	3 – 8
• Methods of analysing and interpreting the information contained in financial statements (Elements 10.1 & 10.2)	18
• Application of the general principles of consolidation (Element 10.2)	19 – 22
• Computing and interpreting accounting ratios (Elements 10.1 & 10.2)	18

Accounting Principles and Theory

• Differences between the published accounts of different types of organisations (Element 10.1)	1
• Generally accepted accounting principles and concepts (Elements 10.1 & 10.2)	2

The Organisation

• Understanding that the accounting systems of an organisation are affected by its roles, organisational structure, its administrative systems and procedures and the nature of its business transactions (Elements 10.1 & 10.2)	Throughout

UNIT 10: DRAFTING FINANCIAL STATEMENTS (ACCOUNTING PRACTICE, INDUSTRY AND COMMERCE)

Element 10.1 Interpret financial statements

Content

*Chapter where
covered in
this text*

Performance criteria

i	Identify the general purpose of financial statements used in various organisations	1, 2
ii	Identify elements in financial statements used in various organisations	2
iii	Identify the relationship of elements within financial statements	Throughout
iv	Interpret the relationship between elements of limited company financial statements	18
v	Unusual features or significant issues are identified within financial statements	18
vi	Valid conclusions are drawn from the information contained within financial statements	18
vii	Conclusions and interpretations are clearly presented	18

Range statement

1 **Financial statements:** balance sheet; income statement

2 **Elements:** assets; liabilities; ownership interest; income; expenditure; contribution from owners; distribution to owners; gains and losses

3 **Relationship between elements:** profitability; liquidity; efficient use of resources; financial position

---

Evidence Requirements

- Competence must be demonstrated consistently, over a period of time with evidence being provided from the interpretation of financial statements from a range of different types of organisation.

Sources of Evidence (these are examples of sources of evidence, but candidates and assessors may be able to identify other, appropriate sources)

- **Observed performance eg,**

    - Resolving discrepancies, unusual features or queries
    - Analysing information
    - Presenting interpretations
    - Reporting on key or unusual features in financial statements
    - Reporting on comparative analysis of financial statements

- **Work produced by candidate eg,**

    - Income and expenditure account
    - Profit and loss account
    - Balance sheet

- **Authenticated testimonies from relevant witnesses**

- **Personal accounts of competence eg,**

    - Report of performance

- **Responses to questions**

- **Other sources of evidence to prove competence or knowledge and understanding where it is not apparent from performance eg,**

    - Report
    - Performance in independent assessment
    - Performance in simulation

UNIT 10: DRAFTING FINANCIAL STATEMENTS (ACCOUNTING PRACTICE, INDUSTRY AND COMMERCE)

Element 10.2 Draft limited company, sole trader and partnership year end financial statements

Content	Chapter where covered in this text
Performance criteria	
i Financial statements are accurately drafted from the appropriate information	3 – 9
ii Subsequent adjustments are correctly implemented	3 – 8
iii Draft accounts comply with domestic standards and legislation and, where relevant, partnership agreement	6 – 17, 20, 21
iv A cash flow statement is correctly prepared and interpreted where required	17
v Year end financial statements are presented for approval to the appropriate person in a clear form	Throughout
vi Confidentiality procedures are followed at all times	Throughout
vii The organisation's policies, regulations, procedures and timescales relating to financial statements are observed at all times	Throughout
viii Discrepancies, unusual features or queries are identified and either resolved or referred to the appropriate person	Throughout

Range statement

1 **Financial statements:** profit and loss account; balance sheet; owners capital and current account; cash flow statement; statement of total recognised gains and losses; the supplementary notes required by statute, SSAPs, FRSs or other relevant pronouncements

2 **Domestic standards:** relevant SSAPs; relevant FRSs; other relevant pronouncements

3 **Limited company financial statements:** unitary; consolidated

Evidence Requirements

- Competence must be demonstrated consistently with evidence of performance being provided of year end financial statements including those of a limited company

Sources of Evidence (these are examples of sources of evidence, but candidates and assessors may be able to identify other, appropriate sources)

- **Observed performance eg,**

  - Gathering year end financial data
  - Preparing a financial statement
  - Resolving discrepancies, unusual features or queries
  - Analysing information
  - Presenting interpretations
  - Investigating balances
  - Consulting with staff

- **Work produced by candidate eg,**

  - Profit and loss account
  - Balance sheet
  - Cash flow statement
  - Notes for inclusion in the accounts
  - Fixed asset schedules for inclusion in the accounts
  - Reports of the treatment of contentious issues in the financial statements

- Schedules drawn up to calculate or support entries in notes to the accounts
- Computer enquiries to extract information for inclusion in year end financial statements
- Owner capital and current account
- Statements of total recognised gains and losses
- Notes of historical cost and profit

- **Authenticated testimonies from relevant witnesses**

- **Personal accounts of competence eg,**

  - Report of performance

- **Other sources of evidence to prove competence or knowledge and understanding where it is not apparent from performance eg,**

  - Reports
  - Performance in independent assessment
  - Performance in simulation
  - Responses to verbal questioning

1 FINANCIAL STATEMENTS AND FRAMEWORK

PATHFINDER INTRODUCTION

This chapter covers the following performance criteria and knowledge and understanding.

- Identify the general purpose of financial statements used in various organisations (performance criteria 10.1)
- An awareness of the elements and purposes of financial statements of different types of organisations (knowledge and understanding 10.1)
- Forms of equity and loan capital (knowledge and understanding 10.2)
- General legal framework of limited companies, partnerships and sole traders; types of limited companies, obligations of Directors, Partners and Sole Traders in respect of the accounts (knowledge and understanding 10.2)
- Differences between the published accounts of different types of organisations (knowledge and understanding 10.2)

Putting the chapter in context – learning objectives.

This first chapter serves as an introduction to the types of business entity that will be studied in this study text and the principles underlying, and purposes behind, the preparation of financial statements for each of these types of entity. In order to put the detailed accounting that is to follow in this text into some context the regulatory framework that underlies financial accounting in the UK is also introduced.

At the end of this chapter you should have learned the following topics.

- Definitions of accounting and the various types of entity to which it can apply.
- Identification of the users of financial statements.
- Identification of the desirable qualities of accounting information.
- Understanding the basics of different types of entities capital structures.
- Describing in general the accounting regulatory framework.

---

1 BUSINESS ENTITIES AND ACCOUNTING

1.1 What is accounting?

Definition Accounting can be considered as consisting of two elements, recording transactions and summarising transactions.

RECORDING the transactions of a business provides information for day-to-day management.

For example, sales to customers on credit must be recorded so that statements of account can be sent to the customers and the money due collected.

SUMMARISING the transactions of a period provides information about the performance and position of a business to interested parties at the end of that period.

Two important summary statements produced during the accounting process are:

- a statement showing the profit or loss made by the business in a year. This is usually called the **profit and loss account** or **income statement**.

- a statement showing the position of the business at the end of the year covered by the profit and loss account. This is called the **balance sheet.** It shows all the assets and liabilities of the business and enables users to judge, for example, whether the business is in a sound financial position and able to pay its debts as they fall due.

1.2   Business entities

Businesses can be organised in several ways.

[Definition]   At its simplest, a business is owned and operated by one person with or without employees – a **sole trader.**

The next level of complexity is the **partnership.**

[Definition]   A partnership is where several people jointly own and run the business.

A third type of entity is the **company.**

[Definition]   A company is formed using contributions from what may be thousands of people, each of whom puts in a share of the total money needed to operate the business. These contributors are called the **shareholders** or **members** of the company. They own it, but they often do not participate in the management. The shareholders appoint **directors** to run the company on their behalf.

Companies are almost always **limited** companies. That means that the possible liability of the shareholders for the debts of the company is limited to the amount of money they put in for their share of the business. This limited liability is achieved by counting the company as a completely separate legal entity. The creditors of the company can lay claim to the assets of the company but cannot, except in rare circumstances, get at the personal assets of the shareholders. If a sole trader goes bust, there is no such separation, and all the trader's assets, business and personal, may be sold to raise money to pay creditors.

For all three types of entity the money put up by the individual, the partners or the shareholders is referred to as the business **capital.** The capital structure of different types of business entity will be considered later in this chapter.

1.3   Types of company

There are about one million limited companies in the UK. Most of them are small, with only a few members, most or all of whom are also directors. These are **private** companies.

Larger companies who wish to ask the general public to buy shares are **public** companies. Only a small proportion of the million companies are public companies, and of these only about 3,000 are **listed** or **quoted** on the London Stock Exchange. A Stock Exchange listing means that a company's shares may be bought and sold easily and cheaply using the market created by the Stock Exchange.

Private companies must have the word 'limited' as the last word of their name, and public companies must have the words 'public limited company', abbreviated to 'plc', at the end of their names. This makes it quite clear to those dealing with them that they have a separate legal identity from their members and that consequently the potential assets available to pay creditors are limited to those of the company.

1.4   Availability of accounting information

The financial statements (profit and loss account and balance sheet) of sole traders and partnerships are completely private and are not seen by anyone other than the trader or partners concerned unless they choose to show them to third parties. A trader might, for example, show his financial statements to a bank manager in support of an application for a loan or overdraft.

The financial statements of all companies, public and private, on the other hand, can be published. First of all, every shareholder gets a copy, but in addition they have to be lodged with the **Registrar of Companies**. The Registrar of Companies maintains a file for each company which is open to public inspection, so the lodged financial statements are available to all.

1.5   Public bodies

As well as the various types of business entity that have been mentioned that prepare accounts there are also a variety of non-business, or non profit-making entities, that are also required to keep accounting records and produce financial statements.

> **Definition**   Public bodies are entities that provide a service to the public normally under governmental control.

Public bodies include local government, central government departments and the National Health Service. Such bodies are accountable to the government and to the public to a certain degree and as such must provide accounting information. As these bodies are generally non-profit making then there will not tend to be a profit and loss account produced although an income and expenditure statement may be appropriate. Accounting information for public bodies will tend to centre more upon control of costs and assets and liabilities.

> **Conclusion**   There are a variety of different types of entity that will produce accounting information. The main types of business entity are the sole trader, partnership, private company and public company. There are also non-business entities or public bodies providing a service to the public under government control.

2   THE USERS OF FINANCIAL ACCOUNTS AND STATEMENTS

2.1   Purpose of accounting

> **Definition**   The purpose of accounting is to provide information to users of financial statements.

It is therefore important to determine the needs of the users. A classification of users into user groups for comparison is given below. The user groups for sole trader, partnership and public bodies will tend to be narrower than this.

2.2   Management

Management will be interested in an analysis of revenues and expenses which will provide information which is useful when plans are formulated and decisions made. Once the budget for a business is complete, the accountant can produce figures for what actually happens as the budget period unfolds, so that they can be compared with the budget. Management will also need to know the cost consequences of a particular course of action to aid their decision making.

2.3   Shareholders and potential shareholders

This group includes the investing public at large and the stockbrokers and commentators who advise them. The shareholders should be informed of the manner in which management has used their funds which have been invested in the business. This is a matter of reporting on past events. However, both shareholders and potential shareholders are also interested in the future performance of the business and use past figures as a guide to the future if they have to vote on proposals or decide whether to disinvest.

Financial analysts advising investors such as insurance companies, pension funds, unit trusts and investment trusts are among the most sophisticated users of accounting information, and the company contemplating a take-over bid is yet another type of potential shareholder.

2.4   Employees and their trade union representatives

These use accounting information to assess the potential performance of the business. This information is relevant to the employee, who wishes to discover whether the company can offer him safe employment and promotion through growth over a period of years, and also to the trade unionist, who uses past profits and potential profits in his calculations and claims for higher wages or better conditions. The viability of different divisions of a company is of interest to this group.

2.5   Lenders

This group includes some who have financed the business over a long period by lending money which is to be repaid at the end of a number of years, as well as short-term creditors such as a bank which allows a company to overdraw its bank account for a number of months, and suppliers of raw materials, which permit a company to buy goods from them and pay in, say, four to twelve weeks' time.

Lenders are interested in the security of their loan, so they will look at an accounting statement to ensure that the company will be able to repay on the due date and meet the interest requirements before that date. The amount of cash available and the value of assets which form a security for the debt are of importance to this group. Credit-rating agencies are interested in accounts for similar reasons.

2.6   Government agencies

These use accounting information, either when collecting statistical information to reveal trends within the economy as a whole or, in the case of the Inland Revenue, to assess the profit on which the company's tax liability is to be computed.

2.7   The business contact group

Customers of a business may use accounting data to assess the viability of a company if a long-term contract is soon to be placed. Competitors will also use the accounts for purposes of comparison.

2.8   The public

From time to time other groups not included above may have an interest in the company eg, members of a local community where the company operates, environmental pressure groups, and so on.

| Conclusion | Financial statements serve a wide variety of user groups, who have different interests and also different levels of financial sophistication. This makes it particularly difficult to produce accounts which are intelligible to the layman but comprehensive for the expert. |

2.9   The groups who make use of financial accounting primarily for decision making purposes

All the above groups use the information in order to make decisions but those who make most use of it are shareholders and potential shareholders in deciding whether to continue their investment in the company or to make an investment in the company. Management would also make use of the information for decision making rather than stewardship but it should be appreciated that management have other sources of information which can also be used for decision making.

2.10   The groups who make use of financial accounting primarily for stewardship purposes

The traditional view of shareholders was that they made use of financial accounting information primarily for stewardship purposes but the modern shareholder is more ready to buy and sell shares rather than stick with one company through thick and thin.

Employees, lenders, government agencies, customers and the public primarily use financial information for stewardship purposes.

2.11   The main financial statements available to users

As we saw in section 1.1 above there are two main financial accounting statements.

(a)   **The balance sheet**- a statement of assets and liabilities at a point in time (the balance sheet date). Each asset and liability is valued according to certain accounting conventions.

(Definition)   An asset is any tangible or intangible possession which has value.

(Definition)   Liabilities are the financial obligations of a business eg, to creditors, debenture-holders and, in the case of a bank loan or overdraft, to a bank.

(b)   **The profit and loss account** - This summarises income and expenditure over a period of time; if income exceeds expenditure there is a profit, if vice versa there is a loss. Note that again income and expenditure are measured using accounting conventions.

Note that the balance sheet is a 'position' statement ie, the financial position at a point in time. On the other hand, the profit and loss account is a 'period statement', explaining changes over time.

2.12   The purpose of each of the main financial statements

The function of the balance sheet is to record the assets owned by the business and the liabilities owed by the business at a particular point in time. It satisfies the stewardship needs of users rather than their decision making needs as, for example, if they are creditors, the balance sheet shows the assets which are available to pay off their debts.

The profit and loss account's primary purpose is to show the amount of profit or loss made in an accounting period ie, a period of time. Generally a business exists in order to make profits for its owners. They will make decisions about the future direction of the business based on its current ability to make profits. For non-profit making bodies an income and expenditure account shows similar information but without the reference to profit.

2.13   Non-financial statements

In general the need for historical financial information has been met by company law and accounting standards requiring detailed notes to the profit and loss account and balance sheet. Some non-financial information is contained in two statements which accompany financial statements in a company's corporate report.

- A Chairman's Statement
- A Directors' Report

A Directors' Report is required by company law to be included within the corporate report. Examples of topics that need to be covered are

Principal activities   Give the principal activities of the company together with any changes in those activities during the financial year.

Business review	A fair review of the activities of the company during the year and the position at the end of it.
Post balance sheet events	Important events affecting the company or group which have occurred since the end of the year.
Future developments	An indication of likely future developments in the business.

In practice much of the general information about the business is actually contained in the Chairman's Statement. The Chairman's Statement is not required by law but is generally included in the report of quoted companies. It provides an opportunity to the company, through the Chairman, to explain what has been happening to the business during the year and what the prospects are next year.

2.14   Activity

How useful do you think that the balance sheet and profit and loss account of a company would be to each of the user groups?

Suggest any alternative information that might be useful.

2.15   Activity solution

Management - historical information is of some use to management as they may be able to learn from it. However management are the decision makers and as such require budgets and plans of future costs and revenues as well as historical information in order to take decisions.

Shareholders are likely to be concerned about the current performance of their investment and therefore the balance sheet and profit and loss account is useful to them. However, they may also be interested in the future plans of the company in order to decide whether to remain as investors.

Potential shareholders are likely to be interested in both the historical performance of the company over a number of years as reflected in the profit and loss accounts for those years but also in the future prospects of the organisation.

Employees will have some interest in the historical information provided by the balance sheet and profit and loss account but they will also be interested in the future plans of the company.

Lenders may either be short term lenders such as a bank overdraft or trade creditors, or longer term lenders. Long-term lenders will probably have some form of security over the assets of the business. They will therefore be interested in the balance sheet to the extent that it shows up to date values for the assets and liabilities of the organisation. Both long and short term lenders will be concerned about the short-term cash flow prospects of the organisation and some form of cash flow budget would be of use to them.

Government agencies collecting statistical information will probably find the balance sheet and profit and loss account provide most of the information that they need.

Customers of the business are likely to be interested in the future viability and prospects of the business which are not clear from the balance sheet and profit and loss account.

The public interest in an organisation will depend upon the reason for the interest and the group concerned.

Conclusion   Different types of entity will have to produce different types of accounting records to satisfy the needs of their different types of users.

3   DESIRABLE QUALITIES OF ACCOUNTING INFORMATION

3.1   Introduction

Having defined the uses of financial statements, the problem arises as to what information is useful. Some criteria can be identified. They are listed briefly here.

3.2   Relevance

The information should be relevant to the needs of the users, so that it helps them to evaluate the financial performance of the business and to draw conclusions from it.

Problem - to identify these needs, given the variety of users.

3.3   Understandability

The information should be in a form which is understandable by user groups.

Problems - users have very different levels of financial sophistication; also the very complexity of business transactions makes it difficult to provide adequate disclosure whilst maintaining simplicity.

3.4   Reliability

The information should be of a standard that can be relied upon by external users, so that it is free from error and can be depended upon by users in their decisions.

Problem - the complexities of modern business makes reliability difficult to achieve in all cases.

3.5   Completeness

Accounting statements should show all aspects of the business.

Problem - the only problem this leads to is the resultant volume of the information.

3.6   Lack of bias

Accounting statements should not be biased towards the needs of one user; they should be objective.

Problem - accounts are prepared by one user group, management. The external audit should remove this bias, but some authorities question the effectiveness of the audit in this respect.

3.7   Timeliness

Accounting statements should be published as soon as possible after the year end.

Problem - there is a conflict between this criterion and that of reliability, in that quicker accounts mean more estimates, and hence reduce reliability.

3.8   Comparability

Accounts should be comparable with those of other similar enterprises, and from one period to the next.

Problem - the main problem has been the use of different accounting policies by different enterprises. Accounting standards have reduced, but not eliminated this problem.

3.9   Activity

Consider the characteristics of useful information. Make a list of any pair of characteristics that you feel may not be compatible.

3.10   Activity solution

Relevance and completeness

If the financial statements show all aspects of the business there will be much information that is not relevant to the needs of individual users.

Reliability and timeliness

If the financial statements are to be produced quickly after the year end they may not be totally reliable.

Relevance and timeliness

If financial statements are tailored to the needs of individual users they may take longer to prepare.

Understandability and completeness

If all aspects of the business are to be shown this may make the financial statements less comprehensible.

> **Conclusion**   Financial statements must be useful to the user of the statement if they are to have any point. In order to be useful accounting information must satisfy a number of criteria, some of which are conflicting.

4   CAPITAL STRUCTURES OF ORGANISATIONS

4.1   Introduction

Each of the different types of entity discussed in this chapter have different owners and providers of capital.

> **Definition**   Capital is the money required by a business to fund its activities. This will be largely contributed at the start of the entity's life but may be added to or withdrawn as the entity's life progresses.

Capital can take the form of money paid into the business by the owners of the business or money borrowed from a variety of third parties.

This capital that is paid into the organisation will form an important part of the information provided by a set of financial statements as users of the statements will wish to know how much capital has been provided in order to be able to judge how well it has been used and managed.

4.2   Types of capital

Capital can take the form of either owner's capital or loan capital.

> **Definition**   Owner's capital is the money paid into a business by the owner or owners.

This therefore includes money contributed by a sole trader, by a number of partners, by many thousands of shareholders in a company or by the government for a public body.

> **Definition**   Loan capital is money raised and borrowed from a party external to the entity such as a bank.

Most entities finance their business with a mixture of owner's capital and loan capital.

4.3　Capital structure

> **Definition**　The capital structure of an entity is the way in which that entity is financed by a mix of owner's capital and loan capital of various forms.

Each individual entity will tend to have a different type of capital structure and this will be reflected in some way in the financial statements of the entity as important and useful information.

4.4　Sole trader

A sole trader is the sole owner of a business and therefore the only provider of owner's capital. Sole traders however may also raise loans from banks or other third parties such as friends or relatives.

This capital structure will tend to be shown in two separate places in the sole trader's balance sheet:

- loan capital will be shown as a long term creditor in the top part of the balance sheet along with all of the other assets and liabilities

- the owner's capital will be shown in the bottom part of the balance sheet together with any profits made by the business to date.

4.5　Activity

A sole trader has business net assets totalling £20,000. These are financed partly by a loan of £2,000 from his mother.

The sole trader's capital at the start of the year was £15,000. During the year he made a profit of £6,300 and took drawings out of the business totalling £3,300.

Show the sole trader's summarised balance sheet at the end of the year.

4.6　Activity solution

	£
Net assets	20,000
Less:　Long term loan	(2,000)
	18,000
Financed by:	
Opening capital	15,000
Add:　Profit for the year	6,300
	21,300
Less:　Drawings for the year	(3,300)
	18,000

4.7　Partnerships

A partnership will have a number of owners all of whom have probably contributed different amounts of capital into the business. The partnership may well also raise external capital in the form of loan capital.

As with the sole trader any loan capital will be shown as a long term creditor in the top part of the balance sheet.

The amount of capital contributed by each of the partners into the business will be accounted for in each partner's capital account (see later in this study text). The balance on each partner's capital account shows the total amount of capital that he has contributed to the business and the balance for each individual partner will be listed in the bottom part of the partnership balance sheet.

4.8   Activity

A partnership has business net assets of £20,000 and has received a bank loan of £2,000. The two partners, A and B, each have balances on their capital accounts of £9,000.

Show the partnership's summarised balance sheet.

4.9   Activity solution

	£
Net assets	20,000
Less: long term loan	(2,000)
	18,000
Financed by:	
Capital accounts - A	9,000
B	9,000
	18,000

4.10   Companies

The funds raised from the owners or shareholders in a company are known as share capital. The reason for this is that the capital is divided into shares with a face value that differs from company to company. Some companies have shares with a face value of £1, so a prospective shareholder wishing to invest £1,000 might buy 1,000 £1 shares. Alternatively the shares might be denominated as having a face value of £10 in which case if the investor wishes to invest £1,000 then it will be in 100 £10 shares.

The value of shares will tend not to remain at their face value but to fluctuate depending upon the fortunes of the company. However for accounting purposes the shares will always be recorded at the value at which they are originally issued.

In the financial statements of a company the share capital will be recorded in the bottom part of the company's balance sheet and the value of the shares may be split between the "Ordinary share capital account" and the "Share premium account" (see later chapter in this study text).

Companies may also raise loan finance which will be shown as part of long term creditors in the top part of the company balance sheet.

4.11   Activity

A company has business net assets of £200,000 which are partly financed by debentures (long term loans) of £20,000. The remaining finance for the company came from the issue of 100,000 £1 ordinary shares at their face value. Since incorporation the company has made profits of £80,000.

Show the company's summarised balance sheet.

4.12   Activity solution

	£
Net assets	200,000
Creditors: amounts falling due after more than one year	
Debenture loans	(20,000)
	180,000
Ordinary share capital	100,000
Profit and loss account	80,000
	180,000

4.13   Public bodies

The various types of public bodies will be funded by different elements of government. However the amount of funding is important information and will be shown in the body's list of assets and liabilities.

> **Definition**   A fund can be defined as a separate pool of monetary and other resources established to support specified activities and operated and accounted for independently of other accounting entities.

A fund is therefore an accounting entity in its own right.

> **Definition**   Fund accounting is the preparation of financial statements for an entity which is a fund.

Funds exist primarily because of stewardship.

> **Definition**   Stewardship is the accountability of management for the resources entrusted to it.

A fund indicates that restrictions have been placed on the use of certain resources. For example, a local authority may receive money from central government specifically for the refurbishment of school buildings. The money may not be used for any other purpose, even if the local authority wishes to do so.

Example

Xwell District Council

Xwell District Council operates a number of funds, using fund accounting in all cases. Two examples are:

(a)   The General Fund (GF) covers general expenditure by the Council. It is financed by a levy on residents of the district.

(b)   The Arts Centre Fund (ACF) is used to account for monies being accumulated to finance the construction of a new arts centre for the district. It receives grants from the GF.

The two funds are effectively separate financial statements despite there being one organisation.

General Fund - Operating Statement

	£	£
Income:		
Allocation of proceeds from local levy		80,000
Expenditure:		
General expenditure	73,000	
Donation to Arts Centre Fund	5,000	
		78,000
Surplus for the year		2,000
Balance b/d		8,000
Balance c/d		10,000

General Fund - Balance sheet

	£
Cash	15,000
Less: Amount due to Arts Centre Fund	5,000
	10,000
Represented by:	
Fund balance	10,000

Arts Centre Fund - Statement of changes in fund balance

	£
Donation from General Fund	5,000
Donation from outside source	3,000
Income from investments	4,000
Net change for year	12,000
Balance b/d	40,000
Balance c/d	52,000

Arts Centre Fund - Balance sheet

	£
Investments	43,000
Cash	4,000
Amount due from General Fund	5,000
	52,000
Represented by:	
Fund balance	52,000

The Council would also produce a consolidated balance sheet which is similar to a consolidated balance sheet for a group of companies except that the 'capitals' of each fund remain on the consolidated statement.

Xwell District Council - Consolidated Balance sheet

		£
Cash 15,000 + 4,000		19,000
Investments		43,000
		62,000
Represented by:		
Fund balances		
General Fund		10,000
Arts Centre Fund		52,000
		62,000

Conclusion   Fund accounting has the advantage of identifying the way specific funds are being utilised. Often the use of fund accounting is unavoidable because of the conditions under which finance is made available.

Each type of business entity discussed will have a different type of capital structure due to the availability of finance for the different types of entity. The different types of capital structure also necessitate different balance sheet presentation in order to give useful information to the users of the financial statements. Further details of the balance sheet presentation will be covered later in this study text.

5   THE REGULATORY SYSTEM

5.1   Introduction

Definition   The regulatory framework of accounting is made up of a number of legislative and quasi-legislative influences.

This section provides an overview of these influences which can be listed as

(a)   Company Law
(b)   Accounting Standards issued by the Accounting Standards Board (ASB)
(c)   EC Directives
(d)   The Stock Exchange (dealt with briefly in the chapters on limited company accounts)

The first three are briefly considered below.

5.2   Company law

The regulatory framework of accounting is affected by company law in a number of areas.

(a)   Financial statements of companies must show a 'true and fair view'.

(b)   Accounting standards issued by the ASB are given legal authority as recognised accounting standards.

(c)   Prescribed formats for the profit and loss account and balance sheet are required.

(d)   Detailed disclosures of information are required.

(e)   A company is limited in the amounts of profits it can distribute to its shareholders.

(f)   Various provisions have to be satisfied if a company wishes to increase or reduce its share capital.

Items (c) to (f) are covered in the chapters on limited company accounts to the extent knowledge is required at this level of accounting. Items (a) and (b) are dealt with below.

5.3   The true and fair view

With regard to accounts of companies prepared under the Companies Act, there is an overriding requirement that those accounts show a true and fair view.

There is no universal definition of 'true and fair view', which is a concept that has dominated UK company accounting since 1948. Effectively it is a concept which has been adapted as the years have passed, in the sense that what was true and fair in 1948 might not be said to be so today, but it remains a concept nonetheless, and a concept of critical importance.

Perhaps the best way of illustrating the flexible and changing nature of 'true and fair' is to consider another definition in a much older statute - the Bill of Rights 1688 - which prohibited 'cruel and unusual' punishments. Those words have similar meanings today as they had in the seventeenth century, but changes in society mean that a judge of today would unquestionably characterise some punishments as cruel, which his predecessor in 1688 would certainly not have considered so.

Whilst this is clearly a more flagrant example, the principle applies equally to the 'true and fair' concept of accountancy.

5.4   Accounting standards

Definition   Accounting standards are authoritative statements of how particular types of transactions and other events should be reflected in financial statements.

The Companies Act is mainly designed to deal with the problem of inadequate information. Accounting standards set out to tackle a different problem: that of the diversity of treatment of certain items in published accounts.

There are many areas of accounting where there is more than one generally accepted method of dealing with particular transactions. Because types of businesses often vary so much as between one another, what is suitable as an accounting policy for one business may be unsuitable for another. It is, however, important for a given business to follow its accounting policies from one year to the next, so that valid comparisons of performance may be made.

The following are examples of the areas where variations in accounting practices are recognised

(a)   Depreciation of fixed assets
(b)   Research and development expenditure
(c)   Hire purchase or instalment transactions
(d)   Stock and work-in-progress

5.5   The introduction of accounting standards

The Accounting Standards Committee was set up in 1970 as a result of considerable criticism during the 1960s of the scope allowed for manipulation of published accounts by the variety of acceptable bases. From its formation, the ASC attempted to build up a definitive body of rules to govern the presentation of published accounts.

Before a standard was introduced, it was first published by the ASC in the form of an Exposure Draft (ED). This was purely a discussion document. Once the discussion (or exposure) period elapsed, the document, amended in the light of the results of that discussion, was issued in the form of a Statement of Standard Accounting Practice (SSAP).

Such statements had binding effect immediately after the operative date (determined by the Consultative Committee of Accountancy Bodies (CCAB)). The CCAB is a committee formed from the representatives of the six UK Professional Accountancy bodies.

5.6   The Dearing Report

In 1987 the CCAB appointed a committee under the chairmanship of Sir Ron Dearing to review and make recommendations on the standard-setting process. The major points which it considered were

(a)   the most appropriate form which accounting standards should take

(b)   the status of standards in relation to company law

(c)   procedures for the monitoring of compliance with standards and the enforcement of standards

(d)   the need for, and nature of, public consultation about draft standards

(e)   the funding of the cost of standard-setting and

(f)   the appropriate composition and powers of any body responsible for standard-setting and the manner in which appointment to that body should be made, taking into account the interests of the users, preparers and auditors of accounts in the standard-setting process.

5.7   Application in the Companies Act 1989

Some of the proposals of the Dearing Report were implemented in the CA 89. In particular

(a)   Accounts must now state that they have been prepared in accordance with applicable accounting standards. The Secretary of State had power to introduce this requirement for different classes of companies and it was introduced for plcs and large private companies.

(b)   The Secretary of State or other 'authorised persons' may apply to the courts to order the revision of defective accounts. There is a procedure whereby a company may revise its defective accounts voluntarily without involving the courts.

5.8   The roles of the FRC, ASB, UITF and Review Panel

Many of the recommendations of the Dearing Report are reflected in the current standard setting process which came into effect in August 1990.

(a)   **The Financial Reporting Council (FRC)**

The FRC comprises around 25 members drawn from the users and preparers of accounts and auditors. It has two operating bodies - the Accounting Standards Board (ASB) and the Review Panel.

The FRC is responsible for guiding the ASB on its planned work programme.

(b)   **The Accounting Standards Board (ASB)**

The ASB has 10 members, so is around half the size of the FRC and the ASC. The ASB, unlike the ASC, has both a full-time chairman and a full-time technical director. Part-time members are encouraged to give more of their time to the task than ASC members could reasonably expect to do.

The part-time members are all well versed in accounting and financial matters. It is the ASB which issues accounting standards now known as Financial Reporting Standards (FRSs).

Prior to their issue a Discussion Draft (DD) may be issued to a restricted number of interested parties setting out a planned approach to an FRS. Later a Financial Reporting Exposure Draft (FRED) is issued for general circulation. The issue of the FRED allows for a further consultation process before the FRS is issued.

(c)   **The Review Panel**

The Review Panel has about 15 members and is concerned with the examination and questioning of departures from accounting standards by large companies.

(d)   **The Urgent Issues Task Force (UITF)**

This is an offshoot of the ASB. Its function is to tackle urgent matters not covered by existing standards and for which, given the urgency, the normal standard-setting process would not be practicable.

The differences between the old and the new structure are

(a)   The FRC contains a much wider field of interested parties than the CCAB.

(b)   The ASB can issue standards on its own authority (unlike the ASC). The CCAB bodies are not now responsible for approving standards.

(c)   Under the CA 89 the accounting standards issued by the ASB are recognised as 'accounting standards' for the purposes of the Act. Directors of public companies are under a statutory duty to disclose whether there has been a material departure from accounting standards.

The authority for SSAPs under the ASC system was derived from the fact that the six professional accountancy bodies expected their members to observe them.

(d)   The Review Panel has an ultimate legal backing to its review; it can apply to the court following a material departure by a public company from an accounting standard. The court may, as a result, order the company concerned to prepare revised accounts.

5.9   The nature of SSAPs and FRSs

In order to avoid the confusion that might result from accounting standards having different sources of authority because they were/are issued by the ASC or the ASB, the ASB formally adopted the 25 SSAPs issued by the ASC as its own SSAPs. They are thus 'accounting standards' under the CA 89 although only a proportion of the 25 are still in issue.

Currently 15 FRSs have been issued.

All SSAPs and FRSs relevant to this syllabus will be covered in the required detail later in the study text.

5.10   **The process leading to Financial Reporting Standards**

Once a topic has been identified, the ASB first commissions its own staff to undertake research in the area. A Discussion Paper will normally be issued to form a basis for discussing the issues involved. On the basis of the feedback received from the Discussion Paper, the ASB may proceed to issue a FRED, which after further feedback will be developed into an FRS.

5.11   **EC Directives**

It is the aim of the EC that its member states will eventually become parts of a single economic entity. To achieve this goal businesses must operate under the same legal and accounting requirements.

The Fourth Company Law Directive resulted in accounts formats and detailed disclosure requirements being contained in sch 4 CA 85. Other European Union members have passed similar legislation.

The Seventh Directive on group accounts was passed by the EC Council in June 1983. The provisions are contained in CA 89.

> **Conclusion**   In the UK the regulatory framework for accounting is made up of the legal framework set out in the Companies Act and the requirements of the accountancy profession set out in SSAPs and FRSs.

6   **SELF TEST QUESTIONS**

1   What are the three main types of business entity? (1.2)

2   What are the two main types of company? (1.3)

3   Who are the main categories of users of financial statements? (2.2 to 2.8)

4   What are the main requirements of management from financial information? (2.2)

5   What would potential shareholders' interests be in the financial statements? (2.3)

6   What is meant by the relevance of information? (3.2)

7   What is meant by information being reliable? (3.4)

8   What is meant by the capital structure of an entity? (4.3)

9   How is the share capital of a company reflected in its financial statements? (4.10)

10   What is the name of the accounting standards currently issued by the Accounting Standards Board (ASB)? (5.8)

2 GAAPs AND CONCEPTS

1 ACCOUNTING CONVENTIONS AND CONCEPTS

1.1 The nature and purpose of accounting conventions

Definition Accounting conventions are principles or accepted practice which apply generally to transactions.

Some of the conventions are of more relevance to some transactions than to others but all have an influence in determining:

- which assets and liabilities are recorded on a balance sheet

- how assets and liabilities are valued

- what income and expenditure is recorded in the profit and loss account

- at what amount income and expenditure is recorded.

It is useful to state and clarify the meaning of accounting conventions so that unusual transactions or situations can be dealt with.

SSAP 2 *Disclosure of accounting policies* was issued by the Accounting Standards Committee in 1971 and it defined four fundamental accounting concepts explained in 1.2 to 1.5 below. All four of these were confirmed in the Companies Act 1985 which also added a fifth (1.6). The other concepts and conventions in Section 1 are 'generally accepted accounting principles' or GAAPs.

1.2   Going concern concept

Definition   The going concern concept assumes that a business (or enterprise) will **continue in operational existence for the foreseeable future**.

This means that the financial statements are drawn up on the assumption that there is no **intention or necessity to liquidate or curtail significantly the scale of operation**.

These words deserve careful reading. Circumstances where the going concern assumption would not be justified would include:

(i)   where there is a specific intention to liquidate the business in the near future;

(ii)   where there is a strong possibility that shortage of finance will force the business into liquidation. This may be revealed by preparing a cash flow forecast for the next twelve months where a month-by-month comparison of expected cash inflows and outflows indicates financing requirements that are unlikely to be satisfied by the bank or by outside lenders;

(iii)   where there is a strong possibility that shortage of finance will result in the sale of a significant part of the business.

In the above circumstances the going concern assumption would not be valid, and the financial statements would be prepared on a basis which takes the likely consequences into account.

In most cases, however, financial statements will be prepared on a going concern basis and the directors will be able to justify the idea that such a basis is valid. The directors and auditors of a company both have a responsibility to ensure that the company is indeed a going concern if the going concern basis is adopted.

1.3   Accruals (or matching) concept

Definition   The accruals or matching concept states that costs and revenues should be matched one with the other and dealt with in the accounting period to which they relate.

The starting position should be to use the concept to determine the accounting period in which revenue (ie, sales) is recognised.

Revenue is usually recognised when it is **realised**. The realisation of revenue is usually taken to occur on the date of sale rather than on the date when the cash relating to the sale is received.

The efforts of expenditure in the past have led to the revenues accruing now. It is thus logical to match the costs or expenses of earning revenue with the revenue reported in any particular period. The operating profit determined in this way is supposed to indicate how efficiently the resources of the business have been utilised.

Although the accruals or matching principle is conceptually simple, it does run into practical difficulties.

For example, expenditure on fixed assets will provide benefits extending over several accounting periods. When a fixed asset is acquired it is necessary to estimate its useful life. The **service potential** of a fixed asset will diminish over its useful life, and this reduction is a cost or expense to be matched against the revenue of each period and is called **depreciation**.

1.4   Prudence concept

Definition   Revenues and profits are not reported and recognised in the financial statements unless realised. Revenues and profits are not deemed realised until the likelihood of conversion to cash is high. In most cases this means the date of sale. By way of contrast, immediate provision is made for anticipated losses, even if such losses are not yet realised.

An example of the prudence concept is the situation in which a liability has been estimated to be between £500 and £600; the accountant will make provision for the highest estimate on the grounds of prudence.

1.5   Consistency concept

Definition   A business should be consistent in its accounting treatment of similar items, both **within** a particular accounting period and **between** one accounting period and the next.

For example, in the case of depreciation of fixed assets, there is more than one accepted accounting treatment. One business may use one method, another business may use another. As far as the consistency concept is concerned, once a business has selected a method, it should use this method consistently for all assets in that class and for all accounting periods. Only in this way can users of financial statements draw meaningful conclusions from reported results. If a business were to change any of its accounting policies (eg, the basis of depreciation) it must have a good reason for doing so and in addition, the financial effect of such a change should be quantified and, if material, reported to the shareholders.

1.6   Determination of value of each asset and liability separately

Definition   In determining the aggregate amount of any item, the amount of any individual asset or liability that falls to be taken into account shall be determined separately.

For example, when stock is valued at the lower of cost and net realisable value, the value must be determined for separate types of stock and then aggregated. In this way anticipated losses on one type of stock will not be offset against expected gains on another.

1.7   Historical cost

Definition   The historical cost accounting system is a system of accounting in which all values are based on the historical costs incurred. This is the basis of accounting prescribed by the Companies Act (although the Act does allow Alternative Accounting Rules that enable certain assets to be revalued and stated at their revalued amounts).

1.8   Stable monetary unit

Business activity involves the undertaking of all types of transactions. These diverse transactions are expressed in terms of a common unit of measurement, namely the monetary unit. Financial statements prepared on a historical cost basis make the assumption that the pound sterling is a stable monetary unit. This means, therefore, that 19X1 £s can be added to 19X9 £s and a meaningful result obtained.

Example

A company balance sheet states its plant and machinery at **cost less aggregate depreciation**, made up as follows:

	Cost	Aggregate depreciation	Net book value
	£	£	£
Assets acquired 19X1	80,000	24,000	56,000
Assets acquired 19X2	100,000	20,000	80,000
Assets acquired 19X3	60,000	6,000	54,000
	240,000	50,000	190,000

If the pound sterling is a stable unit of measurement, the above aggregation is meaningful. The problem arises, however, that even in periods of gradual inflation, the pound sterling is not a stable unit of measurement. The purchasing power of a 19X2 £ is quite different from that of a 19X1 or 19X3 £. This is a severe criticism of accounts prepared on a conventional or historical cost basis.

1.9   Money measurement

Definition   Accounts only record items to which a monetary value can be attributed.

All items, in theory, can have a monetary value attributed to them but not all items can be measured due to the practical difficulties of valuation. Can values be attributed to the worth of employees for example?

Some would argue that it is desirable to value employees and record them as an asset on the balance sheet but it is very difficult to arrive at a value.

1.10   Materiality

Definition   This is the principle that financial statements should separately disclose items which are significant enough to affect evaluation or decisions.

The significance of an item stems from its importance in the overall context of the financial statements.

This convention ensures that only significant items are included in the financial statements in order to improve their clarity. The materiality test ie, what is and is not significant, will differ from organisation to organisation.

Materiality may be considered in the context of the financial statements as a whole or individual items within them. It may also be considered in relative or absolute terms depending upon the item concerned.

1.11   Realisation concept

Definition   The realisation concept states that a transaction should be recognised when the event from which the transaction stems has taken place and the receipt of cash from the transaction is reasonably certain.

Therefore a sale on credit is recognised when the sale is made and the invoice sent out rather than waiting until the cash from the sale is received.

1.12   Objectivity convention

Definition   Financial statements should be as objective as possible. Transactions are to be recorded objectively as historical events.

This is the main basis of historical cost accounting. Certain aspects of historical cost accounting do, however, represent departures from the objectivity convention. For example, although the depreciation charge is often based on the original cost of an asset (objective) it depends also on the estimated useful life and estimated scrap value at the end of that useful life (subjective).

One advantage of the objectivity convention is that it reduces the extent to which financial statements may be influenced by subjective opinion. In the past great importance has been placed on objective or verifiable evidence. At the present time, particularly as a result of inflation, this approach is being increasingly brought into question.

1.13   Business entity

Definition   The business entity concept states that financial accounting information relates only to the activities of the business entity and not to the activities of its owner.

Under this concept accounting is seen as relating to an independent unit, the entity. The entity is seen as being separate from its owners, whatever its legal status. Thus, a company is both legally and for accounting purposes a separate entity distinct from its owners, the shareholders. On the other hand, the business of a sole trader is not a legal entity distinct from its proprietor; however, for accounting purposes, the business is regarded as being a separate entity and accounts are drawn up for the business separately from the trader's own personal financial dealings.

The entity concept is essential in order to be able to account for the business as a separate economic unit. Thus, flows of money between the business and the proprietors may be separately identified from other money flows:

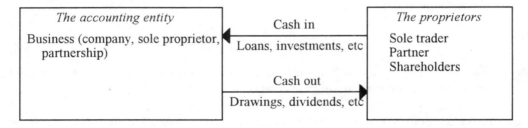

Since we will be concerned with business entities, the correct terms for these cash movements should be established:

Cash movement from/to proprietors	Sole trader, partnership	Company
IN	Either 'loans from proprietors' or 'increase in capital'	Share issue proceeds
OUT	Either 'drawings' or 'reduction in capital'	Dividends

1.14   Duality

Definition   Every transaction has two effects.

The duality concept underpins double entry and the balance sheet.

1.15   Accounting period convention

For accounting purposes the lifetime of the business is divided into arbitrary periods of a fixed length, usually one year. At the end of each arbitrary period, usually referred to as the accounting period, two financial statements are prepared:

(i)   The **balance sheet**, showing the position of the business as at the end of the accounting period.

(ii)   The **profit and loss account** for the accounting period. Profit or loss is arrived at on the basis of the **matching** concept.

Reference has already been made to the difficulties of matching revenues and associated costs, particularly in the case of expenditure on items such as research and development and fixed assets, where the benefits extend to more than one accounting period.

Some accountants argue that profit can only be meaningfully measured over the lifetime of a business, ie, the period starting with the date the business is formed and ending with the date the business goes into liquidation. This is because by avoiding the use of arbitrary accounting periods the problem of matching does not arise. There is also certainty of income and expenditure.

In spite of the arbitrary nature of the accounting period convention, it is necessary to strike a compromise between theoretical accuracy and the needs of the financial community. These needs require periodic financial statements which will form the basis of subsequent financial decisions.

1.16   Substance over form convention

Definition   The economic substance of a transaction should be reflected in the accounts, rather than simply its legal form.

A good example is that of assets acquired on hire purchase terms. Despite the fact that such assets are not owned by the user until the final instalment has been paid, a fixed asset is recorded in his accounts at the start of the hire purchase agreement. The substance of the transaction is that the accounts should reflect the use of a fixed asset in a business.

More recently it has become accepted practice for assets used under long-term leases to be accounted for as if they were owned by the user. This is despite the fact that for most long-term leases the user never becomes the legal owner of the asset.

1.17   Activity

Which accounting conventions or concepts would be likely to be used in the following situations?

(a)   Determining which accounting period an item of expenditure relates to.

(b)   Valuing an asset of the business that is to appear in the balance sheet.

(c)   The accounting treatment of an asset being purchased by the business on hire purchase terms.

1.18   Activity solution

(a)   Accruals or matching concept.
Accounting period convention.

(b)   Historical cost accounting convention.
Prudence concept.
Objectivity convention.
Going concern concept.

(c)   Substance over form convention.

The conventions have the following uses:

- They are of some help in dealing with unusual transactions or situations as they provide some principles which can be applied to a specific transaction.

- They can help a user of accounting information to understand detailed accounting entries.

However it can be argued that they are of limited use for the following reasons.

- Some are statements of the obvious.

- Some are too general to be of practical help.

- They would be much more helpful if integrated. As presented above they are mainly a listing of conventions which by and large are not related to each other. An attempt is being made by the ASB to integrate these principles into a **conceptual framework** (see below).

2   SSAP 2 - DISCLOSURE OF ACCOUNTING POLICIES

2.1   Nature and purpose of SSAP 2

SSAP 2 was published at a time when there were relatively few guidelines laid down for the preparation of accounts. Preparers of accounts were free to use a diversity of methods of accounting without necessarily considering their appropriateness or informing users of the particular methods adopted. Consequently, users had difficulty in gleaning any meaningful information.

The aim of SSAP 2 was to improve a user's understanding and interpretation of the financial statements by

- setting out four fundamental accounting concepts which would apply to all financial statements

- requiring the disclosure of clear explanations of the accounting policies followed by the company

The universal adoption of the fundamental accounting concepts improved quality and consistency as all accounts were now prepared along similar lines. This did not eliminate subjectivity totally from the preparation of accounts: there is still a range of possible ways of dealing with many transactions and items. However, the requirement for the disclosure of the accounting policies used makes the reader aware of these and therefore able to take account of them when making comparisons.

2.2   The four fundamental accounting concepts

Definition **Fundamental accounting concepts** are defined as the broad basic assumptions which underlie the periodic financial statements of business enterprises.

These are the four commonly accepted concepts (sometimes referred to as **assumptions**) which have already been studied, namely:

(a)   the **going concern** concept;
(b)   the **accruals** concept;
(c)   the **consistency** concept; and
(d)   the **prudence** concept.

The use of the above concepts is not normally self-evident from an examination of accounts, but such is their general acceptance that they call for no explanation and their observance is presumed unless otherwise stated.

2.3   Accounting bases and policies

Definition   **Accounting bases** are methods which have been developed for applying fundamental accounting concepts to individual transactions and items for the purpose of financial accounts.

These bases have evolved over the years in response to the variety and complexity of types of business and business transactions. For this reason a number of recognised accounting bases may justifiably exist for dealing with particular items, such as depreciation and amortisation of fixed assets, valuation of stocks and work in progress and translation of foreign currencies.

Accounting bases consider in particular:

(i)   the period in which revenue and costs should be recognised in the profit and loss account; and

(ii)   the amounts at which material items should be stated in the balance sheet.

Definition   **Accounting policies** are the specific accounting bases selected and consistently followed by a specific business enterprise as being, in the opinion of the management, appropriate to its circumstances and best suited fairly to present its results and financial position.

2.4   Significance of disclosure of accounting policies

Since more than one accounting basis may be acceptable, the particular bases chosen to form the accounting policies can significantly affect a concern's reported results and financial position. For this reason, disclosure of accounting policies is essential to the fair presentation of financial accounts.

2.5   Standard accounting practice

(a)   **Disclosure of accounting concepts**

These only require disclosure where there has been a material departure from the fundamental concepts defined earlier. In the absence of a clear statement to the contrary, it is presumed that the four fundamental concepts have been observed.

(b)   **Disclosure of accounting policies**

The accounting policies followed for dealing with material or critical items in the accounts must be disclosed by way of note to the accounts. The explanation should be clear, fair and as concise as possible.

Accounting policies need not be disclosed in a separate statement, but most companies now do so, and it is regarded as the best practice.

2.6   The conflict between accruals and prudence concepts

The prudence concept often conflicts with the accruals concept when considering costs and expenses. If there is a conflict, prudence normally prevails.

Examples include:

Stock

The accruals concept requires that purchased goods not yet sold should be carried forward as stock ie, the cost should be carried forward to match against future sales.

If however there is some doubt that the items can be sold or they are likely to be sold for less than their cost they would only be carried forward up to the amount of expected future sale proceeds (net of any further costs to make the sale).

Thus if items bought for £10,000 can only be sold as scrap for £1,000 (net of delivery costs), the items would be stated at £1,000 in closing stock. The 'excess' cost £9,000 is thus automatically charged against profits.

Development costs

Businesses may undertake research and development work to make a new or improved product. For example an engineering company may be developing a new type of aircraft engine. Costs of development can be considerable. There is an expectation that a saleable product can be developed so the matching concept would require the costs to be carried forward.

However, the prudence concept would require a consideration of the likelihood of profitable commercial production. If it is not reasonably certain that profits will be made in a future period, the costs must be written off in the period in which they are incurred.

2.7 Activity

State which of the four fundamental accounting concepts is being applied in each of the following cases

(a) Valuation of the fixed assets at cost less depreciation

(b) Calculation of a rental prepayment for inclusion in the following year's profit and loss account

(c) Writing down the value of stock to net realisable value due to a fall in popularity of the product

2.8 Activity solution

(a) Going concern: if the appropriateness of this concept were in doubt the fixed assets would have to be valued at net realisable value

(b) Accruals/matching

(c) Prudence

Conclusion   SSAP 2 is a brief standard concerning accounting concepts, bases and policies and yet it pervades every aspect of the financial statements in the application of those concepts.

3   A CONCEPTUAL FRAMEWORK

3.1   The nature and purpose of a conceptual framework

> **Definition**   A conceptual framework is a coherent system of inter-related objectives and fundamentals that can lead to consistent standards and that prescribes the nature, function and limits of financial accounting and financial statements.

The basic objective and need for a conceptual framework is to enable accounting standards to be developed which are less likely to be attacked as they would fit within the agreed principles of a conceptual framework. A conceptual framework would thus avoid what has been termed the 'fire fighting' approach ie, a problem is seen in a particular area and a standard is issued to counter the immediate problem. The end result is a set of standards developed on a piecemeal basis with little overall consensus.

4   STATEMENT OF PRINCIPLES

4.1   Introduction

In order to provide a coherent framework for the issue of accounting standards, the Accounting Standards Board (ASB) is developing a Statement of Principles.

> **Definition**   The **Statement of Principles for Financial Reporting** sets out the principles that the ASB believes should underlie the preparation and presentation of general purpose financial statements.

Its purpose is, among other things, to provide a coherent frame of reference to assist the ASB in the development and review of accounting standards and to provide those interested in its work with an understanding of the ASB's approach to the formulation of accounting standards.

The original exposure draft of the complete Statement of Principles was issued in 1995 and a revised exposure draft issued in 1999. It comprises eight chapters:

1   The objective of financial statements
2   The reporting entity
3   The qualitative characteristics of financial information
4   The elements of financial statements
5   Recognition in financial statements
6   Measurement in financial statements
7   Presentation of financial information
8   Accounting for interests in other entities

4.2   Purpose and status of statement

The purpose of the Statement of Principles is to:

(a)   assist the ASB in the development of future accounting standards and in its review of existing accounting standards;

(b)   assist the ASB by providing a basis for reducing the number of alternative accounting treatments permitted by law and accounting standards;

(c)   assist preparers of financial statements in applying accounting standards and in dealing with topics that do not form the subject of an accounting standard;

(d)   assist auditors in forming an opinion whether financial statements conform with accounting standards;

(e)   assist users of financial statements in interpreting the information contained in financial statements prepared in conformity with accounting standards; and

(f)   provide those who are interested in the work of the ASB with information about its approach to the formulation of accounting standards.

The Statement of Principles will not become an accounting standard. Nothing in the Statement overrides a specific accounting standard.

4.3   Chapter 1 – The objective of financial statements

[Definition]   The objective of financial statements is to provide information about the reporting entity's financial performance and financial position that is useful to a wide range of users for assessing the stewardship of management and for making economic decisions.

The items included in this definition are further discussed in the chapter.

(a)   **Stewardship and economic decisions**

Stewardship in this context is the accountability of management for the resources entrusted to them. Those users who wish to assess the stewardship of management do so in order to make economic decisions, for example whether to hold or sell their investment in the enterprise or whether to re-appoint or replace the management.

Financial statements prepared for this purpose meet the common needs of most users. However, financial statements do not provide all the information that users may need to make economic decisions since they largely portray the financial effects of past events and do not necessarily provide non-financial information.

(b)   **Users and their information needs**

Investors are interested in information that helps them to assess the performance of management. They are also concerned with the risk inherent in, and return provided by, their investments. They need information that helps them to assess the ability of the enterprise to pay dividends, and to determine whether they should buy, hold or sell their investments. Investors also need information on the entity's financial performance and financial position that helps them to assess its cash generation abilities and its financial adaptability.

Employees and their representative groups are interested in information about the stability and profitability of their employers. They are also interested in information that enables them to assess the ability of the enterprise to provide remuneration, employment opportunities and retirement benefits.

Lenders are interested in information that enables them to determine whether their loans will be repaid, and the interest attaching to them paid, when due.

Suppliers and other creditors are interested in information that enables them to decide whether to sell to the enterprise and to assess the likelihood that amounts owing to them will be paid when due.

Customers are interested in information about the ability of an enterprise to continue trading.

Governments and their agencies are interested in the allocation of resources and, therefore, the activities of enterprises. They also require information in order to regulate the activities of enterprises, assess taxation and provide a basis for national statistics.

The public may be interested in information about the trends and recent developments in the prosperity of the enterprise and the range of its activities (for example, an enterprise may make a substantial contribution to a local economy by providing employment and using local suppliers).

The view expressed in the Statement of Principles is that the investors are the defining class of users. The investors are concerned about the entity's cash-generation ability and financial adaptability and this is also of fundamental importance to other users. Therefore if financial statements are prepared according to the interests of the investor group then they will also be focusing on the common interest that all users have in the financial performance and financial position.

(c)   **Information required**

The **financial position** of an enterprise which is affected by:

(i)   the economic resources it controls;
(ii)   its financial structure;
(iii)   its liquidity and solvency; and
(iv)   its capacity to adapt to changes in the environment in which it operates.

Information about financial position is primarily presented in a balance sheet.

The **performance** of an enterprise which comprises the return obtained by the enterprise on the resources it controls, the components of that return and the characteristics of those components, including the cost of its financing. Information on performance is provided in a profit and loss account and a statement of total recognised gains and losses.

Information on **cash flows** which is provided in a cash flow statement. It provides an additional perspective on the performance of an enterprise by indicating the amounts and principal sources of its cash inflows and outflows.

Financial adaptability consists of the ability of an enterprise to take effective action to alter the amount and timing of its cash flows so that it can respond to unexpected events and opportunities. All the primary financial statements provide information that is useful in evaluating the financial adaptability of the enterprise.

The component parts of the financial statements interrelate because they reflect different aspects of the same transactions or other events. Although each statement provides information that is different from the others, none is likely to serve only a single purpose or provide all the information necessary for particular needs of users.

| Conclusion | Users of the financial statements include

-     investors
-     employees
-     lenders
-     creditors
-     customers
-     government
-     the public

They all require information on the financial position, performance and financial adaptability of a company.

4.4   Chapter 2 - The reporting entity

This Chapter of the statement stresses that it is important that entities that ought to prepare and publish financial statements do in fact do so and that those statements report on all the relevant activities and resources. If there is a legitimate demand for the information in financial statements for an entity and that entity is a cohesive economic unit then financial statements should be prepared.

The boundary of the reporting entity is determined by 'control'.

[Definition]   Control has two aspects: the ability to deploy the economic resources involved and the ability to benefit or suffer from their deployment.

The Statement of Principles recognises firstly direct control and secondly direct control plus indirect control. Direct control is used to determine the boundary of the entity that prepares single entity financial statements. Direct plus indirect control is used to determine the boundary of the reporting entity that prepares consolidated financial statements.

One entity will control another if it has the ability to direct that entity's operating and financial policies with a view to gaining economic benefit from the activities of the entity. Such control can be evidenced in a variety of ways but it is important that it is the relationship in practice that is considered rather than the theoretical level of influence.

Group accounts are covered in more detail in this textbook in chapters 19 to 22.

4.5   Chapter 3 - The qualitative characteristics of financial information

Information provided by financial statements needs to be relevant and reliable; if there is a choice of approach then the one chosen is the one that maximises the relevance of the information.

The information provided by the financial statements also needs to be comparable and understandable.

[Definition]   Information is **relevant** if it has the ability to influence the economic decisions of users.

[Definition]   Information is **reliable** when it is free from material error and bias, can be depended upon by users to represent faithfully that which it either purports to represent or could reasonably be expected to represent and a degree of caution has been applied in exercising the judgements necessary.

[Definition]   Information is **comparable** if it enables users to discern and evaluate similarities in, and differences between, the nature and effects of transactions and other events over time and across different reporting entities.

[Definition]   Information is **understandable** if its significance can be appreciated by users that have a reasonable knowledge of business and economic activities and accounting and a willingness to study with reasonable diligence the information provided.

The Statement also considers materiality. Information that is material needs to be given in the financial statements and information that is not material need not be given.

[Definition]   Information is **material** if its misstatement or omission might reasonably be expected to influence the economic decisions of users.

The relationship between these characteristics is shown in the diagram below.

The qualitative characteristics of financial information

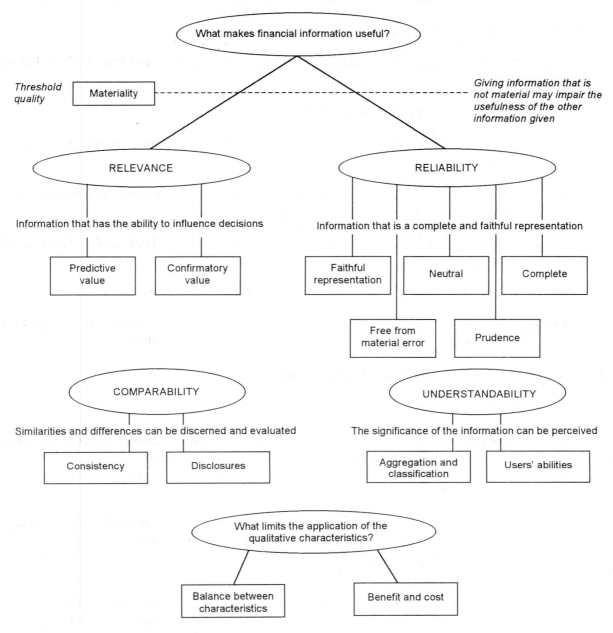

The overriding requirement for financial statements is that they should give a true and fair view of the financial position, performance and financial adaptability of an enterprise. 'A true and fair view' is a dynamic concept whose content evolves in response to such matters as advances in accounting and changes in business practice. Although the Statement of Principles does not deal directly with the concept of 'a true and fair view' it may be expected to contribute over time to the evolution of the interpretation of that concept.

4.6   Activity

Chapter 1 of the statement of principles refers to a 'wide range' of users. Who do you think the users are?

4.7   Activity solution

The normal classification of users is as follows:

(a)   equity investors (existing and potential);

(b)   loan creditors, ie, existing and potential holders of debentures and loan stock, and providers of short-term loans;

(c)   employees (existing, potential and past);

(d)   analysts/advisers including journalists, economists, trade unions, stockbrokers and credit-rating agencies;

(e)   business contacts including customers, trade creditors, competitors and potential takeover bidders;

(f)   government, including tax authorities, the Department of Trade and Industry and local authorities;

(g)   the public, including taxpayers, ratepayers and environmental groups.

[Conclusion]   Relevance and reliability are important qualitative characteristics of financial information, as also are comparability and understandability.

4.8   Chapter 4: The elements of financial statements

(a)   **Assets**

[Definition]   Assets are rights or other access to future economic benefits controlled by an entity as a result of past transactions or events.

(i)   **'Rights or other access'**

For example property is only an asset because of the rights (shared or sole) deriving from ownership or the other rights of occupation and use.

(ii)   **'Future economic benefits'**

These are evidenced by the prospective receipt of cash. This could be cash itself, a debt receivable or any item which may be sold. Although, for example, a factory may not be sold (on a going concern basis) it houses the manufacture of goods. When these goods are sold the economic benefit resulting from the use of the factory is realised as cash.

(iii)   **'Controlled by an entity'**

Control is the ability to obtain the economic benefits and to restrict the access of others (eg, by a company being the sole user of its plant and machinery, or by selling surplus plant and machinery).

(iv)   **'Past transactions or events'**

Transactions will be more common than events, but an event such as a third party's action could lead to a claim for damages. The transaction or event must be 'past' before an asset can arise. For example equipment will only become an asset when there is the right to demand delivery or access to the asset's potential. Depending on the terms of the contract this may be on acceptance of the order or on delivery.

(b)   **Liabilities**

|Definition| Liabilities are the obligations of an entity to transfer economic benefits as a result of past transactions or events.

(i)   **'Obligations'**

These may be legal or not. For example an entity may have no realistic alternative to refunding the price of goods that fail to meet the expectations of customers, even though there is no legal requirement to do so.

Obligation implies that the outflow of resources is **unavoidable**. Costs to be incurred in the future do not represent liabilities as long as the entity can choose to avoid the expenditure. For example, decisions of the board of directors cannot, in themselves, create a liability, because the board of directors has the power to rescind its own decisions.

(ii)   **'Transfer economic benefits'**

This could be a transfer of cash, or other property, the provision of a service, or the refraining from activities which would otherwise be profitable.

(iii)   **'Past transactions or events'**

Similar points are made here to those under assets.

(iv)   **Complementary nature of assets and liabilities**

As should be evident from the above, assets and liabilities are seen as mirror images of each other. Sometimes they are offset, eg, a credit note issued to a customer will be set against his debt rather than being recorded as a separate liability. More on this is considered below.

(c)   **Ownership interest**

|Definition| Ownership interest in the entity is the residual amount found by deducting all of the entity's liabilities from all of the entity's assets.

The above describes the residual nature of ownership interest. Owners' wealth can be increased whether or not a distribution is made. The sharing may be in different proportions.

Ownership interest is usually analysed in financial statements to distinguish that arising from owners' contributions from that resulting from other events. The latter is split into different reserves which may have different applications or legal status.

(d)   **Gains and losses**

These are counted as two of the seven elements.

|Definition| Gains are increases in ownership interest, other than those relating to contributions from owners.

|Definition| Losses are decreases in ownership interest, other than those relating to distributions to owners.

(e)   **Contributions from owners**

|Definition| Contributions from owners are increases in ownership interest resulting from transfers from owners in their capacity as owners.

These will usually be in cash but they could be in other forms of property, by accepting equity in satisfaction of liabilities or by performing services.

The consideration is the granting of rights in the ownership interest.

(f) **Distributions to owners**

Definition Distributions to owners are decreases in ownership interest resulting from transfers made to owners in their capacity as owners.

Distributions include dividends and purchase of own shares but not bonus issues since ownership interest remains constant.

Conclusion The seven elements of financial statements are

- assets
- liabilities
- ownership interest
- gains
- losses
- contributions from owners
- distributions to owners

4.9 Chapter 5: Recognition in financial statements

Definition Recognition involves depiction of the item in words and by a monetary amount and the inclusion of that amount in the financial statement totals.

Only items which meet the definition of an element of the financial statements should be recognised. The definitions are set out in Chapter 4 of the Statement as explained above.

(a) **The stages of recognition**

The recognition of assets and liabilities falls into three stages:

(i) initial recognition (ie, incorporation of an item into financial statements for the first time, for example, where a fixed asset is purchased);

(ii) subsequent remeasurement (ie, changing the monetary amount at which a previously recognised item is recorded, for example, where an existing fixed asset is revalued);

(iii) derecognition (ie, removal from the financial statements of a previously recognised item, for example, where a fixed asset is sold).

(b) **Recognition criteria**

An element should be recognised in the financial statements if

(i) there is sufficient evidence that the new asset or liability has been created or that there has been an addition to an existing asset or liability.

(ii) the element can be measured at a monetary amount with sufficient reliability.

A change in the amount at which an asset or liability is recorded should be recognised if:

(i) there is sufficient evidence that the amount of an asset or liability has changed; and

(ii)   the new amount of the asset or liability can be measured with sufficient reliability.

An asset or liability should be derecognised if sufficient evidence exists that a transaction or other past event has eliminated a previously recognised asset or liability, or the criteria for recognition are no longer met.

4.10 Chapter 6: Measurement in financial statements

[Definition]   **Measurement** is concerned with the monetary amount of the depiction of an element in the financial statements.

The measurement basis, either historical cost or current value, should be the one that best meets the objectives of financial statements.

(a)   Assets and liabilities are initially recognised at the transaction cost. This historical cost is equal to its current replacement cost at that time. They may be remeasured later. In an HCA system this can involve the writing down of an asset to its recoverable amount and the amendment of the monetary amount of liabilities to the amount ultimately expected to be paid.

The main advantage of HCA is familiarity. Procedures for its implementation are well established and therefore cheaper and easier to operate.

(b)   A current value system remeasures assets and liabilities regularly so that changes in value are recorded as they occur. This has the advantage of being more relevant to users who wish to assess the current state or recent performance of the business.

The appropriate current value to be used for assets is the 'value to the business'.

[Definition]   Value to the business is the lower of replacement cost and recoverable amount. Recoverable amount is the higher of net realisable value and value in use.

For liabilities the above rule will always lead to a single current value and thus market values may be used.

4.11 Activity

A company owns a factory which originally cost £80,000. A similar building on the same business park has recently been sold for £120,000. If the company were to sell the building they, too, could expect to receive £120,000, but would incur costs associated with the sale of £10,000. The company estimate that if they continue to use the building it will earn future profits in excess of £900,000 in today's prices.

What is the value to the business of the building?

4.12 Activity solution

Recoverable amount is the higher of net realisable value (£110,000) and value in use (£900,000).

Value to the business is the lower of replacement cost (£120,000) and recoverable amount (£900,000) = £120,000.

It is usually the case that the appropriate current value is the replacement cost.

[Conclusion]   Remeasurement is sometimes used in an HCA system. A current value system of accounting remeasures assets and liabilities on a regular basis.

4.13   Chapter 7: Presentation of financial information

This part of the **Statement of Principles** explores the way in which information should be presented in financial statements in order to meet the objective described in Chapter 1. The presentation decision is taken in the context of a structured set of financial statements comprising **primary statements** and **supporting notes**.

(a)   **The primary statements**

- profit and loss account
- statement of total recognised gains and losses
- balance sheet (the statement of financial position)
- cash flow statement.

} these are statements of financial performance

(b)   **Notes to financial statements**

The notes to financial statements should amplify and explain the primary statements giving more detailed information on items and in certain instances provide an alternative view of a particular transaction or event from that included in those primary statements. The notes and primary statements form an integrated whole. Disclosure in the notes however is not a substitute for recognition and does not correct or justify any misrepresentation or omission in the primary statements.

(c)   **Accompanying information**

Accompanying information is information which is positioned outside the primary statements and notes. This may include voluntary or evolutionary disclosures and information that, perhaps because it is too subjective, is not suitable for inclusion in the primary financial statements and the notes. Accompanying information may include:

(i)   an operating and financial review;

(ii)   information prepared from a different perspective from that adopted in the financial statements;

(iii)   statistical information; and

(iv)   highlights and summary indicators.

Conclusion   Information can be presented in one of the primary statements, in a supporting note to one of these statements or in supplementary accompanying information.

The primary statements are

- the balance sheet
- the profit and loss account
- the statement of total recognised gains and losses
- the cash flow statement.

4.14   Chapter 8: Accounting for interests in other entities

Financial statements need to reflect the effect on the reporting entity's financial performance and position of its interests in other entities.

The classification of investments needs to reflect the way in which they are used to further the business of the investor and the consequent effect on the investor's financial position, performance and financial adaptability. The two key factors for this purpose are the degree of influence of the investor and the nature of the investor's interest in the results, assets and liabilities of its investee.

Control describes the highest degree of influence that an investor can have over its investee. Control is the power to direct. To have control, whether of assets or of other entities, an entity must have both of the following abilities:

(i)   the ability to deploy the economic resources, or direct the entities; and

(ii)   the ability to ensure that any resulting benefits accrue to itself (with corresponding exposure to losses) and to restrict the access of others to those benefits.

Consolidated financial statements recognise the parent's control of its subsidiaries. Consolidation is a process that aggregates the total assets, liabilities and results of the parent and its subsidiaries (the group) so that the consolidated financial statements present financial information about the group as a single reporting entity.

| Conclusion | When one business interest controls another it should prepare a set of financial statements for the group. These are called the consolidated financial statements.

5   THE POTENTIAL BENEFITS AND DRAWBACKS OF AN AGREED CONCEPTUAL FRAMEWORK

5.1   Potential benefits

The potential benefits of a conceptual framework are related to the purposes stated by the ASB for the Statement of Principles (see above). In summary the benefits are:

- A framework for setting accounting standards.

- A basis for resolving disputes.

- Fundamental principles do not have to be repeated in accounting standards.

- There should be a reduction in pressure from vested interests who wish to pursue a particular policy out of self interest rather than satisfying the general needs of users.

5.2   Potential drawbacks

Drawbacks to a conceptual framework include:

- Due to their general nature the principles may not, in practice, reduce the options available.

- There may be further disagreement as to the contents of the framework in addition to disagreement over the contents of standards.

| Conclusion | There is widespread support for a conceptual framework, but aspects of the Statement of Principles have proved to be controversial, particularly the emphasis on the use of current values.

6   SELF TEST QUESTIONS

1   What is the going concern concept? (1.2)

2   What is another name for the accruals concept? (1.3)

3   With what should a business be consistent in its accounting policies? (1.5)

4   What is the objectivity convention? (1.12)

5   What is the accounting period convention? (1.15)

6   What is an accounting basis? (2.3)

7   Does SSAP 2 require disclosure of accounting concepts? (2.5)

8   What is a conceptual framework? (3.1)

9   Describe the factors in financial statements which make information relevant (4.5)

10   Describe the factors in financial statements which make information reliable (4.5)

11   What qualities assist comparability of financial statements? (4.5)

12   How does the Draft Statement of Principles define:
        (a)   assets
        (b)   liabilities
        (c)   ownership interest? (4.8)

3 SOLE TRADERS REVISION - THE TRIAL BALANCE

PATHFINDER INTRODUCTION

This chapter covers the following performance criteria and knowledge and understanding.

- Financial statements are accurately drafted from the appropriate information (performance criteria 10.2)
- Subsequent adjustments are correctly implemented (performance criteria 10.2)
- Form and method of preparation of financial statements (knowledge and understanding 10.2)

Putting the chapter in context – learning objectives.

This chapter concentrates on the preparations necessary for production of a set of fianncial statements for the simplest form of business entity, the sole trader. Before a set of financial statements can be prepared it is vital that all of the relevant balances are correct. Therefore this chapter looks at the preparation of a trial balance and correction of errors using a suspense account prior to actually producing the financial statements in the following chapter.

At the end of this chapter you should have learned the following topics.

- Preparation of a trial balance from the general ledger.
- Correction of different types of error.
- Explanation of the purpose of a suspense account.
- Clearing of a suspense account balance.

---

1 THE TRIAL BALANCE

1.1 Introduction

The large number of transactions recorded in the ledger accounts of any business means that there is the possibility of errors occurring. Periodically some assurance is required as to the accuracy of the procedures. This can be done by extracting a trial balance. In the case of a moderate sized business, final accounts will only be prepared annually, but a trial balance will be extracted at more frequent intervals (say, monthly).

Definition A trial balance is a memorandum listing of all the ledger account balances.

If the double entry procedures have been carefully followed, then the trial balance should show that the total of the debit balances agrees with the total of the credit balances.

This process of drawing up a trial balance can and will be carried out for all types of business entity but for the next three chapters this study text will concentrate on the accounts of a sole trader.

1.2 Producing the trial balance

Step 1 All the ledger accounts in the general ledger must be balanced.

Step 2 Then the trial balance can be drawn up. This is done by listing each of the ledger account names in the business's books showing against each name the balance on that account and whether that balance is a debit or a credit balance brought down.

1.3   Example

Below are the general ledger accounts of Avylon as at 31 December 19X4. Balance the accounts, bring down the balances and show all the balances in a trial balance.

Cash at bank account

Date	Details	£	Date	Details	£
	Capital	1,000		Motor car	400
	Sales	300		Purchases	200
	Debtors	100		Creditors	200
	Loan	600		Drawings	75
				Rent	40
				Insurance	30

Capital account

Date	Details	£	Date	Details	£
				Cash at bank	1,000

Motor car account

Date	Details	£	Date	Details	£
	Cash at bank	400			

Purchases account

Date	Details	£	Date	Details	£
	Cash at bank	200			
	Creditors	400			

Sales account

Date	Details	£	Date	Details	£
				Cash at bank	300
				Debtors	250

Creditors account

Date	Details	£	Date	Details	£
	Cash at bank	200		Purchases	400

Debtors account

Date	Details	£	Date	Details	£
	Sales	250		Cash at bank	100

Drawings account

Date	Details	£	Date	Details	£
	Cash at bank	75			

Rent account

Date	Details	£	Date	Details	£
	Cash at bank	40			

Loan account

Date	Details	£	Date	Details	£
				Cash at bank	600

Insurance account

Date	Details	£	Date	Details	£
	Cash at bank	30			

1.4   Solution

Step 1   Balance each account and bring down the balances

Cash at bank account

Date	Details	£	Date	Details	£
	Capital	1,000		Motor car	400
	Sales	300		Purchases	200
	Debtors	100		Creditors	200
	Loan	600		Drawings	75
				Rent	40
				Insurance	30
				Balance c/d	
		2,000			2,000
	Balance b/d	1,055			

Capital account

Date	Details	£	Date	Details	£
				Cash at bank	1,000

Motor car account

Date	Details	£	Date	Details	£
	Cash at bank	400			

Purchases account

Date	Details	£	Date	Details	£
	Cash at bank	200		Balance c/d	600
	Creditors	400			
		600			600
	Balance b/d	600			

Sales account

Date	Details	£	Date	Details	£
	Balance c/d	550		Cash at bank	300
				Debtors	250
		550			550
				Balance b/d	550

Creditors account

Date	Details	£	Date	Details	£
	Cash at bank	200		Purchases	400
	Balance c/d	200			
		400			400
				Balance b/d	200

Debtors account

Date	Details	£	Date	Details	£
	Sales	250		Cash at bank	100
				Balance c/d	150
		250			250
	Balance b/d	150			

Drawings account

Date	Details	£	Date	Details	£
	Cash at bank	75			

Rent account

Date	Details	£	Date	Details	£
	Cash at bank	40			

Loan account

Date	Details	£	Date	Details	£
				Cash at bank	600

Insurance account

Date	Details	£	Date	Details	£
	Cash at bank	30			

Step 2   Prepare the trial balance showing each of the balances in the ledger accounts.

Avylon
Trial balance as at 31 December 19X4

Account	Debit £	Credit £
Cash at bank	1,055	
Capital		1,000
Motor car	400	
Purchases	600	
Sales		550
Creditors		200
Debtors	150	
Drawings	75	
Rent	40	
Loan		600
Insurance	30	
	2,350	2,350

Conclusion   A trial balance is simply a memorandum listing of all the ledger account balances. It is *not* part of the double entry eg, cash is not being credited with £1,055 and the trial balance debited with £1,055. It merely summarises the net result of all the debits and credits that have been made during the period.

2   TYPES OF ERROR IN DOUBLE ENTRY

2.1   Introduction

The trial balance checks to see whether there have been any errors in the accounting system. However, it is limited in that it will only pick up errors in double entry because, as long as the debits and credits are equal, the trial balance will balance. This section looks at the various types of error that could occur and whether the trial balance would be affected.

2.2   Error of commission

Definition   An error of commission is where a transaction has been recorded in the correct category of account, but in the wrong account.

For example, the purchase of a computer should get recorded in the tangible fixed asset account, office equipment. If the purchase was recorded in the motor vehicles account then this is the correct type of account (tangible fixed assets) but the wrong account within this category.

2.3   Error of principle

Definition   An error of principle is where the transaction is recorded in completely the wrong category of account.

If a sale were to be recorded as a trade creditor (they are both credit entries), then this would be an example of an error of principle.

These types of errors will require a transfer of a transaction between accounts and will not involve a suspense account because there has been no breakdown in the double entry. They might also involve the creation of a journal entry.

To deal with errors of commission and principle

Step 1 Set up the T-accounts affected by the error and put in the balances from the trial balance.

Step 2 Perform the double entry required to remove the transaction from one account to the other.

Step 3 Produce the required journal.

2.4 Error of omission

Definition This error is where a transaction has been completely missed out of the accounting system

Therefore this will not require a suspense account entry simply a completely new correct entry.

The steps to deal with this type of error are identical to the transactions posted to the wrong account error except that the accounts affected may not yet exist in the trial balance and thus new ones may need to be created.

2.5 Compensating error

Definition Compensating errors occur when two transactions have been recorded incorrectly, but by coincidence they are both incorrect by the same amount and cancel one another out.

These errors are very difficult to locate.

2.6 Original entry errors

Definition Original entry errors are where there has been an error in the posting of the amounts of the transaction.

These entries can take two forms:

(1) The wrong amounts for both the debit and the credit entry; and
(2) Different amounts for the debit and the credit.

An example of the first is where £4.00 is misread as £400 and so entered on both the debit and the credit side of the correct accounts.

The second is a result of a breakdown in the double entry and would occur when £3,200 was debited to one account and £2,300 (the first two figures having been transposed) is credited to another account.

2.7 Activity

Which of the above errors would lead to an imbalance on the trial balance?

2.8 Activity solution

The only error that leads to an imbalance in the trial balance is the original entry error when different amounts are debited and credited.

All the other entries maintain the double entry correctly, even though the entries themselves are incorrect.

All the errors mentioned above need to be corrected before financial accounts are produced.   The correction is via the journal.

Conclusion   The correction of the errors requires a sound knowledge of what the correct entry should be and then, having determined that, the required journal to put the entry right.

3   SUSPENSE ACCOUNTS AND THE TRIAL BALANCE

3.1   Introduction

Definition   A suspense account is a multi-purpose account that is used to record errors in the accounting system and also to record entries where the bookkeeper is not sure where the entries should be recorded.

It takes the form of a normal T-account, but does not attach to either the profit and loss account or the balance sheet because the balance on the account should be cleared by the time the financial accounts are prepared.

3.2   Use of a suspense account when unsure as to an entry

Some transactions are quite difficult to record if a bookkeeper has not been fully trained.   When such a transaction occurs, the bookkeeper should always maintain the double entry by recording the unknown entry in the suspense account.

For example, suppose money is received by the business for the sale of an asset.   The correct entries are:

Dr   Cash at bank
     Cr   Disposal account

However, if the bookkeeper does not know what the credit entry is the credit should be posted to the suspense account:

Dr   Cash at bank
     Cr   Suspense account

The entry will then be cleared out by the person producing the financial accounts:

Dr   Suspense account
     Cr   Disposal account

3.3   Error suspense entries

Suspense account entries from errors arise from a variety of sources but all have one common theme, that is there has been a breakdown in the double entry.   This means that the trial balance will not balance without the creation of an entry in a suspense account.   Two categories of error which may give rise to suspense account entries are considered below.

3.4   Incorrect extraction of the trial balance

When a trial balance is produced, debit balances should go under the debit column and credit balances should go under the credit column.   If all the other double entry has been correct, the trial balance will balance.

If one of the debit balances is written on the wrong side, that is on the credit side, then the trial balance will no longer balance.

There are a few account balances that often cause a problem. These are mentioned below, along with a reminder of which side the account balances should go on.

Account	Side of trial balance
Drawings	debit
Discounts received	credit
Discounts allowed	debit
Opening stock	debit
Cash at bank account	debit
Overdraft	credit
Bad (doubtful) debts provision	credit
Provision for depreciation	credit
Closing stock	should not be an entry at all! (see below)

Conclusion   The entry for closing stock is a final adjustment made to the trial balance before the financial accounts are produced and therefore it would not normally appear in the trial balance.

3.5   Activity

The trial balance below is incorrect. Re-create the trial balance with the balances on the correct side.

Incorrect trial balance

Account	Debit £	Credit £
Fixed assets		20,000
Current assets	45,000	
Current liabilities		10,000
Long term liabilities		5,000
Owner's capital		30,000
Drawings	5,000	
Profit		25,000
	50,000	90,000
Imbalance	40,000	
	90,000	90,000

3.6   Activity solution

This imbalance would normally be put into a suspense account. However, no double entry is required to correct this suspense account entry as it only arises because the 'memorandum' trial balance is incorrect, not the underlying accounts. By re-drafting the trial balance correctly, the suspense entry would disappear. The item recorded on the wrong wide of the trial balance is fixed assets which should be a debit balance not a credit balance.

Correct trial balance

Account	Debit £	Credit £
Fixed assets	20,000	
Current assets	45,000	
Current liabilities		10,000
Long term liabilities		5,000
Owner's capital		30,000
Drawings	5,000	
Profit		25,000
	70,000	70,000

3.7 The posting from the day books is incorrect

From your studies on day books and personal ledger accounting, you will remember that the totals of the columns of the day books formed the double entry. If there has been a breakdown in this double entry then a suspense account entry will follow.

The breakdown in double entry can occur from

- one side of the entry being totally missed out; or
- a transposition error in the figures of one of the entries.

3.8 Activity

Using the purchase day book as an example

Summary of purchase day book

	Total £	VAT £	Purchases £	Other etc £
	50,000	15,000	30,000	5,000

If the purchases total were not posted what effect would this have?

3.9 Activity solution

Creditors		VAT		Purchases		Other expenses	
	50,000	15,000		missed out		5,000	

The total has been posted correctly, as have the VAT and other expenses. However the purchases figure has been missed. If the T-accounts were balanced up and a trial balance produced, the debits and the credits would not balance and a suspense account entry would be required until the error is discovered and corrected.

If an exam question states that the total of, for example, the repair column has not been posted, then assume that the creditors ledger column has been posted correctly and therefore there has been a breakdown in the double entry.

3.10   Individual debtor and creditor accounts

Ordinarily, an incorrect posting to the individual account in the debtors or creditors personal ledger from a day book would not affect the general ledger double entry (although it would affect a control account reconciliation). The reason for this is that it is still assumed that the total of the control account column is correct.

However, if the business does not maintain control accounts then the individual posting will affect the double entry.

In an exam, if the question says that control accounts are not maintained, then any incorrect posting to an individual account will create a suspense account entry.

3.11   Creating a suspense account from a trial balance

A step that often proves troublesome is the creation of the initial entry in the suspense account from the trial balance.

An imbalancing trial balance will be presented and the task is to set up a suspense account. This is a straightforward task as long as one thing is remembered:

The suspense account entry is required to bring the smaller total up to the larger total.

The steps required are:

(Step 1)   Total up each side of the trial balance

(Step 2)   Add an amount to the smaller total to make it equal to the larger total

(Step 3)   Put their entry into the suspense account

3.12   Activity

The following trial balance has been incorrectly extracted from the books of F Manning and Co. Re-draft the trial balance, find the suspense account balance and set up a suspense account.

Account	Debit £	Credit £
Motor vehicles	15,000	
Office equipment	10,000	
Opening stock	30,000	
Debtors	20,000	
Bank	12,000	
Creditors		45,000
Loan		20,000
Capital		5,000
Sales		100,000

Purchases	45,000	
Expenses	23,000	
Drawings		10,000
	155,000	180,000

3.13   Activity solution

(*Tutorial note*:   The drawings balance has been shown as a credit balance in the trial balance whereas it is a debit balance and the trial balance must be corrected.)

Account	Debit £	Credit £
Motor vehicles	15,000	
Office equipment	10,000	
Opening stock	30,000	
Debtors	20,000	
Bank	12,000	
Creditors		45,000
Loan		20,000
Capital		5,000
Sales		100,000
Purchases	45,000	
Expenses	23,000	
Drawings (corrected balance)	10,000	
	165,000	170,000
Suspense account	5,000	
	170,000	170,000

Suspense account

	£		£
Balance b/d	5,000		

Conclusion   If a trial balance does not balance then an additional balance must be included on the smaller side in order to make it add up.   This additional amount will be the balance on the suspense account.

4   CORRECTION OF ERRORS AND CLEARING THE SUSPENSE ACCOUNT

4.1   Introduction

Correcting suspense accounts is potentially one of the most difficult problems that can arise in an exam (and real life) situation.   It requires not only a sound grasp of bookkeeping principles but also a degree of logic.

However the best approach to solving the suspense account problem focuses on what the correct entries should be in the accounts and not on the clearing of the suspense account.   Only when the correct entries have been ascertained will the suspense account be even considered.

4.2   **Technique**

The technique to clear a suspense account is:

Step 1   Work out what the correct entry should have been.

This is best done in T-account format.

Step 2   Work out what entries have been made.

Take the entries made in the exam question and put them into T-accounts.

Step 3   Compare the accounts in steps one and two and work out the required entry to correct the entry that has been made.

Step 4   Complete the double entry to the suspense account.

Having decided what entry is required in step three, just make the other half of the double entry to the suspense account.

Step 5   Produce a journal showing the correcting entries.

Sometimes a question requires the clearing of the suspense account via a journal. In this case write out the journal when all the entries have been worked out.

4.3   **Activity**

A trial balance has created a debit suspense account balance of £40,000.

It has been discovered that the purchases total of the purchase day book, £20,000, has been credited to the purchases account.

Show how the suspense account would be cleared.

4.4   **Activity solution**

Step 1   Work out what the correct entry should have been.

	Purchases			Creditors	
	20,000				20,000

Step 2   Work out what entries have been made.

	Purchases			Creditors	
		20,000			20,000

NB assume creditors posted correctly

Step 3   To make the purchase account in step two look like the purchase account of step one, a £40,000 debit is required. This is made up of a £20,000 debit to cancel out the incorrect credit, plus a £20,000 debit to put in the correct entry.

Purchases		Creditors	
40,000	20,000		20,000

Step 4   Opposite entry to the suspense account.

Purchases		Suspense	
40,000	20,000	b/d 40,000	**40,000**

Step 5   Journal entry required.

Dr   Purchases account   £40,000
    Cr   Suspense account   £40,000

Conclusion   Clearing the suspense account is potentially a difficult task. However, using the technique shown along with some bookkeeping knowledge will ensure the task is made that much easier. Such adjustments are frequently examined as they are an excellent test of double entry bookkeeping

5   SELF TEST QUESTIONS

1   What is an error of commission? (2.2)

2   How should an error of principle be dealt with in the preparation of the financial statements? (2.3)

3   How is an error of omission corrected? (2.4)

4   What action should a bookkeeper take if unsure of the full double entry for a transaction? (3.2)

5   If a trial balance does not add up what is the correct procedure for creating a suspense account? (3.11)

6   What are the steps required to clear a suspense account balance caused by an incorrect entry in the ledger accounts? (4.2)

4

SOLE TRADERS - THE ACCOUNTS

PATHFINDER INTRODUCTION

This chapter covers the following performance criteria and knowledge and understanding.

- Financial statements are accurately drafted from the appropriate information (performance criteria 10.2)
- Subsequent adjustments are correctly implemented (performance criteria 10.2)
- Form and method of preparation of financial statements (knowledge and understanding 10.2)

Putting the chapter in context – learning objectives.

Once the trial balance has been correctly prepared for a sole trader and any errors corrected through the suspense account it is then possible to prepare the financial statements for a sole trader. This chapter looks at the period end adjustments that are then required to take the trial balance through to a set of financial statements.

At the end of this chapter you should have learned the following topics.

- An overview of the procedure required for producing a set of financial statements for a sole trader.
- Adjustments required to the ledger accounts for opening and closing stock.
- Entries required to the ledger accounts for depreciation of fixed assets and disposal of a fixed asset.
- Adjustments required to the ledger accounts for bad and doubtful debts.
- Entries required for accruals and prepayments.
- A working method for preparing a set of financial statements from a trial balance for a sole trader.

1 PRODUCTION OF A SET OF ACCOUNTS FOR A SOLE TRADER

1.1 Introduction

A sole trader will periodically wish to produce a set of financial accounts or financial statements for his business. There are no legal or accounting framework requirements as to what type of financial statements are produced nor what information they should contain. There is also no requirement for the sole trader to publish these financial statements.

However it would be normal practice for a sole trader to draw up a balance sheet showing the position of the business at the end of the accounting period and a profit and loss account showing the results of the business for that period.

1.2 Procedure

The procedure that the sole trader will follow in order to produce his set of accounts will be as follows:

Step 1 Prepare a trial balance.

Step 2 Ensure the trial balance balances or insert a suspense account balance if it does not.

Step 3 Clear the suspense account by correcting all of the errors and omissions that have caused the suspense account balance

Step 4 Put through any further accounting adjustments.

Step 5 Prepare the balance sheet and profit and loss account.

Steps 1 to 3 have been revised in the previous chapter.

Step 5, the preparation of the balance sheet and profit and loss account will be considered in the next chapter.

In this chapter Step 4, the accounting adjustments necessary at the end of the period will be revised.

1.3 Accounting adjustments

The accounting adjustments that will be considered in this chapter are:

- stock
- depreciation and disposals
- bad and doubtful debts
- accruals and prepayments.

2 STOCK

2.1 Opening stock

The stock figure shown in the trial balance is last year's closing stock which forms this year's opening stock. It will be a debit balance because it was shown as a current asset in last year's balance sheet. The figure has remained unaltered during the year as all stock movements are recorded as sales (at selling price) and purchases (at cost). It is only at the year end that the stock adjustment is made.

2.2 Closing stock

In practice, to find the closing stock value the stock is counted and valued before the adjustment can be made. In a question the notes to the trial balance will state what the current year's closing stock is.

To deal with this entry:

Step 1 Set up two stock accounts:

- stock - profit and loss account
- stock - balance sheet

Step 2 The stock figure per the trial balance will be on the debit side of the stock - balance sheet account. This is the opening stock in the profit and loss account, so transfer it to the stock - profit and loss account.

    Dr   Stock - profit and loss
          Cr   Stock - balance sheet

with opening stock

There is now no balance on the stock - balance sheet account.

Step 3 There is still a balance on the stock - profit and loss account. Clear this to the P&L a/c.

    Dr   P&L a/c
          Cr   Stock - profit and loss

Step 4   Record this year's closing stock:

> Dr   Stock - balance sheet
> Cr   Stock - profit and loss

with closing stock

Step 5   Clear the closing stock in the stock - profit and loss account to P&L

2.3   Activity

A trial balance for a sole trader shows that the stock figure at the end of the previous year was £10,000. The stock has just been counted and valued at this year end at £12,000.

Prepare the ledger accounts and profit and loss account extract to record these stock figures.

2.4   Activity solution

Stock - balance sheet

	£		£
Opening balance	10,000	Step 2 Stock - profit and loss	10,000
Step 4 Stock - profit and loss	12,000		

Stock - profit and loss account

	£		£
Step 2 Stock - balance sheet	10,000	Step 3 P&L account	10,000
Step 5 P&L account	12,000	Step 4 Stock - balance sheet	12,000

Profit and loss account - extract:

	£	£
Sales		X
Opening stock	10,000	
Purchases	X	
	X	
Less: closing stock	12,000	
Cost of sales		X

Conclusion   The steps involved in dealing with opening and closing stock may appear to be quite complex. However the overall aim is simple. This is to end up with a balance on the stock - balance sheet account at the end of the period which represents the closing stock. This will appear in the balance sheet under the heading of current assets. The stock - profit and loss account should be totally cleared out to the profit and loss account itself.

3   FIXED ASSET ADJUSTMENTS

3.1   Introduction

At the year end there is usually a requirement to work out the depreciation charge for the year from information given in the notes. In addition there may well be a disposal of a fixed asset to deal with as well.

3.2   Depreciation charge

The method to follow for dealing with the depreciation charge for the year is as follows:

Step 1   Calculate the annual depreciation charge as instructed eg, using the straight line method or reducing balance method.

Step 2   Record the charge for the year in the depreciation ledger accounts as follows:

> Dr   Depreciation expense account
> > Cr   Depreciation provision account

Step 3   Transfer the depreciation charge to the P&L account as:

> Dr   P&L account
> > Cr   Depreciation expense account

Step 4   Record the balance on the depreciation provision account on the balance sheet. This is deducted from the cost of the fixed assets to show their net book value.

3.3   Activity

The original cost of the fixed assets of a sole trader on 1 January 19X6 was £20,000 and their net book value at that date was £12,000. He has made additions to those fixed assets costing £4,000 this year but no disposals. His depreciation policy is to provide depreciation on the reducing balance basis at a rate of 20% per annum with a full year's depreciation in the year of addition.

Show the entries in the ledger accounts that are required in order to record the depreciation charge for the year ended 31 December 19X6.

3.4   Activity solution

Depreciation provision account

	£		£
Balance c/d (to balance sheet)	11,200	Opening balance	8,000
		Step 2 Depreciation expense	3,200
	11,200		11,200

(*Tutorial note*: The depreciation provision account has an opening balance being the provision at the end of the previous year. In this case the amount of the opening provision can be calculated as the difference between cost (£20,000) and net book value (£12,000) of the assets at the start of the year.)

Step 1   Calculate the depreciation charge for the year:

$$20\% \times (12,000 + 4,000) \quad = \quad £3,200$$

Depreciation expense account

	£		£
Step 2 Depreciation provision	3,200	Step 3 P&L account	3,200

3.5   Disposal of a fixed asset

The steps to follow when accounting for the disposal of a fixed asset are as follows:

Step 1   Transfer the cost and the accumulated depreciation of the fixed asset being disposed of to the disposal account:

> Dr   Disposal account
> > Cr   Fixed asset at cost account

with the original cost of the asset being disposed of.

> Dr   Depreciation provision account
> > Cr   Disposal account

with the accumulated depreciation on the asset being disposed of.

Step 2   Account for the disposal proceeds in the disposal account.

Step 3   Transfer the balance on the disposal account (the profit or loss on disposal) to the P&L account.

3.6   Activity

A fixed asset which had cost £5,300 and had a net book value of £2,000 has been sold for £1,800.

Show the ledger entries in the disposal account necessary to account for this disposal.

3.7   Activity solution

	Disposal account		
	£		£
Fixed assets at cost	5,300	Depreciation provision	3,300
		Cash – proceeds	1,800
		Loss on disposal - P&L account	200
	5,300		5,300

In most questions students will be expected to deal with the annual depreciation charge in the accounts and often to deal with a disposal as well.   Remember to read the accounting policy information for depreciation carefully particularly if there has been a disposal as this will tell you whether depreciation is to be charged on the asset disposed of or not.

Conclusion   The double entry for recording the annual depreciation charge is:

> Dr   Depreciation expense (profit and loss account)
> Cr   Depreciation provision (balance sheet)

To record a disposal, the double entry is:

Dr   Disposal account
Dr   Fixed asset – depreciation   } with the amounts relating to the asset
Cr   Fixed asset – cost

Dr   Cash   } with the disposal proceeds
Cr   Disposal account

The balance remaining on the disposal account is the profit or loss on disposal, which is taken to the profit and loss account.

4   BAD AND DOUBTFUL DEBTS

4.1   Introduction

A bad debt adjustment may have to be made to the trial balance. This may take the form of a bad debt write off and a change in the provision for doubtful debts.

4.2   Method

Step 1   Set up the required T-accounts

- debtors ledger control;
- provision for doubtful debts; and
- bad debt expense

Step 2   Put in the balances from the trial balance

Step 3   Write off the bad debt

Dr   Bad debt expense account
      Cr   Debtors ledger control account

Step 4   Work out the required doubtful debt provision carried down and account for any increase or decrease with a double entry from the provision for doubtful debts to the bad debt expense account. If there is an increase in provision

Dr   Bad debt expense account
      Cr   Provision for doubtful debts account

If there is a decrease in provision put the double entry in the other way around.

Step 5   Transfer the balance on the bad debts expense account to the profit and loss account for the year. Show the balance on the provision for doubtful debts account netted off against debtors in the balance sheet.

4.3   Activity

A sole trader has year end debtors of £8,000. Of these he has decided that £400 should be written off as bad. At the start of the year the doubtful debt provision was £180 and this is to be adjusted to 2% of the current year end debtors.

Write up the relevant ledger accounts.

4.4   Activity solution

Step 1   Set up the required ledger accounts

Debtors ledger control account

	£		£
Step 2 Balance	8,000	Step 3 Bad debts expense account	400
		Balance c/d	7,600
	8,000		8,000

Provision for doubtful debts

	£		£
Step 4 Bad debts expense (180 - 152)	28	Step 2 Balance	180
Balance c/d	152		
	180		180

Bad debt expense account

	£		£
Step 3 Debtors ledger control	400	Step 4 Provision for doubtful debts	28
		Step 5 P&L account	372
	400		400

Step 4   Doubtful debt provision required:

$2\% \times (8,000 - 400) = £152$

Therefore a decrease in provision is required.

Step 5   The charge to the profit and loss account for the year is £372.

Debtors in the balance sheet would be shown as:

	£
Debtors	7,600
Less: provision for doubtful debts	152
	7,448

Conclusion   If a debt is to be written off then it is taken out of the debtors ledger control account and charged to the profit and loss account as part of the bad debts expense for the year. If a debt is to be provided for this is done through the provision for doubtful debts account but the debtors ledger control account is not altered.

5   ACCRUALS AND PREPAYMENTS

5.1   Introduction

Most trial balance questions require some entries for accruals and prepayments. For each expense which is prepaid or requires an accrual, set up a T-account and follow the usual steps.

5.2   Method

The steps to follow are:

Step 1   Bring down any opening balance representing a prepayment (debit balance) or accrual (credit balance) from the previous year end.

Step 2   Record any cash payments during the year as a debit entry in the expense account.

Step 3   Calculate the closing accrual or prepayment and carry down the balance. If this is an accrual it will be carried down on the debit side and if a prepayment then on the credit side.

Step 4   The balancing figure will be the charge to the profit and loss account.

5.3   Sundry income

Remember that sundry income accounts are the opposite way round from expense accounts. Income received in advance is a credit balance whilst income in arrears is a debit balance. Cash received during the year will be a credit entry in the income account.

There appears to be a lot to think about with these accounting adjustments. However, the next section will outline a disciplined approach to the questions that will demonstrate some of these techniques. It will also show that the key to answering the question is to take each adjustment as a separate mini exercise and not to get overwhelmed with all the adjustments at once.

6   PRODUCING A SET OF FINANCIAL ACCOUNTS FROM A TRIAL BALANCE

6.1   Introduction

The final section of the chapter will now move from a trial balance to the balance sheet and profit and loss account. This generally involves three steps:

Step 1   Working out the double entries for the adjustments;

Step 2   Working out the effect of these entries on the balances in the trial balance; and

Step 3   Slotting the adjusted balances into the balance sheet and profit and loss account.

6.2   Example

The trial balance of Jason and Co at 31 May 19X6 is as follows:

	£	£
Capital		15,258
Drawings		5,970
Purchases	73,010	
Returns inwards	1,076	
Returns outwards		3,720
Discounts	1,870	965
Credit sales		96,520
Cash sales		30,296

Customs duty	11,760	
Carriage inwards	2,930	
Carriage outwards	1,762	
Salesman's commission	711	
Salesman's salary	3,970	
Office salaries	7,207	
Bank charges	980	
Loan interest	450	
Light and heat	2,653	
Sundry expenses	2,100	
Rent and rates	7,315	
Printing and postage	2,103	
Advertising	1,044	
Bad debts	1,791	
Provision for doubtful debts		437
Stock	7,650	
Debtors	10,760	
Creditors		7,411
Cash at bank	2,534	
Cash in hand	75	
New delivery van (less trade-in)	2,200	
Motor expenses	986	
Furniture and equipment:		
Cost	8,000	
Depreciation at 1 June 19X5		2,400
Old delivery van:		
Cost	2,100	
Depreciation at 1 June 19X5		1,000
Loan account at 9% (repayable in five years)		5,000
	163,007	163,007

You ascertain the following information:

(a)   Closing stock has been valued for accounts purposes at £8,490.

(b)   The motor van was sold on 1 June 19X5 and traded in against the cost of a new van. The trade-in price was £1,000 and the cost of the new van was £3,200.

(c)   Depreciation on the straight line basis is to be provided at the following annual rates:

Motor vans	20%
Furniture and equipment	10%

(d)   5% of the closing debtors total is estimated to be doubtful.

You are required to prepare:

(1)   ledger accounts to record the transactions listed in (a) to (d) above;
(2)   a trading and profit and loss account for the year ended 31 May 19X6; and
(3)   a balance sheet as at 31 May 19X6.

6.3   Solution

[Step 1]   Work through the adjustments

T-accounts have been asked for: these will help you to work out the double entries and find the new balances on accounts.

(a)   Closing stock

Stock account (profit and loss)

	£		£
Transfer from balance sheet	7,650	P&L a/c (opening stock)	7,650
P&L a/c (closing stock)	8,490	Accounting adjustment	8,490
	16,140		16,140

Stock account (balance sheet)

	£		£
Per trial balance	7,650	Transfer to stock (profit	
Accounting adjustment	8,490	and loss)	7,650
		Balance c/d	8,490
	16,140		16,140
Balance b/d (closing stock)	8,490		

(b)   Van disposal

Van cost account

	£		£
Old van per trial balance	2,100	Disposal account	2,100
New van - cash paid (per		Balance c/d	3,200
trial balance)	2,200		
Part exchange value (disposal			
proceeds)	1,000		
	5,300		5,300
Balance b/d	3,200		

Van provision for depreciation account

	£		£
Disposal account	1,000	Old van per trial balance	1,000

Old van disposal account

	£		£
Van cost account	2,100	Accumulated depreciation	1,000
		Part exchange value	1,000
		Loss on disposal (bal fig) P&L a/c	100
	2,100		2,100

Note that the part exchange value is given in the question as £1,000. This is treated in the disposal account in just the same way as cash proceeds.

(c)   Depreciation

Calculation

Motor van (3,200 × 20%)   £640
Furniture and equipment (8,000 × 10%)   £800

Double entry

Van provision for depreciation account

	£		£
Disposal account	1,000	Old van per trial balance	1,000
Balance c/d	640	Depreciation expense a/c	
		(P&L)	640
	1,640		1,640
		Balance b/d	640

Furniture and equipment provision for depreciation account

	£		£
Balance c/d	3,200	Per trial balance b/d	2,400
		Depreciation expense a/c	
		(P&L)	800
	3,200		3,200
		Balance b/d	3,200

(d)   Bad debt provision

Calculation of provision

Closing debtors per trial balance	=		£10,760
5% of debtors (5% × £10,760)	=		£538
Increase in provision required	=	(538 – 437)	£101

Double entry

Provision for doubtful debts account

	£		£
Required bal c/d	538	Per trial balance	437
(see working above)		Bad debt expense (bal fig)	101
	538		538
		Balance b/d	538

Bad debt expense account

	£		£
Per trial balance	1,791	P&L a/c	1,892
Provision for doubtful debts	101		
	1,892		1,892

Step 2 Produce the adjusted trial balance from the original trial balance and your journals and workings. It is important to keep neat workings to support your figures.

Adjusted trial balance

	£	£
Capital		15,258
Drawings		5,970
Purchases	73,010	
Returns inwards	1,076	
Returns outwards		3,720
Discounts	1,870	965
Credit sales		96,520
Cash sales		30,296
Customs duty	11,760	
Carriage inwards	2,930	
Carriage outwards	1,762	
Salesman's commission	711	
Salesman's salary	3,970	
Office salaries	7,207	
Bank charges	980	
Loan interest	450	
Light and heat	2,653	
Sundry expenses	2,100	
Rent and rates	7,315	
Printing and postage	2,103	
Advertising	1,044	
Bad debts (1,791 + 101)	1,892	
Provision for doubtful debts (437 + 101)		538
Stock (balance sheet)	8,490	
Debtors	10,760	
Creditors		7,411
Cash at bank	2,534	
Cash in hand	75	
Motor expenses	986	
Furniture and equipment		
Cost	8,000	
Depreciation at 31 May 19X6		3,200
Delivery van		
Cost	3,200	
Depreciation at 31 May 19X6		640
Loan account at 9% (repayable in five years)	5,000	
Stock (P&L)	7,650	8,490
Depreciation expense	640	
	800	
Loss on sale of van		100
	172,038	172,038

Step 3   Prepare the profit and loss account and balance sheet

(a)   **Trading and profit and loss account for the year ended 31 May 19X6**

		£	£	£
Sales:				
	Credit			96,520
	Cash			30,296
				126,816
Less:	Sales returns			(1,076)
				125,740
Opening stock			7,650	
Purchases		73,010		
Less:	Purchase returns	(3,720)		
		69,290		
Carriage inwards		2,930		
Customs duty		11,760		
			83,980	
			91,630	
Closing stock			(8,490)	
Cost of sales				83,140
Gross profit				42,600
Discount received				965
				43,565
Less:	Expenses			
Depreciation:				
	Van		(640)	
	Equipment		(800)	
Loss on disposal			(100)	
Bad debts			(1,892)	
Light and heat			(2,653)	
Rent and rates			(7,315)	
Discount allowed			(1,870)	
Carriage outwards			(1,762)	
Salesman's commission			(711)	
Salesman's salary			(3,970)	
Office salaries			(7,207)	
Bank charges			(980)	
Loan interest			(450)	
Sundry expenses			(2,100)	
Printing and postage			(2,103)	
Advertising			(1,044)	
Motor expenses			(986)	
				(36,583)
Net profit				6,982

(b)

Balance sheet at 31 May 19X6

	Cost £	Acc dep'n £	£
Fixed assets:			
Motor van	3,200	(640)	2,560
Furniture and equipment	8,000	(3,200)	4,800
	11,200	(3,840)	7,360
Current assets:			
Stock		8,490	
Debtors	10,760		
Less: Provision for doubtful debts	(538)		
		10,222	
Cash at bank		2,534	
Cash in hand		75	
		21,321	
Less: Current liabilities:			
Trade creditors		(7,411)	
			13,910
			21,270
Less: Long-term liability			(5,000)
			16,270
Capital account:			
Balance at 1 June 19X5			15,258
Net profit for the year			6,982
			22,240
Less: Drawings			(5,970)
			16,270

Notes on presentation

(a)   The trading account includes all expenditure incurred in bringing the goods to their present location and condition. This includes:

(i)   purchase cost including import duty;
(ii)   carriage inwards and freight costs.

In contrast carriage outwards is treated as an expense of selling and is included with all the other expenses. Note that both carriage inwards and carriage outwards are debits (ie, expenses).

[Definition]   Carriage inwards is the cost of bringing in raw materials from suppliers. Carriage outwards is the delivery charge incurred in supplying goods to customers.

(b)   'Returns' often causes difficulties. Returns inwards are the same as sales returns. Since sales are credits, sales returns are debits. For presentation purposes, sales returns are deducted from sales. In the same way purchase returns are deducted from purchases.

(c)   The discounts are shown as one line in the trial balance with both a debit and a credit balance. Remember that expenses are debit balances while items of income are credit balances. Therefore the discount allowed is the debit balance and the discount received the credit balance.

(d)   In examinations the answers should precede the workings, which should clearly be labelled as such. The idea behind this is that the examiner only wishes to look at the workings if errors have been made - hopefully he will not need to.

If the workings are numbered then a reference to the working can be made in the final accounts.

Therefore, in an examination, the trading and P&L a/c and balance sheet should be shown before the workings above.

Conclusion   All that has been covered in this chapter should have been revision from your previous studies. Subsequent chapters of this study text will now take this accounts preparation process further.

7   SELF TEST QUESTIONS

1   In a trial balance if stock is shown as a debit balance will this normally be the opening stock or the closing stock figure? (2.1)

2   After all of the double entry has been carried out for stock at the year end what does the balance on the stock - balance sheet account represent? (2.4)

3   What is the double entry for recording the annual depreciation charge on fixed assets? (3.2)

4   What is the double entry for cash proceeds from the sale of a fixed asset? (3.7)

5   What does any balance on a fixed asset disposal account represent? (3.7)

6   What is the double entry for writing off a bad debt? (4.2)

7   What is the double entry for an increase in the doubtful debt provision? (4.2)

8   If income is received in advance will this be a debit balance or a credit balance? (5.3)

9   What is carriage inwards? (6.3)

10   How are carriage inwards and carriage outwards treated in a set of financial statements? (6.3)

THE EXTENDED TRIAL BALANCE - SOLE TRADERS

PATHFINDER INTRODUCTION

This chapter covers the following performance criteria and knowledge and understanding.

- Financial statements are accurately drafted from the appropriate information (performance criteria 10.2)
- Subsequent adjustments are correctly implemented (performance criteria 10.2)
- Form and method of preparation of financial statements (knowledge and understanding 10.2)

Putting the chapter in context – learning objectives.

The previous chapter covered the preparation of a basic set of financial statements for a sole trader from a trial balance. However a further method of preparing a set of financial statements, particularly where a number of adjustments are necessary, is to use as a working method an extended trial balance. Therefore in this chapter again, the financial statements of a sole trader will be produced but this time the extended trial balance will be used to take the initial trial balance figures through to the final balance sheet and profit and loss account.

At the end of this chapter you should have learned the following topics.

- Preparing a proforma extended trial balance.
- Entering the initial trial balance figures on the extended trial balance.
- Entering the period end adjustments onto the extended trial balance.
- Entering the period end accruals and prepayments on the extended trial balance.
- Entering stock figures correctly on the extended trial balance.
- Completing the extended trial balance.

---

1 EXTENDED TRIAL BALANCE

1.1 Introduction

The chapter on the trial balance showed how general ledger accounts were balanced and the balances listed to check the accuracy of the accounting. The chapter on producing the final accounts showed how the trial balance, via a series of adjustments, was used to produce a profit and loss account and balance sheet.

In practice, producing the set of financial accounts combines these two steps by using a technique called an 'extended trial balance'.

Definition   An extended trial balance is a worksheet which takes a trial balance, makes all the year end adjustments and produces a draft balance sheet and profit and loss account.

1.2 Proforma extended trial balance

An extended trial balance can be seen in the illustration. The layout is explained below.

(a)   Account - the first column is used to list all the general ledger accounts.

(b)   Trial balance - the next section containing two columns is used to list the balances on all the general ledger accounts. The balance on an account is put into either the debit column or the credit column as usual. The total of the debit column should equal the total of the credit column.

(c)   Ref and adjustments - these sections are used to record any period-end adjustments to the trial balance made via journals. The reference of the journals is put into the 'ref' column to enable the figures in the adjustment section to be traced back to source documentation. A double entry is performed for each adjustment using the debit and credit columns.

(d)   Profit and loss - account balances that belong in the profit and loss account will finally be put in this section.

(e)   Balance sheet - account balances that belong in the balance sheet will be put in this section.

It is of vital importance that the debit column total and credit column total of the trial balance and adjustments sections balance before moving on to the next sections.

Illustration:

**Extended trial balance
at 31 December 19X2**

Account	Trial balance		Ref	Adjustments		Profit and loss		Balance sheet	
	Dr	Cr		Dr	Cr	Dr	Cr	Dr	Cr
	£	£		£	£	£	£	£	£

Conclusion	An extended trial balance is a worksheet used to produce final profit and loss account and balance sheet figures from a trial balance.

2   FROM TRIAL BALANCE TO EXTENDED TRIAL BALANCE

2.1   Introduction

The starting point for any extended trial balance is the trial balance. A trial balance is extracted from the general ledger in the normal way. If the double entry has been correct, then the trial balance will balance and can be inserted directly into the extended trial balance. If the double entry has broken down somewhere, then the trial balance will not be in balance and a suspense account will be needed. In this instance correct the suspense account first so that the trial balance entered into the extended trial balance balances (covered in the previous chapter).

2.2   Activity

The following balances have been extracted from the books of XYZ, a small shower manufacturing firm.

	Dr £	Cr £
Capital account		12,000
Opening stock	15,000	
Sales		100,000
Purchases	40,000	
Rent and rates	10,000	
Drawings	12,000	
Electricity	2,000	
Motor van cost	8,000	
Motor van accumulated depreciation		4,000
Bank balance	4,500	
Trade debtors	20,000	
Trade creditors		21,000
Sundry expenses	500	
Wages and salaries	25,000	
	137,000	137,000

Begin the extended trial balance for this business.

2.3   Activity solution

Step 1   Draw up a proforma extended trial balance using the account names given

Extended trial balance at 31 December 19X2

Account	Trial balance Dr £	Trial balance Cr £	Ref	Adjustments Dr £	Adjustments Cr £	Profit and loss Dr £	Profit and loss Cr £	Balance sheet Dr £	Balance sheet Cr £
Capital account									
Stock									
Sales									
Purchases									
Rent and rates									
Drawings									
Electricity									
Motor van cost									
Motor van provision for depreciation									
Bank balance									
Trade debtors									
Trade creditors									
Sundry expenses									
Wages and salaries									

Step 2   Put in the figures from the trial balance

Extended trial balance at 31 December 19X2

Account	Trial balance Dr £	Trial balance Cr £	Ref	Adjustments Dr £	Adjustments Cr £	Profit and loss Dr £	Profit and loss Cr £	Balance sheet Dr £	Balance sheet Cr £
Capital account		12,000							
Stock	15,000								
Sales		100,000							
Purchases	40,000								
Rent and rates	10,000								
Drawings	12,000								
Electricity	2,000								
Motor van cost	8,000								
Motor van provision for depreciation		4,000							
Bank balance	4,500								
Trade debtors	20,000								
Trade creditors		21,000							
Sundry expenses	500								
Wages and salaries	25,000								
	137,000	137,000							

Step 3   Check that the trial balance balances, i.e. that the debits equal the credits.

Conclusion   The opening trial balance is entered into the first two columns of the extended trial balance.

3   PERIOD END ADJUSTMENTS

3.1   Introduction

Definition   Period end adjustments are accounting adjustments to the trial balance required for the preparation of the period end financial accounts. They include items like bad debt provisions and write offs, depreciation adjustments, disposals of fixed assets and correction of mis-postings.

All the period end adjustments likely to arise have already been covered in previous chapters. The purpose of this section is to demonstrate how those adjustments are shown on the extended trial balance.

3.2   Activity

Continuing with the activity already started in this chapter produce the journals and make the following adjustments to the trial balance:

(a)   a depreciation charge for the year of £500;
(b)   a bad debt write off amounting to £1,000; and
(c)   an adjustment for drawings of £200 included in sundry expenses.

3.3   Activity solution

Step 1   Produce the journals

		Dr £	Cr £
(a)	Depreciation expense	500	
	Provision for depreciation		500
	Being depreciation for the year		
(b)	Bad debts expense	1,000	
	Trade debtors		1,000
	Being the write off of a bad debt		
(c)	Drawings	200	
	Sundry expenses		200
	Being the transfer of an incorrect posting		

Step 2   Enter the adjustments on to the extended trial balance

Extended trial balance at 31 December 19X2

Account	Trial balance Dr £	Trial balance Cr £	Ref	Adjustments Dr £	Adjustments Cr £	Profit and loss Dr £	Profit and loss Cr £	Balance sheet Dr £	Balance sheet Cr £
Capital account		12,000							
Stock	15,000								
Sales		100,000							
Purchases	40,000								
Rent and rates	10,000								
Drawings	12,000		c	200					
Electricity	2,000								
Motor van cost	8,000								
Motor van provision for depreciation		4,000	a		500				
Bank balance	4,500								
Trade debtors	20,000		b		1,000				
Trade creditors		21,000							
Sundry expenses	500		c		200				
Wages and salaries	25,000								
Depreciation expenses			a	500					
Bad debt expense			b	1,000					
	137,000	137,000							

Step 3   Check the debit and credit adjustments columns balance but do not enter the totals yet.

They both total to £1,700

Note that the total of the debit and credit columns must balance, that is, the double entry has been maintained. If the column totals are not checked at this point and the columns do not balance there are two main effects. Firstly, the extended trial balance will not balance and secondly, it is a major headache trying to find out what has gone wrong at a later stage. Whilst it appears a little slower working through methodically, it will be a lot quicker than having to go back through the whole extended trial balance to find errors when it does not balance at the final stage.

Conclusion   Year end adjustments, such as depreciation charges and charges for bad and doubtful debts, are entered in the adjustments column of the extended trial balance.

4   ACCRUALS AND PREPAYMENTS

4.1   Introduction

In practice, accruals and prepayments are often shown as separate adjustments with their own columns in the extended trial balance but they can also be included with other year end adjustments. Their treatment warrants separate attention only because it is slightly different in the extended trial balance compared with the ledger accounts. If anything, it is more straightforward.

4.2   How to enter accruals into the extended trial balance

When an expense accrual is calculated, it is entered in the expense account by carrying down a balance. The balance c/d (above the total) is a debit and has the effect of increasing the expense taken to the profit and loss account. The credit balance c/d (below the total) is the accrual shown in the balance sheet. This process may be thought of as a kind of double entry, as follows:

Dr   Profit and loss expense account
      Cr   Accruals in the balance sheet

In the extended trial balance the individual accruals are entered in the debit column. The total of all the accruals is entered in the credit column. This credit entry is on a newly created account line called 'accruals' and it will eventually give the accruals figure in the balance sheet.

4.3   Activity

Continuing with the activity, the following accruals are needed at the year end:

Electricity   £150
Sundry expenses   £50

4.4   Activity solution

Step 1   Write in accruals in the debit adjustments column on the appropriate account line.

Step 2   Total up the accruals and enter the amount in the credit adjustments column opposite a new account heading, accruals. (The reference column just shows the references for the new entries.)

Extended trial balance at 31 December 19X2

Account	Trial balance		Ref	Adjustments		Profit and loss		Balance sheet	
	Dr	Cr		Dr	Cr	Dr	Cr	Dr	Cr
	£	£		£	£	£	£	£	£
Capital account		12,000							
Stock	15,000								
Sales		100,000							
Purchases	40,000								
Rent and rates	10,000								
Drawings	12,000			200					
Electricity	2,000		d	150					
Motor van cost	8,000								
Motor van provision for depreciation		4,000			500				
Bank balance	4,500								
Trade debtors	20,000				1,000				
Trade creditors		21,000							
Sundry expenses	500		d	50	200				
Wages and salaries	25,000								
Depreciation expenses				500					
Bad debt expense				1,000					
Accruals			d		200				
	137,000	137,000		1,900	1,900				

4.5   How to enter prepayments into the trial balance

A prepayment on an expense account comprises a debit balance b/d which is the prepayment shown in the balance sheet and a credit entry for the balance c/d (above the total) which has the effect of reducing the expense taken to the profit and loss account. Again, this may be represented by a double entry:

Dr   Prepayments in the balance sheet
      Cr   Profit and loss account expenses

In the extended trial balance the prepayments are listed individually in the credit adjustments column. This will form the credit side of the account line of the double entry. Total prepayments are placed in a new account line, prepayments, in the debit column. This debit will eventually appear in the balance sheet as 'prepayments'.

4.6   Activity

Carrying on the activity, a prepayment of rent of £800 is to be recognised.

4.7   Activity solution

Step 1   Enter the individual prepayment in the credit column for each expense account.

Step 2   Total the individual prepayment and enter as a debit in a new line entitled 'prepayments'.

Extended trial balance at 31 December 19X2

Account	Trial balance Dr £	Trial balance Cr £	Ref	Adjustments Dr £	Adjustments Cr £	Profit and loss Dr £	Profit and loss Cr £	Balance sheet Dr £	Balance sheet Cr £
Capital account		12,000							
Stock	15,000								
Sales		100,000							
Purchases	40,000								
Rent and rates	10,000		e		800				
Drawings	12,000			200					
Electricity	2,000			150					
Motor van cost	8,000								
Motor van provision for depreciation		4,000			500				
Bank balance	4,500								
Trade debtors	20,000				1,000				
Trade creditors		21,000							
Sundry expenses	500			50	200				
Wages and salaries	25,000								
Depreciation expenses				500					
Bad debt expense				1,000					
Accruals					200				
Prepayment			e	800					
	137,000	137,000		2,700	2,700				

When all the accruals and prepayments have been entered, total up the debit and credit columns and make sure they balance.

Conclusion | Adjustments for accruals and prepayments are entered into the adjustments columns of the extended trial balance.

5   STOCK AND THE EXTENDED TRIAL BALANCE

5.1   Introduction

Earlier it was shown that the period end required an adjustment to account for the closing stock as follows:

Dr   stock account (balance sheet)
    Cr   stock account (profit and loss account)

An entry was also required to transfer last year's closing stock, now forming this year's opening stock, to the profit and loss account:

Dr   stock (profit and loss account) and then cleared to P&L a/c
Cr   stock (balance sheet)

Both entries will be looked at in this section on stock in the extended trial balance.

5.2   Entering closing stock into the extended trial balance

The closing stock entries are made in the adjustments column. A new account is required called stock (profit and loss). Remember, the stock account appearing in the trial balance is the stock (balance sheet) account which currently has on it the figure for opening stock ie last year's closing stock.

5.3   Activity

XYZ's closing stock was valued at £17,000. Enter this information on the extended trial balance.

5.4   Activity solution

Step 1 | Write the new stock (profit and loss) account in the account column.

Step 2 | Make the closing stock entry in the adjustments columns. (The reference column only shows the reference for the new entries.) Debit the stock (balance sheet) account and credit the stock (profit and loss) account.

Extended trial balance at 31 December 19X2

Account	Trial balance Dr £	Trial balance Cr £	Ref	Adjustments Dr £	Adjustments Cr £	Profit and loss Dr £	Profit and loss Cr £	Balance sheet Dr £	Balance sheet Cr £
Capital account		12,000							
Stock (balance sheet)	15,000		f	**17,000**					
Sales		100,000							
Purchases	40,000								
Rent and rates	10,000				800				
Drawings	12,000			200					
Electricity	2,000			150					
Motor van cost	8,000								
Motor van provision for depreciation		4,000			500				
Bank balance	4,500								
Trade debtors	20,000				1,000				
Trade creditors		21,000							
Sundry expenses	500			50	200				
Wages and salaries	25,000								
Depreciation expenses				500					
Bad debt expense				1,000					
Accruals					200				
Prepayments				800					
Stock (profit and loss)			f	**17,000**					
	137,000	137,000		19,700	19,700				

5.5 Opening stock and the extended trial balance

For extended trial balance purposes, the opening stock can be cleared to the stock (profit and loss) account as an adjustment by crediting the stock (balance sheet) account and debiting the stock (profit and loss) account.

5.6 Activity

Adjust the extended trial balance for the opening stock.

5.7   Activity solution

Extended trial balance at 31 December 19X2

Account	Trial balance Dr £	Trial balance Cr £	Ref	Adjustments Dr £	Adjustments Cr £	Profit and loss Dr £	Profit and loss Cr £	Balance sheet Dr £	Balance sheet Cr £
Capital account		12,000							
Stock	15,000		g	**17,000**	**15,000**				
Sales		100,000							
Purchases	40,000								
Rent and rates	10,000				800				
Drawings	12,000			200					
Electricity	2,000			150					
Motor van cost	8,000								
Motor van provision for depreciation		4,000			500				
Bank balance	4,500								
Trade debtors	20,000				1,000				
Trade creditors		21,000							
Sundry expenses	500			50	200				
Wages and salaries	25,000								
Depreciation expenses				500					
Bad debt expense				1,000					
Accruals					200				
Prepayments				800					
Stock (profit and loss)			g	**15,000**	**17,000**				
	137,000	137,000		34,700	34,700				

Note that the stock (profit and loss) account shows the opening and closing stock figures that will be cleared to the profit and loss account.

At this point total the debit and credit adjustment columns as all of the period end adjustments are now completed. If the adjustments have been correctly entered then the debit total should equal the credit total.

Conclusion   Adjustments to stock are entered into the adjustments column of the extended trial balance.

5.8   Short cut method

To satisfy the double entries for the year end stock adjustments two stock accounts have been used on the extended trial balance.

The figures for XYZ will actually eventually appear as follows:

	Trial balance		Adjustments		Profit & loss a/c		Balance sheet	
	Dr	**Cr**	**Dr**	**Cr**	**Dr**	**Cr**	**Dr**	**Cr**
Stock (balance sheet)	15,000		17,000	15,000			17,000	
Stock (profit and loss)			15,000	17,000	15,000	17,000		

However there is an easier way of doing this that gives the same result.

The two double entries in the adjustments column may be simplified to one if only one stock account is used, for both balance sheet and profit and loss account purposes. In this case, all that is needed is to introduce closing stock with one double entry:

	Trial balance		Adjustments		Profit & loss a/c		Balance sheet	
	Dr	**Cr**	**Dr**	**Cr**	**Dr**	**Cr**	**Dr**	**Cr**
Stock	15,000		17,000	17,000				

The account line is not cross cast; each individual entry is placed in the profit and loss account or balance sheet, as appropriate

	Trial balance		Adjustments		Profit & loss a/c		Balance sheet	
	Dr	**Cr**	**Dr**	**Cr**	**Dr**	**Cr**	**Dr**	**Cr**
Stock	15,000		17,000	17,000	15,000	17,000	17,000	

This simpler approach gives the same final result in the profit and loss account and balance sheet column.

6 COMPLETING THE EXTENDED TRIAL BALANCE

6.1 Introduction

The final step in preparing an extended trial balance is to complete the profit and loss and balance sheet columns.

6.2 Extending the account balances across the trial balance

Extending the account balances across the extended trial balance requires two skills:

(a)   Knowledge of which accounts go into the profit and loss account and which accounts go into the balance sheet.

(b)   Careful addition (casting).

6.3 Activity

Continue the earlier activity to complete the extended trial balance.

6.4   Activity solution

Extended trial balance at 31 December 19X2

Account	Trial balance Dr £	Cr £	Ref	Adjustments Dr £	Cr £	Profit and loss Dr £	Cr £	Balance sheet Dr £	Cr £
Capital account		12,000							12,000
Stock	15,000			17,000	15,000			17,000	
Sales		100,000					100,000		
Purchases	40,000					40,000			
Rent and rates	10,000				800	9,200			
Drawings	12,000			200				12,200	
Electricity	2,000			150		2,150			
Motor van cost	8,000							8,000	
Motor van provision for depreciation		4,000			500				4,500
Bank balance	4,500							4,500	
Trade debtors	20,000				1,000			19,000	
Trade creditors		21,000							21,000
Sundry expenses	500			50	200	350			
Wages and salaries	25,000					25,000			
Depreciation expenses				500		500			
Bad debt expense				1,000		1,000			
Accruals					200				200
Prepayments				800				800	
Stock (profit and loss)				15,000	17,000	15,000	17,000		
	137,000	137,000		34,700	34,700				

Notes:

(a)   *Capital account*

A balance sheet account with only one credit entry (in the trial balance column), therefore carry that figure across to the credit column of the balance sheet section.

(b)   *Stock*

The stock account is the balance sheet stock therefore the final figure will go into the balance sheet. There are three entries on the stock line.

Trial balance debit	£15,000
Debit adjustment	£17,000
Credit adjustment	£15,000

Treating a debit as a 'plus' and a credit as a 'minus', add across the various columns. If the result is a plus then the account balance is a debit, whilst a minus would mean a credit balance.

Cross casting this line: 15,000 + 17,000 − 15,000 = £17,000

So the final balance is a debit balance of £17,000 in the balance sheet column.

(c)   *Sales and purchases*

Single figure profit and loss account figures - a credit and a debit respectively.

(d)   *Rent and rates*

This is a profit and loss account item with more than one figure. Following the same procedure as for the stock: 10,000 (debit) − 800 (credit) = £9,200 (debit)

Continue to cross cast the remaining account lines, except for stock (profit and loss) to confirm that they follow the same procedure.

(e)   *Accruals and prepayments*

These are the totals to appear on the balance sheet therefore a credit for accruals and a debit for prepayments.

(f)   *Stock (profit and loss)*

Rather than cross casting this line, transfer each figure to the profit and loss account, as both will be shown separately. One is opening stock (£15,000) and the other closing stock (£17,000). This is the exception to the rule.

6.5   Finding the profit and loss for the period

Having completed the profit and loss and balance sheet columns, the final step of the extended trial balance is to find the profit or loss for the period.

The steps for doing this are as follows.

Step 1   Add up the credit column of the profit and loss section.

Step 2   Add up the debit column of the profit and loss section.

Step 3   Take the debit away from the credit.

If there are more credits than debits, a profit has been made, whereas an excess of debits over credits means a loss has been incurred.

This makes sense, because if the income (credit) is bigger than the expenses (debit) a profit is made.

Step 4   Insert the figure to make the two balances equal.

Step 5   If a profit has been made (more credits) a balancing figure will be required in the debit column of the profit and loss account. A loss (more debits) would go as a balancing figure on the credit side of the profit and loss account.

Step 6   Cast the two balance sheet columns.

Step 7   Insert the same profit (or loss) figure as a balancing figure in the balance sheet. However, this time the profit figure goes as a balancing figure on the credit side whereas a loss would have to sit on the debit side.

Do not worry unduly about which side the profit figure or loss figure goes on. If the double entry has been maintained it will be obvious where the resultant figure lives.

6.6 Activity

Determine the profit and loss for the period for the activity and complete the extended trial balance.

6.7 Activity solution

Extended trial balance at 31 December 19X2

Account	Trial balance Dr £	Trial balance Cr £	Ref	Adjustments Dr £	Adjustments Cr £	Profit and loss Dr £	Profit and loss Cr £	Balance sheet Dr £	Balance sheet Cr £
Capital account		12,000							12,000
Stock	15,000			17,000	15,000			17,000	
Sales		100,000					100,000		
Purchases	40,000					40,000			
Rent and rates	10,000				800	9,200			
Drawings	12,000			200				12,200	
Electricity	2,000			150		2,150			
Motor van cost	8,000							8,000	
Motor van provision for depreciation		4,000			500				4,500
Bank balance	4,500							4,500	
Trade debtors	20,000				1,000			19,000	
Trade creditors		21,000							21,000
Sundry expenses	500			50	200	350			
Wages and salaries	25,000					25,000			
Depreciation expenses				500		500			
Bad debt expense				1,000		1,000			
Accruals					200				200
Prepayments				800				800	
Stock (profit and loss)				15,000	17,000	15,000	17,000		
	137,000	137,000		34,700	34,700	93,200	117,000	61,500	37,700
Profit						23,800			23,800
						117,000	117,000	61,500	61,500

The profit and loss account columns show that a profit of £23,800 has been made. This also appears in the balance sheet as owing to the owner of the business.

Conclusion The figures are extended into the profit and loss account and the balance sheet columns of the extended trial balance to produce the final accounts. The balancing figure in the profit and loss account columns is the net profit or loss for the year.

7 SELF TEST QUESTIONS

1 What are the columns required in an extended trial balance? (1.2)

2 How would a year end bad debt write off be adjusted for in the extended trial balance? (3.3)

3 How would year end accruals be entered into the extended trial balance? (4.4)

4   How would year end prepayments be entered into the extended trial balance? (4.7)

5   What does the stock figure in the original trial balance represent? (5.2)

6   How is the closing stock adjusted for in the extended trial balance? (5.4)

7   How is the opening stock adjusted for in the extended trial balance? (5.7)

8   What is the short cut method for entering opening and closing stock onto the extended trial balance? (5.8)

9   How is the profit for the period determined from an extended trial balance? (6.5)

10   If a profit for the period is made how will this appear in the balance sheet columns of the extended trial balance? (6.5)

6 | BASIC PARTNERSHIP ACCOUNTING

PATHFINDER INTRODUCTION

This chapter covers the following performance criteria and knowledge and understanding.

- Financial statements are accurately drafted from the appropriate information (performance criteria 10.2)
- Subsequent adjustments are correctly implemented (performance criteria 10.2)
- Draft accounts comply with domestic standards and legislation and, where relevant, partnership agreement (performance criteria 10.2)
- Form and method of preparation of financial statements (knowledge and understanding 10.2)

Putting the chapter in context – learning objectives.

This chapter moves on to deal with the financial statements of the next relevant type of business entity, the partnership. The vast majority of the accounting is the same as that covered for a sole trader in the previous chapters. However there are differences in some of the details of accounting for capital and the split of profit that will be considered in this chapter before moving on to more complex partnership situations in the next chapter.

At the end of this chapter you should have learned the following topics.

- An introduction to the basic principles of partnerships and partnership accounting.
- Accounting for the appropriation of profit amongst the partners.
- Preparing a simple set of financial statements for a partnership from a trial balance.

---

1 PARTNERSHIPS - BASIC PRINCIPLES

1.1 Introduction

 A partnership is a natural progression from a sole trader, the sole proprietor taking in one or more partners (co-proprietors) in common with a view to profit. A partnership is not a corporate entity, but a collection of individuals jointly carrying on business.

Although partnerships are covered by statutory rules, mainly by the Partnership Act 1890, these are often varied by agreement between the partners. Since no limitation of the liability of the partners is (usually) involved, there is no need for the detailed statutory rules to protect creditors typical of the Companies Act. Therefore, those matters which the partners agree between them provide the legal structure within which the partners operate.

1.2 The advantages and disadvantages of a partnership

Comparing a partnership to sole trading, the advantages of operating as a partnership are as follows.

(a) Business risks are spread among more than one person.

(b) Individual partners can develop special skills upon which the other partners can rely rather than being a jack of all trades.

(c)   Certain partners may be able to draw upon larger capital resources to set up the partnership or expand the partnership.

The disadvantages are:

(a)   There may be disputes between partners on such matters as the direction the business is taking or how much money individual partners are taking out of the business. Some partners may feel they are contributing more time and effort to the partnership than others and not being sufficiently financially rewarded as a result.

(b)   A partner is 'jointly and severally liable' for his partners. This means that if one partner is being sued in relation to the business of the partnership, the other partners share in the responsibility.

1.3   Partnership agreement

Definition   A partnership agreement, which need not necessarily be in written form, will govern the relationships between the partners.

Important matters to be covered include

(a)   name of firm, the type of business, and duration
(b)   capital to be introduced by partners
(c)   distribution of profits between partners
(d)   drawings by partners
(e)   arrangements for dissolution, or on the death or retirement of partners
(f)   settling of disputes
(g)   preparation and audit of accounts.

The division of profit stated in the partnership agreement may be quite complex in order to reflect the expected differing efforts and contributions of the partners. For example, some or all of the partners may be entitled to a salary to reflect the differing management involvement in the business. Interest on capital may be provided to reflect the differing amounts of capital contributed. The profit shares may differ to reflect seniority or greater skills.

It is important to appreciate however that all of the above examples are means of dividing the profits of the partnership and are not expenses of the business. A partnership salary is merely a device for calculating the division of profit; it is not a salary in the normal meaning of the term.

Conclusion   A partnership is made up of a number of sole traders trading together normally with some agreement drawn up between them.

1.4   Accounting for partnerships

The accounting techniques developed for sole traders are generally applicable to partnerships, but there are certain important differences. These can be summarised:

Item	*Sole trader's books*	*Partnership's books*
Capital introduced	Capital account	Partners' fixed capital accounts
Drawings and share of the profit	Capital account	Partners' current accounts
Division of profits	Inapplicable - one proprietor only	Appropriation account

Definition   The appropriation account is an account used to split the profit of the partnership amongst the individual partners.

1.5   Capital accounts

At the commencement of the partnership an agreement will have to be reached as to the amount of capital to be introduced. This could be in the form of cash or other assets. Whatever the form of assets introduced and debited to asset accounts, it is normal to make the credit entry to fixed capital accounts. These are so called because they are not then used to record drawings or shares of profits but only major changes in the relations between partners. In particular, fixed capital accounts are used to deal with

(a)   capital introduced or withdrawn by new or retiring partners

(b)   revaluation adjustments (see later in this study text).

The balances on fixed capital accounts do not necessarily bear any relation to the division of profits. However, to compensate partners who provide a larger share of the capital, it is common for notional interest on capital accounts to be paid to partners. This is dealt with through the appropriation account.

1.6   Current accounts

These are used to deal with the regular transactions between the partners and the firm ie, matters other than those sufficiently fundamental to be dealt with through the capital accounts. Most commonly these are

(a)   share of profits, interest on capital and partners' salaries usually computed annually

(b)   monthly drawings against the annual share of profit.

1.7   Example

Nab and Crag commenced business in partnership on 1 January 19X6, contributing as fixed capital £5,000 and £10,000 cash respectively. All profits and losses are shared equally. The profit for the year ended 31 December 19X6 amounted to £10,000. Drawings for Nab and Crag amounted to £3,000 and £4,000 respectively.

You are required to prepare the capital and current accounts, appropriation account and balance sheet extracts.

1.8   Solution

Partners' capital accounts

	Nab	*Crag*				*Nab*	*Crag*
	£	£				£	£
			19X6				
			1 Jan	Cash		5,000	10,000

Appropriation account

	£			£
19X6			19X6	
31 Dec Share of profit -			31 Dec Net profit b/d	10,000
current account				
Nab	5,000			
Crag	5,000			
	10,000			10,000

Partners' current accounts

	Nab £	Crag £		Nab £	Crag £
19X6			19X6		
1 Dec Drawings	3,000	4,000	31 Dec Share of profits	5,000	5,000
Balance c/d	2,000	1,000			
	5,000	5,000		5,000	5,000
			19X7		
			1 Jan Balance b/d	2,000	1,000

The above accounts are presented in a columnar format. This is quite common in a partnership set of books as each partner will have similar transactions during the year. A columnar format allows two (or more) separate accounts to be shown using the same narrative. It is important to remember though that each partner's account is separate from the other partner(s).

Balance sheet at 31 December 19X6 (extract)

	Capital accounts £	Current accounts £	Total £
Partners' accounts:			
Nab	5,000	2,000	7,000
Crag	10,000	1,000	11,000
	15,000	3,000	18,000

Note that the current account balances of £2,000 and £1,000 will be credited in the following year with profit shares and debited with drawings.

One of the main differences between the capital section of the balance sheet of a sole trader and a partnership is that the partnership balance sheet will often only give the closing balances whereas the sole trader's movements in capital are shown. The main reason for the difference is simply one of space. Movements in the capital and current accounts for a few partners cannot be easily accommodated on the face of the balance sheet.

1.9   Activity

The information is the same as in the previous activity, except that Nab's drawings are £5,300. Rewrite the partners' current accounts.

1.10   Activity solution

Partners' current accounts

		Nab £	Crag £			Nab £	Crag £
19X6				19X6			
	Drawings	5,300	4,000		Share of profits	5,000	5,000
31 Dec	Balance c/d		1,000	31 Dec	Balance c/d	300	
		5,300	5,000			5,300	5,000
19X7				19X7			
1 Jan	Balance b/d	300		1 Jan	Balance b/d		1,000

Note that Nab's current account is overdrawn. How do we present this in the balance sheet?

Balance sheet at 31 December 19X6 (extract)

	Capital accounts £	Current accounts £	Total £
Partners' accounts:			
Nab	5,000	(300)	4,700
Crag	10,000	1,000	11,000
	15,000	700	15,700

> **Conclusion**   Partners' drawings and share of the annual profit are recorded in their current accounts. Their capital accounts are used to record fixed capital introduced.

2   PROFIT APPROPRIATION

2.1   Appropriation account

> **Definition**   The appropriation account is a ledger account dealing with the allocation of net profit between the partners.

In practice it is often included as the final part of the trading and profit and loss account.

An important point is that all allocations of profit to partners in their capacity as partners, and during the time they actually are partners, are made through the appropriation account. This applies even though such allocations may be described as partners' salaries, interest on capital or a share of profits.

2.2   Activity

Pike and Scar are in partnership and have the following profit-sharing arrangements

(a)   interest on capital is to be provided at a rate of 8% pa
(b)   Pike and Scar are to receive salaries of £6,000 and £8,000 pa respectively
(c)   the balance of profit or loss is to be divided between Pike and Scar in the ratio 3 : 2

Net profit for the year amounts to £20,000 and capital account balances are Pike £12,000 and Scar £9,000.

You are required to prepare

(a)   a statement showing the allocation of profit between the partners and
(b)   relevant entries in the trading and profit and loss and appropriation account.

2.3   Activity solution

(a)   **Allocation of net profit of £20,000**

	Pike £	Scar £	Total £
Interest on capital (8% × £12,000/9,000)	960	720	1,680
Salaries	6,000	8,000	14,000
			15,680
Balance of profits (£20,000 − £15,680) in ratio 3 : 2	2,592 (3/5)	1,728 (2/5)	4,320
Totals	9,552	10,448	20,000

Note that this is only a calculation of the allocation of profit and not part of the double entry bookkeeping system, merely providing the figures for the appropriation account.

(b)   **Extract from trading and profit and loss and appropriation account for the year ended**

	£	£
Sales		x
Cost of sales		x
Gross profit		x
Expenses		x
Net profit		20,000
Allocated to:		
Pike	9,552	
Scar	10,448	
		20,000

The profit and loss appropriation account is closed by transferring the profit shares to the credit of the partners' current accounts. The double entry is therefore

Debit	Credit	With
Profit and loss appropriation account	Pike's current account	£9,552
Profit and loss appropriation account	Scar's current account	£10,448

For the purposes of examinations (and in practice) parts (a) and (b) above can be amalgamated as follows

Extract from trading and profit and loss and appropriation account for the year ended ...

	£
Sales	X
Cost of sales	X
Gross profit	X
Expenses	X
Net profit for year	20,000

Appropriation statement

	Pike £		Scar £		Total £
Interest on capital	960		720		1,680
Salaries	6,000		8,000		14,000
Balance of profits (£20,000 – £15,680) in ratio 3 : 2	2,592	(3/5)	1,728	(2/5)	4,320
Totals	9,552		10,448		20,000

The debits actually being made are as before (£9,552 and £10,448)

This treatment of the appropriation of profit in the appropriation statement is exactly the same as debiting an appropriation ledger account and crediting the partner's current accounts.

Conclusion   The appropriation account is used to deal with the allocation of net profit between the partners.

2.4   Profits and losses

It is entirely possible for a partnership to make such a small profit that this will not cover all of the agreed appropriation such as interest on capital and salaries. Nevertheless these appropriations must be carried out first as they are part of the partnership agreement. Then the remaining loss is split amongst the partners in the profit share ratio.

2.5   Activity

The facts are the same as for the previous activity, except that net profit is now only £3,680.

You are required to show the allocation of profit between the partners.

2.6   Activity solution

Allocation of net profit of £3,680

	Pike £	Scar £	Total £
Interest on capital	960	720	1,680
Salaries	6,000	8,000	14,000
Balance of loss £3,680 – £15,680			
= (£12,000) to be shared in ratio 3 : 2	(7,200)	(4,800)	(12,000)
Totals	(240)	3,920	3,680

The profit share is always carried out last after all other appropriation eg interest, salaries, even if this means that it becomes a loss share.

The double entry in this case is

Debit	*Credit*	*With*
Profit and loss appropriation account	Scar's current account	£3,920
Pike's current account	Profit and loss appropriation account	£240

The relevant part of the profit and loss account would show

	£	£
Net profit		3,680
Allocated to:		
Scar	3,920	
Pike	(240)	
		3,680

2.7   Partners' salaries

One point which regularly causes difficulties is the partners' salaries. The key is to remember at the outset that a partner's salary is an appropriation of profit, whereas a salary paid to an employee is an expense.

Accordingly a salary to which a partner is entitled is included as part of the appropriation statement. Questions sometimes state that a partner has withdrawn his salary. In this case

(a)   include the salary in the appropriation statement as usual and

(b)   quite separately treat the withdrawal of the salary as drawings.

Debit	*Credit*	*With*
Partners' current account	Bank	Amount withdrawn

2.8   Guaranteed minimum profit share

In certain partnership agreements a partner may be guaranteed a minimum share of profits. The appropriation of profit would proceed in the normal way. If the result is that the partner has less than this minimum, the deficit will be made good by the other partners (normally in profit-sharing ratio).

2.9   Activity

Tessa, Laura and Jane are in partnership and have the following profit-sharing arrangements

(a)   Tessa and Laura are to receive salaries of £20,000 and £30,000 respectively
(b)   the balance of profit or loss is to be divided Tessa 1, Laura 2, Jane 3
(c)   Tessa is guaranteed a minimum profit share of £25,000.

The net profit for the year is £68,000.

You are required to show the appropriation account for the year.

2.10   Activity solution

Appropriation account

	Tessa £	Laura £	Jane £	Total £
Net profit				68,000
Salaries	20,000	30,000	-	(50,000)
				18,000
Balance of profits in ratio 1 : 2 : 3	3,000	6,000	9,000	(18,000)
	23,000	36,000	9,000	
Adjustment	2,000			
Laura 2/5 × 2,000		(800)		
Jane 3/5 × 2,000			(1,200)	
Totals	25,000	35,200	7,800	68,000

Conclusion   The partner with the guaranteed minimum profit share must receive that amount. Any shortfall must be made up by the remaining partners.

2.11   Interest on drawings

Occasionally there is a provision in a partnership agreement for a notional interest charge on the drawings by each partner. The interest charges are merely a negative profit share - they are a means by which total profits are allocated between the partners.

The reason for an interest on drawings provision is that those partners who draw out more cash than their colleagues in the early part of an accounting period should suffer a cost.

2.12   Activity

Dick and Dastardly are in partnership. The capital and current accounts as at 1 January 19X7 show

	Capital £	Current £
Dick	50,000	2,500
Dastardly	20,000	3,000

The partnership agreement provides for the following

(a)   profits and losses are shared between Dick and Dastardly in percentages 60 and 40
(b)   interest on capital at 10% per annum is allowed
(c)   interest on drawings is charged at 12% per annum.

Drawings for the year to 31 December 19X7 are

	Dick £	Dastardly £
1 February 19X7	5,000	2,000
30 September 19X7	2,000	5,000

The profit for the year is £20,000.

You are required to prepare the appropriation account and the current accounts for the year ended 31 December 19X7.

2.13   Activity solution

Appropriation account for the year ended 31 December 19X7

	Dick £	Dastardly £	£
Profit for the year			20,000
Add: Interest on drawings (see working)	(610)	(370)	980
			20,980
Less: Interest on capital:			
50,000 × 10%	5,000		
20,000 × 10%		2,000	(7,000)
			13,980
Balance in profit-sharing ratio:			
13,980 × 60%	8,388		
13,980 × 40%		5,592	(13,980)
Total allocation	12,778	7,222	20,000

Current accounts

		Dick £	Dastardly £				Dick £	Dastardly £
19X7:				**19X7:**				
1 Feb	Drawings	5,000	2,000		Balance b/d		2,500	3,000
30 Sep	Drawings	2,000	5,000	31 Dec	Share of			
	Balance c/d	8,278	3,222		profits		12,778	7,222
		15,278	10,222				15,278	10,222

WORKING

		Dick £	Dastardly £
Interest on drawings:			
1 February 19X7	5,000 × 12% × 11/12	550	
	2,000 × 12% × 11/12		220
30 September 19X7	2,000 × 12% × 3/12	60	
	5,000 × 12% × 3/12		150
		610	370

(*Tutorial note:* interest on drawings is charged for the period of time that the cash has been withdrawn out of the business.)

Interest on drawings is in effect the opposite of interest on capital. Interest on drawings is effectively credited to the appropriation account and debited to the partners' current accounts.

Conclusion   Appropriations of net profit may take the form of:
- interest on capital
- 'salaries'
- a share of the remaining profit (in the agreed ratio)
- interest on drawings (occasionally).

2.14   The provisions of the Partnership Act 1890

The essence of a partnership is the mutual agreement of the partners. The Partnership Act 1890 allows partners wide powers in determining their relationships with each other. Partnership agreements may be written or oral, although the former are preferable in order to prevent misunderstandings or disputes. However, in the absence of a specific agreement, Section 24 of the Act lays down the following rules:

(1)   Partners' capitals to be contributed equally.
(2)   No partner is entitled to interest on capital.
(3)   No partner is entitled to a salary.
(4)   Profits and losses, both of a capital and revenue nature are to be shared equally.
(5)   Any loan made to the business by a partner is to carry interest at the rate of 5% pa.

3   PARTNERSHIP FINANCIAL STATEMENTS

3.1   Introduction

The profit and loss account and balance sheet for a partnership are generally very similar to those for a sole trader. The differences are in the areas of appropriation and capital and current accounts dealt with earlier in this chapter.

3.2   Activity

You are provided with the following information regarding the partnership of Dacre, Hutton and Tod.

(a)   **The trial balance at 31 December 19X6 is as follows**

	Dr £	Cr £
Sales		50,000
Stock at 1 January 19X6	6,000	
Purchases	29,250	
Carriage inwards	250	
Carriage outwards	400	
Creditors		4,000
Cash at bank	3,900	
Current accounts:		
Dacre		900
Hutton		750
Tod		1,350
Capital accounts:		
Dacre		4,000
Hutton		5,000
Tod		6,000
Drawings:		
Dacre	2,000	
Hutton	3,000	
Tod	5,000	
Sundry expenses	2,800	
Debtors	13,000	
Shop fittings:		
Cost	8,000	
Accumulated depreciation		1,600
	73,600	73,600

(b)   Closing stock is valued for accounts purposes at £5,500.

(c)   Depreciation of £800 is to be provided on the shop fittings.

(d)   The profit-sharing arrangements are as follows

    (i)   Interest on capital is to be provided at a rate of 10% per annum

    (ii)   Dacre and Tod are to receive salaries of £3,000 and £4,000 per annum respectively

    (iii)   the balance of profit or loss is to be divided between Dacre, Hutton and Tod in the ratio of 3 : 8 : 4.

You are required to prepare final accounts together with current accounts of the partners.

3.3   Activity solution

Step 1   Prepare the trading and profit and loss account as if it were for a sole trader.

Step 2   Calculate the total appropriation of profit to each partner using an appropriation statement.

Dacre, Hutton and Tod

Trading and profit and loss account for the year ended 31 December 19X6

	£	£
Sales		50,000
Opening stock	6,000	
Purchases	29,250	
Carriage inwards	250	
	35,500	
Less: Closing stock	5,500	
		30,000
Gross profit		20,000
Sundry expenses	2,800	
Carriage outwards	400	
Depreciation	800	
		4,000
Net profit		16,000
Allocated to:		
Dacre	4,900	
Hutton	4,500	
Tod	6,600	
		16,000

Profit appropriation

The new development is that, having calculated the profit for the period, it has to be appropriated between Dacre, Hutton and Tod. To calculate their respective shares an appropriation statement is used:

	Dacre £	Hutton £	Tod £	Total £
Interest on capital	400	500	600	1,500
Salaries	3,000	-	4,000	7,000
Balance of profit (£16,000 – £8,500) in ratio 3 : 8 : 4	1,500	4,000	2,000	7,500
	4,900	4,500	6,600	16,000

This gives us the figures for the double entry

Dr   Profit and loss appropriation
      Cr   Partners' current accounts

Step 3   Prepare balance sheet as for a sole trader.

Balance sheet as at 31 December 19X6

	Cost £	Acc dep'n £	£
Fixed assets			
Shop fittings	8,000	2,400	5,600
Current assets			
Stock		5,500	
Debtors		13,000	
Cash		3,900	
		22,400	
Current liabilities			
Creditors		4,000	
Net current assets			18,400
			24,000

Step 4   Prepare partners' capital and current accounts and put balances onto the capital section of the balance sheet.

Partners' accounts

	Capital accounts £	Current accounts £	Total £
Dacre	4,000	3,800	7,800
Hutton	5,000	2,250	7,250
Tod	6,000	2,950	8,950
	15,000	9,000	24,000

Partners' current accounts

		Dacre £	Hutton £	Tod £			Dacre £	Hutton £	Tod £
19X6:					19X6:				
	Draw-ings	2,000	3,000	5,000	1 Jan	Balance b/d	900	750	1,350
31 Dec	Balance c/d	3,800	2,250	2,950		P&L app	4,900	4,500	6,600
		5,800	5,250	7,950			5,800	5,250	7,950
					19X7:				
					1 Jan	Balance b/d	3,800	2,250	2,950

A final point

The majority of examination questions specify separate capital and current accounts. Occasionally you may be faced with a question specifying only one account for each partner. Such an account acts as a capital and current account combined.

[Conclusion]   To prepare a set of partnership accounts:

1.   Draw up a proforma balance sheet and profit and loss account and enter figures as soon as you calculate them.

2.   Work through any adjustments required.

3.   Complete the profit and loss account and appropriate the profit as per the partnership agreement.

4.   Open up partners' current accounts; enter the opening balances, appropriation of profit and drawings.

5.   Find the new balances on the partners' current accounts.

6.   Complete the balance sheet.

4   SELF TEST QUESTIONS

1   What is a partnership? (1.1)

2   What advantages does trading as a partnership have over sole trading? (1.2)

3   What typical points might be covered in a partnership agreement? (1.3)

4   What is recorded in partners' fixed capital accounts? (1.5)

5   What is recorded in partners' current accounts? (1.6)

6   What is the purpose of the appropriation account? (2.1)

7   How is a partner's salary always treated in partnership accounts? (2.7)

8   What is a guaranteed profit share system for a partner? (2.8)

9   What is the double entry for interest on drawings? (2.13)

10   How would partners' capital accounts and current accounts be shown in the partnership balance sheet? (3.3)

7 ACCOUNTING FOR PARTNERSHIP CHANGES

PATHFINDER INTRODUCTION

This chapter covers the following performance criteria and knowledge and understanding.

- Financial statements are accurately drafted from the appropriate information (performance criteria 10.2)
- Subsequent adjustments are correctly implemented (performance criteria 10.2)
- Draft accounts comply with domestic standards and legislation and, where relevant, partnership agreement (performance criteria 10.2)
- Form and method of preparation of financial statements (knowledge and understanding 10.2)

Putting the chapter in context – learning objectives.

This chapter takes accounting for partnerships a step further by looking at the accounting necessary for any changes in the partnership agreement. These changes might be due to the admission of a new partner, the retirement or death of an existing partner, a simple change in the details of the profit-sharing agreement or the sale or dissolution of the partnership. The accounting adjustments necessary for many of these changes are similar and these adjustments and the methods of applying them to each situation will be considered in some detail. Finally the chapter will continue from the chapters on sole traders and consider how a set of partnership financial statements might be drawn up from an extended trial balance.

At the end of this chapter you should have learned the following topics.

- The general principles of accounting for partnership changes.
- The specific methods of dealing with the admission or retirement of a partner.
- The importance of, and accounting for, revaluations of partnership assets.
- The treatment of goodwill when there is a change in the partnership.
- The accounting treatment of a merger of two sole traders in order to form a partnership.
- The accounting treatment of a dissolution of a partnership.
- The preparation of a set of financial statements for a partnership from an extended trial balance.

1 PARTNERSHIP CHANGES

1.1 Introduction

Changes in a partnership may occur for a variety of different reasons:

- a partner leaves, dies or retires from the partnership;
- a new partner enters the partnership;
- the existing partners change their profit-sharing arrangements;
- the partnership is merged or sold;
- the partnership is dissolved.

1.2 Accounting aspects

From the accounting viewpoint there are two main aspects:

(a) dividing profits between old and new partners when the change occurs during the course of the financial period.

(b)   the problem of valuing partnership assets, especially goodwill, at the time of the change.

1.3   Division of profits

There will be many occasions when a partnership change does not take place at a convenient date (such as the accounting year end!).

For the purpose of dividing profits equitably between the partners concerned, it is necessary to apportion (or allocate) profits between those arising before the change, and those arising afterwards.

In most cases where the trade is not of a seasonal nature, sales occur at an even rate during the year. It will then be reasonable to apportion sales and profit on a time basis. Having apportioned the profit between the different parts of the year, it is then allocated between the partners according to their arrangements for sharing profits during those periods.

1.4   Activity

Gavel and Kirk are in partnership, sharing profits in the ratio 3 : 2, after Gavel has received a salary of £2,000 per annum. The accounting year-end of the partnership is 31 December. On 30 June 19X6 Blea is admitted to the partnership. The new profit-sharing arrangements provide for Gavel's salary of £2,000 per annum to be maintained, and for Blea to receive a salary of £3,000 per annum. The balance is to be shared between Gavel, Kirk and Blea in the ratio 2 : 2 : 1.

The net profit for the year to 31 December 19X6 is £22,000.

You are required to show the transfer to the partners' current accounts for the year ended 31 December 19X6.

1.5   Activity solution

Step 1   Apportion the profit to the pre and post change periods.

Assuming that the net profit of £22,000 accrues evenly over the year, it may be apportioned on a time basis as follows

		£
1 January 19X6 to 30 June 19X6	$\frac{6}{12} \times £22,000$	11,000
1 July 19X6 to 31 December 19X6	$\frac{6}{12} \times £22,000$	11,000
		22,000

Step 2   Allocate each periods profit to the partners according to the profit share agreement in that period.

The net profit relating to each six month period is allocated according to the profit-sharing arrangements operating during that period.

Statement of allocation of profit

	Gavel £	Kirk £	Blea £	Total £
Six months to 30 June 19X6				
Salary:				
Gavel 6/12 × £2,000	1,000	-	-	1,000
Balance of profit (£11,000 – £1,000)				
in ratio 3 : 2	6,000	4,000	-	10,000
	7,000	4,000	-	11,000

	Gavel £	Kirk £	Blea £	Total £
Six months to 31 December 19X6				
Salary:				
Gavel 6/12 × £2,000	1,000	-	-	1,000
Blea 6/12 × £3,000	-	-	1,500	1,500
Balance of profit (£11,000 – £2,500)				
in ratio 2 : 2 : 1	3,400	3,400	1,700	8,500
	4,400	3,400	3,200	11,000
Totals - 12 months	11,400	7,400	3,200	22,000

Remember that the salaries are expressed at an annual rate! Interest on capital percentages are also expressed at an annual rate so a similar problem of time apportionment could apply elsewhere.

Partners' current accounts - Extract

	Gavel £	Kirk £	Blea £		Gavel £	Kirk £	Blea £
				Profit and loss appropriation:			
				To 30 June	7,000	4,000	-
				To 31 Dec 19X6	4,400	3,400	3,200

1.6   Apportionment of profit

Unless otherwise instructed, it is acceptable to apportion profits (step 1) on a time basis. However, occasionally the question may specify some alternative basis.

1.7   Activity

Assume that in the previous example the net profit of £22,000 was arrived at as follows

	£	£
Sales (£96,000 in six months to 30 June 19X6)		160,000
Cost of sales		118,000
Gross profit		42,000
Selling and distribution expenses	5,500	
Administrative expenses	12,500	
Financial expenses	2,000	
		20,000
Net profit		22,000

You are required to show the apportionment of profit between the two parts of the year. Assume that gross profit and selling expenses are to be apportioned on a turnover basis and all other items on a time basis. The allocation of profit between the partners is not required.

1.8   Activity solution

Step 1   Apportion profit to the pre and post change periods.

	£
Turnover:	
Six months to 30 June 19X6	96,000
Six months to 31 December 19X6	64,000
	160,000

The ratio of turnover is therefore 96 : 64 or 3 : 2.

	Six months to 30 June 19X6		Six months to 31 December 19X6		Total	
	£	£	£	£	£	£
Gross profit (3:2)		25,200		16,800		42,000
Selling expenses (3:2)	3,300		2,200		5,500	
Administrative expenses (1:1)	6,250		6,250		12,500	
Financial expenses (1:1)	1,000		1,000		2,000	
		10,550		9,450		20,000
Net profit		14,650		7,350		22,000

The apportionment of net profit is therefore

	£
Six months to 30 June 19X6	14,650
Six months to 31 December 19X6	7,350
	22,000

As can be seen, in a seasonal business, where sales fluctuate greatly from month to month, the apportionment of a net profit on a time basis may give a misleading picture.

Conclusion   Where there is a change of profit share arrangement part way through an accounting period then the profit must be apportioned to the pre and post change periods on an equitable basis.

2   RETIREMENT AND ADMISSION

2.1   Retirement of an existing partner

Definition   Retirement of a partner is where he leaves the partnership and therefore requires repayment of all amounts due to him from the partnership.

When a partner retires it is important first of all to ensure that his current account is credited with his share of profits and debited with his drawings up to the date of retirement. The balances on his current and capital accounts are then transferred to a loan account and becomes a liability of the business. The manner and timing of the payment of this liability are likely to be regulated by the partnership agreement. In practice the amount will probably be paid in instalments, with allowance for interest on the unpaid balance. Since the former partner is no longer a partner of the business, the interest cannot be regarded as an appropriation of profit and must be regarded as an expense of the partnership (in the same way as interest on a bank overdraft).

2.2   Example

Birk, How and Stile have been in partnership for many years. Birk retired from the partnership on 1 July. At 30 June the summarised balance sheet showed the following position

	£
Sundry assets	27,296

Partners' accounts	Capital accounts £	Current accounts £	Total £
Birk	12,000	1,735	13,735
How	8,000	2,064	10,064
Stile	3,000	497	3,497
	23,000	4,296	27,296

Show the partnership balance sheet after Birk's retirement.

2.3   Solution

It is assumed that the current account balances reflect profit shares and drawings up to 30 June. At that date the balances on Birk's capital and current accounts should be transferred to a loan account and regarded as a liability of the partnership. The double entry for this is:

> Dr Birk's capital/current account
> Cr Loan account - Birk

A balance sheet at 1 July would then appear

	£
Sundry assets	27,296
Less: Loan account - Birk	13,735
Net assets	13,561

Partners' accounts	*Capital accounts* £	*Current accounts* £	*Total* £
How	8,000	2,064	10,064
Stile	3,000	497	3,497
	11,000	2,561	13,561

The retiring partner is now a creditor of the partnership as he is no longer a partner. The loan account will eventually be paid off according to the partnership agreement.

2.4   Admission of a new partner

A new partner will often be required to bring in cash as a contribution to the fixed capital of the partnership. This cash is therefore credited to this new partner's capital account.

2.5   Example

The facts are as in the previous example but this time instead of Birk retiring Tarn is admitted to the partnership on 3 July. He brings in cash of £2,500 as his fixed capital.

Write up the partners' capital accounts.

2.6   Solution

Partners' capital accounts

	Birk £	How £	Stile £	Tarn £		Birk £	How £	Stile £	Tarn £
					1 July:				
					Bal b/d	12,000	8,000	3,000	
					3 July:				
					Cash -	-	-	2,500

A summarised balance sheet at 3 July would then show the following position

			£
Sundry assets (£27,296 + £2,500)			29,796

Partners' accounts	*Capital accounts*	*Current accounts*	*Total*
	£	£	£
Birk	12,000	1,735	13,735
How	8,000	2,064	10,064
Stile	3,000	497	3,497
Tarn	2,500	-	2,500
	25,500	4,296	29,796

2.7   New capital other than cash

If Tarn had contributed his capital share in the form of an asset other than cash, for example a car valued at £2,500, the double entry would have been

Dr Motor car account   £2,500
      Cr Tarn's capital account   £2,500

The only effect on the balance sheet would then be the make-up of the sundry assets figure of £29,796 as between fixed and current assets.

[Conclusion]   Withdrawals of capital are recorded as:
                          Dr: Capital (and current) account
                              Cr: Cash / other assets / loan

                      Introductions of capital are recorded as:
                          Dr: Cash / other assets
                              Cr: Capital account.

3   REVALUATION OF PARTNERSHIP ASSETS

3.1   Introduction

Two unrealistic assumptions have been made so far when dealing with changes in a partnership:

(a)   No notice was taken of any difference between the current value of individual tangible assets and the amount at which they were stated in the books of account. On a change in profit-sharing arrangements such account must be taken as partners are entitled to share capital profits in the same ratio as they share revenue profits.

         Thus, just as we time-apportion profits between periods before and after the change, so we need to take account of capital gains or losses at the date of change.

(b)   Goodwill was ignored. Its nature and measurement will be dealt with in the next section.

3.2   Why a revaluation is required on a partnership change

[Definition]   A revaluation of partnership assets occurs where the current value of the assets differs from the book value and the book values are to be updated to reflect this.

Any change in a partnership (and remember a change can be an admission of a new partner, the retirement of an old partner or a change in profit sharing ratios) affects partners' rights to profits and assets. The entitlement to a one third share in profits means an entitlement to a one third share in the assets which exist in the partnership as well.

To the extent that the current worth of the assets is different from their book value a profit or loss will have accrued on the asset from the date of acquisition of the asset to the date of the partnership change. This profit or loss will need to be allocated to each partner in the old profit sharing ratio as the partnership change triggers off new profit sharing ratios.

The gain/loss is computed by revaluing the net assets at the date of change.

3.3   Accounting adjustments

Wherever there is a change in profit-sharing arrangements, a partnership will take account of changes in the value of its tangible assets.

In this instance use will be made of a revaluation account to calculate the overall gain or loss on the revaluation; this will then be shared between the old or original partners in their old profit-sharing ratios.

Step 1   Revalue the partnership assets using a revaluation account.

The initial bookkeeping entries are as follows

Debit	*Credit*	*With*
Assets	Revaluation	Increases in asset values
Revaluation	Assets	Decreases in asset values
Liabilities	Revaluation	Decreases in liability values
Revaluation	Liabilities	Increases in liability values

Step 2   The balance on the revaluation account will represent the surplus or deficiency on the revaluation, which will be shared between the old partners in their old profit-sharing ratios.

Debit	*Credit*	*With*
Revaluation	Partner's capital accounts	Surplus on revaluation
or		
Partner's capital accounts	Revaluation	Deficit on revaluation

3.4   Example

Trooper, Tremlett and Arkle are in partnership; sharing profits in the ratio 4 : 3 : 3. As at 1 January 19X6 Randall is to be admitted to the partnership, thereafter profits are to be shared equally. Randall is to introduce capital of £30,000.

The partnership's balance sheet as at 31 December 19X5 shows the following

	£	£
Fixed assets:		
Property		70,000
Plant and machinery		30,000
Fixtures and fittings		25,000
		125,000
Current assets:		
Stock	35,000	
Debtors	28,000	
Bank	17,000	
	80,000	
Less: Current liabilities:		
Creditors	27,250	
	52,750	
		177,750

	Capital £	Current £	Total £
Partners' accounts:			
Trooper	50,000	2,000	52,000
Tremlett	53,750	4,000	57,750
Arkle	65,000	3,000	68,000
	168,750	9,000	177,750

For the purposes of the revaluation the assets of the partnership are to be revalued as follows

	£
Property	80,000
Plant and machinery	27,500
Fixtures and fittings	32,100
Stock	36,350
Debtors	27,750

You are required to show

(a)   the revaluation account
(b)   the partners' capital accounts
(c)   the balance sheet of the partnership as at 1 January 19X6.

3.5   Solution

(a)

Step 1   Revalue the assets.

Step 2   Allocate the revaluation surplus/deficiency to the old partners in the old profit sharing ratio.

Revaluation

	£	£		£
Plant and machinery		2,500	Property	10,000
Debtors		250	Fixtures and fittings	7,100
Profit on realisation:			Stock	1,350
Trooper (4)	6,280			
Tremlett (3)	4,710			
Arkle (3)	4,710			
		15,700		
		18,450		18,450

The overall revaluation surplus of £15,700 relates only to the original or old partners and is therefore credited to their capital accounts only.

Step 3   Bring in the new partner's capital.

(b)   **Partners' capital accounts**

	Trooper £	Tremlett £	Arkle £	Randall £		Trooper £	Tremlett £	Arkle £	Randall £
Balance c/d	56,280	58,460	69,710	30,000	Balance b/d	50,000	53,750	65,000	
					Revaluation	6,280	4,710	4,710	
					Bank				30,000
	56,280	58,460	69,710	30,000		56,280	58,460	69,710	30,000

(c)   **Trooper, Tremlett, Arkle and Randall**
Balance sheet as at 1 January 19X6

	£	£
Fixed assets:		
Property		80,000
Plant and machinery		27,500
Fixtures and fittings		32,100
		139,600
Current assets:		
Stock	36,350	
Debtors	27,750	
Bank	47,000	
	111,100	
Less: Current liabilities:		
Creditors	27,250	
		83,850
		223,450

	Capital £	Current £	Total £
Partners' accounts			
Trooper	56,280	2,000	58,280
Tremlett	58,460	4,000	62,460
Arkle	69,710	3,000	72,710
Randall	30,000	-	30,000
	214,450	9,000	223,450

Conclusion   All increases and decreases in the value of assets and liabilities at the date of a partnership change are included in the revaluation account:
- increases in assets are credit entries
- increases in liabilities are debit entries.

4   GOODWILL

4.1   Introduction

In the previous section it was noted that when there was a change in a partnership of any sort that it was necessary to ensure that the correct values were assigned to all of the assets of the partnership. It will also be necessary to ensure that all of the assets of the partnership themselves are recognised.

One asset that is not normally recognised on a business balance sheet but may well exist is the asset of goodwill. If goodwill exists in a partnership then at the time of any change in partnership it will become necessary to recognise and value this asset if only briefly.

4.2   The nature of goodwill

Definition   Goodwill is the difference in value between the partnership as a whole and the current value of the assets of the partnership.

Goodwill is known as an intangible asset as unlike other assets such as buildings or stock it cannot be physically identified. However for most businesses it does exist.

A business may generate goodwill for a variety of reasons:

- good reputation of the business's products;
- good pre and post sales service;
- quality of the business's staff;
- good location; etc.

In general circumstances goodwill is not normally shown on the balance sheet of the business because of generally accepted accounting practices (which will be covered in more detail in a later chapter). However the goodwill that a business has is quite clearly an asset.

For the purposes of partnership accounting the goodwill that a partnership has should be recognised at the time of any change in the partnership. Therefore the first step will be to attempt to place a value on this goodwill.

4.3   Measurement of goodwill

There can be no precise valuation of goodwill, which has to be essentially the result of an exercise of judgement of the worth of the business as a whole by the parties involved.

In examination questions the examiner will either tell you the valuation to be placed on the goodwill, or give sufficient information to enable you to calculate the figure. The most likely possibilities are as follows.

(a)   Goodwill is valued at £12,000. Self-explanatory.

(b)   X introduces £3,000 in payment for his share of one quarter of the goodwill. If a quarter share is valued at £3,000, then the total value for goodwill is £12,000.

(c)   Goodwill is to be valued at three times last year's profit of £4,000. Three times last year's profit is £12,000, giving the total value for goodwill.

(d)   The business is worth £200,000 and the fair value of the tangible net assets is £160,000. Goodwill is therefore £40,000.

4.4   Accounting adjustments

There are two main situations as regards goodwill:

(a)   the partners wish to include goodwill as an asset in their balance sheet, (which is the least likely situation in practice) or

(b)   the partners do not wish to include goodwill as an asset in their balance sheet but the effect of goodwill needs to be reflected in their capital accounts.

4.5   Goodwill included as an asset in the balance sheet

On rare occasions partners may wish to recognise the value of goodwill and include it as an asset on the balance sheet.

The goodwill is an asset of the business which belongs to the partners therefore this value is credited to the partners' capital accounts.

The double entry for this is:

Dr Goodwill account
        Cr Partners capital accounts

This entry takes place at the time of any partnership change and is therefore credited to the old partners' capital accounts in the old profit sharing ratio.

4.6   Activity

Laid, Back and Gower are in partnership sharing profits 5 : 3 : 2. As at 1 January 19X7 Gooch is to be admitted to the partnership; thereafter profits are to be shared equally. Gooch is to introduce capital of £40,000, of which £10,000 represents a payment for his share of the goodwill, which is subsequently to be disclosed in the books.

The partnership's balance sheet as at 31 December 19X6 shows the following

	£	£
Fixed assets:		
Property		42,500
Plant and machinery		16,750
Fixtures and fittings		12,800
		72,050
Current assets:		
Stock	15,800	
Debtors	29,471	
Bank	18,623	
	63,894	
Less: Current liabilities:		
Creditors	24,713	
		39,181
		111,231
Partners' capital accounts:		
Laid		61,237
Back		18,476
Gower		31,518
		111,231

For the purposes of the revaluation the assets of the partnership are to be revalued as follows

	£
Property	75,000
Plant and machinery	21,250
Fixtures and fittings	11,000

You are required to show

(a)   the revaluation account
(b)   the partners' capital accounts
(c)   the balance sheet of the partnership as at 1 January 19X7.

4.7   Activity solution

(a)

Step 1   Revalue the tangible assets.

Step 2   Allocate the revaluation surplus to the OLD partners in the OLD profit sharing ratio.

Revaluation account

	£	£		£
Fixtures and fittings		1,800	Property	32,500
Profit on revaluation:			Plant and machinery	4,500
Laid (5)	17,600			
Back (3)	10,560			
Gower (2)	7,040			
		35,200		
		37,000		37,000

Step 3   Calculate the value of goodwill.

If Gooch is introducing £10,000 for his share of the goodwill (one quarter thereof) the total value of goodwill must be £40,000.

Step 4   Apportion the value of the goodwill to the OLD partners in the OLD profit sharing ratio.

(b)

Partners' capital accounts

	Laid £	*Back* £	*Gower* £	*Gooch* £		*Laid* £	*Back* £	*Gower* £	*Gooch* £
Balance					Balance				
c/d	98,837	41,036	46,558	40,000	b/d	61,237	18,476	31,518	
					Bank				40,000
					Reval-				
					uation	17,600	10,560	7,040	
					Goodwill		.		
					(5:3:2)	20,000	12,000	8,000	
	98,837	41,036	46,558	40,000		98,837	41,036	46,558	40,000

Step 5   Introduce the new partner's capital.

Step 6   Draw up the balance sheet after the partnership change.

(c)   **Laid, Back, Gower and Gooch**
Balance sheet as at 1 January 19X7

	£	£
Fixed assets:		
Goodwill		40,000
Property		75,000
Plant and machinery		21,250
Fixtures and fittings		11,000
		147,250

Current assets:

Stock	15,800	
Debtors	29,471	
Bank	58,623	
	103,894	

Less: Current liabilities:

Creditors	24,713	
		79,181
		226,431

Partners' capital accounts:

Laid	98,837	
Back	41,036	
Gower	46,558	
Gooch	40,000	
		226,431

Conclusion   If goodwill is to remain as an asset on the balance sheet then it must be shown at the top of the balance sheet as an intangible fixed asset.

4.8   Goodwill not included as an asset in the balance sheet

In most cases goodwill will not be shown on the balance sheet after a partnership change despite the fact that a new partner, for example, has paid for a share.

There are a number of reasons why partnerships do not wish to record goodwill in the balance sheet.

(a)   **Subjective nature of valuation**

The value attached to goodwill on a partnership change is either a matter of negotiation between the partners or derived from a formula in the partnership agreement.

It only represents a value attached to the asset at the time of the change.   In changing business conditions in the future its value may be very different.

(b)   **Taxation**

For capital gains tax purposes it is generally disadvantageous to record partnership goodwill as an asset.

(c)   **Amortisation (depreciation)**

If goodwill is recorded as an asset should it not be depreciated like any other fixed asset?

Some would say yes and some no. The argument is however avoided if goodwill is not shown in the first place.

This will not change the need to make entries; the old partners by allowing another person into partnership are sharing their business with him. They are thus selling some of the past goodwill to him and this fact needs to be recorded in the capital accounts.

The approach to be adopted in this instance is to open up temporarily an account for goodwill, using the following journal entries

Debit	Credit	With
Goodwill	Old partners' capital accounts	Their share of the goodwill (using old profit-sharing ratio)
New partners' capital accounts	Goodwill	Their share of the goodwill (using new profit-sharing ratio)

In simple terms this can be described as

Write up goodwill in the old profit-sharing ratios (OPSR); and
Write it down in the new profit-sharing ratios (NPSR).

4.9   Activity

Francis, Robson and Hateley are in partnership sharing profits 7 : 2 : 1. As at 1 January 19X8 Harford is to be admitted to the partnership; thereafter profits are to be shared 3 : 3 : 3 : 1. Harford is to introduce capital of £50,000, of which £12,000 represents a payment for his share of the goodwill, not to be disclosed in the books.

An extract from the partnership balance sheet as at 31 December 19X7 shows the following

	£
Capital accounts:	
Francis	36,761
Robson	27,304
Hateley	29,287
	93,352

Assuming that there are no other revaluations necessary to other assets you are required to show

(a)   partners' capital accounts and
(b)   goodwill account.

4.10   Activity solution

(a)

Step 1   Determine the total value of the goodwill. Harford is paying £12,000 for his 1/10 share therefore the total goodwill is £120,000.

Step 2   Dr Goodwill account.
Cr Old partners' capital account in the old profit sharing ratio.

Partners' capital accounts

	Francis £	Robson £	Hateley £	Harford £		Francis £	Robson £	Hateley £	Harford £
Good-will	36,000	36,000	36,000	12,000	Balance b/d	36,761	27,304	29,287	
Balance c/d	84,761	15,304	5,287	38,000	Bank				50,000
					Good-will	84,000	24,000	12,000	
	120,761	51,304	41,287	50,000		120,761	51,304	41,287	50,000

(b)

Step 3   Dr New partners' capital account.
Cr Goodwill account - in the new profit sharing ratio.

Goodwill

	£		£
Francis (7)	84,000	Francis (3)	36,000
Robson (2)	24,000	Robson (3)	36,000
Hateley (1)	12,000	Hateley (3)	36,000
		Harford (1)	12,000
	120,000		120,000

Goodwill invariably appears as a complication in questions involving partnerships. The key is to follow the requirements of the question.

Confusion often arises in the case of goodwill not shown in the books in the sense that it appears most unfair that Harford, in the previous example, for instance pays in £50,000 on admission to the partnership and yet ends up with only £38,000 on his capital account. However, the point to remember is that the balance sheet does not include goodwill.

If goodwill were subsequently to be included in the books, say on 2 January 19X8, Harford's capital account would be credited with his share of the goodwill (1/10 × £120,000 = £12,000).

Similarly, if the partnership were dissolved, Harford would be entitled to a one-tenth share in the profit on the disposal of the partnership, which would include the valuation placed on the goodwill.

In any event the key is to follow the requirement in the question, which is likely to treat the partners fairly.

4.11   Goodwill and retirement of a partner

So far all of the examples have concentrated on the admission of a new partner. However if an existing partner retires it is equally important to recognise the value of the goodwill at the time of the retirement to ensure that the retiring partner is repaid his share of the value of all of the assets of the partnership including the unrecorded intangible fixed asset, goodwill.

4.12   Activity

A, B and C are in partnership sharing profits and losses in the ratio of 3:2:1. On 31 December 19X7 A retires from the partnership. From that date onwards B and C are to share profits equally. At that date the partnership balance sheet is as follows:

			£	£
Fixed assets				60,000
Net current assets				20,000
				80,000
Capital accounts	-	A	20,000	
		B	20,000	
		C	15,000	
				55,000
Current accounts	-	A	15,000	
		B	5,000	
		C	5,000	
				25,000
				80,000

At the same date the goodwill of the business was valued at £30,000. Any amounts owing to A are to be left as a loan to the partnership.

Prepare the partners' capital accounts to reflect the retirement and the balance sheet after the retirement.

4.13   Activity solution

Step 1   Account for the goodwill in the partners' capital accounts.

Dr	Goodwill account		£30,000	
	Cr	Old partners' capital accounts in old profit sharing ratio		£30,000

Then:

Dr	New partners capital accounts in new profit sharing ratio		£30,000	
	Cr	Goodwill account		£30,000

Partners' capital accounts

	A £	B £	C £		A £	B £	C £
Goodwill		15,000	15,000	Balance b/d	20,000	20,000	15,000
Loan account				Goodwill			
- A	35,000			(3:2:1)	15,000	10,000	5,000
Balance c/d		15,000	5,000				
	35,000	30,000	20,000		35,000	30,000	20,000

[Step 2]   Transfer the balance on A's capital and current account to a loan account.

The loan account will total:

	£
Capital account balance	35,000
Current account balance	15,000
	50,000

[Step 3]   Draw up the balance sheet after the retirement.

Balance sheet for the B and C partnership at 1 January 19X8

			£	£
Fixed assets				60,000
Net current assets				20,000
Loan account	-	A		(50,000)
				30,000
Capital accounts	-	B	15,000	
	-	C	5,000	
				20,000
Current accounts	-	B	5,000	
		C	5,000	
				10,000
				30,000

[Conclusion]   The treatment of goodwill is precisely the same whether the change in partnership is a retirement of an old partner or the admission of a new partner. In a retirement the retiring partner must be given credit for his share of the goodwill that he has earned whilst being a partner. In an admission the incoming partner must pay for and be charged for his share of the goodwill that he is buying.

5   PARTNERSHIP BALANCE SHEET AFTER A MERGER OF TWO SOLE TRADER BUSINESSES

5.1   Procedure

If two sole traders merge their businesses then they become a partnership and must be accounted for as such.

The merger of the businesses of two sole traders presents similar problems to the admission of a partner.

[Step 1]   Each trader will record the capital profit or loss accruing to him at the date of the merger. Values will be placed on the tangible net assets and goodwill of each trader's business and these values can be incorporated into the trader's books by use of a revaluation account. The entries will be similar to the revaluation of assets on a partnership change. The balancing figure in the revaluation account will be transferred to the trader's capital account.

Step 2   Any assets not being taken over by the partnership are removed from the trader's books by transferring the book value of the asset to the debit of the trader's capital account.

Step 3   The separate books can now be merged at the agreed values. The partnership assets will be the sum of the assets of the two sole traders and each person's capital account will be their opening balance of capital in the partnership.

If goodwill is not to appear as an asset in the balance sheet, the combined amount needs to be written off against each partner's capital account in the new profit sharing ratio.

5.2   Example

A agrees to amalgamate with C to form X and Co.

The balance sheets of the two businesses at the date of the merger were as follows:

	A £	C £
Fixed assets:		
Freehold property	10,000	
Plant and machinery	4,000	7,000
Motor vehicle	3,000	
	17,000	7,000
Current assets:		
Stock	4,000	3,000
Debtors	2,000	1,000
Cash at bank	2,000	4,000
	25,000	15,000
Loan from F	2,000	
Current liabilities:		
Trade creditors	5,000	6,000
Capital accounts:		
A	18,000	
C		9,000
	25,000	15,000

X & Co was to take over all the assets and liabilities of the two businesses except

(a)   F's loan, for which A agreed to take over responsibility
(b)   A was to take over the car.

The following were the agreed values placed on the assets of the old businesses.

	A £	C £
Goodwill	9,000	3,000
Freehold property	14,000	-
Plant and machinery	3,000	6,000
Stock	4,000	2,000

Trade creditors were taken over at their book value.

Profit sharing in the new firm is 3:1 between A and C.

Goodwill was not to appear in the new firm's balance sheet.

You are required

- to prepare the closing entries in the books of A and C to record the revaluation and the entries in their capital accounts.
- to prepare the balance sheet of X & Co immediately following the amalgamation.

5.3   Solution

Books of A

Step 1   Revalue the assets/liabilities of each trader in their own books to the agreed values. Transfer the surplus on revaluation to the capital account of the trader.

Revaluation account

	£		£
Plant and machinery - loss	1,000	Goodwill - profit	9,000
Capital account	12,000	Freehold property - profit	4,000
	13,000		13,000

Step 2   Transfer any assets/liabilities taken over by the sole traders to their capital accounts.

A's capital account

	£		£
Motor car	3,000	Balance b/d	18,000
		F's loan	2,000
Balance c/d to new firm	29,000	Profit on revaluation	12,000
	32,000		32,000

Books of C

Step 1   Revalue the assets/liabilities of each trader in their own books to the agreed values. Transfer the surplus on revaluation to the capital account of the trader.

Revaluation account

	£		£
Plant and machinery - loss	1,000	Goodwill - profit	3,000
Stock - loss	1,000		
Capital account	1,000		
	3,000		3,000

C's capital account

	£		£
Balance c/d	10,000	Balance b/d	9,000
		Profit on revaluation	1,000
	——		——
	10,000		10,000
	——		——

Step 3   Amalgamate the two individual capital accounts. Remove the goodwill in the profit sharing ratio and carry down the balances.

Partners' capital accounts

	A	C		A	C
	£	£		£	£
Goodwill written down			Balance b/d		
3 : 1 × 12,000	9,000	3,000	from old business	29,000	10,000
Balance c/d	20,000	7,000			
	——	——		——	——
	29,000	10,000		29,000	10,000
	——	——		——	——

Step 4   Prepare the balance sheet after the merger using the agreed asset values.

X & Co - Balance sheet after merger

	£	£
Fixed assets:		
Freehold property		14,000
Plant and machinery (3,000 + 6,000)		9,000
		——
		23,000
Current assets:		
Stock (4,000 + 2,000)	6,000	
Debtors (2,000 + 1,000)	3,000	
Cash (2,000 + 4,000)	6,000	
	——	
	15,000	
Current liabilities:		
Trade creditors (5,000 + 6,000)	11,000	
	——	
		4,000
		——
		27,000
		——
Capital accounts		
A		20,000
B		7,000
		——
		27,000
		——

Conclusion   A merger of two sole traders is treated in much the same way as the admission of a new partner. However before any partnership accounting takes place the individual sole traders' assets, liabilities and capital accounts must all be adjusted to reflect their agreed current values.

6   DISSOLUTION OF PARTNERSHIP

6.1   Reasons for dissolution

Possible reasons for the dissolution of a partnership include:

(a)   death or retirement of a partner
(b)   disagreement among the partners
(c)   continuing trading losses
(d)   the completion of the purpose for which the partnership was formed.

Whatever the reason, the accounting treatment is the same. The partnership has come to an end and the accounting must reflect this.

6.2   Objective of dissolution

The objective of a dissolution is to dispose of the partnership assets, pay off the liabilities and distribute the balance to the partners according to their entitlements.

The amount each partner receives is the balance on his or her capital account plus his or her share of the profit arising on the disposal of the assets (or minus any share of loss). If the final result is that a partner's account is in deficit, he or she has to pay the money in to allow the other partners to draw out their full entitlement.

6.3   The realisation account

 A realisation account is used to transfer all of the assets being sold by the partners and to account for the proceeds of sale and any other expenses relating to the dissolution.

The first bookkeeping step in dealing with a dissolution is to open a **realisation account**, sometimes called a **dissolution account**. All the asset balances except cash in hand and cash at bank are transferred in to the debit of the realisation account. The proceeds of sale of these assets will be credited to the realisation account, the balance on which will then be the profit or loss on the dissolution, subject to some minor items. This profit or loss is then taken to the partners' capital accounts in their profit sharing ratio.

The assets could be sold separately or as a single going concern unit. In either case the proceeds are credited to the realisation account.

6.4   Dealing with liabilities

The liabilities of the partnership have to be paid - credit cash and debit the liability accounts.

It may be that liabilities are paid off for a little more or less than the book amounts perhaps because of cash discounts or negotiated settlements. Any such difference is debited or credited to the realisation account as representing the loss or profit arising on the final settlement of the liabilities.

6.5   Expenses of dissolution

The expenses of dissolution are simply debited to the realisation account when paid.

6.6   Assets taken over by the partners

It may be that partners agree to takeover certain partnership assets at dissolution. To record this, we simply credit realisation account and debit the capital account of the partner concerned. This is one method of paying off the amounts owing to the partners.

6.7   Partners' accounts

Partners may have both capital accounts and current accounts. The distinction between them ceases to have any meaning on dissolution and current account balances should be transferred to the capital accounts. This will then give the total amount owed to each partner.

6.8   Sale of business as a going concern - liabilities taken over

A purchaser of the business may agree to take over all or some of the partnership's liabilities. The easiest way to deal with this is to credit the liabilities taken over to the realisation account, so that the profit or loss arising on the sale in the realisation account is the difference between the consideration and the **net** assets taken over.

6.9   The final settlement with the partners

When all the entries described above have been recorded, there will remain only the partners' capital accounts and the cash at bank. It only remains to draw cheques to pay the partners the balances due to them. Any partner with a debit balance on his or her capital account will pay in cash to clear the balance.

6.10   Example

A, B and C share profits 4 : 3 : 3. They agree to dissolve their partnership at the end of the financial year, when the balance sheet appeared as follows:

		£	£
Fixed assets, at cost less depreciation:			
Freehold			40,000
Plant and machinery			15,000
Motor vehicles (three cars)			16,000
			71,000
Current assets:			
Stock		50,000	
Debtors		25,000	
Cash		15,000	
		90,000	
Current liabilities		21,000	
			69,000
Loan account - D			(20,000)
			120,000

Partners' accounts:

	A	B	C	
	£	£	£	
Capital	40,000	30,000	20,000	90,000
Current	15,000	10,000	5,000	30,000
	55,000	40,000	25,000	120,000

The following are sold for cash:

		£
Freehold, for		80,000
Plant and machinery, for		13,000
Stock, for		43,000
		136,000

The creditors are settled for £20,000.

C takes over the debtors at an agreed value of £22,000.

A takes over D's loan at its book value.

A, B and C take over the cars at the following valuations:

A	£6,000
B	£8,000
C	£4,000

Realisation expenses are £2,000.

You are required to prepare the ledger accounts to show the closing of the partnership records.

6.11   Solution

Step 1   Enter the assets (other than cash) into the realisation account at their book value.

Step 2   Enter the cash proceeds on realisation.

Dr   Cash account
Cr   Realisation account

Step 3   Deal with the creditors by crediting the profit on settlement to the realisation account.

Step 4   Deal with the assets and liabilities taken over by individual partners through the realisation account and the partners' accounts.

Step 5   Enter the realisation expenses in the cash account and realisation account.

Step 6   Split any profit/loss on realisation (the balance on the realisation account) amongst the partners in profit sharing ratio.

Step 7   Pay off each of the partners the amount showing as owing to them on their accounts.

Numbers in brackets refer to sequence of entries

Realisation account

		£	£			£
(1)	Freehold account		40,000	(2)	Cash - sale proceeds	136,000
(1)	Plant and machinery			(3)	Discount received on	
	account		15,000		creditors	1,000
(1)	Motor vehicles				Partners' accounts -	
	account		16,000		assets taken over:	
(1)	Stock account		50,000	(4)	C debtors	22,000
(1)	Debtors account		25,000	(4)	A motor car	6,000
(5)	Cash - realisation			(4)	B motor car	8,000
	expenses		2,000	(4)	C motor car	4,000
(6)	Partners' accounts -					
	profit on realisation:					
	A 40% 11,600					
	B 30% 8,700					
	C 30% 8,700					
			29,000			
			177,000			177,000

Partners' accounts

		A	B	C			A	B	C
		£	£	£			£	£	£
(4)	Debtors					Balances b/d:			
	taken over			22,000		Capital			
(4)	Motor cars					accounts	40,000	30,000	20,000
	taken over	6,000	8,000	4,000		Current			
(7)	Cash to					accounts	15,000	10,000	5,000
	settle	80,600	40,700	7,700			55,000	40,000	25,000
					(4)	D's loan			
						account	20,000		
					(6)	Realisation			
						account -			
						profit	11,600	8,700	8,700
		86,600	48,700	33,700			86,600	48,700	33,700

Creditors' account

		£		£
(3)	Cash	20,000	Balance b/d	21,000
(3)	Realisation account -			
	discount received			
	on settlement	1,000		
		21,000		21,000

D's loan account

		£			£
(4)	A's partner account	20,000	Balance b/d		20,000

Cash account

		£	£				£	£
	Balance b/d		15,000	(3)	Creditors			20,000
	Sale proceeds to			(5)	Realisation expenses			2,000
	realisation account:				Partners' accounts to settle:			
(2)	Freehold	80,000		(7)	A			80,600
(2)	Plant and			(7)	B			40,700
	machinery	13,000		(7)	C			7,700
(2)	Stock	43,000						
			136,000					129,000
			151,000					151,000

Conclusion To account for a dissolution:

1 Transfer the current account balance of each partner to the capital account.

2 Open up a realisation account and transfer in all the assets and liabilities of the partnership:

Dr: Realisation account   with the value
     Cr: Asset account   of the assets

Dr: Liability account   with the value
     Cr: Realisation account   of the liabilities

3 Deal with any assets taken over by a partner

Dr: Capital account
     Cr: Realisation account

4 Deal with the cash received on sale of the assets and cash paid to settle liabilities and realisation expenses:

Dr: Cash account   with the sale proceeds
     Cr: Realisation account   of the assets

Dr: Realisation account   with the amounts paid to
     Cr: Cash account   settle liabilities and
         expenses of dissolution

5 Share the balance on realisation account amongst the partners in their profit-sharing ratio.

6 Settle the balances on the capital accounts with cash.

7   PARTNERSHIP FINANCIAL STATEMENTS FROM AN EXTENDED TRIAL BALANCE

7.1   Introduction

In an earlier chapter it was seen how the financial statements of a sole trader could be prepared using an extended trial balance as a working paper. In much the same way the financial statements of a partnership can also be prepared using an extended trial balance.

The majority of the accounts and entries on the extended trial balance for a partnership will be exactly the same as those for a sole trader. For example all of the balance sheet and profit and loss account ledger account balances will appear, adjustments will be made for errors, opening and closing stock entries will be made and entries will be made for accruals and prepayments. There may however be some additional account items for a partnership that will be briefly considered in this final section.

7.2   Partner's capital accounts

Instead of a sole trader's extended trial balance showing only a single capital account there will of course be a capital account balance for each of the partners. If assets have been revalued or goodwill has been assessed and valued then there will be entries for these items to be made in the adjustments column. If a retiring partner's capital account balance is transferred to a loan account or a new partner introduces additional capital then again these items will appear in the adjustments column.

7.3   Partner's current accounts

The partner's current account balances will appear as balances from the initial trial balance. They must then be adjusted for each partner's profit share for the period and drawings for the period.

7.4   Profit and loss appropriation account columns

The extended trial balance for a partnership is likely to have two columns in addition to those of a sole trader in order to reflect the appropriation of the net profit for the period to the partners.

7.5   Revaluation and goodwill accounts

If there is a change in the partnership and the assets are revalued or there is goodwill to be dealt with then additional account lines will be necessary to reflect these two additional accounts.

7.6   Activity

Given below is the summarised draft trial balance for the AB partnership as at 31 December 19X2. Up to that date the partnership agreement was that A should receive an annual salary of £10,000 and all remaining profits should be split in the ratio of 2:1.

On that date C was admitted to the partnership and paid in £24,000. The goodwill of the partnership on that date was estimated as £12,000 (this is not to remain in the books) and the partnership agreement from 19X3 onwards was simply that all profits should be shared equally between A, B and C.

Summarised draft trial balance at 31 December 19X2

	£	£
Sales		144,000
Purchases	91,000	
Expenses	35,000	
Stock	7,000	
Fixed assets - cost	70,000	
Fixed assets - accumulated depreciation		14,000
Debtors	6,200	
Bank	5,800	
Creditors		4,000
Loan account - D		10,000
Current accounts - A		1,000
- B		2,000
Capital accounts - A		20,000
- B		20,000
	215,000	215,000

The following information is to be taken into consideration:

* depreciation for the year of £2,000 has still to be charged;
* accruals of £3,000 and prepayments of £4,000 are yet to be accounted for;
* the closing stock figure is £8,000.

Prepare the extended trial balance for the year showing the entries required for the admission of C on 31 December. Prepare the final partnership balance sheet on 31 December 19X2 after the admission of C.

7.7   Activity solution

Step 1   Enter the trial balance figures onto the extended trial balance and ensure that it balances.

Step 2   Enter the year end adjustments in the adjustments column.

Step 3   Extend the profit and loss account figures into the profit and loss account column in order to determine the net profit for the year.

Step 4   Extend the net profit figure into the P&L Appropriation column and determine how this profit is split amongst the partners for the year. This appropriation of profit will eventually appear in the balance sheet as additions to the partners' current account balances.

Step 5   Deal with the admission of the new partner. Enter the cash paid into the partnership and the adjustment required for goodwill.

Step 6   Extend all of the balance sheet balances across to the balance sheet column. Ensure that the balance sheet columns balance and then prepare the final partnership balance sheet.

		Trial balance		Adjustments		Profit and loss account		Profit and loss appropriation account		Balance sheet	
		£	£	£	£	£	£	£	£	£	£
			Step (1)								Step (6)
Sales			144,000				144,000 (3)				
Purchases		91,000				91,000 (3)					
Expenses		35,000		3,000 (2)	4,000 (2)	34,000 (3)					
Stock		7,000		8,000 (2)	8,000 (2)	7,000 (3)	8,000 (3)			8,000	
Fixed assets											
- cost		70,000								70,000	
- depreciation			14,000		2,000 (2)						16,000
Debtors		6,200								6,200	
Bank		5,800		24,000 (5)						29,800	
Creditors			4,000								4,000
Loan a/c	D		10,000								10,000
Current a/c	A		1,000								1,000 (4)
	B		2,000								2,000 (4)
Partner salary	A							10,000 (4)			10,000 (4)
Profit share	A							5,333 (4)			5,333 (4)
	B							2,667 (4)			2,667 (4)
Capital a/c	A		20,000	4,000 (5)	8,000 (5)						24,000
	B		20,000	4,000 (5)	4,000 (5)						20,000
	C			4,000 (5)	24,000 (5)						20,000
Dep exp				2,000 (2)		2,000 (3)					
Accruals					3,000 (2)						3,000
Prepayments				4,000 (2)						4,000	
Net profit						18,000 (3)			18,000 (4)		
Goodwill				12,000 (5)	12,000 (5)						
		215,000	215,000	65,000	65,000	152,000	152,000	18,000	18,000	118,000	118,000

AB partnership balance sheet at 31 December 19X2

		£	£
Fixed assets	- cost		70,000
	- depreciation		16,000
			54,000
Stock		8,000	
Debtors		6,200	
Prepayments		4,000	
Bank		29,800	
		48,000	
Less: Creditors and accruals (4,000 + 3,000)		7,000	
Net current assets			41,000
			95,000
Less: Loan - D			10,000
			85,000

Capital accounts	A		24,000
	B		20,000
	C		20,000
			———
			64,000
Current accounts	A (1,000 + 10,000 + 5,333)	16,333	
	B (2,000 + 2,667)	4,667	
		———	
			21,000
			———
			85,000
			———

8   SELF TEST QUESTIONS

1   How is a retiring partner normally paid his share of the partnership assets? (2.1)

2   What is the double entry for capital introduced by a new partner? (2.4)

3   Why is it necessary to revalue the assets of a partnership when there is a change in the partnership? (3.2)

4   How is the revaluation of partnership assets dealt with in the ledger accounts of the partnership? (3.3)

5   What is goodwill? (4.2)

6   If goodwill is to remain as an asset on the partnership balance sheet what is the double entry required to record this? (4.5)

7   If goodwill is not to remain as an asset on the balance sheet then what is the double entry required to adjust for it if there is a change in partnership? (4.8)

8   What are the steps necessary to account for the merger of two sole traders in order to form a partnership? (5.1)

9   In the dissolution of a partnership what does the balance on the realisation account represent and how is it treated? (6.3)

10   In the dissolution of a partnership what is the double entry required if a partner takes over an asset of the partnership? (6.6)

8 LIMITED COMPANIES - INTRODUCTION

PATHFINDER INTRODUCTION

This chapter covers the following performance criteria and knowledge and understanding.

- Financial statements are accurately drafted from the appropriate information (performance criteria 10.2)
- Subsequent adjustments are correctly implemented (performance criteria 10.2)
- Draft accounts comply with domestic standards and legislation (performance criteria 10.2)
- General legal framework of limited companies: types of limited companies, obligations of directors in respect of the accounts (knowledge and understanding 10.2)
- Forms of equity and loan capital (knowledge and understanding 10.2)
- Form and method of preparation of financial statements (knowledge and understanding 10.2)

Putting the chapter in context – learning objectives.

This chapter moves on to the third type of business entity that must be accounted for, the limited company. It concentrates on the legal framework within which companies operate and the legal background to company accounting. It also considers the main differences between a sole trader and a company in terms of accounting and covers the methods required to prepare a set of draft financial statements for a company. The draft financial statements prepared in this chapter are at a very basic level. In subsequent chapters the detailed company accounting requirements of the Companies Acts and Accounting Standards will be considered.

At the end of this chapter you should have learned the following topics.

- The various types of limited company.
- The records which a limited company is required to keep by law.
- The various types of company finance available.
- The preparation of a set of financial statements for a company.
- The detailed accounting for share capital.
- The detailed accounting for reserves.
- The preparation of financial statements for a company from an extended trial balance.

1 TYPES OF LIMITED COMPANY

1.1 Introduction

In the UK the predominant form of business enterprise is the **limited company**.

 Most companies are limited by **shares**, meaning that in the event of the failure of a company, the amount the shareholders can lose is restricted to the amount paid for their shares.

It is important to appreciate that not all limited companies are large - they vary in size from the very small to the huge quoted company which operates world-wide.

1.2   Key factors distinguishing companies

There are four key factors which distinguish companies from other forms of business enterprise:

(a)   The fundamental concept of the **separate legal entity** of the company: the company is a separate entity in law. From this flow (b) and (c) below.

(b)   The **separation of the ownership** (shareholders) **from the management** (directors) of the company. It is most important to understand this.

> **Definition**   **Shareholders** own shares in the company and therefore own the company itself.

> **Definition**   The **directors** of a company manage the company on the shareholders' behalf.

(c)   The **limited liability** of shareholders for the debts of a company. Generally speaking their liability will be limited to any portion of the nominal value of shares which is unpaid. Today it is unusual for shares to be issued other than fully paid.

(d)   The formalities required. A sole trader or partnership can operate with little or no formalities. In return for the privilege of limited liability, companies must comply with a great many rules, many of which are covered in this chapter and the next.

1.3   Financial differences between sole traders and companies

The main financial differences between companies and sole traders are in the following respects:

(a)   the form of the capital accounts;
(b)   the form of loans to the company;
(c)   the way in which profits are withdrawn by the proprietors;
(d)   the form in which retained funds are presented.

The differences may be summarised as follows:

	Item	*Sole trader*	*Company*
(a)	Capital introduced by proprietors	Capital account	Issued share capital
(b)	Loans from third parties	Loan account	Debentures
(c)	Profits withdrawn by proprietors	Drawings	Dividends
(d)	Profits retained in the business	Capital account	Reserves

These differences will all be considered later in this chapter.

1.4   The advantages and disadvantages of operation as a limited company rather than as a sole trader

The advantages of operation as a limited company rather than as a sole trader can be as follows.

(a)   The liability of the shareholders is limited to the capital already introduced by them.

(b)   There is a formal separation of the business from the owners of the business, which may be helpful to the running of the business. For example if several members of a family are the shareholders in a company but only two of the family are directors, it is clear to all concerned who is running the company.

(c)   Ownership of the business can be shared between people more easily than other forms of business organisation eg, a partnership.

(d)   Shares in the business can be transferred relatively easily.

(e)   There may be tax advantages.

The disadvantages of operation as a limited company rather than as a sole trader can be as follows.

(a)   The costs of formation of the company. Documentation needs to be prepared to form the company, although these costs are only about £100 for a company with 'normal' type of memorandum and articles of association.

(b)   The annual running costs of the company. Annual returns need to be completed and sent to the Registrar of Companies. The audit fee is a further additional cost though companies obviously derive a benefit from having their accounts audited, not least from the greater reliability they acquire as a result of the audit.

(c)   Directors of a company are subject to greater legislative duties than others running an unincorporated business.

(d)   It is difficult/expensive to return capital surplus to the business's requirements back to the shareholders.

(e)   Shares in the business can be transferred relatively easily.

(f)   There may be tax disadvantages.

1.5   Private companies and public companies

Whether a particular company is a private company or a public company is a matter of law.

Definition   A **public** company is a company which must have a minimum allotted share capital of £50,000, of which at least one quarter and the whole of any premium are paid up. Such a company has the letters plc after its name: these stand for 'public limited company'.

Definition   A **private** company is a company that is not a public company: such a company has the letters Ltd after its name.

1.6   Quoted and unquoted companies

Definition   A quoted (or listed) company is a company the shares of which are traded on the Stock Exchange.

Clearly a quoted company must, by definition, be a public company, though of course not all public companies are quoted companies.

At this stage neither of these distinctions is very important as far as accounting is concerned.

Conclusion   Four key factors distinguish companies from other forms of business:
-       a company is a separate legal entity
-       its ownership is separated from its management
-       shareholders have limited liability
-       formalities

      A company may be public or private.

2   THE RECORDS WHICH A LIMITED COMPANY IS REQUIRED TO KEEP BY LAW

2.1   Registered office

A company must always have a registered office and give notice of its situation because

- any writ or other legal process is validly served on the company by delivery to its registered office and

- certain statutory books and other documents of the company open to inspection (by members or in some cases by third parties) are held at the registered office or other specified place. Most books should be available for public inspection for at least two hours per day during business hours.

2.2   Statutory books

The statutory books a company must keep are registers of:

(a)   **Members**

Contents - details of shareholders showing name, address, date of ownership of shares, number and type of shares held.

On a total disposal of a person's shareholding the entry would be closed off by inserting the date he ceased to be a member.

(b)   **Directors and Secretary**

Contents - personal details (name and address, nationality, details of other directorships).

(c)   **Debenture holders**

Contents - details of debenture holders showing name, address and amount of holding.

(d)   **Mortgages and charges**

Contents - details of charges on the company's assets. Certain creditors of the company will have advanced money to the company. One condition of such loans is often some security being given by the company.

(e)   **Beneficial interests of directors in shares or debentures of the company**

Contents - similar information to that contained in the register of members, but included with the directors' interests will be shares owned by the spouse and children. The purpose of a separate register is to enable interested parties to ascertain the extent of financial involvement of each director in the company.

(f)   **Substantial beneficial interests in the company's shares (only required for quoted companies)**

A person whose holding exceeds 3% of the nominal value of issued ordinary shares must notify the company (within two days of the percentage being exceeded). The register records the interests that are notified to the company.

In addition, copies of registered charges, minutes of general meetings and directors' service agreements must be held in the same way.

Items (a) or (c) may be held at some place in England and Wales or (for a Scottish company) in Scotland other than at the registered office provided that notice of that other address is given to the Registry.   Items (e) and (f) may be kept wherever the register of members is held and so may directors' service agreements (which may also be at the company's principal place of business in the country of domicile).

2.3   Statutory accounts

At least once in every calendar year the directors must lay before the company in general meeting a profit and loss account and balance sheet made up to a date within seven days of an accounting reference date.   This must be done not more than seven or ten months (for public and private companies respectively) from the end of the accounting reference period which ended on the relevant accounting reference date.   This interval may be extended by three months if the company gives notice to the Registrar that it carries on business or has interests abroad. Within the same time limits all companies (other than exempt unlimited companies) must deliver a copy of the accounts to the Registrar.

Members, debenture holders and auditors are to receive a copy twenty-one days before the general meeting.

> **Definition**   The accounting reference period is the twelve month period for which accounts are made up (ie to within seven days of the accounting reference date).

> **Definition**   An accounting reference date is the anniversary of the last day of the month of incorporation (ie formation) of a company.

2.4   Annual return

A company is required to deliver to the Registrar of Companies once a year the annual return.   The return should be delivered within 28 days of a return date.   The return date is either

(a)   the anniversary of incorporation or

(b)   if the company's last return was made in accordance with legislation existing before the CA 89 the anniversary of that date.

If the company has a share capital its return must contain the following information:

- the address of the registered office and, if the register of members or the register of debenture holders is not kept at that office, the address (eg, of a professional registrar) at which it is kept

- a summary of authorised and issued share capital with consideration received for issued shares and other details

- a list of members (made up to the return date) showing individual shareholdings and changes which have occurred during the year.   However, to avoid the annual submission of a lengthy list, companies may submit a full list once every three years and particulars of changes in the intermediate years and

- particulars of directors and secretary taken from the register.   The annual return must be signed by one director and the secretary.

> **Conclusion**   A limited company is legally required to:
> -   have a registered office
> -   keep statutory books
> -   prepare annual accounts
> -   complete an annual return.

3   **COMPANY FINANCE**

3.1   **Introduction**

The way in which the assets of a company (fixed assets, stock, debtors and cash) are financed will vary from one company to another. Part of the finance may be provided by the owners or proprietors of the company (referred to as shareholders), while part may be provided by outsiders including trade creditors, banks and other lenders of funds.

Companies will also normally be partly financed by their own accumulated profits known as reserves.

3.2   **The nature and purpose of share capital and reserves**

(Definition)   Share capital represents the capital invested in the company by its shareholders by the purchase of shares.

(Definition)   Reserves represent the balance of net assets belonging to the shareholders. These may include part of past issues of share capital (known as share premium), retained trading profits and revaluation gains on the revaluation of fixed assets.

The total of share capital and reserves represents the book value of the net assets of the company.

3.3   **Distinction between nominal value and market value of share capital**

(Definition)   The nominal value of a share is its face value, eg £1 ordinary shares or 50p ordinary share.

Each share has a stated nominal (or par) value. This has little practical significance except as a base line price below which further shares may not generally be issued. The nominal value is also used as a means of calculating dividends to shareholders.

(Definition)   The market value of a share is the price at which that share could be bought or sold.

The market value of a share is not fixed at any particular date. The market value is related to the market value of the business of the company. For example if a business is worth £100,000 and there are 1,000 £1 shares in issue in the company, the market value of each share is £100 whereas the nominal value is £1.

If the company is listed on a stock exchange then a price will be quoted for the shares based upon recent transactions between purchasers and sellers of shares. This is also referred to as the market value of a share, but this may not be the same value that would apply if the entire business was sold and thus all the shares were sold as one transaction.

3.4   **Why companies are concerned with the value of their shares**

Companies are concerned with the value the stock market places on the shares for two main reasons.

(a)   Shareholders will look at a steadily rising price of the shares as evidence of sound management of the company by the directors. It would indicate additional profits being made every year.

(b)   If the company wishes to raise further finance through the issue of shares, the current market price will be used as a basis for issuing more shares. The higher the price, the less number of shares will need to be issued and the less dilution there will be of the existing shareholders' effective interest in the company.

It is important to appreciate that the market value of a share quoted on the Stock Exchange has no direct relationship to the nominal value.

3.5   Share capital

The share capital of a company may be divided into various classes. The company's internal regulations (the Articles of Association) define the respective rights attached to the various shares eg, as regards dividend entitlement or voting at company meetings. The various classes of share capital are dealt with below. In practice it is usually only larger companies which have different classes of share capital.

3.6   Ordinary shares

Definition   Ordinary shares are the normal shares issued by a company. The normal rights of ordinary shareholders are to vote at company meetings and to receive dividends from profits.

Ordinary shares are often referred to as equity shares. A special class of ordinary share is the redeemable ordinary share where the terms of issue specify that it is repayable by the company.

3.7   Preference shares

Definition   Preference shares are shares carrying a fixed rate of dividend, the holders of which have a prior claim to any company profits available for distribution.

The rights and advantages of the shares will be specified in the articles of association.

Special categories of preference shares include:

(i)   Participating preference shares - where shareholders are entitled to participate together to a specified extent in distributable profits and surpluses on liquidation. Again, the rights of the shareholders are set out in the articles.

(ii)   Redeemable preference shares - the terms of issue specify that they are repayable by the company.

3.8   Deferred shares

Definition   The right to a dividend on deferred shares is deferred until the preference shareholders have received their fixed amounts, and the ordinary shareholders have received a stated minimum dividend.

These are sometimes referred to as founders' shares. Ordinary and preference shares can be compared.

Aspect	Ordinary shares	Preference shares
Voting power	Carry a vote.	Do not carry a vote.
Distribution of profits (dividends)	A dividend which may vary from one year to the next after the preference shareholders have received their dividend.	A fixed dividend (fixed percentage of nominal value) in priority to ordinary dividend.
Liquidation of the company	Entitled to surplus assets on liquidation after liabilities and preference shares have been repaid.	Priority of repayment over ordinary shares but not usually entitled to surplus assets on liquidation.

3.9   Debentures or loan stock

Definition   A debenture is a written acknowledgement of a loan to a company, given under the company's seal, which carries a fixed rate of interest.

A debenture may relate to a loan from one person. Debenture stock, on the other hand, rather like shares, may be held by a large number of individuals. The conditions and regulations are set out in a debenture trust deed.

Debentures are not part of a company's share capital - they are third party liabilities. Debenture interest is therefore a charge against profit and must be paid whether or not the company makes a profit.

Debenture or loan stock may be secured or unsecured.

3.10   Secured loan stock

The security given may be either:

(i)   fully or partly secured by a fixed charge which mortgages specific assets;

(ii)   fully or partly secured by a floating charge on the general assets of the company. The charge is said to **crystallise** if the company does not comply with the provisions of the debenture deed. A receiver may then be appointed to take over the company's assets in order to pay out the debenture holders.

3.11   Unsecured loan stock

On a liquidation this would rank equally with other unsecured liabilities such as trade creditors.

Both secured and unsecured loan stock are usually redeemable at a specified future date.

3.12   Convertible loan stock

Definition   A loan which gives the holder the right to convert to other securities, normally ordinary shares, at a predetermined rate and time.

This is a hybrid, having characteristics both of loan stock and of ordinary shares. On issue, the stock starts off with the characteristics of loan stock. The conditions of issue state that at certain specified future dates holders of the stock may, if they wish, convert their stock into a specified number of ordinary shares.

3.13   Bank overdraft

Often a bank overdraft is secured on specific assets of the company, thus taking the form of a secured loan.

Conclusion   The principal sources of finance may be summarised as follows:

-	Ordinary shares	
-	Preference shares	Share capital
-	Deferred shares	
-	Secured loan stock (debentures)	
-	Unsecured loan stock (debentures)	
-	Convertible loan stock	Liabilities
-	Bank overdraft	

4   **FINANCIAL STATEMENTS**

4.1   **Introduction**

Two important considerations directly affect the financial statements of a company:

(a)   the *Companies Act 1985* contains detailed rules governing the form and content of company accounts;

(b)   Financial Reporting Standards (FRSs) and Statements of Standard Accounting Practice (SSAPs).

4.2   **Purpose of financial statements**

A distinction must be made between:

(i)   Financial statements which the *Companies Act* require to be presented to shareholders, and lodged with the Registrar. These must comply with the requirements of (a) and (b) above.

(ii)   Financial statements which are prepared for internal purposes, eg, for management. These statements need not comply with legal and accountancy requirements and will give more detail than the statutory accounts.

You need to know the detailed requirements of the *Companies Act*, FRSs or SSAPs only to the extent that they are covered in this text.

4.3   **Balance sheet**

A vertical form balance sheet of a company might appear as follows:

	£	£
Fixed assets:		
Intangible assets:		
Goodwill		50,000
Tangible assets:		
Freehold land and buildings	124,700	
Plant and machinery	29,750	
		154,450
		204,450
Investments		20,000
		224,450
Current assets:		
Stocks	59,670	
Debtors	49,350	
Cash at bank and in hand	4,645	
	113,665	
Creditors: amounts falling due within one year:		
Trade creditors	31,690	
Taxation	26,735	
Dividend payable	30,000	
	88,425	

Net current assets	25,240
Total assets less current liabilities	249,690
Creditors: amounts falling due after more than one year:	
8% Debenture 19X4	100,000
	149,690
Capital and reserves	
Called up share capital - 50p ordinary shares	75,000
Profit and loss account	74,690
	149,690

In a sole trader's accounts the proprietor's capital consists of the original capital introduced to set up the business plus, each year, the profit that has been made minus drawings taken out.

In the case of a company the initial capital is the share capital, and this is held in the balance sheet at the same figure year after year unless new shares are issued. The company's profit for the year minus dividends paid to the members is accumulated under the heading 'profit and loss account' in the balance sheet.

It is important to realise that the shareholders' interest in the company consists of the share capital plus reserves (£149,690 in the above example) and not merely the share capital figure.

4.4   Capital and reserves

The profit and loss account balance represents the retained profits of the company, ie, those profits of the company which have not yet been paid out by way of dividend to the shareholders.

The profit and loss account is an example of a **reserve.** Any balances in a company balance sheet representing profits or surpluses, whether they are realised or not, are collectively referred to as **reserves.** There is more about reserves in later in this chapter.

It is helpful if you can produce company balance sheets in the form shown above when practising questions, highlighting the words shown in this particular example in bold.

4.5   Activity

List the ways in which the balance sheet shown above differs from that of a sole trader.

4.6   Activity solution

(a)   Fixed assets divided into tangible assets and intangible assets.
(b)   Current liabilities described as 'Creditors: amounts falling due within one year'.
(c)   Creditors for taxation and dividend payable.
(d)   Long term creditors described as 'Creditors: amounts falling due after more than one year'.
(e)   Capital and reserves section.
(f)   Called up share capital.
(g)   Profit and loss account.

4.7   The nature and purpose of a dividend

One of the creditors in the balance sheet is described as "dividend payable".

Definition   A dividend is a return of part of the profits made by the company to the shareholders.

Dividends can be stated as a percentage based on the nominal value of the share or alternatively as an amount per share eg,

An 8p dividend on a £1 share can be expressed either as 8% or 8p per share.

Modern practice tends to state dividends on a pence per share basis and not as a percentage.

Dividends are **declared** by the company in general meeting. This can only be done if the directors recommend payment of a dividend and it cannot exceed the amount recommended by them. The directors on their own responsibility declare an interim dividend during the accounting period on account of the total dividend for the year, if allowable in the articles of the company.

4.8   The recording of dividends in the ledger accounts

The bookkeeping for payment of an interim dividend is:

Dr   Profit and loss account
        Cr   Bank

Whilst the bookkeeping for a proposed final dividend is:

Dr   Profit and loss account
        Cr   Dividend payable (creditor in the balance sheet)

Both the interim and final dividend appear in the profit and loss account but it will only be the final proposed dividend that is a creditor in the balance sheet.

4.9   Profit and loss account

The format of the profit and loss account for the year can vary. Costs can be analysed in different ways, and the various statutory headings for costs will be considered in the next chapter.

XY Ltd
Profit and loss account for the year ended 31 December 19X9

				£	£
Sales					X
Costs - various analyses can be made					(X)
Net profit before taxation				say	150,000
Corporation tax					48,000
Net profit after taxation					102,000
Dividends					
Preference dividend	-	paid	10,000		
	-	proposed	10,000		
Ordinary dividend	-	paid	18,000		
	-	proposed	36,000		
					74,000
Profit retained for the year					28,000

4.10   The nature of corporation tax

There is a special cost to a company shown in their profit and loss account which is not a cost to a sole trader business or a partnership - **corporation tax**.

Definition   Corporation tax is a tax levied on companies as a percentage of their taxable profits

As it is a form of appropriation of profit (appropriated by the Government rather than the shareholders), it is shown as a separate cost after **net profit before taxation**.

As shareholders' dividends are not tax deductible, taxation is shown **before** shareholders' dividends.

4.11   The recording of taxation in the ledger accounts

Corporation tax is payable in most cases nine months after the end of the accounting period. In order to agree the corporation tax payable, the company must submit the accounts to the Inland Revenue (the tax authority). Thus at the time of the preparation of the accounts the corporation tax is an estimate of the liability. The double entry is:

Dr   Profit and loss account
      Cr   Corporation tax creditor (see the balance sheet)

with the estimated amount of tax charge.

4.12   Activity

The following trial balance at 31 December 19X3 has been extracted from the books of Tefex Ltd:

	Dr £	Cr £
Creditors		3,600
Debtors	8,300	
Land at cost	2,000	
Machinery at cost	12,000	
Proceeds of sale of machinery		400
Doubtful debt provision at 31 Dec 19X2		500
Depreciation provision at 31 Dec 19X2		4,500
Cash in hand	500	
Wages	2,400	
Insurance	600	
Interest paid	800	
Bank balance		4,300
Stock at 31 Dec 19X2	4,800	
Sales		24,200
Purchases	22,000	
Share capital		10,000
Profit and loss account at 31 Dec 19X2		5,900
	53,400	53,400

Additional information:

(1)   Stock at 31 December 19X3 was £5,200.

(2)   Machinery costing £1,200 on which £700 depreciation had been provided was sold for £400 in the year.

(3)   Depreciation on machinery is provided on the reducing balance basis on the net book value at the end of the year at the rate of 10%.

No depreciation is provided on land.

(4)   The doubtful debt provision is to be £600..

You are required:

(a)   to prepare a trading and profit and loss account for the year ended 31 December 19X3;
(b)   to prepare a balance sheet at that date.

4.13   Activity solution

(a)   **Tefex Ltd**

Trading and profit and loss account for the year ended 31 December 19X3

	£	£
Sales		24,200
Opening stock	4,800	
Purchases	22,000	
	26,800	
Closing stock	5,200	
Cost of goods sold		21,600
Gross profit		2,600
Expenses:		
Wages	2,400	
Insurance	600	
Interest	800	
Depreciation (Working (1))	700	
Loss on sale (Working (2))	100	
Bad debts (600 – 500)	100	
		4,700
Loss for year		(2,100)
Profit and loss account b/d		5,900
Profit and loss account c/d		3,800

WORKINGS

(W1)   **Depreciation**

	Cost £	Depn £
Opening balances	12,000	4,500
Sale	(1,200)	(700)
	10,800	3,800
	(3,800)	
NBV	7,000	

Depreciation charge 10% × £7,000 = **£700**

	Cost £	Depn £
Balance after sale	10,800	3,800
Depreciation charge for year		700
	10,800	4,500

(W2)   **Loss on sale of machinery**

	£
Cost	1,200
Depreciation	700
	500
Sold for	400
Loss	100

(b)   **Balance sheet as at 31 December 19X3**

	Cost £	Depn £	£
Fixed assets:			
Tangible assets:			
Land	2,000	-	2,000
Machinery (working 1)	10,800	4,500	6,300
	12,800	4,500	8,300
Current assets:			
Stock		5,200	
Debtors (£8,300 – 600)		7,700	
Cash		500	
		13,400	
Creditors: amounts falling due within one year:			
Bank overdraft		4,300	
Trade creditors		3,600	
		7,900	

Net current assets	5,500
Total assets less current liabilities	13,800
Capital and reserves:	
Called up share capital	10,000
Profit and loss account	3,800
	13,800

Conclusion The preparation of a set of financial statements for a company is very similar to that for a sole trader or partnership. The financial statements will be prepared from a trial balance or extended trial balance and there will be the familiar types of accounting adjustments. The main differences will be in the format and wording of the statements and in accounting areas such as dividends, corporation tax, capital and reserves.

5 ACCOUNTING FOR SHARE CAPITAL

5.1 Authorised and issued share capital

Definition The **authorised** share capital is the maximum number of shares a company may issue.

Definition The **issued** share capital is the actual number of shares in issue at any point in time.

It is the issued share capital which appears on a company's balance sheet.

5.2 Called up and paid up share capital

Definition The **called up** share capital is the amount of nominal value paid by a shareholder plus further amounts agreed to be paid by shareholders on set dates in the future.

Most capital is issued on a fully called basis and it is the only type of share capital which we will have to deal with at this level of examinations.

Definition **Paid up** share capital is the amount of nominal value paid at the current date.

Thus if there are further calls the paid up share capital will be less than the called up share capital.

5.3 Issue of shares at nominal value

The double entry is:

Dr   Cash account
       Cr   Share capital account

with the issue proceeds.

5.4 Activity

A company issues 200,000 50p ordinary shares at their nominal value. Write up the ledger accounts.

5.5   Activity solution

Cash book

	£		£
Ordinary share capital	100,000		

Ordinary share capital account

	£		£
		Cash	100,000

5.6   Issue at a value in excess of nominal value

In this case the amount by which the issue price exceeds the nominal value (the premium) must by law be transferred to a share premium account. The double entry is

Dr   Cash - with total proceeds
      Cr   Share capital account - with nominal value of shares issued
      Cr   Share premium account - with premium

5.7   Activity

A company issues 200,000 50p ordinary shares at an issue price of 75p.

Write up the ledger accounts.

5.8   Activity solution

Cash book

	£		£
Ordinary share capital	100,000		
Share premium	50,000		

Ordinary share capital account

	£		£
		Cash	100,000

Share premium account

	£		£
		Cash	50,000

Balance sheet extract:

	£
Capital and reserves:	
Called up share capital - 50p ordinary shares	100,000
Share premium account	50,000
Profit and loss account	X

The *Companies Act 1985* prohibits the issue of shares at a discount - in other words at a value less than their nominal value.

Conclusion   Whenever shares are issued at a price which is greater than their nominal value the excess of the issue price over the nominal value must always be taken to the share premium account. This means that the ordinary share capital account will always represent the nominal value of the shares issued only.

6   ACCOUNTING FOR RESERVES

6.1   Introduction

Reserves have already been introduced as the profits of the company that have not been paid out on a dividend. The nature and types of reserves will now be considered further.

6.2   Distinction between capital and revenue reserves.

Capital reserves must be established in certain circumstances by law. They include:

(a)   Share premium account;

(b)   Capital redemption reserve (not within the syllabus);

(c)   Revaluation reserve.

These reserves are sometimes referred to as **statutory reserves**

Revenue reserves arise when the company makes profits and does not pay out all the profits to the shareholders. There is no statutory requirement for a company to have any amounts in its revenue reserves.

6.3   The permitted uses of capital and revenue reserves

Revenue reserves can be used for any purpose by the company. The most important practical effect is that they can be distributed to shareholders as dividends.

Capital reserves cannot be so used but this does not mean they cannot be used for other things.

6.4   Uses of the share premium account

The share premium account arises on the issue of shares (ie, capital). It follows that there should be restrictions as to its use.

The share premium account may be used for the following purposes:

(a)   financing the issue of fully paid bonus shares;

(b)   writing off preliminary expenses on the formation of a company;

(c)   writing off expenses, commission or discount on share or debenture issues;

(d)   providing the premium payable on the redemption of debentures and in certain cases on redeemable shares.

Note that the balance on share premium account is either a credit balance or nil - never a debit balance.

6.5   Revenue reserves

The profit for the year (after allowing for expenses and taxation) may be dealt with as follows:

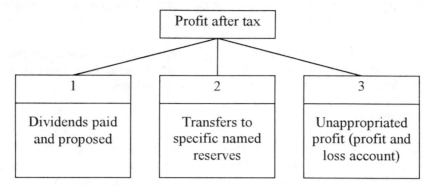

Where profit is transferred to a named reserve, the directors are indicating that these amounts are not available to support a dividend payment (although there is nothing in law to prevent their distribution).

Examples of reserves given special names or titles include:

(a)   **Plant replacement reserve**

During a period of rising prices the replacement cost of new plant will be far greater than its original cost, and consequently the assets representing the historical cost depreciation will fall short of the required amount. Setting up a plant replacement reserve will help to solve this problem.

Therefore an amount may be transferred to the plant replacement reserve by:

Dr   Profit and loss account
       Cr   Plant replacement reserve

(b)   **Stock replacement reserve**

A similar problem arises with stock: during a period of increasing prices, each successive unit of stock costs more. By reducing distributable profits, amounts which might otherwise have been distributed as dividends are retained within the business. The double entry is:

Dr   Profit and loss account
       Cr   Stock replacement reserve

(c)   **General reserve**

Questions often state, for example, that 'the directors wish to transfer £3,000 to a general reserve' without indicating a specific purpose for the reserve. Although legally the reserve can be distributed as a dividend, the directors are indicating that it is not available for distribution. The double entry is:

Dr   Profit and loss account
       Cr   General reserve

6.6   Profit and loss account (reserve)

As shown in the diagram in the previous paragraph any unappropriated profits remain in the profit and loss account.

It is however important to distinguish between:

(a)   the 'normal' profit and loss account, for the year, which is made up in a similar fashion to that of the sole trader; and

(b)   the profit and loss account (reserve), which is the total accumulated unappropriated profit of the company to date - effectively, the amount the company regards as distributable to shareholders. It is this balance that appears in the balance sheet.

6.7   Statement of reserves

In order to cope with the double entry involved in and disclosure of the transfers between various reserves, it is helpful to present the movement in the various reserves in columnar format. This statement can be put immediately below the profit and loss account for the year.

6.8   Activity

ZZ Ltd's summarised balance sheet at 31 December 19X7 showed:

	£
Net assets	280,000
Capital and reserves	
Called up share capital	
- 50p ordinary shares	75,000
- £1 8% preference shares	60,000
Share premium account	25,000
Plant replacement reserve	30,000
Profit and loss account	90,000
	280,000

The net profit for the year to 31 December 19X8 has been computed as £180,000.

The following additional information is available:

(a)   Corporation tax is estimated at £70,000.

(b)   An interim dividend of 2p has been paid on the ordinary shares, and one half of the dividend on the preference shares.

(c)   It is proposed to pay the remaining dividend on the preference shares and a final dividend of 5p on the ordinary shares.

(d)   £20,000 is to be transferred to the plant replacement reserve.

You are required:

(a)   to construct the profit and loss account for the year;
(b)   to show the balance sheet at the end of the year to the extent that information is available.

6.9 Activity solution

Profit and loss account for the year ended 31 December 19X8

		£	£
Profit before taxation			180,000
Corporation tax			70,000
Profit after taxation			110,000
Dividends			
Preference	- paid (60,000 × 4%)	2,400	
	- proposed (60,000 × 4%)	2,400	
			(4,800)
Ordinary	- paid (150,000 × 2p)	3,000	
	- proposed (150,000 × 5p)	7,500	
			(10,500)
Profit retained for the year			94,700

Balance sheet (extracts) as at 31 December 19X8

	£
Creditors: amounts falling due within one year	
Corporation tax	70,000
Dividends (2,400 + 7,500)	9,900
Capital and reserves	
Called up share capital	
- 50p ordinary shares	75,000
- £1 8% preference shares	60,000
Share premium account	25,000
Plant replacement reserve	50,000
Profit and loss account	164,700
	374,700

Note: the total amount of capital and reserves (and thus the net assets) has increased by the amount of **retained** profits of the company, proved below.

	£
Net assets last year	280,000
Retained profit	94,700
Net assets this year	374,700

Statement of reserves

	Profit and loss £	Plant replacement £	Share premium £
Balance at 1 January 19X8	90,000	30,000	25,000
Profit for the year	94,700		
Transfer	(20,000)	20,000	
Balance at 31 December 19X8	164,700	50,000	25,000

6.10   Alternative presentation of profit and loss account

An alternative presentation of the profit and loss account is to show all the appropriation and the opening and closing balances on the face of the profit and loss account:

Profit and loss account for the year ended 31 December 19X8

	£	£
Profit before taxation		180,000
Corporation tax		70,000
Profit after taxation		110,000
Dividends		
Preference - paid (60,000 × 4%)	2,400	
- proposed	2,400	
		(4,800)
Ordinary - paid (150,000 × 2p)	3,000	
- proposed (150,000 × 5p)	7,500	
		(10,500)
Profit retained for the year		94,700
Transfer to plant replacement reserve		(20,000)
		74,700
Balance brought forward		90,000
Balance carried forward		164,700

Conclusion   Capital reserves cannot be distributed to the shareholders as dividends. Revenue reserves can be used for any purpose.

7   PREPARATION OF FINANCIAL STATEMENTS FROM AN EXTENDED TRIAL BALANCE

7.1   Introduction

The use of an extended trial balance to prepare a set of financial statements for a sole trader was considered in detail in an earlier chapter. This method of working can also be used to prepare the financial statements of a company.

Most of the entries on the extended trial balance for a company will be similar to those of a sole trader, for example, stock entries, period end adjustments and accruals and prepayments. However due to the nature of accounting for a company there will be some additional accounts to deal with.

7.2   Share capital

As has already been considered in this chapter the capital of a company is made up of shares and these are recorded in a share capital account and possibly a share premium account. These accounts will appear on the extended trial balance and will be extended across to the balance sheet columns.

7.3   Corporation tax

There will be two accounts for corporation tax in the extended trial balance. One is for the tax charge in the profit and loss account and the other the balance sheet liability for Corporation Tax.

7.4   Dividends

As with tax there will be two accounts in the extended trial balance for dividends. One will be the dividends paid and proposed that are to appear in the profit and loss account and the other will be the balance sheet liability for the proposed dividend at the end of the period.

7.5   Reserves

Finally there will be potentially a variety of account lines in the extended trial balance for the reserves of the company. Any transfers to reserves for the period will be accounted for through these accounts.

7.6   Activity

An activity from earlier in the chapter is now repeated below.

This time the profit and loss account and the balance sheet for the company will be produced using an extended trial balance.

ZZ Ltd's summarised balance sheet at 31 December 19X7 showed:

	£
Net assets	280,000
Capital and reserves	
Called up share capital	
- 50p ordinary shares	75,000
- £1 8% preference shares	60,000
Share premium account	25,000
Plant replacement reserve	30,000
Profit and loss account	90,000
	280,000

The net profit for the year to 31 December 19X8 has been computed as £180,000.

The following additional information is available:

(a)   Corporation tax is estimated at £70,000.

(b)   An interim dividend of 2p has been paid on the ordinary shares, and one half of the dividend on the preference shares.

(c)   It is proposed to pay the remaining dividend on the preference shares and a final dividend of 5p on the ordinary shares.

(d)   £20,000 is to be transferred to the plant replacement reserve.

You are required:

(a)   to construct the profit and loss account for the year;
(b)   to show the balance sheet at the end of the year to the extent that information is available.

7.7   Activity solution

Step 1   Enter the initial trial balance figures onto the trial balance column of the extended trial balance.

Step 2   Enter the net profit against the net profit line and as an increase (debit) in net assets.

Step 3   Enter the corporation tax estimate as a debit to the CT charge account and credit to the balance sheet liability account.

Step 4   Put through the dividend entries. Both dividends paid and proposed appear as a debit in the dividends line. The dividends paid are a credit against net assets (cash payment); the proposed dividend appears on a separate line ready to be extended across to the balance sheet.

Step 5   The transfer to the plant replacement reserve is a debit to the net profit figure and a credit to the reserve itself.

Step 6   Extend the profit and loss account items across to the P&L account columns. Put in the final net profit figure as the balancing figure and also enter it in the balance sheet column in the account, Profit and loss account.

Step 7   Extend the balance sheet figures across to the balance sheet columns and the debits and credits should agree.

Step 8   Prepare the final profit and loss account and balance sheet.

Account	Trial balance £	£	Adjustments £	£	Profit and loss account £	£	Balance sheet £	£
	Step 1				Step 6		Step 7	
Net assets	280,000		180,000 (2)	2,400 (4) 3,000 (4)			454,600	
Called up share capital								
-50p ordinary shares		75,000						75,000
-£1 8% preference shares		60,000						60,000
Share premium		25,000						25,000
Plant replacement reserve		30,000		20,000 (5)				50,000
Profit and loss a/c		90,000						90,000
Net profit			20,000 (5)	180,000 (2)		160,000		74,700
Corporation tax								
- charge			70,000 (3)		70,000			
- balance sheet				70,000 (3)				70,000
Dividends								
- paid and proposed			2,400 (4) 3,000 (4) 2,400 (4) 7,500 (4)		15,300			
Dividends								
- balance sheet				2,400 (4) 7,500 (4)				9,900
Final net profit					74,700			
	280,000	280,000	285,300	285,300	160,000	160,000	454,600	454,600

Profit and loss account for the year ended 31 December 19X8

			£	£
Net profit				180,000
Corporation tax				70,000
Profit after taxation				110,000
Dividends				
Preference	-	paid	2,400	
		proposed	2,400	
Ordinary	-	paid	3,000	
		proposed	7,500	
				(15,300)
				94,700
Transfer to plant replacement reserve				(20,000)
Retained profit				74,700
Profit and loss account b/f				90,000
Profit and loss account c/f				164,700

Balance sheet as at 31 December 19X8

	£
Net assets	454,600
Creditors: amounts falling due within one year	
Corporation tax	(70,000)
Proposed dividend	(9,900)
	374,700
Called up share capital	
- 50p ordinary shares	75,000
- £1 8% preference shares	60,000
Share premium account	25,000
Plant replacement reserve	50,000
Profit and loss account	164,700
	374,700

8   SELF TEST QUESTIONS

1   What are the three key factors that distinguish a company from a sole trader? (1.2)

2   Who are the owners of a company? (1.2)

3   Who are the managers of a company? (1.2)

4   What is the difference between a private and a public company? (1.5)

5   What is the relationship between the nominal value and the market value of a company's shares? (3.3)

6   What are preference shares? (3.7)

7   What are debentures? (3.9)

8   What is the double entry for a proposed final dividend? (4.8)

9   How is an issue of shares at a price in excess of their nominal value accounted for? (5.6)

10   What are the names of three capital reserves? (6.2)

9 PUBLISHED ACCOUNTS

PATHFINDER INTRODUCTION

This chapter covers the following performance criteria and knowledge and understanding.

- Financial statements are accurately drafted from the appropriate information (performance criteria 10.2)
- Draft accounts comply with domestic standards and legislation (performance criteria 10.2)
- Statutory form of accounting statements: disclosure requirements (knowledge and understanding 10.2)

Putting the chapter in context – learning objectives.

In the previous chapter a background understanding of the accounting context within which companies operate was given. The previous chapter also concentrated on the preparation of a draft company balance sheet and profit and loss account. In this chapter the legal requirements for a company's financial statements must also be considered. The Companies Act then goes further and prescribes a vast array of detailed notes to the balance sheet and profit and loss account that companies must also provide in order to give users of the financial statements the information that they require. This chapter concentrates on the key disclosures that are required for this syllabus (by no means all of them!).

The chapter is long and there appears to be a lot of detailed formats and notes to be learnt. However this knowledge will gradually be acquired particularly with the help of question practice. The chapters following this one consider further accounting requirements of SSAPs and FRSs for a variety of elements of the balance sheet and profit and loss account such as taxation, fixed assets, stocks etc. It will often be useful to refer back to the relevant areas of this chapter in conjunction with these subsequent chapters.

The content of this chapter cannot be learnt in one sitting! It is the type of area of knowledge that will be gradually assimilated and acquired.

At the end of this chapter you should have learned the following topics.

- Company law background.
- The balance sheet format.
- Balance sheet notes for fixed assets.
- Balance sheet notes for current assets and liabilities.
- Preparation of a balance sheet.
- The profit and loss account formats.
- Notes to the profit and loss account.
- Contents of the directors report.
- Accounts preparation for small and medium sized companies.

1 COMPANY LAW

1.1 The duty to prepare annual accounts

The directors of a company are responsible for presenting to the company in general meeting a profit and loss account and balance sheet within eighteen months of incorporation, and subsequently at least once in every calendar year. Additionally, all such accounts laid before the company in general meeting must contain a report by the auditors in which they are required to state **(inter alia)** whether in their opinion the company's balance sheet and profit and loss account have been prepared in accordance with the provisions of the Companies Act 1985 (CA 85).

1.2 Prescribed formats

Until the Companies Act 1981 (CA 81) there was no prescribed form of accounts laid down by law, and provided the statutory requirements on disclosure were met, there was allowed a certain latitude in the presentation of financial statements. Sch 4 CA85 now contains specific formats for a company balance sheet and profit and loss account although some choice in overall layout is still allowed.

1.3 Accounting concepts

The SSAP 2 concepts (prudence, accrual, consistency and going concern) are embodied in the Companies Act 1985 as four of the five 'Accounting Principles'. The fifth principle states that in determining the aggregate amount of any item the amount of any individual asset or liability that falls to be taken into account shall be determined separately. For example, when stock is valued at the lower of cost and net realisable value the value must be determined for separate types of stock and then aggregated. In this way anticipated losses on one type of stock will not be offset against expected gains on another.

More detailed accounting provisions are also included in the legislation for certain items. These are detailed in later sections of this chapter when the relevant items are considered.

1.4 Accounting rules

Accounting rules are contained in the CA85. They relate to the amount at which assets are stated in financial statements of companies. There are no statutory accounting rules for the measurement of liabilities.

Companies may use either HISTORICAL COST accounting rules or ALTERNATIVE accounting rules which are based upon current costs or market value. It is possible for a company to use a mixture of these rules as in the 'Modified Historical Cost Convention' when historical cost accounts are modified by the revaluation of certain fixed assets.

The accounting rules are contained in Sch 4 CA85. The table below summarises the rules.

ACCOUNTING RULES

Relate to amount at which ASSETS are stated in accounts

HISTORICAL COST ACCOUNTING RULES	ALTERNATIVE ACCOUNTING RULES
Assets should be stated at the PURCHASE PRICE or PRODUCTION COST	Any of the following assets may be stated at alternative amounts:
Modifications to stating asset at purchase price/production cost:	FIXED ASSETS
FIXED ASSETS / CURRENT ASSETS	(i) Tangible fixed assets. Market value (at last valuation date) or current cost.
Reduce cost by provisions for depreciation with special rules for development costs and goodwill / Reduce cost to net realisable value.	(ii) Intangible fixed assets (except goodwill). Current cost.
	(iii) Investments. Market value (at last valuation date) or any other appropriate basis.
	CURRENT ASSETS
	(i) Investments. Current cost.
	(ii) Stock. Current cost.
	Application of the alternative accounting rules for any of the assets may result in:
	(i) Amendment to the depreciation charge.
	(ii) Additional disclosure of information.
	(iii) Treatment of revaluations.

1.5 The 'true and fair view override'

The Companies Act 1985 requires the directors to depart from any specific provision of the Act in the overriding interest that the individual accounts and group accounts shall present a true and fair view. Where the override is invoked, the Act requires that 'particulars of any such departure, the reasons for it and its effect shall be given in a note to the accounts'.

Where the true and fair view override is being invoked, this should be stated clearly and unambiguously. The statutory disclosure requirement should be interpreted as follows:

(i) Particulars - a statement of the treatment which the Act would normally require in the circumstances and a description of the treatment actually adopted.

(ii) Reasons - a statement as to why the treatment prescribed would not give a true and fair view.

(iii) Effect - a description of how the position shown in the accounts is different as a result of the departure, normally with quantification.

Conclusion   The Companies Act embodies five accounting principles:

- prudence
- accruals
- consistency
- going concern
- separate valuation

Companies may use either the historical cost accounting rules or the alternative accounting rules.

2   THE BALANCE SHEET

2.1   The format

As already mentioned there are some choices in the format of the balance sheet. The most popular, Format 1 (the vertical balance sheet) is reproduced below:

A   Called up share capital not paid (1)

B   Fixed assets

     I   Intangible assets

         1   Development costs
         2   Concessions, patents, licences, trade marks and similar rights and assets (2)
         3   Goodwill (3)
         4   Payments on account

     II   Tangible assets

         1   Land and buildings
         2   Plant and machinery
         3   Fixtures, fittings, tools and equipment
         4   Payments on account and assets in course of construction

     III   Investments

         1   Shares in group undertakings
         2   Loans to group undertakings
         3   Participating interests
         4   Loans to undertakings in which the company has a participating interest
         5   Other investments other than loans
         6   Other loans
         7   Own shares (4)

C   Current assets

     I   Stocks

         1   Raw materials and consumables
         2   Work in progress
         3   Finished goods and goods for resale
         4   Payments on account

II   Debtors (5)

    1   Trade debtors
    2   Amounts owed by group undertakings
    3   Amounts owed by undertakings in which the company has a participating interest
    4   Other debtors
    5   Called up share capital not paid (1)
    6   Prepayments and accrued income (6)

III   Investments

    1   Shares in group undertakings
    2   Own shares (4)
    3   Other investments

IV   Cash at bank and in hand

D   Prepayments and accrued income (6)

E   Creditors: amounts falling due within one year

    1   Debenture loans (7)
    2   Bank loans and overdrafts
    3   Payments received on account (8)
    4   Trade creditors
    5   Bills of exchange payable
    6   Amounts owed to group undertakings
    7   Amounts owed to undertakings in which the company has a participating interest
    8   Other creditors including taxation and social security (9)
    9   Accruals and deferred income (10)

F   Net current assets (liabilities) (11)

G   Total assets less current liabilities

H   Creditors: amounts falling due after more than one year

    1   Debenture loans (7)
    2   Bank loans and overdrafts
    3   Payments received on account (8)
    4   Trade creditors
    5   Bills of exchange payable
    6   Amounts owed to group undertakings
    7   Amounts owed to undertakings in which the company has a participating interest
    8   Other creditors including taxation and social security (9)
    9   Accruals and deferred income (10)

I   Provisions for liabilities and charges

    1   Pensions and similar obligations
    2   Taxation, including deferred taxation
    3   Other provisions

J   Accruals and deferred income (10)

K   Capital and reserves

      I   Called up share capital (12)

      II   Share premium account

      III   Revaluation reserve

      IV   Other reserves

            1   Capital redemption reserve
            2   Reserve for own shares
            3   Reserves provided for by the articles of association
            4   Other reserves

      V   Profit and loss account

Notes on the balance sheet formats

(1)   Called up share capital not paid
      (Items A and C.II.5.)
      This item may be shown in either of the two positions given.

(2)   Concessions, patents, licences, trade marks and similar rights and assets (Item B.I.2.)
      Amounts in respect of assets shall only be included in a company's balance sheet under this item if either –

      (a)   the assets were acquired for valuable consideration and are not required to be shown under goodwill; or

      (b)   the assets in question were created by the company itself.

(3)   Goodwill

      (Item B.I.3.)
      Amounts representing goodwill shall only be included to the extent that the goodwill was acquired for valuable consideration.

(4)   Own shares

      (Items B.III.7 and C.III.2.)
      The nominal value of the shares held shall be shown separately.

(5)   Debtors

      (Items C.II.1 to 6.)
      The amount falling due after more than one year shall be shown separately for each item included under debtors.

(6)   Prepayments and accrued income

      (Items C.II.6 and D.)
      This item may be shown in either of the two positions given.

(7)   Debenture loans

(Items E.1 and H.1)
The amount of any convertible loans shall be shown separately.

(8)   Payments received on account

(Items E.3 and H.3)
Payments received on account of orders shall be shown for each of these items in so far as they are not shown as deductions from stocks.

(9)   Other creditors including taxation and social security

(Items E.8 and H.8)
The amount for creditors in respect of taxation and social security shall be shown separately from the amount for other creditors.

(10)   Accruals and deferred income

(Items E.9, H.9 and J.)
The two positions given for this item at E.9 and H.9 are an alternative to the position at J, but if the item is not shown in a position corresponding to that at J it may be shown in either or both of the other two positions (as the case may require).

(11)   Net current assets (liabilities)

(Item F.)
In determining the amount to be shown for this item any amounts shown under 'prepayments and accrued income' shall be taken into account wherever shown.

(12)   Called up share capital

(Item K.1)
The amount of allotted share capital and the amount of called up share capital which has been paid up shall be shown separately.

2.2   The balance sheet – an example of presentation

In the example which follows, the financial statements for Seaton plc are given under the CA85 disclosure and accounting requirements. The example is annotated by tutorial notes (which would not, of course, appear in a set of published accounts) giving the full disclosure and accounting requirements of the Companies Act.

Seaton plc
Balance sheet at 31 December 19X4

	Notes	£'000	19X3 £'000
Fixed assets			
Intangible assets	(3.2)	153	101
Tangible assets	(3.4)	1,986	1,753
Investments	(3.5)	29	33
		2,168	1,887

Current assets			
Stocks	(4.2)	1,637	1,598
Debtors	(4.3)	2,079	1,635
Investments	(4.4)	126	39
Cash at bank and in hand		75	41
		3,917	3,313
Creditors: amounts falling due within one year	(4.5)	3,010	2,980
Net current assets		907	333
Total assets less current liabilities		3,075	2,220
Creditors: amounts falling due after more than one year	(4.6)	910	495
Provisions for liabilities and charges	(4.7)	27	13
		937	508
		2,138	1,712
Capital and reserves			
Called up share capital	(4.8)	1,500	1,500
Share premium account		23	23
Revaluation reserve		25	25
Other reserves	(4.9)	67	67
Profit and loss account	(4.9)	523	97
		2,138	1,712

The accounts were approved by
the directors on 3 March 19X5

Colyn Seaton

Director

2.3   Approval and signing of accounts

A company's individual (and consolidated) accounts must be approved by the board of directors and the company's individual **balance sheet** must be signed on behalf of the board by **a** director. The copy of the balance sheet which is sent to the registrar of companies must also be signed by **a** director but not necessarily the same director.

In addition, the directors' report must be approved by the board of directors and signed on behalf of the board by **a** director **or** the secretary of the company. (The directors' report is dealt with later.)

2.4   Accounting policies

The notes to the accounts must state the accounting policies adopted by the company for all material items in the financial statements, for example depreciation of fixed assets and valuation of stocks.

Conclusion   Format 1 is the balance sheet format most commonly used and it is important that you learn it thoroughly.

3   NOTES TO THE BALANCE SHEET - FIXED ASSETS

3.1   Introduction

Definition   Assets are to be shown as fixed assets if they are intended for use on a continuing basis in the company's activities. All other assets are to be shown as current assets.

3.2   Intangible assets

		£'000	*19X3* £'000
(a)	Development costs	73	31
(b)	Concessions, patents, licences and trade marks	26	13
(c)	Goodwill	40	50
(d)	Payments on account for intangible assets	14	7
		153	101

Examples of further disclosure required.

(a)   **Development costs**

Development costs relate to a special project for the manufacture, design and marketing of a new range of Seatons. Development commenced in 19X2 and was concluded during the year. Sales commenced during the current year. The costs are being written off over the five year expected life of the new product range.

	£'000
Cost:	
At 1 January 19X4	31
Additions	60
At 31 December 19X4	91

	£'000
Accumulated depreciation:	
At 1 January 19X4	-
Provision for the year	18
At 31 December 19X4	18
Net book amount at 31 December 19X4	73
Net book amount at 31 December 19X3	31

(b)   **Goodwill**

	£'000
Cost:	
At 1 January 19X4 and 31 December 19X4	50
Accumulated depreciation:	
At 1 January 19X4	-
Provision for the year	10
At 31 December 19X4	10
Net book amount at 31 December 19X4	40
Net book amount at 31 December 19X3	50

The goodwill arose on the acquisition of the partnership business of Seapound & Co in 19X3 and was equal to three times the average profits of that partnership during its last five years of trading. It is being written off in equal instalments over five years, being its estimated useful economic life.

3.3   Disclosure of fixed assets

Movements on each of the four categories (may be shown in notes) giving cost or revalued amount (whichever is appropriate), additions, disposals, transfers and any revision of revalued amount. Movements on cumulative depreciation and provisions for diminution in value must also be shown, including provision for the year, the effect of disposals and any other adjustment.

(a)   **Valuation of fixed assets**

Where any class of tangible fixed assets has been revalued, the notes must disclose:

(i)   The date and amounts of the valuations

(ii)   The basis of valuation

(iii)   The name and qualifications of the valuer and a description of the nature of the valuer's organisation

(iv)   All historical cost information that would be required if there were no valuation

(v)   Whether the valuer is internal or external to the entity

(vi)   Where the directors are not aware of any material change in value, and therefore the valuation has not been updated, a statement to that effect

(vii)   Where the valuation has not been updated, or is not a full valuation, the date of the last full valuation.

(b)   **Land and buildings**

There must be disclosure of the division between freehold and leasehold interests in respect of amounts shown in the balance sheet or its related notes in respect of land and buildings. Leasehold interest must be further sub-divided between long leases (unexpired terms of 50 years or more) and short leases (unexpired terms of less than 50 years).

3.4 **Tangible assets**

	Land and buildings	Plant and machinery	Fixtures, fittings, tools and equipment	Payments on account and assets in course of construction	Total
	£'000	£'000	£'000	£'000	£'000
Cost or valuation:					
At 1 January 19X4	871	998	207	27	2,103
Additions	74	809	25	13	921
Disposals	-	(23)	(5)	-	(28)
At 31 December 19X4	945	1,784	227	40	2,996
Accumulated depreciation:					
At 1 January 19X4	33	292	25	-	350
Provision for year	11	622	27	8	668
Disposals	-	(4)	(4)	-	(8)
At 31 December 19X4	44	910	48	8	1,010
Net book amount:					
at 31 December 19X4	901	874	179	32	1,986
at 31 December 19X3	838	706	182	27	1,753

The net book amount of land and buildings comprises:

	19X4 £'000	19X3 £'000
Freehold	629	555
Long leasehold	129	129
Short leasehold	143	154
	901	838

3.5 **Investments**

	1 Jan. 19X4 £'000	Additions £'000	Disposals £'000	31 Dec. 19X4 £'000
Listed shares (market value £28,500) **(£31,000)**	24	1	5	20
Unquoted investments in shares	8	-	-	8
Loans	1	-	-	1
	33	1	5	29

4   NOTES TO THE BALANCE SHEET - CURRENT ASSETS & LIABILITIES

4.1   Accounting principles for current assets

Current assets should generally be stated at purchase price or production cost except where net realisable value is lower.

Provisions to reduce to net realisable value must be written back if the reasons for which they were made have ceased to apply.

[Definition]   Purchase price is the actual price paid plus any expenses incidental to the acquisition and includes any consideration (whether in cash or otherwise) given in respect of an asset.

[Definition]   Production cost includes raw materials, consumables and direct production costs. A reasonable proportion of indirect production costs and interest on capital borrowed to finance production of the asset may also be included. In the case of a current asset, distribution costs may not be included in production costs.

4.2   Stocks

	£'000	19X3 £'000
Raw materials and consumables	437	505
Work in progress	306	281
Finished goods and goods for resale	871	803
Payments on account	23	9
	1,637	1,598

Disclosure

Any material difference between the balance sheet amount of stocks and replacement cost or, if more appropriate, the most recent actual purchase price must be disclosed for each category of stocks.

4.3   Debtors

	£'000	19X3 £'000
Trade debtors	1,327	1,191
Other debtors	408	250
Prepayments and accrued income	344	194
	2,079	1,635

Presentation

(a)   Amounts falling due after more than one year must be shown separately for each item.

(b)   There are six categories:

     (i)   Trade debtors;
     (ii)   Amounts owed by group undertakings;
     (iii)   Amounts owed by undertakings in which the company has a participating interest;
     (iv)   Other debtors;
     (v)   Called up share capital not paid;
     (vi)   Prepayments and accrued income.

Notes:

     (1)   Called up share capital not paid may be shown as the first item on the balance sheet, before fixed assets, if preferred.

     (2)   Prepayments and accrued income may be shown as a separate category, after cash at bank and in hand, if preferred.

4.4   Investments

All investments disclosed as current assets are in shares listed on a recognised stock exchange and are shown at the lower of cost and market value. The aggregate market value is £143,000 (19X3 £45,000).

4.5   Creditors: amounts falling due within one year

	£'000	*19X3* £'000
Debenture loans	200	-
Bank loans and overdrafts	20	20
Trade creditors	1,281	1,007
Taxation and social security	35	11
Proposed dividends	30	-
Other creditors	62	613
Accruals and deferred income	1,382	1,329
	3,010	2,980

Presentation

There are nine categories illustrated in the pro-formas in **CA85.** These are expanded as follows to include other items which, if they arose, would require to be shown separately:

(a)   Debenture loans (showing convertible loans separately);
(b)   Bank loans and overdrafts;
(c)   Other loans;
(d)   Payments received on account (if not shown as deductions from stocks);
(e)   Trade creditors;
(f)   Bills of exchange payable;
(g)   Amounts owed to group undertakings;
(h)   Amounts owed to undertakings in which the company has a participating interest;
(i)   Taxation and social security;
(j)   Proposed dividends;
(k)   Other creditors;
(l)   Accruals and deferred income.

4.6   Creditors: amounts falling due after more than one year

	£'000	*19X3* £'000
Debenture loans	100	300
Bank loans and overdrafts	29	115
Other loans	224	24
Taxation and social security	400	23
Deferred income	157	33
	910	495

Further disclosure required:

(a)   **Debenture loans**

Interest is payable at a rate of 10% pa. The loans are redeemable in 19X9. £200,000 of the long-term debenture loans outstanding in 19X3 are redeemable during 19X5 and are included in arriving at net current assets.

(b)   **Other loans**

	£'000	*19X3* £'000
Medium-term (repayable within five years from the current balance sheet date)	15	15
Long-term	209	9
	224	24

The long-term loan is from Seascrew Finance plc. It is repayable on demand after 19X8, and carries a rate of interest of 18% pa. The loan is secured by a floating charge on the undertaking, property and assets of the company.

Notes:

(1)   Presentation should be as for current liability creditors, with a maximum of twelve categories.

(2)   Debentures and loan stocks:

Where debentures or any form of loan stock have been issued during a financial year, there must be shown:

(i)   The classes of debenture issued;
(ii)   For each class, the amount issued and the consideration received.

(3)   **All creditors**

For each item under creditors show the aggregate of both:

(i)   non-instalment debts that fall due for repayment after five years; and
(ii)   instalment debts some of which fall due for payment after five years.

The terms of repayment and the rate of interest payable should be shown for each debt which falls to be taken into account in the above disclosure. However, it will be sufficient to provide a general indication of repayment terms and interest rates if compliance with this requirement would result in a statement of excessive length.

For each category of creditors, there must be shown the amount for which security has been given and an indication of the nature of the security.

4.7   Provisions for liabilities and charges

	£'000	*19X3* £'000
Pensions and similar obligations	16	2
Taxation, including deferred taxation	8	8
Other provisions	3	3
	27	13

Pensions and similar obligations:	
At 1 January 19X4	2
Transfer from profit and loss account	14
At 31 December 19X4	16

The taxation provision is wholly in respect of deferred taxation. There has been no movement on this account during the year.

Notes:

(1)   Movements:

Where there is a movement on any provision for liabilities and charges (other than a transfer from a provision for the purpose for which it was established) there must be disclosure of the movements on that provision, consisting of:

(i)   The amount at the beginning and the end of the year;
(ii)   Transfers to or from the provision during that year;
(iii)   The source and application of the amounts transferred.

Corresponding amounts need not be given.

(2)   [Definition]   Provisions are amounts retained for any liability or loss which either is likely to be incurred, or certain to be incurred but uncertain as to amount or date on which it will arise.

Deferred taxation, which is not defined in the Act, is expected to be treated as a 'provision' since it is likely that there will be some uncertainty regarding either the amount required or the date on which timing differences may reverse. Other tax 'provisions' are likely to be classified as 'creditors' unless there is some uncertainty as to either the amount of the liability or the date on which it will arise. (See later chapter on Taxation.)

4.8   Called up share capital

	£'000	*19X3* £'000
Allotted and fully paid:		
Ordinary shares of £1 each	1,200	1,200
6% cumulative preference shares of 50p each	300	300
	1,500	1,500

Disclosure

(a)   The amount of allotted share capital and the amount of called up share capital which has been paid up must be shown separately.

(b)   The authorised share capital and, where there is more than one class of shares, the number and aggregate nominal value of each class allotted must be disclosed.

(c)   Where shares have been allotted during a financial year there must be shown:

    (i)   the class of shares allotted;

    (ii)   for each class, the number allotted, their aggregate nominal value and the consideration received.

(d)   If there are any redeemable shares, there must be disclosed:

    (i)   The earliest and latest dates of redemption;
    (ii)   Whether the redemption is obligatory or at the option of the company;
    (iii)   Whether any premium is payable on redemption.

(e)   If any fixed cumulative dividends on shares are in arrears, there must be shown:

    (i)   The amount of the arrears;
    (ii)   The period for which the dividends are in arrears (by class of shares).

[Definition]   Called up share capital is the aggregate amount of calls made on shares, share capital paid up without being called and share capital to be paid on a specified future date under the terms of allotment.

Allotted share capital is not defined but is presumed to be the full nominal value of shares allotted.

4.9   Reserves

	Profit and loss account £'000
At 1 January 19X4	97
Currency translation differences	(28)
Amount set aside from profit for the financial year	454
At 31 December 19X4	523

All movements on any reserve account must be shown.

5   PREPARING BALANCE SHEETS IN ACCORDANCE WITH THE PRESCRIBED FORMATS

5.1   Approach to computational questions

Computational balance sheet disclosure questions do not generally specify a particular format to be used and thus Format 1 should be followed.

Allow a whole page for the balance sheet, a page for the notes and a separate page for the workings.

Few workings will be required as the notes to the accounts can often act as workings as well. For example a fixed asset note per the CA 85 requires an analysis of each major type of fixed asset showing brought forward figures, additions and disposals for both cost and depreciation. Thus the working out of the year end figures for fixed assets is effectively done by producing the note.

When presenting the balance sheet

(a)   write out a heading in full

(b)   use the same narrative as in the CA 85 format

(c)   leave some space between the various parts and allow for the later insertion of figures that you may have forgotten to include. The examiner will not deduct marks if there is a lot of 'white space'. He will deduct marks if the statement is so cramped as to be illegible.

Much use can be made of the combination provisions of the CA 85 to show a summarised balance sheet and the detailed figures in the notes. For example

Approach 1

Face of balance sheet

	£
Creditors: amounts falling due within one year	300,000

Notes to the accounts

Creditors: amounts falling due within one year:	
Bank overdraft	160,000
Trade creditors	120,000
Accruals	5,000
Proposed dividend	15,000
	300,000

Approach 2

Face of balance sheet

	£
Creditors: amounts falling due within one year:	
Bank overdraft	160,000
Trade creditors	120,000
Accruals	5,000
Proposed dividend	15,000
	300,000

The advantages of approach 1 are

(a)   it is often neater and
(b)   it is easier to add missed out creditors without the end result being cramped.

The advantage of approach 2 is that less writing is involved.

The choice really depends on how tidy and methodical you are.

It is helpful to allow two or three columns for the figures on the balance sheet (comparative figures are rarely required).

5.2   Activity

Small plc is a quoted company with an authorised share capital of £250,000, consisting of ordinary shares of £1 each. The company prepares its accounts as on 31 March in each year and the trial balance, before final adjustments, extracted on 31 March 19X5 showed:

	£	£
Ordinary share capital, issued and fully paid		200,000
Retained profits as on 1 April 19X4		61,000
6% Debenture stock (secured on leasehold factory)		60,000
Leasehold factory:		
Cost at beginning of year	200,000	
Accumulated depreciation at beginning of year		76,000
Plant and machinery :		
Cost at beginning of year	80,000	
Accumulated depreciation		30,000
Additions in year	10,000	
Creditors and accrued expenses		170,000
Stock as on 31 March 19X5	160,000	
Debtors	100,000	
Prepayments	80,000	
Balance at bank	90,000	
Profit for the year (subject to any items		
in the following notes)		111,000
Sale proceeds of plant		12,000
	720,000	720,000

You ascertain that:

(1)   The debenture stock is repayable at par by six equal annual drawings starting on 31 December 19X5.

(2)   The lease of the factory has 56 years remaining at 31 March 19X5.

(3)   Annual depreciation is calculated as to:

Leasehold factory   –   2% on cost

Plant and machinery   –   20% reducing balance on NBV as at 31 March 19X4 plus additions less disposals in the year

(4)   Plant disposed of originally cost £16,000. Accumulated depreciation is £3,200.

(5)   Stock has been valued consistently at the lower of cost and net realisable value.

(6)   A dividend of 20% is proposed.

(7)   The directors have placed contracts for new plant costing £5,000. These have not been provided for, but should be disclosed.

You are required to prepare in a form suitable for publication and in conformity with the provisions of the Companies Act 1985, the balance sheet as on 31 March 19X5 together with accompanying notes.

5.3   **Activity solution**

Small plc

Balance sheet as at 31 March 19X5

	£	£
Fixed assets		
Tangible assets		157,760
Current assets		
Stocks	160,000	
Debtors	180,000	
Cash at bank and in hand	90,000	
	430,000	
Creditors: amounts falling due within one year	220,000	
Net current assets		210,000
Total assets less current liabilities		367,760
Creditors: amounts falling due after more than one year		50,000
		317,760
Capital and reserves		
Called up share capital		200,000
Profit and loss account		117,760
		317,760

The accounts were approved by the directors on ....

Signed A Director

Notes to the balance sheet

(a)   **Statement of accounting policies**

    (i)   The accounts have been prepared in accordance with applicable accounting standards.

    (ii)   Depreciation

        (1)   Leasehold factory - 2% on cost.

        (2)   Plant and machinery - depreciation is calculated on the reducing balance method at a rate of 20% pa. Assets acquired during the year are charged with a full year's depreciation.

    (iii)   Stock

    Stock has been valued at the lower of cost and net realisable value.

(b)   **Tangible assets**

	Long leasehold property £	Plant and machinery £	Total £
Cost:			
At 1 April 19X4	200,000	80,000	280,000
Additions	-	10,000	10,000
Disposals	-	(16,000)	(16,000)
At 31 March 19X5	200,000	74,000	274,000
Aggregate depreciation:			
At 1 April 19X4	76,000	30,000	106,000
Eliminated on disposals		(3,200)	(3,200)
Amount provided	4,000	9,440	13,440
At 31 March 19X5	80,000	36,240	116,240
Net book value:			
at 31 March 19X5	120,000	37,760	157,760
at 31 March 19X4	124,000	50,000	174,000

Note: future capital expenditure

	£
Contracted for but not provided in the accounts	5,000

(c)   **Debtors**

	£
Trade debtors	100,000
Prepayments and accrued income	80,000
	180,000

(d)   **Creditors: amounts falling due within one year**

	£
Debenture loan	10,000
Trade creditors	170,000
Proposed dividend	40,000
	220,000

(e)   **Creditors: amounts falling due after more than one year**

This consists of 6% debenture stock repayable at par by five equal annual drawings commencing 31 December 19X6. £10,000 is payable more than five years from the balance sheet date. The debenture stock is secured.

(f)   **Called up share capital**

	Authorised £	*Allotted fully paid* £
Ordinary shares of £1 each	250,000	200,000

(g)   **Profit and loss account**

	£
Retained profit as at 1 April 19X4	61,000
Add: Retained profit for the year (W3)	56,760
Retained profit as at 31 March 19X5	117,760

WORKINGS

(W1)   Depreciation

	£	£
Leasehold factory 2% of £200,000		4,000
Plant and machinery		
NBV b/d	50,000	
Additions	10,000	
Disposals at NBV	(12,800)	
	47,200	
Depreciation 20% ×	47,200	= 9,440
		13,440

(W2)   Disposal of plant

	£	£
Proceeds		12,000
Cost	16,000	
Less: Depreciation	3,200	
		12,800
		800

(W3)   Profit for year per TB

		£
Profit for year per TB		111,000
Less: Depreciation (4,000 + 9,440)	13,440	
Loss on sale (W2)	800	
Proposed dividend (20% × 200,000)	40,000	
		54,240
		56,760

6   THE PROFIT AND LOSS ACCOUNT – FORMATS

6.1   The formats

As with the balance sheet the CA 85 offers a choice of profit and loss account formats.

The two vertical formats are reproduced below. Format 1 is the 'operational' statement and format 2 is the 'type of expenditure' statement. Format 1 is the more common.

Profit and loss account - Format 1

1	Turnover
2	Cost of sales (14)
3	Gross profit or loss
4	Distribution costs (14)
5	Administrative expenses (14)
6	Other operating income
7	Income from shares in group undertakings
8	Income from participating interests
9	Income from other fixed asset investments (15)
10	Other interest receivable and similar income (15)
11	Amounts written off investments
12	Interest payable and similar charges (16)
13	Tax on profit or loss on ordinary activities
14	Profit or loss on ordinary activities after taxation
15	Extraordinary income
16	Extraordinary charges
17	Extraordinary profit or loss
18	Tax on extraordinary profit or loss
19	Other taxes not shown under the above items
20	Profit or loss for the financial year

Format 2

1	Turnover	
2	Change in stocks of finished goods and in work in progress	
3	Own work capitalised	
4	Other operating income	
5	(a)	Raw materials and consumables
	(b)	Other external charges
6	Staff costs:	
	(a)	Wages and salaries
	(b)	Social security costs
	(c)	Other pension costs
7	(a)	Depreciation and other amounts written off tangible and intangible fixed assets
	(b)	Exceptional amounts written off current assets
8	Other operating charges	
9	Income from shares in group undertakings	
10	Income from participating interests	
11	Income from other fixed asset investments (15)	
12	Other interest receivable and similar income (15)	
13	Amounts written off investments	
14	Interest payable and similar charges (16)	
15	Tax on profit or loss on ordinary activities	
16	Profit or loss on ordinary activities after taxation	
17	Extraordinary income	
18	Extraordinary charges	
19	Extraordinary profit or loss	

20   Tax on extraordinary profit or loss
21   Other taxes not shown under the above items
22   Profit or loss for the financial year

6.2   Comments on the profit and loss account

(a)   As there are no alphabetical or Roman numerals assigned to items in the profit and loss account none of these items have to be disclosed on the face of the profit and loss account. The items which must appear in a profit and loss account do not in fact appear in any of the formats but every profit and loss account must show:

   (i)   the company's profit or loss on ordinary activities before taxation

   (ii)   any amount set aside or proposed to be set aside to, or withdrawn or proposed to be withdrawn from, reserves and

   (iii)   the aggregate amount of any dividends paid and proposed, showing separately the amount of proposed dividends if this is not disclosed in a note.

(b)   The extent to which items included in the formats need to be disclosed on the face of the profit and loss account is subject to the same principles as the balance sheet:

   (i)   items must be rearranged or adapted where the special nature of the company's business requires such adaptation

   (ii)   items may be combined if either (1) the individual amounts are not material to assessing the profit and loss of the company or (2) the combination of items facilitates the assessment of the profit and loss of the company.

In the latter case the individual amounts of the combined items must be disclosed in a note to the accounts.

6.3   The profit and loss account – An example of presentation

Seaton plc

Profit and loss account for the year ended 31 December 19X4

	Notes	£'000	*19X3* £'000
Turnover	(7.1)	4,910	3,505
Cost of sales		(2,475)	(1,210)
Gross profit		2,435	2,295
Distribution costs		(716)	(946)
Administrative expenses		(756)	(1,198)
Other operating income		13	7
Income from fixed asset investments	(7.5)	4	6
Other interest receivable and similar income		15	5
Interest payable and similar charges	(7.6)	(85)	(57)
Profit on ordinary activities before taxation	(7.2)	910	112
Tax on profit on ordinary activities	(7.7)	386	22
Profit for the financial year		524	90
Dividends paid and proposed		70	-
Amount set aside to reserves		454	90

Conclusion Two profit and loss account formats are used: Format 1 (operational) and Format 2 (type of expenditure). Both these formats should be thoroughly learned.

7   NOTES TO THE PROFIT AND LOSS ACCOUNT

Note: not all these notes are cross referenced directly to the profit and loss account. Accounting policies are required where relevant.

7.1   Segmental information

	Turnover	
	19X4	*19X3*
	£'000	£'000
Class of business:		
Seaton	2,378	1,650
Seatex	1,831	1,583
Seatan	701	272
	4,910	3,505

	Turnover	
	19X4	*19X3*
	£'000	£'000
Geographical market:		
United Kingdom	2,490	2,112
United States of America	1,012	989
Europe	987	182
India	151	63
Australia	270	159
	4,910	3,505

Turnover and profit disclosure

(a)   Notes must show turnover broken down by classes of business and by geographical markets, having regard to the manner in which the company's activities are organised, in so far as these classes and markets differ substantially.

(b)   SSAP 25 contains additional requirements for larger companies to disclose the segmental breakdown of profits before tax as well as turnover. (SSAP 25 is covered later in this study text).

7.2   Profit on ordinary activities before taxation

Various items that have been charged in reaching this figure must be disclosed:

	£'000	£'000
Profit before taxation is stated after the following amounts:		
Depreciation and amortisation	701	450
Auditors' remuneration	28	22

7.3   Directors' emoluments

The directors' emoluments will be included in the relevant cost heading eg, cost of sales, distribution costs but the detailed amounts must be disclosed separately in a note:

	£'000	*19X3* £'000
Aggregate emoluments	225	114
Gains made on exercise of share options	10	8
Amounts receivable under long-term incentive schemes	10	5
Company pension contributions to money purchase schemes	25	20
Compensation for loss of office	45	–
Sums paid to third parties for directors' services	–	3
	315	150

Retirement benefits are accruing to six directors under a money purchase pension scheme and to two directors under a defined benefit scheme.

The highest paid director received emoluments as follows:

	£'000	*19X3* £'000
Aggregate emoluments, gains on share options exercised and benefits under long-term incentive schemes	47	21
Company pension contributions to money purchase scheme	-	-
Defined benefit pension scheme:		
Accrued pension at end of year	20	17
Accrued lump sum at end of year	50	40

Where the combined total of directors' emoluments, gains on the exercise of share options and amounts receivable under long term incentive schemes is £200,000 or more the following additional information must be given in respect of the **highest paid director**:

(a) Emoluments (including gains on the exercise of share options and amounts receivable under long term incentive schemes).

(b) Company contributions paid to a pension scheme.

(c) Accrued retirement benefits (where the highest paid director is a member of a defined benefit scheme).

7.4 Staff costs – employees

Staff costs for employees will also be split up and included in the relevant P&L a/c cost headings. The totals however must be disclosed in a note as follows:

	£'000	*19X3* £'000
Staff costs:		
Wages and salaries	1,600	1,885
Social security costs	235	280
Other pension costs	187	125

The average number of people employed by the group during the year was:

		19X3
United Kingdom	55	82
United States of America	38	42
Europe	47	25
India	30	20
Australia	35	29

7.5   Income from investments

Within the headings 'Income from other fixed investments' and 'Other interest receivable and similar income', the income and interest derived from group companies should be shown separately.

7.6   Interest payable and similar charges

	£'000	*19X3* £'000
Interest payable on bank loans and overdrafts	80	52
Interest payable on other loans	5	5
	85	57

7.7   Tax on profit on ordinary activities

	£'000	*19X3* £'000
Taxation on the profit for the year:		
UK corporation tax at 31%	356	19
Relief for overseas tax	(15)	(10)
	341	9
Overseas tax	45	13
	386	22

The charge for taxation on the profit for the year has been reduced by £107,000 (19X3 £28,000) in respect of fixed asset timing differences for which no deferred taxation has been provided. (Taxation will be covered in more detail in the next chapter.)

7.8   Exceptional items

Definition   Items within the normal activities of the business which require disclosure on account of their abnormal size or incidence eg, large bad debts, stock write-offs and losses on long-term contracts.

These should be disclosed in arriving at the profit on ordinary activities.

(This will be studied in more depth in a later chapter of this study text.)

7.9   Activity

Jot down notes explaining which of the items below would require to be disclosed in notes to the profit and loss account.

(a)   Audit fee – £6,000.
(b)   Auditors' expenses – £250.
(c)   Bad debts – £6,000.
(d)   Auditors' preparation of taxation computations – £200.
(e)   Rent of office accommodation – £1,000.
(f)   Capital expenditure of £20,000 authorised by directors, but no contract placed.

7.10   Activity solution

(a)
(b)   require disclosure in notes to the profit and loss account;

(c)   would require disclosure only if the amount were exceptional for the company concerned;

(d)   requires disclosure in notes to the profit and loss account;

(e)   does not require disclosure;

(f)   does not require disclosure - would only be disclosed in a note if the contract has been entered into.

> **Conclusion**   The detailed disclosure requirements for the profit and loss account are best learnt by memorising the statutory formats and then using each caption as a mental 'peg' on which to hang the information disclosed by notes.

8   PREPARING PROFIT AND LOSS ACCOUNTS IN ACCORDANCE WITH THE PRESCRIBED FORMATS

8.1   Approach to computational questions

Most computational questions do not specify a particular format to be used. Format 1 is generally the easiest to use.

Allow a whole page for the profit and loss account and a page for the notes to the profit and loss account. A working paper may also be needed to show how the various costs given in the question have been allocated to cost of sales, distribution costs and administrative expenses. There are no definitions in the Companies Acts of these cost headings and so, provided a working is submitted which is clear, any reasonable allocation of costs will be marked as correct.

It is important however, to keep the notes to the accounts on a separate page to the workings. In the note to the accounts, you are trying to reproduce information in a published document. The most common notes that are required are:

(a)   Detailed expenses (depreciation, auditors' fees and expenses)
(b)   Directors' emoluments
(c)   Details of tax charge
(d)   Earnings per share (see later).

When presenting the profit and loss account use the same principles as for the balance sheet:

(a)   write out a heading in full

(b)   use the same narrative as in the CA85 format

(c)   leave some space between various parts and allow for the later insertion of figures that you may have forgotten to include.

8.2   Reserves note

In addition a separate statement of reserves either at the foot of the profit and loss account for the year or in a note to the accounts is the clearest way to compute the year end reserves for the balance sheet and also to comply with the CA85 disclosure requirements (the CA85 requires an analysis of each reserve).

A suggested layout is

Statement of reserves

	Profit and loss account	Revaluation reserve	Share premium	Plant replacement
	£	£	£	£
As at 1 Jan 19X1	90,000	20,000	Nil	Nil
Profit for the year	89,000			
Revaluation		30,000		
Issue of shares			40,000	
Transfers	(15,000)			15,000
As at 31 Dec 19X1	164,000	50,000	40,000	15,000

A further advantage of the layout is that further reserves can be added as you progress through the question.

8.3   The profit and loss account - format 2

The layout of format 2 needs to be known and occasionally there may be a requirement to use this method. Most cost headings are easily understood, the exceptions being item 5(b), other external charges and item 8, other operating charges. Neither term is defined but a sensible split would be to include factory costs under 5(b) and administrative costs under 8.

8.4   Activity

An extract from the trial balance of Production Ltd as at 30 September 19X3 is given below

	£	£
Turnover		900,000
Stocks:		
Raw materials	40,000	
Work-in-progress	70,000	
Finished goods	60,000	
Raw materials	300,000	
Wages	200,000	
Production overheads	80,000	
Administration salaries	100,000	
Office rent and rates	20,000	
Closing stocks are:		
Raw materials	30,000	
Work-in-progress	62,000	
Finished goods	80,000	

Prepare the profit and loss accounts using Format 1 and Format 2.

8.5   Activity solution

Format 1 - Profit and loss account for the year ended 30 September 19X3

	£
Sales	900,000
Cost of sales (working)	578,000
Gross profit	322,000
Administrative expenses (working)	120,000
	202,000

WORKING

Allocation of costs	Cost of sales £	Administrative £
Opening stocks:		
Raw materials	40,000	
Work-in-progress	70,000	
Finished goods	60,000	
Raw materials	300,000	
Wages	200,000	
Production overheads	80,000	
Administrative salaries		100,000
Office rent and rates		20,000
Closing stocks:		
Raw materials	(30,000)	
Work-in-progress	(62,000)	
Finished goods	(80,000)	
	578,000	120,000

Format 2 - Profit and loss account for the year ended 30 September 19X3

	£	£
Sales		900,000
Change in stock of finished goods and work-in-progress (W1)		12,000
Raw materials and consumables (W2)	310,000	
Other external charges	80,000	
Staff costs (200 + 100)	300,000	
Other operating charges	20,000	
		(710,000)
		202,000

WORKINGS

			£
(W1)	Closing stock		
	Finished goods		80,000
	Work-in-progress		62,000
	Opening stock		
	Finished goods		(70,000)
	Work-in-progress		(60,000)
	Increase		12,000
(W2)	Raw materials		
	Opening stock		40,000
	Purchases		300,000
	Closing stock		(30,000)
			310,000

9   THE DIRECTORS' REPORT

9.1   Introduction

The company's annual report and accounts must include a Directors' Report. The information to be disclosed is set out in Sch 7 CA85. A checklist of the requirements is given here.

9.2   Checklist of requirements

(1)   *Principal activities* Give the principal activities of the company or group together with any changes in those activities during the financial year.

(2)   *Business review* A fair review of the activities of the company or group during the year and the position at the end of it.

(3)   *Post balance sheet events* Important events affecting the company or group which have occurred since the end of the year.

(4)   *Future developments* An indication of likely future developments in the business.

(5)   *Research and development* An indication of the activities of the company or group in the field of research and development.

(6)   *Dividend* The amount which the directors recommend to be paid as dividends.

(7)   *Asset values* Significant differences between the balance sheet value and market value of freehold or leasehold interests in land.

(8)   *Directors* The names of those who were directors of the company at any time during the financial year.

(9)   *Interests of directors* For each director who holds office at the end of the year disclose the following:

(a)   Number of shares held.
(b)   Amount of debentures held.
(c)   Options for shares or debentures.

(Nil figures should be given if no interest exists.)

The information should be given for the following dates:

(i)   At the beginning of the financial year or on the date of appointment if appointed during the year; and

(ii)   At the end of the financial year.

(10)   *Purchase of own shares*   Where a company purchases its own shares, or acquires its own shares by forfeiture or in any other manner, there must be disclosure of:

(a)   number and nominal value of shares purchased;
(b)   amount paid;
(c)   reasons for purchases;
(d)   percentage of called-up share capital which they represent.

(11)   *Disabled employees*   If the average number of the company's UK employees exceeds 250, a statement of its policy:

(a)   for giving full and fair consideration to applications for employment by the company made by disabled persons, having regard to their particular aptitudes and abilities;

(b)   for continuing the employment of, and for arranging appropriate training for, employees of the company who have become disabled persons during the period when they were employed by the company; and

(c)   otherwise for the training, career development and promotion of disabled persons employed by the company.

(12)   *Employee involvement*   If the average number of the company's UK employees exceeds 250, a statement of its policy for:

(a)   providing employees systematically with information on matters of concern to them as employees;

(b)   consulting employees or their representatives on a regular basis so that the views of employees can be taken into account in making decisions which are likely to affect their interests;

(c)   encouraging the involvement of employees in the company's performance through an employees' share scheme or by some other means;

(d)   achieving a common awareness on the part of all employees of the financial and economic factors affecting the performance of the company.

(13)   *Donations*   Disclose the total of political and charitable donations if the total is in excess of £200. The total must be split between those for charitable purposes and those for political purposes.

In respect of political donations only disclose for each donation of more than £200:

(a)   the name of the party or organisation concerned; and
(b)   the amount given.

(14)   *Creditor payment policy* Plcs and large private companies whose parent is a plc, must disclose their payment policy for their suppliers. The directors must state, for the financial year *following* that covered by the annual report, whether it is the company's policy to follow any code or standard on payment practice. If so, the name of the code/standard must be given, together with information on how a copy can be obtained. If not, it must state its policy.

The directors must also state whether it is the company's policy to:

(a)   settle the terms of payment with suppliers when agreeing the terms of each transaction;

(b)   ensure that suppliers are made aware of the terms of payment;

(c)   abide by the terms of payment.

The directors must also state the following figure, expressed in days:

$$\frac{\text{Amount owed to trade creditors at the year end}}{\text{Amount invoiced by suppliers during the year}} \times 365$$

(15)   *Approval* The board of directors must approve the directors' report and authorise either a director or the company secretary to sign the directors' report on behalf of the board.

Conclusion   The items listed above are the minimum required to meet the requirements of CA85. There is no particular order of these matters which must be followed to meet legal requirements.

10   SMALL AND MEDIUM SIZED COMPANIES

10.1   Introduction

CA85 introduced into law a distinction between the requirements in relation to the accounts prepared by a small or medium company for circulation to its members and those which it files with the Registrar of Companies. Small and medium companies (as defined below) may file 'abbreviated' accounts with the Registrar of Companies. They are, however, still required to send full accounts to their members (although they may be able to take advantage of some exemptions from disclosure requirements - see below).

The *CA89* removed the term 'modified' accounts from the legislation, and made some amendments to the requirements. In addition, small or medium companies are not required to state in their full accounts whether the accounts have been prepared in accordance with applicable accounting standards.

In 1992 a statutory instrument was issued which:

(a)   amended the small and medium sized company limits;
(b)   reduced the extent of disclosure of small companies in their 'full' financial statements.

10.2   Criteria

A company qualifies as small or medium if, for the financial year in question and the immediately preceding financial year, it is within the limits of at least two of the following three criteria:

Size criteria	*Small*	*Medium*
Balance sheet total (ie, total assets)	£1,400,000	£5,600,000
Turnover*	£2,800,000	£11,200,000
Average number of employees	50	250

* adjust pro rata where period more or less than twelve months.

Having once qualified as small or medium, a company does not cease to qualify unless it fails to satisfy the conditions for two consecutive years, in which case it ceases to qualify in the second such year. For example, a company which satisfies the criteria for a small company in, say, 19X2 and 19X3, but not in 19X4, may still file small company accounts in 19X4. If in 19X5 it still does not satisfy the criteria for a small company (but does for a medium company) it may file medium company accounts (but not small company accounts) in 19X5.

10.3   Exemptions and abbreviations permitted for small companies

(a)   A directors' report is not required.

(b)   A profit and loss account is not required.

(c)   An 'abbreviated balance sheet' is allowed. This need contain only the items preceded by capital letters or roman numerals in the formats in *Sch 4 CA85*. This means that the sub-headings preceded by Arabic numerals need not be shown.

(d)   Only a limited number of the notes to the accounts.

(e)   Comparative figures are required for (c) and (d) above.

10.4   Exemptions and abbreviations permitted for medium-sized companies

(a)   A full directors' report is required.

(b)   An abbreviated profit and loss account is allowed which begins with the item 'gross profit or loss'. This is done by combining the following items:

(i)   Using Format 1 combine items 1, 2, 3 and 6.
(ii)   Using Format 2 combine items 1, 2, 3, 4 and 5.

(c)   A full balance sheet is required.

(d)   A full set of notes is required except that the particulars of turnover attributable to different classes of business and geographical markets need not be disclosed.

(e)   A company is not entitled to file abbreviated accounts if it is:

   (i)   a public company; or
   (ii)   a banking or insurance company; or
   (iii)   an authorised person under the *Financial Services Act 1986*; or
   (iv)   a member of a group containing any such company.

10.5   Responsibility of directors and auditors

When abbreviated individual accounts are filed with the Registrar of Companies, they must be signed by directors of the company and include a statement by the directors, above their signatures, that they have relied on the exemptions for individual accounts on the grounds that the company is entitled to be treated as a small or medium company, as the case may be. Where abbreviated group accounts are filed, the directors' statement must also include a reference to this fact.

Where abbreviated accounts are filed, the auditors must provide a special report, stating that the company is entitled to deliver abbreviated accounts and that the accounts have been properly prepared. Where the full accounts have been qualified, the auditors' report on the full accounts must also be attached.

10.6   Small company statutory accounts

Classification as a small company entitles a company to reduce the extent of disclosure in its annual reports for **members**. This new basis considerably reduces the amount of disclosure required, both in the financial statements and in the directors' report.

Details are given below. There is no need to learn the reduced disclosures, but you need to have an appreciation of their extent.

In the balance sheet the items preceded by letters and roman numerals are unchanged and continue to have to be disclosed. However many of the sub-items preceded by Arabic numerals can be aggregated together and renamed as appropriate. In the profit and loss account there are no changes to the standard formats. What has changed is the level of disclosure in the notes to the accounts.

10.7   Modifications to the notes to the accounts

The notes relating to the following may be omitted:

(a)   debentures;

(b)   split of freehold, long leasehold and short leasehold within land and buildings;

(c)   provision for taxation and other particulars of tax;

(d)   particulars of long-term debts (terms of repayment, rate of interest, security etc);

(e)   proposed and paid dividends;

(f)   separate statement of certain items of income and expenditure, ie:

       (i)   interest payable;
       (ii)   auditors' remuneration;

(g)   particulars of staff (numbers, emoluments etc);

(h)   breakdown of aggregate amount of directors' emoluments;

(i)   turnover and geographical analysis.

10.8   Modification to the directors' report

The following information need not be given:

(a)   fair review of business and amount to be paid as dividend;
(b)   employee involvement;
(c)   post balance sheet events;
(d)   likely future developments;
(e)   research and development activities;
(f)   asset values.

10.9   Financial reporting standard for smaller entities (FRSSE)

The ASB has issued a revised Financial Reporting Standard for Smaller Entities (FRSSE) in December 1998.

The FRSSE is a comprehensive standard containing the measurement and disclosure requirements most relevant to smaller entities. It contains the requirements in existing accounting standards and UITF Abstracts that are relevant to most smaller entities, in simplified form.

The FRSSE applies to:

(a)   companies incorporated under companies legislation and entitled to the exemptions available for small companies when filing accounts with the Registrar of Companies; or

(b)   entities that would have come into category (a) above had they been companies incorporated under companies legislation.

Adoption of the FRSSE is optional. An entity that chooses to adopt the FRSSE is exempt from all other accounting standards and UITF Abstracts.

10.10   Delivery and publication of additional accounts in ECUs

The *Companies Act 1985* includes an optional facility for all companies to prepare and file at Companies House an additional set of statutory accounts translated into ECUs (European Currency Units).

This additional copy is treated as the statutory accounts of the company and therefore must include the auditors' report as it appears in the sterling statutory accounts.

The translation rate used must be the rate at the balance sheet date, and that rate must be disclosed.

Conclusion	There are several ways in which the Companies Act requirements are modified for small and medium sized companies. The most important are:

-     abbreviated accounts may be filed with the Registrar of Companies
-     simplified statutory accounts may be circulated to shareholders (small companies only).
-     small companies may follow the requirements of the FRSSE.

11   SELF TEST QUESTIONS

1   What are the five accounting principles stated in the Companies Act 1985? (1.3)

2   What are the alternative accounting rules from the CA 85? (1.4)

3   What disclosure is required for tangible fixed assets? (3.3/3.4)

4   What are the general rules for valuing current assets? (4.1)

5   What are the categories of creditors: amounts falling due within one year that must be shown? (4.5)

6   Distinguish between format 1 and format 2 profit and loss account formats. (6.1)

7   What must be disclosed under the heading of directors' emoluments? (7.3)

8   What must be disclosed under the heading of staff costs? (7.4)

9   What are the main modifications to financial statements that are allowed for small companies? (10.3)

10   What are the main modifications to financial statements that are allowed for medium-sized companies? (10.4)

10 TAXATION IN COMPANY ACCOUNTS

PATHFINDER INTRODUCTION

This chapter covers the following performance criteria and knowledge and understanding.

- Draft accounts comply with domestic standards and legislation (performance criteria 10.2)
- Main requirements of relevant SSAPs, FRSs and other relevant pronouncements and their application to this element (knowledge and understanding 10.2)
- The presentation of Corporation Tax in financial statements (knowledge and understanding 10.2)

Putting the chapter in context – learning objectives.

This chapter looks at the accounting for taxation of various types in financial statements. The first tax to be considered is VAT which may appear in the financial statements of sole traders, partnerships or companies. This area of the syllabus should be largely revision. The second tax to be considered is income tax in the context of the receipt and payment of debenture interest. This is only relevant to companies. The detailed requirements of SSAP 8 are then considered. This involves some understanding of the tax system for Corporation Tax as well as the related accounting requirements. This is an area that again is relevant only to company financial statements but some taxation aspects are almost bound to appear in any set of company accounts.

At the end of this chapter you should have learned the following topics.

- SSAP 5 – Accounting for VAT.
- Accounting for income tax.
- Accounting for Corporation Tax in accordance with SSAP 8.
- Basic accounting for deferred tax in accordance with SSAP 15.
- Applying the taxation and accounting requirements to a published set of accounts.

1 SSAP 5 – ACCOUNTING FOR VALUE ADDED TAX

1.1 Introduction

 VAT is a form of indirect taxation introduced to the UK on 1 April 1973. It is levied on most goods and services at a standard rate of 17.5%.

Although it is eventually borne by the final consumer, VAT is collected at each stage of the production and distribution chain.

1.2 Accounting treatment

The majority of traders act as collection agents (unpaid) for HM Customs and Excise, accounting on a quarterly basis for VAT levied on their sales (or outputs), less VAT suffered on their purchases (or inputs).

The simplest way in which this operation can be reflected in the books of account is by opening a VAT account which acts as a personal account with HM Customs and Excise. The VAT account is debited with all VAT suffered on inputs and credited with all VAT charged on outputs. The balance on the account will, therefore, represent the amount due to or from HM Customs and Excise. Entries in the account will be made as follows:

(a)   VAT suffered on inputs:

Dr	Purchases account	with cost excluding VAT
Dr	VAT account	with VAT
	Cr Supplier's account	with cost including VAT

(b)   VAT charged on outputs:

Dr	Customer's account	with sales price including VAT
	Cr Sales account	with sales price excluding VAT
	Cr VAT account	with VAT

(c)   Payments over to Customs and Excise:

Dr	VAT account
	Cr Cash book

(d)   Refunds of excess VAT suffered from Customs and Excise:

Dr	Cash book
	Cr VAT account

1.3   Activity

A trader's purchase and sales analysis shows the following information for the last quarter of his financial year:

	£
Taxable inputs (purchases)	211,500
Taxable outputs (sales)	302,143

Both figures include VAT at 17.5%. During this time he paid £17,550 in settlement of the previous quarter's return.

Draft the profit and loss account extracts and the VAT account to record these transactions (to the nearest £).

1.4   Activity solution

Profit and loss account - extracts

	£
Sales (302,143 × 100/117.5)	257,143
Purchases (211,500 × 100/117.5)	180,000

VAT account (a personal account with HM Customs and Excise)

	£		£
VAT on inputs:		VAT on outputs:	
Purchases		Balance b/d	17,550
(17.5/117.5 ×		Sales	
£211,500)	31,500	(17.5/117.5 ×	
Cash paid	17,550	£302,143)	45,000
Balance c/d	13,500		
	———		———
	62,550		62,550
	———		———
		Balance b/d	13,500

Note: as the balance on this account represents a normal trade liability, it can be included in creditors on the balance sheet. It would only require separate disclosure in exceptional circumstances.

[Conclusion] Both sales and purchases are shown net of VAT in the profit and loss account. VAT normally only appears in the balance sheet as a short term creditor.

1.5   Rates of VAT

The standard rate of VAT is 17.5%. There is also a zero rate and exempt items but neither of these complications is required for this syllabus.

1.6   Standard accounting practice

SSAP 5 requires that:

(a)   Turnover shown in the profit and loss account should exclude VAT on taxable outputs (see also para 95 Sch 4 CA85).

(b)   Irrecoverable VAT on fixed assets and other items disclosed separately in published accounts (eg, capital commitments) should be included in their cost.

[Conclusion] For traders whose supplies are taxable (either standard-rated or zero-rated) VAT will have no effect on the profit and loss account, other than in exceptional cases where input VAT is non-recoverable (eg, on the purchase of a car, or expenditure on entertaining).

2   ACCOUNTING FOR INCOME TAX

2.1   The company as a collecting agent

Just as a company acts as a collecting agent for VAT, it acts as a collecting agent for income tax (IT). Certain payments by companies are made under deduction of income tax at source

(i)   loan stock and debenture interest
(ii)   patent and mineral output royalties
(iii)   covenants
(iv)   annuities.

Any income tax collected by a company is paid over to the Inland Revenue every quarter.

2.2   Unfranked investment income (UFII)

A company in receipt of debenture interest will receive it net of income tax (at 20%) which the paying company will have deducted at source. This income is known as unfranked investment income.

	£	£
Dr Cash (net receipt)	x	
Cr Debenture interest received		x

It follows that the company (which suffers corporation tax, not income tax) may reclaim the income tax deducted at source from the Inland Revenue. The double entry is to gross up the receipt using an income tax account

	£	£
Dr Income tax account	x	
Cr Debenture interest received		x

Conclusion   The gross debenture interest is therefore credited to profit and loss account and the amount of IT deducted recorded in the IT account.

2.3   Payments of debenture interest

When a company pays debenture interest it will pay the net amount in cash and the income tax element must eventually be paid to the Inland Revenue. The double entry for a payment is:

	£	£
Dr Debenture interest payable (gross amount)	x	
Cr Cash (net amount)		x
Cr Income tax account (IT deducted)		x

2.4   Activity

	£
Loan interest received (gross)	28,000
Loan interest paid (gross)	48,000

Assuming that income tax has been deducted at 20%, complete the income tax account.

2.5   Activity solution

Income tax account

	£		£
Interest received account		Interest paid account	
(20% × £28,000)	5,600	(20% × £48,000)	9,600
Balance c/d	4,000		
	———		———
	£9,600		£9,600
	———		———
		Balance b/d	4,000

£4,000 is subsequently paid to the Inland Revenue. However if there is a balance on the IT account at the year end this will appear in the balance sheet as a creditor or debtor.

Note that in computational questions in the examination, the question will give the **gross** amount of interest unless there is a specific mention that the sum referred to is a net amount. This is because the information given is normally in the form of a trial balance and the above entries will have already been made.

Conclusion   Debenture interest receivable and payable appear at their gross amounts in the profit and loss account. The balance on the IT account shows the amount owing to/from the Inland Revenue.

3 SSAP 8 – THE TREATMENT OF TAXATION UNDER THE IMPUTATION SYSTEM IN THE ACCOUNTS OF COMPANIES

3.1 Tax on profit on ordinary activities

The double entry for the corporation tax charge for the year is

	£	£
Dr Profit and loss account	x	
Cr Corporation tax account		x

Although the tax payable is only an estimate and often referred to as a corporation tax **provision,** it should be included in creditors and not under provisions.

If the estimate is wrong, the under or over provision is dealt with by increasing or decreasing the following year's tax charge.

Prior to April 1999 the accounting requirements for taxation were made complicated by the need for companies to pay Advance Corporation Tax, ACT, whenever a dividend was paid. However ACT has now been abolished by the government and the only remaining requirement is to deal with dividends received.

3.2 Dividends received

Dividends received are known as franked investment income (FII) and must be shown at a gross amount in the profit and loss account although paid out of post tax income by the paying company.

This is achieved by adding a tax credit to the amount of cash dividend received and also increasing the tax charge for the period by the same tax credit amount.

The full double entry for this is:

	£	£
DR Tax charge (P&L a/c)	X	
CR Dividend receivable (P&L a/c)		X

with the tax credit. The exam question will tell you what rate to use for the tax credit, for example it might be calculated as $^{10}/_{90}$ of the amount of the cash dividend received.

3.3 Activity

A cash dividend is received by a company of £7,500. The company's estimated tax charge for the year is £20,000. Tax credits are available at $^{10}/_{90}$ of the cash amount of dividend received.

Calculate the figures that will appear in the profit and loss account.

3.4 Activity solution

	£	£
Dividend receivable		
$(7,500 + (7,500 \times {}^{10}/_{90}))$		8,333
Tax on profit on ordinary activities		
Corporation tax charge	20,000	
Tax credit on FII		
$(7,500 \times {}^{10}/_{90})$	833	
	———	
		20,833

> **Conclusion** A dividend received is grossed up in the profit and loss account by the tax credit attached to it and this tax credit is then added to the tax charge in the profit and loss account.

4 SSAP 15 – ACCOUNTING FOR DEFERRED TAX

4.1 Introduction

The amount of taxation payable on the profits of a particular period may bear little relationship to the reported profit appearing in the published accounts. This results from the profit for taxation purposes being determined on a different basis from the accounting profit shown in the financial statements. This difference derives from two main sources, permanent differences and timing differences.

> **Definition** **Permanent differences** are due to the fact that certain types of income are not chargeable to tax, and certain expenditure is disallowable eg, disallowable entertaining expenditure.

> **Definition** **Timing differences** are where items of income and expenditure are included in taxation computations in periods different from those in which they are included in financial statements eg, capital allowances as opposed to the annual depreciation charge. Timing differences originate in one period and potentially reverse in one or more subsequent periods.

> **Definition** **Deferred taxation** is an attempt to eliminate the distorting effect of timing differences. Deferred taxation is not concerned with permanent differences.

4.2 The purpose of deferred taxation

Full deferred taxation accounting attempts to eliminate the effect of timing differences so that the tax charge appearing in the published accounts is directly related to the reported profit.

However SSAP 15 requires deferred tax to be accounted for on the basis of partial provision.

> **Definition** Partial provision requires that tax deferred or accelerated by the effect of timing differences should be accounted for only to the extent it is probable that an asset or liability will crystallise.

The most common cause of deferred tax liabilities is due to accelerated capital allowances, the timing difference between capital allowances and the annual depreciation charge.

To determine whether a deferred tax asset or liability will crystallise gives rise to a number of complex calculations and is outside the syllabus. The bookkeeping entries, once the decision has been made as to the amount of deferred tax to provide, are required to be known, but are fortunately relatively straightforward.

4.3 Bookkeeping

The bookkeeping for the main components of the deferred taxation account is as follows:

(a) Deferred tax provided on accelerated capital allowances, and other timing differences occurring in the year (often referred to as the **transfer to deferred tax for the year**):

Dr	Profit and loss account, tax charge	Tax on timing
Cr	Deferred taxation account	differences

(b)   Reversal of timing differences during the year will result in a transfer **from** deferred tax.

Dr   Deferred taxation account   Tax on reversal of timing
Cr   Profit and loss account,   difference
         tax charge

4.4   Activity

X Ltd is preparing its accounts for the year ended 31 December 19X6. The deferred tax account as at 31 December 19X5 was £50,000. The current corporation tax charge for the year is £60,000 and a transfer of £20,000 is required to the deferred tax account. A dividend of £7,500 is proposed. Prepare the relevant extracts from the profit and loss account, the balance sheet and the notes to the accounts.

4.5   Activity solution

Extract from profit and loss account for the year ended 31 December 19X6

	£	£
Taxation		
UK corporation tax at ..%	60,000	
Deferred taxation	20,000	
		80,000
Proposed dividend		7,500

Extract from balance sheet as at 31 December 19X6

	£
Creditors: amounts falling due within one year	
Proposed dividend	7,500
Corporation tax	60,000
Provisions for liabilities and charges	
Deferred taxation (note 1)	70,000

Notes to the accounts

(1)   Deferred taxation

	£
Balance brought forward	50,000
Transfer from profit and loss account	20,000
Balance carried forward	70,000

5   PUBLISHED ACCOUNTS QUESTIONS INVOLVING TAXATION

5.1   Introduction

The treatment of taxation in published accounts often causes considerable difficulties for students. The entries required will vary depending upon the information given but a general approach is given below which should be sufficient for most questions. The main point to remember is to deal with the profit and loss account entries before the computation of the balance sheet liabilities.

5.2   Activity

An extract from the trial balance of More Complex Ltd as at 31 December 19X8 shows:

	£	£
Sales		1,500,000
Cost of sales, distribution and admin expenses	950,000	
Taxation:		
- (last years provision £20,000 – agreed liability £22,500)	2,500	
Interim dividend	22,500	
Dividend received		8,000
Deferred taxation		30,000

Additional information:

(a)   The tax provision for the year on ordinary operations is estimated at £170,000.

(b)   The corporation tax rate is 30% and tax credits are $^{10}/_{90}$ of net dividends received.

(c)   The transfer to deferred taxation for the year is £15,000.

(d)   The directors are not proposing a final dividend.

Prepare the figures to appear in the profit and loss account and balance sheet.

5.3   Activity solution

Step 1   Completing the profit and loss account:

Profit and loss account for the year ended 31 Dec 19X8

	£	£
Sales		1,500,000
Costs		950,000
		550,000
Investment income (8,000 + 889 [1])		8,889
Profit on ordinary activities before taxation		558,889
Taxation:		
On profits of the year	170,000	
Under-provision in prior year [2]	2,500	
Deferred taxation [3]	15,000	
Tax credits on franked investment income [1]	889	
		188,389
Profit for the financial year		370,500
Dividends		22,500
Profits retained for the year		348,000

Step 2   A working should be set up to record the entries made from the profit and loss account to the balance sheet:

	Current tax liability £	Deferred tax £
Per trial balance	–	30,000
From profit and loss:		
- tax section	170,000	15,000 (3)
Year end balance	170,000	45,000

Notes

(1)   The dividend received must be grossed up in the profit and loss account by an amount equivalent to its related tax credit ($£8,000 \times {}^{10}/_{90} = £889$).

The tax charge is also increased by this amount and the full double entry is:

Dr   Tax charge in P&L a/c   £889
        Cr   Investment income   £889

(2)   The trial balance shows an under provision in last year's profit and loss account for tax of £2,500 (22,500 – £20,000). This is accounted for by increasing this year's tax charge by £2,500.

(3)   The double entry for the transfer to deferred taxation for the year is:

Dr   Tax charge in P&L a/c   £15,000
        Cr   Deferred taxation a/c   £15,000

Conclusion   **Disclosure requirements: profit and loss account**

- The taxation charge should include the following items. Where any of the individual items is material, it should be disclosed separately:

  (i)   UK corporation tax (remember to state the rate used for the provision);
  (ii)   transfer to or from deferred tax
  (iii)   tax credit on FII;

- Dividends paid and proposed are shown **net** ie, the actual cash amount paid or payable to shareholders.

Disclosure requirements: balance sheet

- Proposed dividends should be shown **net** under current liabilities.

6   **SELF TEST QUESTIONS**

1   What is the double entry for a credit sale on which VAT has been charged? (1.2)

2   What does a credit balance on the VAT account represent? (1.4)

3   What type of payments are made after a deduction of income tax at source? (2.1)

4   What is unfranked investment income? (2.2)

5   What is the double entry for the payment of debenture interest? (2.3)

6   What is the double entry for the tax charge for the year? (3.1)

7   What is franked investment income? (3.2)

8   How are dividends received recorded in the profit and loss account? (3.2)

9   What is deferred tax? (4.1)

10   What are timing differences? (4.1)

11 TANGIBLE FIXED ASSETS

PATHFINDER INTRODUCTION

This chapter covers the following performance criteria and knowledge and understanding.

- Draft accounts comply with domestic standards and legislation (performance criteria 10.2)
- Main requirements of relevant SSAPs, FRSs and other relevant pronouncements and their application to this element (knowledge and understanding 10.2)

Putting the chapter in context – learning objectives

The fixed assets of any business entity will normally be a large element of the balance sheet total of that entity. The majority of fixed assets are classed as tangible fixed assets ie, those that are physical in nature. The accounting requirements of FRS 15 and SSAPs 19 and 4 will all be considered in this chapter. Published financial statements for a limited company must comply with the accounting and disclosure requirements of these accounting standards, as well as with the requirements of the Companies Act considered in an earlier chapter. Intangible fixed assets and the accounting requirements relevant to them will be considered in the next chapter.

At the end of this chapter you should have learned the following topics.

- The accounting requirements of FRS 15.
- The further accounting and disclosure requirements for fixed assets and depreciation.
- The accounting and disclosure requirements for investment properties from SSAP 19.
- The accounting and disclosure requirements for the receipt of governments grants from SSAP 4.

---

1 FRS 15: TANGIBLE FIXED ASSETS

1.1 Introduction

In February 1999 the ASB issued FRS 15, *Tangible fixed assets*. The FRS deals with the accounting principles relating to the initial measurement of tangible fixed assets, any subsequent valuations and depreciation, and replaces the requirements of SSAP 12. However investment properties are still to be accounted for according to SSAP 19 which is dealt with later in this chapter.

Definition Tangible fixed assets are assets that have physical substance and are held for use in the production or supply of goods or services, for rental to others, or for administrative purposes on a continuing basis in the reporting entity's activities.

1.2 Objective of FRS 15

The FRS codifies much of existing best practice regarding accounting for tangible fixed assets and its objective is to ensure that these assets are accounted for on a consistent basis and where revaluations are made to ensure that the revaluations are kept up-to-date.

1.3   Initial measurement

A tangible fixed asset should initially be measured at its cost.

Definition   The cost of a fixed asset is its purchase price (after deducting any trade discounts and rebates) and any costs directly attributable to bringing it into working condition for its intended use.

1.4   Subsequent expenditure

Many fixed assets will require subsequent expenditure such as repairs and maintenance. These are usually undertaken in order to maintain the asset's standard of performance and as such should be recognised in the profit and loss account as they are incurred.

The FRS states that there are only three circumstances in which subsequent expenditure should be capitalised in the balance sheet:

(a)   where the expenditure enhances the economic benefits of the asset and increases its previously assessed standard of perfomance. For example modifying an item of plant to increase its capacity;

(b)   where the expenditure is to replace or restore a component of the asset that is being treated separately for depreciation purposes by being depreciated over its individual useful economic life. An example given is the lining of a furnace which may need to be replaced say, every five years;

(c)   expenditure that relates to a major overhaul of the asset that restores the economic benefits that have already been consumed such as the requirement to overhaul aircraft on a regular basis in order to continue flying the aircraft.

1.5   Revaluation of fixed assets

The FRS then goes on to consider revaluation of fixed assets. Entities are given the option whether or not to revalue their fixed assets but if they do then the policy of revaluation should be applied to all the assets in a particular class although not necessarily to all classes of fixed asset.

The basic principle of the FRS is that where fixed assets are revalued they should be shown in the balance sheet at their current value. This requires frequent checks on the valuation and the FRS sets out guidelines here.

1.6   Frequency of valuations

Maintaining a current value can generally be done by a full valuation at least every five years and an interim valuation in year 3. However if it appears likely that there has been a material change in value in any intervening years then an interim valuation is also required then.

This policy is most appropriate for properties but for other fixed assets that are not properties there may be an active second hand market in the asset or reliable indices. In such cases annual revaluation by the directors will be sufficient.

1.7   Valuation bases

On what basis should the valuations be made? This will depend upon the type of asset being revalued:

(a)   non-specialised properties - existing use value

(b)   specialised properties - depreciated replacement cost

(c)   property surplus to requirements - open market value

(d)   other non-property fixed assets - market value or depreciated replacement cost if market value is not available.

1.8   Accounting for revaluation gains

Revaluation gains should be reported in the statement of total recognised gains and losses. However if the gain is the reversal of a previous loss on the same asset that had been charged to the profit and loss account then the gain also goes to the profit and loss account.

1.9   Accounting for revaluation losses

If a revaluation loss is caused by a consumption of economic benefits, for example physical damage to the asset, then this loss should be charged to the profit and loss account.

However some falls in value are also due to general falls in prices. Therefore any other revaluation losses should be recognised as follows:

(a)   charged to the statement of total recognised gains and losses until the carrying amount reaches the equivalent of depreciated historical cost; then

(b)   any further loss charged to the profit and loss account unless the recoverable amount of the asset is greater than the revalued amount in which case the difference is taken to the statement of total recognised gains and losses instead.

1.10   Activity

A non-specialised property has a book value of £480,000 at the year end. Its existing use value at that date is £350,000, its recoverable amount is £380,000 and its depreciated historical cost is £400,000.

How would the revaluation loss at the year end be treated in the financial statements?

1.11   Activity solution

Total revaluation loss	=	£480,000 - £350,000
	=	£130,000
Loss down to depreciated historical cost - taken to STRGL	=	£480,000 - £400,000
	=	£80,000
Remaining loss	=	£130,000 - £80,000
	=	£50,000

Normally this £50,000 would be taken to the profit and loss account, however the recoverable amount of £380,000 is higher than the revalued amount of £350,000. This £30,000 difference is also taken to the STRGL with only the remaining £20,000 of revaluation loss being taken to the profit and loss account.

Summary:

	£
Revaluation loss taken to STRGL (£80,000 + £30,000)	110,000
Revaluation loss taken to P&L	20,000
Total revaluation loss	130,000

1.12   Profits and losses on disposal

The profit or loss on disposal of a fixed asset is to be calculated as the difference between the sale proceeds and the carrying amount of the asset in the balance sheet.

2   DEPRECIATION OF FIXED ASSETS

2.1   Introduction

The final area that FRS 15 deals with is the depreciation of fixed assets.

> **Definition**   Depreciation is the measure of the cost or revalued amount of the economic benefits of the tangible fixed asset that have been consumed during the period.

> Consumption includes the wearing out, using up or other reduction in the useful economic life of a tangible fixed asset whether arising from use, effluxion of time or obsolescence through either changes in technology or demand for the goods and services produced by the asset.

2.2   What is the purpose of depreciation?

Clearly the fundamental objective of depreciation is to reflect the use of the fixed asset in the profit and loss account for the period. The expense of using the fixed assets is then being matched with the revenue that the fixed assets have helped to earn.

The depreciation provision is not intended as a fund for the replacement of the fixed assets concerned it is simply a method of charging the profit and loss account with the amount of economic benefit in that fixed asset consumed in the period.

2.3   Mechanics of depreciation

The monetary amount that is to be written off as depreciation over the life of an asset is called the depreciable amount.

> **Definition**   The depreciable amount is the cost of a tangible fixed asset (or, where an asset is revalued, the revalued amount) less its residual value.

> **Definition**   The residual value of an asset is the net realisable value of an asset at the end of its useful economic life. Residual values are based on prices prevailing at the date of the acquisition (or revaluation) of the asset and do not take account of expected future price rises.

The depreciable amount is written off to the profit and loss account over the asset's useful economic life.

> **Definition**   The useful economic life of a tangible fixed asset is the period over which the entity expects to derive economic benefit from that asset.

2.4   Activity

An asset costs £100,000 and has an expected useful life of ten years. The purchaser intends to use the asset for six years at which point the expected residual value will be £40,000 (at current prices). If inflation is taken into account the residual value is expected to be £55,000. What is the depreciable amount?

2.5   Activity solution

The depreciable amount is £(100,000 – 40,000) £60,000 spread over six years. Which method of depreciation is used to allocate the charge is left for the purchaser to decide.

2.6   Methods of depreciation

A variety of methods of depreciation are available and FRS 15 does not state that a particular method should be used. The only guidance is that the method chosen should result in a depreciation charge throughout the asset's useful economic life and not just towards the end of that life or when the asset is falling in value.

The main methods of depreciation are as follows:

(a)   Straight-line (or fixed instalment)
(b)   Reducing balance (or decreasing charge)
(c)   Sum of the years' digits
(d)   Output or usage

2.7   Straight line or fixed instalment method

This method requires three items of information:

(a)   original cost of the asset (C);
(b)   estimated useful life of the asset (n years);
(c)   estimated scrap or realisable value at end of useful life (S), the residual value.

Annual depreciation charge, d, is given by $d = \dfrac{(C - S)}{n}$

2.8   Activity

Original cost of asset   £4,200
Estimated useful life   4 years
Estimated scrap value   £200

Using the straight line method, calculate the annual depreciation charge.

2.9   Activity solution

Annual depreciation charge $\dfrac{£(4,200 - 200)}{4}$ = £1,000 pa

Advantages of the straight line method	*Disadvantages of the straight line method*
Simple to operate, and revenues of successive accounting periods are charged with equal amounts of depreciation.	If revenue is constant, the return on the asset (measured on net book value) will increase as the asset becomes older.

2.10   Reducing balance or decreasing charge method

The depreciation charge is calculated by applying a fixed percentage to the net book amount (or written down value) of the asset. In the year in which the asset is acquired, the percentage is applied to the original or historical cost.   In successive periods, the percentage is applied to the asset's written-down value.

The aim of this method is to reduce the net book amount to its scrap value at the end of the estimated useful life of the asset.   In order to achieve this objective, the depreciation rate percentage for the reducing balance method must be higher than for the straight-line method.

2.11   Activity

An asset cost £1,000. Its estimated useful life was four years with a scrap value at the end of four years of approximately £60.

Calculate the depreciation charge for each of the four years on a reducing balance basis at a rate of 50%.

2.12   Activity solution

	£
Cost	1,000
Year 1 (£1,000 × 50%)	(500)
NBV	500
Year 2 (£500 × 50%)	(250)
NBV	250
Year 3 (£250 × 50%)	(125)
NBV	125
Year 4 (£125 × 50%)	(63)
Final NBV	62

One particular feature of the reducing balance method is that the net book value never equals zero.

Advantages of the reducing balance method	*Disadvantages of the reducing balance method*
This method results in a higher depreciation charge in the early years of the life of an asset (as compared, say, with the straight-line method). This is justified by the fact that the asset has a greater earning capacity in its earlier years and also by the fact that repair and maintenance charges are probably heavier in later years.	There may be a tendency for a company to use a rate of depreciation that is too low, and thus not bring net book value down to estimated scrap value at the end of an asset's useful life.

2.13   Sum of the years' digits method

This is a further variation on the reducing balance method. As with the latter method, the aim is to show a higher depreciation charge in the early years of the life of an asset.

2.14   Activity

Cost of asset	£4,200
Scrap value	£200
Estimated useful life	4 years

Using the sum of the digits method, calculate the depreciation charge for each year.

2.15   Activity solution

Sum of digits of asset's life $4 + 3 + 2 + 1 = 10$

£

Depreciation year 1 $= \dfrac{4}{10} \times$ £(4,200 – 200)   1,600

Depreciation year 2 $= \dfrac{3}{10} \times$ £4,000   1,200

Depreciation year 3 $= \dfrac{2}{10} \times$ £4,000   800

Depreciation year 4 $= \dfrac{1}{10} \times$ £4,000   400

Total depreciation   4,000

The general sum of the years' digits formula is: $\text{Sum} = \dfrac{n(n+1)}{2}$ where n is the number of years.

2.16   Output or usage method

The aim is to express the estimated useful life of an asset in terms of its output or usage, rather than in terms of accounting periods.

2.17   Activity

The useful life of a motor van is estimated to be 60,000 miles, with a nil scrap value at the end of this mileage. The cost of the van is £1,800.

If the mileage of the van is 12,000 miles in year 1 and 9,000 miles in year 2 what is the depreciation charge each year?

2.18   Activity solution

	Mileage	Depreciation charge
		£
Year 1	12,000	$\dfrac{12,000}{60,000} \times$ £1,800 = 360
Year 2	9,000	$\dfrac{9,000}{60,000} \times$ £1,800 = 270

Conclusion   One advantage of this method is that the original cost of the asset is allocated over accounting periods according to usage of assets. The depreciation charge becomes a function of output or usage rather than of time. Where there is variable use of the asset over time, it can be argued that this method satisfies the matching concept more satisfactorily than the earlier methods.

2.19   Change of method of depreciation

A change from one method of depreciation to another is only permissible on the grounds that the new method will give a fairer presentation of the results and financial position. This is not treated as a change of accounting policy.

The carrying amount of the asset is depreciated using the new method over the remaining useful economic life, starting in the period in which the change of method was made.

2.20   Depreciation of buildings

In the past many companies with well-maintained buildings such as pubs or hotels have made no depreciation charge on these buildings. FRS 15 addresses this issue and states that the only grounds for not charging depreciation are that the depreciation charge and accumulated depreciation are immaterial. This may be the case where assets have a very long useful economic life and/or a high residual value.

If depreciation is not charged on these grounds of immateriality then the FRS states that the relevant assets must be reviewed for impairment in value at the end of each accounting period.

2.21   Useful economic life

 The useful economic life of an asset is the period over which the entity expects to derive economic benefit from that asset.

The useful economic lives of assets should be reviewed at the end of each accounting period and, when necessary, revised. The carrying value should then be written off over the revised remaining useful economic life.

2.22   Activity

An asset was purchased for £100,000 on 1 January 19X5, and straight line depreciation of £20,000 per annum was charged (five year life, no residual value). A general review of asset lives is undertaken and for this particular asset, the remaining useful life as at 31 December 19X7 is seven years.

What is the effect on the accounts for the year ended 31 December 19X7?

2.23   Activity solution

NBV as at 31 December 19X6 (60% × £100,000)	£60,000
Remaining useful life as at 1 January 19X7	8 years
Annual depreciation charge	£7,500

Note: that the estimated remaining life is seven years from 31 December 19X7, but this information is used to compute the current year's charge as well.

2.24   Residual value

 The residual value is the net realisable value at the end of the asset's useful economic life. Residual values are based on prices prevailing at the date of the acquisition or revaluation and do not take account of expected future price changes.

If the residual value is material then it should be reviewed at the end of each accounting period to take account of reasonably expected technological changes. A change in the estimated residual value should be accounted for over the asset's remaining useful economic life.

2.25   Revalued assets

Where it is an enterprise's policy to include some or all of its fixed assets in the financial statements at revalued amounts, the charge for depreciation of such assets should be based on the revalued amounts and the remaining useful economic lives.

Usually any accumulated depreciation at the date of revaluation is eliminated and the asset is restated at its revalued amount.

2.26   Activity

A company's building is currently included in the balance sheet at its original cost as follows:

	£
Cost	200,000
Depreciation	40,000
Net book value	160,000

It is being depreciated over its useful economic life of 50 years and it has already been owned for 10 years.

It is now to be revalued to its current market value of £450,000.

Write up the accounting entries for this revaluation and explain how the building will be depreciated from now on.

2.27   Activity solution

Step 1   Bring the fixed asset - cost account up to the revalued amount.

Fixed asset - cost

	£		£
Balance b/d	200,000	Balance c/d	450,000
Revaluation reserve	250,000		
	450,000		450,000

Step 2   Remove the accumulated depreciation already charged on the asset.

Fixed asset - accumulated depreciation

	£		£
Revaluation reserve	40,000	Balance b/d	40,000

Step 3   Write up the revaluation reserve account.

Revaluation reserve

	£		£
Balance c/d	290,000	Fixed asset - cost	250,000
		Fixed asset – accumulated	
		depreciation	40,000
	290,000		290,000

The balance on the revaluation reserve is the amount required to take the building from its current carrying value of £160,000 to its revalued figure of £450,000 (£290,000).

The depreciation charge for the building for each year will now be based upon the carrying value on the balance sheet, £450,000, and the remaining useful life, 40 years.

$$\text{Annual depreciation charge} \quad = \quad \frac{£450,000}{40 \text{ years}}$$

$$= \quad £11,250 \text{ per annum.}$$

Conclusion   When a fixed asset is revalued the amount required to increase its net book value to the current valuation is taken to the revaluation reserve. The annual depreciation charge through the profit and loss account is then based upon this new revalued amount, the carrying value in the balance sheet.

2.28   Depreciated replacement cost

If the asset is to be revalued at depreciated replacement cost then both the cost and the accumulated depreciation at the date of the revaluation should be restated so that the carrying amount after the revaluation equals its revalued amount.

3   SSAP 19 – ACCOUNTING FOR INVESTMENT PROPERTIES

3.1   Introduction

Definition   SSAP 19 regards an investment property as an asset which is held as a disposable investment rather than an asset consumed in the business operations of a company over a number of years.

With such a property the most useful information to give a user of the accounts is the current value of the investment. Systematic annual depreciation would be of little relevance.

SSAP 19 requires that investment properties should not suffer a depreciation charge and should be stated at their current values.

3.2   Standard accounting practice

• Investment properties should not be subject to periodic charges for depreciation except for properties held on lease which should be depreciated when the unexpired term is 20 years or less.

• Note that the CA85 requires all fixed assets with a finite useful life to be depreciated, so a true and fair override will be required to follow the SSAP 19 accounting treatment involving the non-depreciation of investment properties. This means that a note to the accounts should explain what the company has done and why.

•   Investment properties should be included in the balance sheet at their open market value.

•   The names of the persons making the valuation, or particulars of their qualifications, should be disclosed together with the bases of valuation used by them. If a person making a valuation is an employee or officer of the company or group which owns the property this fact should be disclosed.

•   Changes in the value of investment properties should not be taken to the profit and loss account but should be taken to the statement of total recognised gains and losses (being a movement on an investment revaluation reserve), unless a deficit on an individual investment property is expected to be permanent, in which case it should be charged in the profit and loss account of the period.

3.3   Definition of an investment property

An investment property is an interest in land and/or buildings:

(a)   in respect of which construction work and development have been completed; and

(b)   which is held for its investment potential, any rental income being negotiated at arm's length.

The following are exceptions from the definition:

(a)   A property which is owned and occupied by a company for its own purposes is not an investment property.

(b)   A property let to and occupied by another group company is not an investment property for the purposes of its own accounts or the group accounts.

3.4   Activity

Industrial Ltd produces accounts to 31 December. On 1 January 19X8 it moved from its factory in Bolton to a new purpose-built factory in Rochdale (expected life of fifty years). The old premises were available for letting from 1 January 19X8 and a lease was granted on 30 September 19X8 to B Ltd at an annual rental of £8,000. A valuation of the old premises at 31 December 19X8 was £160,000.

Extracts from the balance sheet as at 31 December 19X7 were:

Fixed assets

	Cost £	Depreciation £	NBV £
Land and buildings:			
Old premises	200,000	80,000	120,000
New premises	450,000		450,000

Show relevant extracts from the balance sheet as at 31 December 19X8.

3.5   **Activity solution**

Fixed assets

	Cost £	Depreciation £	NBV £
Land and buildings	450,000	9,000	441,000
Investment property at valuation			160,000
Reserves			
Investment revaluation reserve (160,000 − 120,000)			40,000

3.6   **Treatment of annual valuations**

SSAP 19 regards the total investment property revaluation reserve as being available to cover deficits, with only permanent deficits having to be charged to profit and loss.

3.7   **Activity**

Newline Investment Co Ltd purchased three investment properties on 31 December 19X1, and the following valuations have been made during the period to 31 December 19X4:

	31 Dec 19X1 £'000	31 Dec 19X2 £'000	31 Dec 19X3 £'000	31 Dec 19X4 £'000
Property A	200	180 *	120 *	90**
Property B	300	330	340	340
Property C	400	440	450	450
Total	900	950	910	880

*   deficit believed to be temporary
**   deficit believed to be permanent

Show the balance on the investment revaluation reserve for each balance sheet date.

3.8   **Activity solution**

The investment revaluation reserve would be disclosed for the various years as follows:

	Year ended 31 December		
	19X2 £'000	19X3 £'000	19X4 £'000
Balance b/d	Nil	50	10
Net revaluation (including temporary deficits)			
(30 + 40 − 20)	50		
(10 + 10 − 60)		(40)	-
Balance c/d	50	10	10

The permanent deficit of £30,000 arising from property A in the year ended 31 December 19X4 will be charged through the profit and loss account.

Conclusion   Investment properties are an exception to the rules of FRS 15 and are not normally depreciated. This requires a routine true and fair override note in the published accounts.

4   SSAP 4 – ACCOUNTING FOR GOVERNMENT GRANTS

4.1   Introduction

SSAP 4 was originally introduced following the advent of regional development grants under the Industry Act 1972. These grants were often related to capital expenditure and thus a standard was necessary to state how the grant should be accounted for.

Since the issue of SSAP 4 the variety of forms of government assistance available to industry has greatly increased: many are discretionary in nature both as to whether they are given at all and as to the amount given. Frequently the terms on which grants are given do not make clear precisely the expenditure to which they are related. The problem facing accountants today is thus how to relate grants to specific expenditure.

A revised SSAP 4 was issued in July 1990.

Definition   **Government** is widely defined to include national government and all tiers of local and regional government. It also includes EU bodies.

Definition   **Grants** include cash or transfers of assets.

4.2   General principles

Grants should not be recognised in the profit and loss account until the conditions for receipt have been complied with and there is reasonable assurance that the grant will be received. (This is prudent.)

Subject to this condition, grants should be recognised in the profit and loss account so as to match them with the expenditure towards which they are intended to contribute. (Application of the accruals concept.)

4.3   Revenue grants

In the absence of evidence to the contrary, grants should be assumed to contribute towards the expenditure that is the basis for their payment. The explanatory foreword illustrates this principle by stating that if the grant is paid when evidence is produced that certain expenditure has been incurred, the grant should be matched with that expenditure.

However, if the grant is paid on a different basis, for example achievement of a non-financial objective, such as the creation of a specified number of new jobs, the grant should be matched with the identifiable costs of achieving that objective.

4.4   Capital grants

Grants for fixed asset purchases should be recognised over the expected useful lives of the related assets.

SSAP 4 permits two treatments. The explanatory foreword states that both treatments are acceptable and capable of giving a true and fair view:

(a)   write off the grant against the cost of the fixed asset and depreciate the reduced cost; or

(b)   treat the grant as a deferred credit and transfer a portion to revenue each year, so offsetting the higher depreciation charge on the original cost.

Method (a) is obviously far simpler to operate. Method (b), however, has the advantage of ensuring that assets acquired at different times and in different locations are recorded on a uniform basis, regardless of changes in government policy.

However, the CA85 requires that fixed assets should be stated at purchase price and this is defined as actual price paid plus any additional expenses. The latest legal opinion on this matter is that companies should not deduct grants from cost, because if they do, they are contravening the fixed asset valuation rules of the CA85. Thus method (a) may only be adopted by unincorporated bodies.

4.5   Activity

A company opens a new factory in a development area and receives a government grant of £15,000 in respect of capital equipment costing £100,000. It depreciates all plant and machinery at 20% pa straight-line.

Show the balance sheet extracts to record the grant in the first year under methods (a) and (b) above.

4.6   Activity solution

(a)   **Write off against asset**

Balance sheet extract

	£
Fixed assets:	
Plant and machinery at cost (100 – 15)	85,000
Less: Depreciation (20% × £85,000)	17,000
	68,000

(b)   **Deferred credit method**

Government grant deferred credit account

	£		£
P&L a/c transfer for year:		Cash grant	15,000
20% × £15,000	3,000		
Balance c/d	12,000		
	15,000		15,000
		Balance b/d	12,000

Balance sheet extract

	£
Fixed assets:	
Plant and machinery at cost	100,000
Less: Depreciation (20% × £100,000)	20,000
	80,000
Deferred income:	
Government grant	12,000

Conclusion   When dealing with capital based grants the deferred credit method is to be preferred and must be used in limited company financial statements. Remember to include the balance on the deferred income account as a credit on the balance sheet.

4.7   Other grants

Purpose of grant	Recognise in profit and loss account
To give immediate financial support	When receivable
To reimburse previously incurred costs	When receivable
To finance general activities over a period	In relevant period
To compensate for a loss of income	In relevant period

4.8   Contingent liabilities

The explanatory foreword states that enterprises should consider regularly whether there is a likelihood of a breach of conditions on which the grant was made. If such a breach has occurred or appears likely to occur, the likelihood of having to make a repayment should be considered.

If repayment is probable then it should be provided for. It should be accounted for by setting off against any unamortised deferred income relating to the grant. Any excess should be immediately charged to profit and loss account.

4.9   Disclosure

The following information should be disclosed:

(a)   accounting policy

(b)   effects of government grants (amount credited to profit and loss account; balance on deferred income account)

(c)   if other forms of government assistance have had a material effect on the results, the nature of the assistance and an estimate of the effects

(d)   potential liabilities to repay grants should if necessary be disclosed in accordance with FRS 12.

5   SELF TEST QUESTIONS

1   What is a tangible fixed asset? (1.1)

2   What is the objective of FRS 15? (1.2)

3   When can subsequent expenditure on a fixed asset be capitalised? (1.4)

4   How are revaluation gains dealt with? (1.8)

5   What is the purpose of depreciation? (2.2)

6   How should the residual value of a fixed asset be determined for depreciation purposes? (2.3)

7   What are the main accounting requirements for investment properties from SSAP 19? (3.2)

8   How is an investment property to be distinguished from other fixed asset properties? (3.3)

9   How is a revenue grant from government to be accounted for? (4.3)

10   What are the two possible methods of accounting for a capital based government grant according to SSAP 4? (4.4)

12 INTANGIBLE FIXED ASSETS

PATHFINDER INTRODUCTION

This chapter covers the following performance criteria and knowledge and understanding.

- Draft accounts comply with domestic standards and legislation (performance criteria 10.2)
- Main requirements of relevant SSAPs, FRSs and other relevant pronouncements and their application to this element (knowledge and understanding 10.2)

Putting the chapter in context – learning objectives

This chapter considers the accounting treatment of intangible fixed assets. These are assets that have no physical form but are still required for long term use within the business. The basic principles relating to tangible fixed assets apply here in that the rule is normally that if an intangible asset is included in the balance sheet as a fixed asset then it must be written off or amortised over a suitable period in just the same way as tangible fixed assets would be depreciated. However the nature of intangible assets makes their identification, valuation and accounting treatment a little more complicated. For the purposes of this syllabus the intangible fixed assets that are of concern are research and development expenditure, covered by SSAP 13, and goodwill, dealt with in FRS 10.

At the end of this chapter you should have learned the following topics.

- SSAP 13 – Accounting for research and development.
- FRS 10 - Goodwill and intangible assets.

1   SSAP 13 – ACCOUNTING FOR RESEARCH AND DEVELOPMENT

1.1   Introduction

SSAP 13 was first issued in 1977 and revised in January 1989.

The term **research and development** can be used to cover a wide range of activity. SSAP 13 follows the OECD classification in defining three broad areas of activity:

Definition **Pure (or basic) research:** experimental or theoretical work undertaken primarily to acquire new scientific or technical knowledge for its own sake rather than directed towards any specific aim or application.

Definition **Applied research:** original or critical investigation undertaken in order to gain new scientific or technical knowledge and directed towards a specific practical aim or objective.

Definition **Development:** use of scientific or technical knowledge in order to produce new or substantially improved materials, devices, products or services, to install new processes or systems prior to the commencement of commercial production or commercial applications, or to improving substantially those already produced or installed.

Development is therefore concerned with using **existing** knowledge to introduce new products or processes.

1.2   Classification of costs

Expenditure on research and development does not consist only of the salaries of scientists or the cost of test tubes. Many costs can properly be regarded as being incurred for research and development purposes. These include:

(a)   Costs of materials.

(b)   Salaries, wages, and other employment costs of workers involved in research and development.

(c)   Depreciation of scientific and other equipment and land and buildings.

(d)   A proportion of overhead costs.

(e)   Related costs, such as patents, licence fees, etc.

1.3   Accounting problems

The problems in accounting for research and development revolve around two of the fundamental accounting concepts: accruals and prudence. Should the expenditure be matched with any related future income? - the accruals concept. Or should it be written off immediately? - the prudent approach.

1.4   Pure and applied research

Under the accruals concept, income is matched with the costs involved in generating that income. Yet how can expenditure on pure and applied research be matched with any particular period's income? There may be no direct benefit from the expenditure, or it may benefit many periods.

Expenditure on pure and applied research can, therefore, be regarded as part of the continuing cost of running the business. Since no one period can be expected to benefit more than another, such expenditure should be written off as incurred. Carrying expenditure forward to future periods would conflict not only with the accruals concept, but with prudent accounting practice.

| Conclusion | Pure and applied research costs should be written off as an expense in the profit and loss account immediately that they are incurred. |

1.5   Development expenditure

In the case of development expenditure, it is likely that future income, or cost reduction, can be directly attributable to a development project. An example of this is a motor car manufacturer who is developing a new model of car. He is incurring costs now in the expectation that they will be recovered from future sales of the car. On the accruals basis, such expenditure should not be written off against the current year's income, but carried forward and set against income from the project in future years.

However, prudence dictates that it is impossible to determine whether future benefits will arise from a development project unless the project and its related expenditure are clearly identifiable. SSAP 13 therefore concludes that development expenditure should normally be written off as incurred, but *may* be carried forward in certain circumstances.

| Conclusion | Development expenditure can be capitalised in the balance sheet and carried forward but only if certain criteria are met. |

1.6   SSAP 13 criteria

Development expenditure should be written off in the year of expenditure except in the following circumstances when it may be deferred to future periods:

(a)   there is a clearly defined project; and

(b)   the related expenditure is separately identifiable; and

(c)   the outcome of such a project has been assessed with reasonable certainty as to:

   (i)   its technical feasibility; and

   (ii)   its ultimate commercial viability considered in the light of factors such as likely market conditions (including competing products), public opinion, consumer and environmental legislation; and

(d)   the aggregate of the deferred development costs, any further development costs, and related production, selling and administration costs is reasonably expected to be exceeded by related future sales or other revenues; and

(e)   adequate resources exist, or are reasonably expected to be available, to enable the project to be completed and to provide any consequential increases in working capital.

In the foregoing circumstances development expenditure may be deferred to the extent that its recovery can reasonably be regarded as assured.

If an accounting policy of deferral of development expenditure is adopted, it should be applied to all development projects that meet the criteria above.

1.7   Further problems with development expenditure

If development expenditure is deferred to future periods, three further problems arise:

(a)   How and when should the expenditure be written off?
(b)   What should be done if circumstances surrounding the project change?
(c)   How should development expenditure be shown in the balance sheet?

These problems are considered in turn.

1.8   Writing off deferred development expenditure

The aim in carrying forward such expenditure is to match it against future benefits arising from the developed product. This can be in the form either of revenue from the sale of the product, or of reduced costs from improved production processes.

Deferred development expenditure should be matched against benefits in a sensible and consistent manner. It is not enough to write off the expenditure over an arbitrary number of years: writing off should start when the product begins to be produced commercially.

1.9   Activity

Improve plc has deferred development expenditure of £600,000 relating to the development of New Miracle Brand X. It is expected that the demand for the product will stay at a high level for the next three years. Annual sales of 400,000, 300,000 and 200,000 units respectively are expected over this period. Brand X sells for £10.

How might this expenditure be amortised?

1.10 Activity solution

There are two possibilities for writing off the development expenditure:

(a) in equal instalments over the three year period, i.e. £200,000 pa; or

(b) in relation to total sales expected (900,000 units):

$$\text{Year 1} \quad \frac{400,000}{900,000} \times £600,000 = £266,667$$

$$\text{Year 2} \quad \frac{300,000}{900,000} \times £600,000 = 200,000$$

$$\text{Year 3} \quad \frac{200,000}{900,000} \times £600,000 = 133,333$$

1.11 Changing circumstances

Deferred development expenditure should be reviewed at the end of each accounting period and where the circumstances which have justified the deferral of the expenditure no longer apply, or are considered doubtful, the expenditure, to the extent to which it is considered to be irrecoverable, should be written off immediately project by project.

1.12 Accounting presentation

- The accounting policy on research and development expenditure should be stated and explained.

- The total amount of research and development expenditure charged in the profit and loss account should be disclosed, analysed between the current year's expenditure and amounts amortised from deferred expenditure.

- Movements on deferred development expenditure and the amount carried forward at the beginning and the end of the period should be disclosed. Deferred development expenditure should be disclosed under intangible fixed assets in the balance sheet.

- The requirement to disclose the expenditure charged in the profit and loss account does **not** apply to 'small' unquoted companies. A small company is one which satisfies the criteria (multiplied in each case by ten) for defining a medium-sized company under the CA85 abbreviated accounts provisions. Thus all quoted companies and large unquoted companies have to disclose the information.

1.13 Companies Act disclosure

The Companies Act 1985 requires deferred development expenditure to be included as an intangible fixed asset.

An example of an appropriate note to the balance sheet would be as follows:

	£'000	£'000
Deferred development expenditure b/d		320
Expenditure incurred in the period	70	
Expenditure written off in the period	(64)	
		6
Deferred development expenditure c/d		326

The profit and loss account or a note to the profit and loss account would disclose the **total** amount of research and development expenditure. For example:

	£'000
Research and development expenditure:	
Expenditure in year charged	130
Development expenditure amortised	64
	194

The £130,000 does not include the £70,000 appearing in the balance sheet note as it has not been charged in the profit and loss account.

Conclusion Expenditure on pure and applied research should be written off as it is incurred. Expenditure on development may, if desired, be carried forward provided certain criteria are satisfied.

2 ACCOUNTING FOR GOODWILL - FRS 10

2.1 Introduction

The concept of goodwill of a business was introduced in the chapter on partnership accounting. It was seen then that in general terms goodwill will tend not to be recognised in the balance sheet. In the context of a company there are more detailed rules stemming from the requirements of the Companies Act and accounting standards.

FRS 10 *Goodwill and intangible assets* was published in 1997 in order to replace the previous accounting standard on goodwill, SSAP 22.

2.2 Activity

Consider why goodwill may exist.

2.3 Activity solution

Goodwill may exist because of any combination of a number of possible factors, for example:

(a) Reputation for quality and/or service.
(b) A good location.
(c) Technical 'know-how' and experience.
(d) Possession of favourable contracts/significant market share.
(e) Good management and/or technical personnel.

2.4 Types of goodwill

Goodwill is classified as a type of intangible asset.

Definition Intangible assets are non-financial fixed assets that do not have physical substance but are identifiable and are controlled by the entity through custody or legal rights.

There are two readily identifiable types of goodwill. These are inherent goodwill and purchased goodwill.

Definition Inherent goodwill is the internally generated goodwill that most businesses possess due to their reputation, products, service, location etc.

> **Definition** Purchased goodwill is the difference between the cost of an acquired entity and the aggregate of the fair values of that entity's identifiable assets and liabilities.

The basic distinction between these two types of goodwill for accounting purposes is that inherent goodwill should never appear on a company's balance sheet as a fixed asset. However purchased goodwill should appear on the balance sheet as an intangible fixed asset and should generally be amortised over its useful economic life.

It is the detailed treatment of purchased goodwill in the balance sheet that is dealt with by FRS 10.

> **Conclusion** Inherent goodwill (or non-purchased goodwill) should never appear as an intangible fixed asset on a company's balance sheet. Purchased goodwill however should be capitalised and amortised.

2.5   Purchased goodwill

FRS 10 states that purchased goodwill (and other intangible assets) should be capitalised as assets on the balance sheet. This goodwill should then be amortised over its useful economic life.

> **Definition** Amortisation is the description given to the annual depreciation of intangible fixed assets.

2.6   Amortisation of goodwill

It is generally assumed by FRS 10 that the useful economic life of purchased goodwill will not exceed 20 years. Therefore this will be the normal maximum period over which the goodwill will be amortised. The amount amortised or written off the goodwill each year will be charged to the profit and loss account.

2.7   Useful economic life

Although the presumption of FRS 10 is that the useful economic life of goodwill will not exceed 20 years the FRS does recognise that in some cases the life of goodwill may be longer than 20 years or indeed indefinite.

If the life of the goodwill is deemed to be longer than 20 years then it will be amortised over this longer period.

If the life of the goodwill is deemed to be indefinite then it will not be amortised at all.

2.8   Useful economic life

However for either of these treatments of goodwill to be acceptable under FRS 10 then the durability of the acquired business must be demonstrated and justify the longer useful economic life. In addition, the goodwill itself must be capable of remeasurement each year in order to ascertain that it has not fallen in value to an amount that is below its balance sheet value. This check on value is known as an impairment review.

> **Definition** Impairment is a reduction in the recoverable amount of a fixed asset or goodwill below its carrying value.

> **Definition** The recoverable amount of a fixed asset or goodwill is the higher of its net realisable value and value in use.

> **Definition** The net realisable value of goodwill is the amount at which it could be disposed of, less any direct selling costs.

Definition   The value in use of goodwill is the present value of the future cash flows from continued use of the asset, including those resulting from its ultimate disposal.

Definition   The carrying value of goodwill is the amount at which it is currently valued in the balance sheet.

If the impairment review indicates that the recoverable amount of the goodwill has fallen below the carrying value of the asset in the balance sheet then it must be written down to the recoverable amount immediately.

Impairment reviews are generally only necessary for goodwill that is amortised over a period exceeding 20 years or not amortised at all. All other goodwill that is amortised over a period of less than 20 years is only subject to an impairment review at the end of the first full year after its recognition.

2.9   Negative goodwill

It is possible for a business to acquire what is known as negative goodwill.

Definition   Negative goodwill arises where a company pays less for another business than the separable net assets of that business are worth.

Negative goodwill is a credit balance and FRS 10 states that it should be shown on the balance sheet of a company immediately below the goodwill heading within intangible fixed assets. This negative goodwill should then be credited back to the profit and loss account over the periods expected to benefit from the acquisition.

2.10   Disclosure requirements

As goodwill is a fixed asset then the normal disclosures for fixed assets e.g., brought forward and carried forward amounts are all required as notes to the accounts (see Chapter 9).

In addition the following disclosures are required by FRS 10:

- the bases of valuation of the goodwill and intangible assets;
- the grounds for believing that a useful economic life exceeds 20 years or is indefinite (where applicable);
- the treatment adopted for any negative goodwill.

The Companies Act requires all fixed assets, including goodwill, to be amortised over a limited period. Therefore if any goodwill is not amortised due to its indefinite life then a note is required to the accounts stating that this policy has been adopted in order to give a true and fair view and in accordance with FRS 10 (ie, a 'true and fair view override' note). This note must also detail the reasons for and the effect of the departure from the Companies Act requirements.

Conclusion   Most purchased goodwill should be amortised over a period of 20 years or less. However if a company's directors feel that the useful economic life of its goodwill is greater than 20 years or indeed indefinite then it can be amortised over this longer period or not amortised at all provided that an impairment review is performed each year. If the impairment review shows that the value of the goodwill has fallen below its carrying value then it should be written down to this new value immediately.

3   SELF TEST QUESTIONS

1   What are the three broad categories of research and development expenditure defined in SSAP 13? (1.1)

2   Which two accounting concepts conflict when considering the accounting treatment of research and development costs? (1.3)

3   What is the acceptable SSAP 13 accounting treatment for pure and applied research costs? (1.4)

4   What are the five SSAP 13 criteria for capitalising development expenditure? (1.6)

5   How should deferred development expenditure be written off? (1.8)

6   Distinguish between inherent goodwill and purchased goodwill. (2.4)

7   How should purchased goodwill normally be dealt with in a company's financial statements? (2.5)

8   What is an impairment review and when should it be carried out? (2.8)

9   What is the recoverable amount for goodwill? (2.8)

10   What is the FRS 10 treatment of negative goodwill? (2.9)

13 STOCKS AND LONG TERM CONTRACTS

PATHFINDER INTRODUCTION

This chapter covers the following performance criteria and knowledge and understanding.

- Draft accounts comply with domestic standards and legislation (performance criteria 10.2)
- Main requirements of relevant SSAPs, FRSs and other relevant pronouncements and their application to this element (knowledge and understanding 10.2)

Putting the chapter in context – learning objectives

This chapter considers the accounting treatment and disclosure of stocks and long term contracts. The material on valuation of stocks should be familiar from your earlier studies.

Long term contracts are dealt with in outline only as the detailed requirements of SSAP 9 are outside the scope of your syllabus.

At the end of this chapter you should have learned the following topics.

- SSAP 9 – Stocks.
- Methods of calculating cost of purchase.
- Balance sheet presentation of stocks.
- Long term contract work in progress.

1 SSAP 9 - STOCKS

1.1 What is 'stock'?

At any point in time, most manufacturing and retailing enterprises will hold several categories of stock, including:

(a) Goods purchased for resale.
(b) Consumable stores (such as oil).
(c) Raw materials and components used in the production process.
(d) Partly-finished goods (usually called work-in-progress).
(e) Finished goods (which have been manufactured by the enterprise).

1.2 Accounting concepts

As regards stock, two concepts are of particular importance. These are:

(a) The accruals (or matching) concept. The buying and manufacturing costs of the goods sold and the current revenues earned must be matched up (or compared).

(b) The prudence concept. Profit is not taken until sales revenue has been earned and realised. For a credit sale, this usually means the date of delivery (when a debtor balance is created). For a cash sale, the date of delivery and receipt of cash are the same.

However, if goods are expected to be sold below cost (say, because they are damaged or obsolete), immediate account must be taken of the loss as soon as it is recognised.

The prudence concept leads to the following basic rule, from SSAP 9:

The amount at which stocks and work-in-progress, other than long-term contract work-in-progress, is stated in periodic financial statements should be the total of the lower of cost and net realisable value of the separate items of stocks and work-in-progress or of groups of similar items.

1.3   Cost

Definition   Cost includes all that expenditure which has been incurred in the normal course of business in bringing the product or service to its present location and condition (para 17 SSAP 9).

This includes:

(a)   Cost of purchase: material costs, import duties, freight.
(b)   Cost of conversion: this includes direct costs and production overheads.

1.4   Net realisable value

Definition   Net realisable value is the estimated proceeds of sale less any further costs to completion and all costs to be incurred in distributing, marketing and selling.

Conclusion   Cost is all the expenditure which has been incurred in bringing the product or service to its present location and condition. It includes cost of purchase and cost of conversion.

2   METHODS OF CALCULATING COST OF PURCHASE

2.1   Introduction

There are several possible methods.

(a)   Identified, actual or unit cost.
(b)   Average cost.
(c)   First in first out (FIFO).
(d)   Last in first out (LIFO).
(e)   Base stock.
(f)   Adjusted selling price.
(g)   Standard cost.

2.2   Identified, actual or unit cost

Unsold or unused stocks are linked with their purchase. This method is limited to large or valuable items where individual units can be easily identified with their cost of acquisition eg, diamonds. This method, therefore, has limited usefulness in practice, but is acceptable under SSAP 9.

2.3   Average cost

Where raw materials or goods go, for example, into a large store, it may be impossible or impracticable to identify particular items. All units going into and out of the store are pooled and an average price determined. This average price should be calculated as a weighted average (this is preferable to a simple average).

2.4   Activity

200 units   Purchased day 1 at £15 per unit

100 units   Purchased day 2 at £21 per unit

200 units   Sold   day 3 at £25 per unit

Calculate the gross profit earned on day 3 and the valuation of stock remaining at the end of day 3, using the weighted average method.

2.5   Activity solution

Weighted average price at end of day 2 $=$ $\dfrac{(200 \times £15) + (100 \times £21)}{300}$

                                               $=$ £17 per unit

Calculation of gross profit

			£
Proceeds of sale	200 × £25 =		5,000
Less: Cost of goods sold	200 × £17 =		3,400
Gross profit			1,600

Calculation of stock in the balance sheet

		£
100 units stated at	100 × £17 =	£1,700

Note: calculations based on a simple average would give a different gross profit of £1,400.

The aim of the weighted average method is to even out price fluctuations. It is complex to operate, but acceptable under SSAP 9.

2.6   First-in-first-out (FIFO)

This method assumes that goods are sold or used in production in the order in which they are brought into stock. The first items sold will be the earliest purchases.

2.7   Activity

Using the figures from the previous activity calculate the gross profit on day 3 and the value of stock at the end of day 3 using FIFO.

2.8   Activity solution

The assumption here is that the 200 units sold on day 3 were the 200 units acquired on day 1.

Calculation of gross profit

			£
Proceeds of sale	200 × £25 =		5,000
Less: Cost of goods sold	200 × £15 =		3,000
Gross profit			2,000

Calculation of stock in the balance sheet

100 units stated at   100 × £21 =   £2,100

One of the features of FIFO is that stock in the balance sheet tends to be stated at the most recent values, whereas cost of goods sold is based on the more historical values. In a period of inflation FIFO tends to overstate gross profit because current revenues are matched with historical costs. This method is acceptable under SSAP 9.

| Conclusion | The FIFO method assumes that goods will be sold or used in the order in which they were purchased (first-in-first-out).

2.9   Last-in-first-out (LIFO)

The LIFO method assumes that goods sold or used in production are those most recently acquired. Goods still in stock, on the other hand, are those that have been in stock for the longest time.

2.10   Activity

Using the figures from the previous activity calculate the gross profit and closing stock value using LIFO.

2.11   Activity solution

This method assumes that the 200 units sold on day 3 were: firstly, 100 of the goods purchased on day 2, and, secondly, 100 of the 200 goods purchased on day 1.

Calculation of gross profit

		£	£
Proceeds of sale	200 × £25 =		5,000
Less: Cost of goods sold:			
100 units (day 2)	100 × £21 =	2,100	
100 units (day 1)	100 × £15 =	1,500	
			3,600
Gross profit			1,400

Calculation of stock in the balance sheet

100 units stated at   100 × £15 =   £1,500

SSAP 9 does not regard LIFO as being suitable for financial reporting, although it is accepted in the relevant International Accounting Standard. LIFO has the advantage over FIFO in that it takes some account of changes in the price level, but suffers from the disadvantage that it may reveal out-of-date cost figures for stock in the balance sheet.

Comparison of weighted average, FIFO and LIFO (using activity results).

	Sales	Trading account Cost of goods sold	Gross profit	Balance sheet Closing stock
	£	£	£	£
Weighted average	5,000	3,400	1,600	1,700
FIFO	5,000	3,000	2,000	2,100
LIFO	5,000	3,600	1,400	1,500

2.12   Base stock

This method ascribes a fixed unit value to a predetermined number of units of stock, any excess over that number being valued on the basis of some other method. If the number of units is less than the base number, the fixed unit value is applied to the number in stock. This would not normally provide a valuation near enough to actual cost to be acceptable under SSAP 9.

2.13   Adjusted selling price

This method requires knowledge of the mark-up or gross profit percentage. The cost of stock is calculated at selling price and then converted into cost terms by deducting the mark-up. This method is acceptable only if it can be demonstrated that it does give a reasonable approximation to actual cost under SSAP 9.

2.14   Standard cost

This method will only give realistic results if the standard costs are reviewed regularly. This method is acceptable under SSAP 9.

2.15   Costs of conversion

To the costs of purchase must be added the costs of conversion.

(a)   **Direct production expenses**

These expenses can all be attributed to units of production, and include direct labour and direct expenses.

(b)   **Production overheads**

These may be included, provided they relate to the production function. Furthermore, the production overheads included in closing stock must be based on a normal level of activity. Thus, overheads attributable to time during a strike or a machine breakdown are not attributable to closing stock.

(c)   **Other overheads**

The overriding criterion is that they should relate to bringing the product or service to its present location and condition. SSAP 9 gives the example of design and selling costs relating to products manufactured to a customer's specification. Normally, however, selling overheads do not form part of stock valuation.

Conclusion   There are a number of methods of arriving at the cost of stocks held. The most commonly used methods are FIFO (first-in-first-out) and average cost.

3   BALANCE SHEET PRESENTATION OF STOCKS

3.1   Lower of cost and market value rule

SSAP 9 states that stock and work in progress should be stated at the total of the lower of cost and net realisable value of the separate items of stock or of groups of similar items.

Definition   Net realisable value is the estimated proceeds of sale less all further costs to completion and less all costs to be incurred in distributing, marketing and selling.

The comparison of cost and net realisable value should take place for each individual line or category of stock.

3.2   Activity

The following information relates to five dissimilar stock items:

	Cost	Net realisable value	Lower of cost and net realisable value	Unrealised loss
	£	£	£	£
Item A	480	510	480	–
Item B	220	200	200	20
Item C	170	220	170	–
Item D	150	200	150	–
Item E	600	450	450	150
	1,620	1,580	1,450	170

At what figure would the stock be valued?

3.3   Activity solution

In accordance with accepted practice, one would state stock in the balance sheet at £1,450. The figure is made up of cost (£1,620) less unrealised losses (£170).

If the calculation were performed on an aggregate basis, stock would be stated at £1,580. This would be regarded as unacceptable under SSAP 9.

3.4   Disclosure requirements - SSAP 9

The disclosure requirements (excluding long-term contracts) are:

- The accounting policies which have been used in calculating cost, net realisable value, attributable profit and foreseeable losses (see later) should be stated.

- Stocks and work-in-progress should be sub-classified in balance sheets or in notes to the financial statements in a manner which is appropriate to the business and so as to indicate the amounts held in each of the main categories in the standard balance sheet formats of the CA85.

Conclusion   The basic rule is that stocks are valued at the lower of cost and net realisable value.

4   LONG-TERM CONTRACT WORK-IN-PROGRESS

4.1   Introduction

> **Definition** SSAP 9 defines a long-term contract as 'a contract entered into for the design, manufacture or construction of a single substantial asset or the provision of a service (or of a combination of assets or services which together constitute a single project) where the time taken substantially to complete the contract is such that the contract activity falls into different accounting periods.'

Because they extend over more than one accounting period, long term contracts can cause particular accounting problems.

Example

A company enters into a long term contract which runs for twelve months from 1 July 19X7. Total costs on the contract are expected to amount to £300,000 and the total contract price is £1,000,000. The company prepares accounts to 31 December each year.

No profit is recognised until the contract is complete. At 31 December 19X7, costs of £200,000 have been incurred.

Assuming that the costs of £200,000 are treated as work in progress and included as an asset on the balance sheet, this gives rise to a profit of £Nil for the year ended 31 December 19X7, but a profit of £700,000 for the year ended 31 December 19X8.

Given that a large proportion of the work was carried out in 19X7, this treatment does not give a true and fair view of the activities of the company.

4.2   Standard accounting practice

SSAP 9 applies the accruals concept to long term contract accounting by requiring entities to recognise attributable profit in the profit and loss account as the contract progresses.

> **Definition** **Attributable profit** is that part of the total profit currently expected to arise over the duration of the contract that fairly reflects the profit attributable to that part of the work performed at the accounting date.

Long term contracts should be assessed on a contract by contract basis and reflected in the profit and loss account by recording turnover and related costs as contract activity progresses. Turnover is ascertained in a manner appropriate to the stage of completion of the contract, the business and the industry in which it operates.

Where it is considered that the outcome of a contract can be assessed with reasonable certainty before its conclusion, the prudently calculated attributable profit should be recognised in the profit and loss account as the difference between the reported turnover and related costs for that contract.

If it is expected that there will be a loss on a contract as a whole, all of the loss should be recognised as soon as it is foreseen (in accordance with the prudence concept).

> **Definition** **Foreseeable losses** are losses which are currently estimated to arise over the duration of the contract.

The full accounting and disclosure requirements of SSAP 9 are very complex and are outside the scope of your syllabus.

4.3   Example

A company enters into a long term contract which runs for twelve months from 1 July 19X7. The total contract price is £1,000,000. At 31 December 19X7 costs incurred on the contract were £400,000 and the value of the work done was certified as £500,000.

How should this contract be treated in the accounts for the year ended 31 December 19X7 if:

(a)   Total costs are expected to be £600,000.
(b)   Total costs are expected to be £1,100,000?

4.4   Solution

(a)   The contract as a whole is expected to make a profit of £400,000, so a portion of this profit can be recognised in the 19X7 accounts.

There are several possible ways of calculating attributable profit of which two are shown below:

(i) $\dfrac{\text{Costs to date}}{\text{Total costs}}$ × Total profit $\dfrac{400,000}{600,000} \times 400,000 = £266,667$

(ii) $\dfrac{\text{Work certified to date}}{\text{Total turnover}}$ × Total profit $\dfrac{500,000}{1,000,000} \times 400,000 = £200,000$

Using method (ii), the figures that appear in the profit and loss account are:

	£
Turnover (value of work certified)	500,000
Cost of sales (balancing figure)	(300,000)
Gross profit	200,000

In addition, long term contract work in progress would be stated in the balance sheet as:

	£
Costs incurred to date	400,000
Less: costs transferred to cost of sales	(300,000)
	100,000

(b)   The contract is expected to make a loss of £100,000. The whole of the loss must be recognised as soon as it is foreseen:

	£
Turnover (value of work certified)	500,000
Cost of sales (balancing figure)	(600,000)
Gross loss	(100,000)

A provision for losses on long term contracts would appear in the balance sheet and would be calculated as:

	£
Cost of sales	600,000
Less: costs incurred to date	(400,000)
	200,000

Conclusion The accounting treatment of long term contracts required by SSAP 9 reflects the accruals concept and the prudence concept.

5   SELF TEST QUESTIONS

1   Which two fundamental accounting concepts are most relevant to the accounting treatment of stocks? (1.2)

2   What is the SSAP 9 definition of the cost of stocks? (1.3)

3   What is the net realisable value of stocks? (1.4)

4   What is the assumption behind a FIFO cost valuation for stocks? (2.6)

5   What effect does using a LIFO valuation for cost of stock have on closing stock values in the balance sheet? (2.11)

6   What is the adjusted selling price method of determining the cost of stock? (2.13)

7   What is the basic SSAP 9 rule regarding the valuation of stocks for balance sheet purposes? (3.1)

8   What is a long term contract? (4.1)

9   What is attributable profit in the context of long term contracts? (4.2)

10   How should long term contracts be treated in the profit and loss account? (4.2)

14 | SUBSTANCE OF TRANSACTIONS

PATHFINDER INTRODUCTION

This chapter covers the following performance criteria and knowledge and understanding.

- Draft accounts comply with domestic standards and legislation (performance criteria 10.2)
- Main requirements of relevant SSAPs, FRSs and other relevant pronouncements and their application to this element (knowledge and understanding 10.2)

Putting the chapter in context – learning objectives.

This chapter considers a variety of accounting standards that deal with an important area of accounting. This is the principle that the financial statements of a company should reflect the commercial substance of the transactions of the entity rather than simply their legal form. This is an area of accounting that has concerned the accounting bodies for some considerable period of time and there are a number of SSAPs and FRSs that tackle this subject. This chapter considers some of the older standards from the ASC, SSAP 17 and SSAP 21. SSAP 21 looked at a specific problem area, that of accounting for lease transactions and hire purchase transactions. The ASB has continued to work in this area of substance over form with the issue of the general FRS, FRS 5 Reporting the Substance of Transactions, and the disclosure FRS, FRS 8 Related Party Disclosures. More recently the ASB has also issued FRS 12, Provisions, Contingent Liabilities and Contingent Assets.

At the end of this chapter you should have learned the following topics.

- SSAP 17 Accounting for post balance sheet events.
- FRS 12 Provisions, contingent liabilities and contingent assets.
- FRS 5 Reporting the substance of transactions.
- SSAP 21 Accounting for leases and hire purchase contracts.
- FRS 8 Related party disclosures.

---

1 SSAP 17 – ACCOUNTING FOR POST BALANCE SHEET EVENTS

1.1 Introduction

Suppose the year end of a company is 31 December 19X7 and the directors approve the financial statements at a board meeting held on 22 March 19X8. Certain events occurring during the intervening period will provide information which will help in preparing the financial statements.

These post balance sheet events fall into two categories: adjusting events and non-adjusting events.

Definition   **Post balance sheet events** are those events, both favourable and unfavourable, which occur between the balance sheet date and the date on which the financial statements are approved by the board of directors.

Definition   **The date on which the financial statements are approved by the board of directors** is the date the board of directors formally approves a set of documents as the financial statements. In respect of unincorporated enterprises, the date of approval is the corresponding date.

Definition **Adjusting events** are post balance sheet events which provide additional evidence of conditions existing at the balance sheet date.

Definition **Non-adjusting events** are post balance sheet events which concern conditions which did not exist at the balance sheet date.

1.2 Adjusting events

These events provide additional evidence of conditions existing at the balance sheet date. For example, bad debts arising one or two months after the balance sheet date may help to quantify the bad debt provision as at the balance sheet date. Adjusting events may, therefore, affect the amount at which items are stated in the balance sheet.

1.3 Examples of adjusting events

Examples include:

- Provisions for stock and bad debts confirmed by later sales/receipts.

- Amounts received or receivable in respect of insurance claims which were being negotiated at the balance sheet date.

- Certain special items occurring after the balance sheet date which, for various reasons, are reflected in the current year's financial statements:

    (i)   Proposed dividends.
    (ii)   Appropriations to reserves.
    (iii)   Effects of changes in taxation.

1.4 Non-adjusting events

These are events arising after the balance sheet date but which, unlike those events above, do **not** concern conditions existing at the balance sheet date. Such events will not, therefore, have any effect on items in the balance sheet or profit and loss account. However, in order to prevent the financial statements from presenting a misleading position, some form of additional disclosure is required if the events are material, say by way of memorandum note indicating what effect the events would have had on the year end balance sheet.

1.5 Examples of non-adjusting events

Examples include:

- The issue of new share or loan capital.
- Financial consequences of losses of fixed assets or stock as a result of fires or floods.

1.6 'Window dressing'

Definition 'Window dressing' refers to the practice of entering into certain transactions before the year end and reversing those transactions after the year end.

Thus no real transaction has occurred (ie, no substance, only legal form) but the balance sheet reflects the transaction (as it normally records the legal form of assets and liabilities). The hoped-for effect is to improve the appearance of the balance sheet.

SSAP 17 requires a **disclosure** of such transactions if they are material. They are **not**, however, adjusting events.

1.7   Standard accounting practice – SSAP 17

SSAP 17 *Accounting for post balance sheet events* requires that:

- Financial statements should be prepared on the basis of conditions existing at the balance sheet date.

- A material post balance sheet event requires changes in the amounts to be included in financial statements where:

    (a)   it is an adjusting event; or

    (b)   it indicates that application of the going concern concept to the whole or a material part of the company is not appropriate.

- A material post balance sheet event should be disclosed where:

    (a)   it is a non-adjusting event of such materiality that its non-disclosure would affect the ability of the users of financial statements to reach a proper understanding of the financial position; or

    (b)   it is the reversal or maturity after the year-end of a transaction entered into before the year-end, the substance of which was primarily to alter the appearance of the company's balance sheet (window dressing).

- In respect of each post balance sheet event which is required to be disclosed, the following information should be stated by way of notes in financial statements:

    (a)   the nature of the event; and

    (b)   an estimate of the financial effect, or a statement that it is not practicable to make such an estimate.

- The estimate of the financial effect should be disclosed before taking account of taxation, and the taxation implications should be explained where necessary for a proper understanding of the financial position.

- The date on which the financial statements are approved by the board of directors should be disclosed in the financial statements.

1.8   Activity

How would the following matters be dealt with?

(a)   When drafting the final accounts, a company's accountant includes a figure of £2,000 as the net realisable value of damaged items of stock.

   The cost of these items was £3,000, and the normal selling price would be £4,000. Between the balance sheet date and the approval of the accounts the items are sold for £3,100.

(b)   A company is engaged in the construction of its own factory. The estimated value on completion is £200,000, costs to date are £80,000 and at the balance sheet date expected further costs to completion were £90,000.

After the balance sheet date serious defects – which must have existed unnoticed for some time – are discovered in the foundations of the building, necessitating partial demolition and rebuilding at an estimated cost of £70,000 (in addition to the estimated further costs to completion of £90,000).

1.9   Activity solution

(a)   This is an adjusting post balance sheet event.   The valuation in the accounts should be adjusted to £3,000 ie, cost, since net realisable value has, in the event, turned out to be greater than cost.

(b)   This is an adjusting post balance sheet event. There is an anticipated loss on the factory of £40,000 (value £200,000 less costs to date £80,000 less estimated further costs £160,000). The asset should, therefore, be valued at £40,000 (costs to date £80,000 less attributable loss £40,000).

1.10   CA85

Para 6 Sch 7 CA85 requires the directors' report to contain:

(a)   particulars of any important events affecting the company or any of its subsidiaries which have occurred since the end of that year;

(b)   an indication of likely future developments in the business of the company and of its subsidiaries.

[Conclusion]   Adjusting events give rise to changes in the accounts figures. Non-adjusting events are disclosed by way of note.

2   FRS 12 - PROVISIONS, CONTINGENT LIABILITIES AND CONTINGENT ASSETS

2.1   Objective of FRS 12

The objective of FRS 12 is to ensure that appropriate recognition criteria and measurement bases are applied to provisions, contingent liabilities and contingent assets. The FRS is also concerned that sufficient information is disclosed in the notes to the financial statements to enable users to understand the nature, timing and amount of these items.

2.2   Recognition of provisions

[Definition]   A provision is a liability that is of uncertain timing or amount, to be settled by the transfer of economic benefits.

A provision should be recognised when:

(a)   an entity has a present obligation as a result of a past event; and
(b)   a transfer of economic benefits to settle the liability is probable; and
(c)   a reliable estimate can be made of the amount of the obligation.

If these conditions are not met then the provision should not be recognised.

2.3   Measurement of provisions

The amount at which a provision should be recognised will be the best estimate of the expenditure required to settle the liability. There will tend to be a number of risks and uncertainties surrounding this estimate and care should be taken to avoid duplicating adjustments for these risks and consequently overstating the provision.

Provisions should be reviewed at the end of each accounting period and adjusted to reflect the current best estimate. If a transfer of economic benefits to settle the provision is no longer probable then the provision should be reversed.

2.4 Use of a provision

A provision should only be used for expenditure for which the provision was originally recognised.

2.5 Disclosure of provisions

For each class of provision the following should be disclosed:

(a)   the opening and closing balance on the provision and details of any movements during the year;

(b)   a brief description of the nature of the obligation and the expected timing of the cash flows;

(c)   an indication of the uncertainties surrounding the amount or timing.

2.6 Contingent liabilities

Definition   A contingent liability is either:

(a)   a possible obligation arising from past events whose existence will be confirmed only by the occurrence of one or more uncertain future events not wholly within the entity's control; or

(b)   a present obligation that arises from past events but is not recognised because it is not probable that a transfer of economic benefits will be required to settle the obligation or because the amount of the obligation cannot be measured with sufficient reliability.

A contingent liability should never be recognised. However details should be disclosed unless the possibility of any transfer is remote.

2.7 Disclosure of contingent liabilities

A brief description of the nature of the contingent liability should be given, an estimate of its financial effect and an indication of the uncertainties surrounding its amount or timing.

2.8 Contingent assets

Definition   A contingent asset is a possible asset arising from past events whose existence will be confirmed only by the occurrence of one or more uncertain future events not wholly within the entity's control.

A contingent asset should never be recognised. Details of any contingent asset should only be disclosed where the inflow is probable.

2.9 Disclosure of contingent assets

If the inflow is probable then the notes should provide a brief description of the nature of the contingent asset and an estimate of its financial effect.

Conclusion   Contingent liabilities and assets should never be recognised in the financial statements. Contingent liabilities should be disclosed in the notes unless their likelihood is remote. Contingent assets should only be disclosed in the notes if they are probable.

3   FRS 5 - REPORTING THE SUBSTANCE OF TRANSACTIONS

3.1   Introduction

FRS 5 was issued in April 1994.

Its main thrust is to ensure that financial statements report the substance of transactions and not merely their legal form. The view held by the ASB was that, previously, users could be left unaware of the total assets employed in a business and of its overall financing. Detailed disclosure in the notes is no substitute for inclusion in the accounts.

3.2   The ways in which companies have tried to keep items off the balance sheet

'Reporting the substance of transactions' is a reaction to the practice of 'off balance sheet financing' which became popular in the 1980s. As the term indicates, the most widely recognised effect is the omission of liabilities from the balance sheet. However the assets being financed are also excluded with the result that the resources of the company and its financing are understated.

Ways in which companies have tried to keep items off the balance sheet in the past include the following.

- **Leasing of assets**

    Prior to the issue of SSAP 21 leases were not capitalised ie, the asset and its related financial commitment were not shown on the lessee's balance sheet. (SSAP 21 will be considered later in this chapter).

- **Window dressing**

    Companies may enter into transactions shortly before the year end to 'improve' the look of the balance sheet. These transactions reverse shortly after the year end. Such transactions are covered by SSAP 17 but this only requires disclosure in the notes, not changes in the financial statements.

- **Innovations in the financial markets**

    A number of (often complex) arrangements were developed for which the accounting entries were not immediately obvious. It was the growth in these arrangements which resulted in the determination of the ASB to issue an accounting standard on the substance of transactions.

3.3   Determining the substance of a transaction

FRS 5 recognises that its provisions will not be relevant to the vast majority of transactions. However there are circumstances where the substance of the transaction will not be clear.

Common features of transactions whose substance is not readily apparent are

- the separation of the legal title to an item from the ability to enjoy the principal benefits and exposure to the principal risks associated with it. An example of this might be certain types of lease (see later in this chapter);
- the linking of a transaction with one or more others in such a way that the commercial effect cannot be understood without reference to the series as a whole - an example of this might be a sale and repurchase agreement which is really only a loan with security;
- the inclusion in a transaction of one or more options whose terms make it highly likely that the option will be exercised.

3.4 FRS 5 approach

A key step in determining the substance of a transaction is to identify its effect on the assets and liabilities of the entity.

Definition Assets are rights or other access to future economic benefits controlled by an entity.

Definition Liabilities are an entity's obligations to transfer economic benefits.

Risk often indicates which party has an asset. Risk is important, as the party which has access to benefits (and hence an asset) will usually also be the one to suffer or gain if the benefits ultimately differ from those expected.

3.5 Inclusion of assets and liabilities in the balance sheet

Assets and liabilities should be included in the balance sheet where there is both

(a) sufficient evidence that an asset or liability exists, and
(b) that the asset or liability can be measured at a monetary amount with sufficient reliability.

3.6 Derecognition of assets

An asset should cease to be recognised (derecognised) only where two conditions are both fulfilled:

- the entity retains no significant access to material benefits

- any risk it retains is immaterial in relation to the variation in benefits likely to occur in practice.

3.7 Disclosures

Disclosure of a transaction should be sufficiently detailed to enable the user of the financial statements to understand its commercial effect.

To the extent that a transaction has not resulted in the recognition of assets or liabilities it is still necessary to consider whether disclosure of its nature and effect is required in order to give a true and fair view. For example the transaction may give rise to guarantees or other obligations.

Conclusion FRS 5 is a long and complex standard. However its requirements are only relevant to a limited number and type of transactions. For the purposes of this syllabus students will not be required to identify the substance of transactions. However an awareness of the problem dealt with in FRS 5 and an overview of its approach to asset and liability recognition is required.

4 SSAP 21 - ACCOUNTING FOR LEASES AND HIRE PURCHASE CONTRACTS

4.1 Introduction

If a business 'acquires' an asset on hire purchase (rather than outright purchase), the strict legal position is that title to the asset does not pass from 'seller' to 'buyer' until the final HP instalment is paid. In the meantime, however, the 'buyer' will have enjoyed full use of the asset, just as though he were the legal owner.

An alternative method for a business to acquire the use of an asset is to lease the asset.

The required accounting treatment for leases depends on whether they are classified as finance leases or operating leases.

The aim of SSAP 21 is to ensure that the accounting procedures for HP and leasing reflect the economic reality or substance of the transactions rather than the strict legal position.

4.2 Hire purchase agreement

 Hire purchase: a contract for the hire of an asset which contains a provision giving the hirer an option to acquire legal title to the asset upon the fulfilment of certain conditions stated in the contract.

Under a hire purchase agreement, goods are supplied on hire to customers on terms that, once an agreed number of instalments have been paid, they may exercise an option to purchase the goods for a nominal sum. Until the option is exercised, the goods remain the legal property of the supplier.

4.3 Lease agreement

[Definition] Under a *lease* agreement, a customer (the lessee) agrees to hire goods, normally for a fixed minimum period with rights of renewal. The goods remain the property of the lessor throughout the period.

Lease agreements can involve a **finance lease**, a long term lease where the rights and responsibilities in the asset (but not the legal ownership) pass to the user (lessee) or an **operating lease**, where such rights remain with the owner (lessor).

4.4 Accounting requirements for finance leases and hire purchase agreements

A finance lease is required by SSAP 21 *Accounting for leases and hire purchase contracts* to be dealt with in the same way as a hire purchase agreement. The lessee (user) treats the 'fair value' of the asset as a fixed asset and sets up a liability for this amount. Payments made are split between payment of this capital amount and payment of finance charges, with the latter debited to profit and loss account.

4.5 Accounting requirement for operating leases

The lease rentals under an operating lease are simply charged to profit and loss account and no asset is shown in the books of the lessee.

4.6 Finance leases

[Definition] A **finance lease** is a lease that transfers substantially all the risks and rewards of ownership of an asset to the lessee. It should be presumed that such a transfer of risks and rewards occurs if at the inception of a lease the present value of the minimum lease payments, including any initial payment, amounts to substantially all (normally 90% or more) of the fair value of the leased asset. The present value should be calculated by using the interest rate implicit in the lease.

This definition is complex as there is a fine dividing line between finance and operating leases and this needs to be clearly drawn as the accounting treatment is so different.

For accounting purposes the treatment of finance leases and HP agreements is exactly the same.

At the start of the lease the initial accounting entries for a finance lease would be

Dr   Fixed asset account
     Cr   Obligations under finance leases account

with the fair value of the asset or its cash price.

4.7   Finance leases – depreciation

As the finance lease asset is classified as a fixed asset it should be depreciated over the shorter of:

(a)   the economic useful life of the asset (as in FRS 15); and

(b)   the lease term.

4.8   Finance leases – allocation of finance charges

Over the period of the lease, the total finance charge is the amount by which the rentals paid to the lessor exceed the fair value of the asset.

Each individual rental payment should be split between:

(i)   finance charge (P/L account item); and

(ii)   repayment of obligation to pay rentals (thus reducing the balance sheet liability - obligations under finance leases).

The basic aim of the allocation of finance charge is to allocate the charge in such a way as to produce a reasonably constant periodic rate of return on the remaining balance of liability.

4.9   Activity

A company has two options. It can buy an asset for cash at a cost of £5,710 or it can lease it by way of a finance lease. The terms of the lease are as follows:

(1)   primary period is for four years from 1 January 19X2 with a rental of £2,000 pa payable on the 31 December each year;

(2)   the lessee is required to pay all repair, maintenance and insurance costs as they arise;

(3)   the interest rate implicit in the lease is 15%.

The lessee estimates the useful economic life of the asset to be four years. Depreciation is provided on a straight-line basis.

Show the accounting necessary for this lease if it is classified as a finance lease.

4.10   Activity solution

Step 1   The asset is shown in the balance sheet at £5,710 (subject to depreciation).

Depreciation is over four years.

Annual depreciation charge = 1/4 × £5,710 = £1,428 (assuming no residual value)

Step 2   The liability is shown in the balance sheet at £5,710 but subsequently reduced by the capital portion of the leasing payments

The total finance charge is the difference between the total payment and the fair value £(8,000 – 5,710) = £2,290. The allocation of this to each rental payment and the consequent capital sum outstanding is calculated as follows:

Period (year ended 31 December)	Capital sum at start of period	Finance charge at 15% pa	Sub-total	Rental paid	Capital sum at end of period

	£		£		£		£		£
19X2	5,710	+	856	=	6,566	–	(2,000)	=	4,566
19X3	4,566	+	685	=	5,251	–	(2,000)	=	3,251
19X4	3,251	+	488	=	3,739	–	(2,000)	=	1,739
19X5	1,739	+	261	=	2,000	–	(2,000)	=	-
			2,290				8,000		

Step 3 The accounting entries are then made in the ledger accounts and balance sheet and profit and loss account.

Obligation under finance leases

	£		£
31 Dec 19X2 Cash	2,000	1 Jan 19X2 Fixed assets	5,710
31 Dec 19X2 Bal c/d	4,566	31 Dec 19X2 P&L a/c	
(see balance sheet extract		(Finance charge)	
below)		Step 2	856
	6,566		6,566
31 Dec 19X3 Cash	2,000	1 Jan 19X3 Bal b/d	4,566
31 Dec 19X3 Bal b/d	3,251	31 Dec 19X3 P&L a/c	
(see balance sheet extract		(Finance charge)	
below)		Step 2	685
	5,251		5,251

Balance sheet (extracts)

		19X2 £	*19X3* £
Fixed asset -	Cost	5,710	5,710
	Depreciation	1,428	2,856
Net book value		4,282	2,854
Creditors:			
Obligations under finance leases		4,566	3,251

Notes to the financial statements (extracts):

	19X2 £	*19X3* £
Operating profit is stated after charging:		
Depreciation of assets held under finance leases	1,428	1,428
Interest payable and similar charges		
Finance lease charges	856	685

Step 4 The creditor balance in the balance sheet 'Obligations under finance leases' needs to be split between "Creditors: amounts falling due within one year" and "Creditors: amounts falling due after more than one year".

	19X2 £	*19X3* £

Falling due within one year		
(2,000 - 685)	1,315	
(2,000 - 488)		1,512
Falling due after more than		
one year (bal fig)	3,251	1,739
	4,566	3,251

The calculation of the amount falling due within one year is the following year's total lease payment (capital and finance charge) minus the finance charge element for the following year. This will leave only the capital element due next year which is the figure required.

4.11 Operating leases

Definition An operating lease is any lease other than a finance lease.

In terms of accounting for operating leases there are no balance sheet aspects. The total lease rental is simply charged to the profit and loss account by the lessee as an expense.

Conclusion The purpose of SSAP 21 is to ensure that leased assets and assets purchased under hire purchase agreements are accounted for according to their commercial substance rather than their strict legal form. The commercial substance of both a finance lease and an HP agreement is that the purchaser has the rights and benefits inherent in the asset. Therefore for these agreements the asset and related liability appear on the purchaser's or lessee's balance sheet. However for an operating lease there are no balance sheet entries for the lessee simply a charging of the full lease rental to the profit and loss account in each period.

5 FRS 8 - RELATED PARTY DISCLOSURES

5.1 Introduction

When transactions take place between related parties they may not be on arm's length terms. Disclosure of the existence of such transactions, and of the relationships underlying them, gives important information to users of financial statements.

One striking example of the need for disclosure is that related party transactions have been a feature of a number of financial scandals in recent years, many of which have had in common the dominance of the company by a powerful chief executive who was also involved with the related party.

More generally, transactions between related parties - eg, companies in the same group - are now a common feature of business operations. Disclosure of these transactions, some of which may not have been at arm's length, together with information about the underlying relationship, gives the user of accounts an important indication of their significance to the operating results and financial position of the reporting company. For the same reasons disclosure is called for where transactions take place with a wide range of other related parties - eg, directors, associates, pension funds and key management.

Definition A related party transaction is the transfer of assets or liabilities or the performance of services by, to or for a related party irrespective of whether a price is charged.

FRS 8 requires the disclosure of:

(a)   all material related party transactions, and

(b)   the name of the party controlling the reporting entity and, if different, that of the ultimate controlling party whether or not any transactions between the reporting entity and those parties have taken place.

5.2   Definition of related parties

FRS 8 defines related parties as follows:

Definition   Two or more parties are related parties when for all or part of the financial period:

> (i)   one party has control over the other party; or
>
> (ii)   the parties are subject to common control from the same source; or
>
> (iii)   one party has significant influence over the other party; or
>
> (iv)   the parties are subject to influence from the same source to such an extent that one of the parties has subordinated its own separate interests.

5.3   Intragroup transactions

No disclosure is required in consolidated accounts of intragroup transactions and balances eliminated on consolidation.

5.4   Activity

Which of the following are related parties of a company?

(i)   its ultimate parent company;
(ii)   a fellow subsidiary;
(iii)   a subsidiary;
(iv)   an associated company;
(v)   a joint venture;
(vi)   directors of the company;
(vii)   a pension fund for the benefit of the company's employees.

5.5   Activity solution

All of them are related parties.

Conclusion   FRS 8 requires the disclosure of all material transactions with related parties.

6   SELF TEST QUESTIONS

1   What is an adjusting post balance sheet event? (1.1)

2   Give examples of an adjusting post balance sheet event. (1.3)

3   What is the accounting treatment of a non-adjusting post balance sheet event? (1.4)

4   What is window dressing? (1.6)

5   Distinguish between the accounting treatment of a contingent liability and a contingent asset. (2.6, 2.8)

6   What is the FRS 5 basic approach to determining the substance of transactions? (3.4)

7   Distinguish between a finance lease and an operating lease. (4.3)

8   What are the initial accounting entries for a finance lease? (4.6)

9   How is an operating lease treated in financial statements? (4.11)

10   What is the main purpose of FRS 8 *Related party disclosures*? (5.1)

15 REPORTING FINANCIAL PERFORMANCE

PATHFINDER INTRODUCTION

This chapter covers the following performance criteria and knowledge and understanding.

- Draft accounts comply with domestic standards and legislation (performance criteria 10.2)
- Main requirements of relevant SSAPs, FRSs and other relevant pronouncements and their application to this element (knowledge and understanding 10.2)

Putting the chapter in context – learning objectives.

This chapter considers the further accounting requirements for presentation of a company's profit and loss account over and above those contained in the CA 85 and covered in an earlier chapter. These accounting requirements are largely the domain of FRS 3 which was introduced by the ASB in order to radically alter the presentation of the profit and loss account. FRS 3 changed the way in which the face of the profit and loss account appears in the financial statements, changed the method reporting unusual items, introduced a new primary statement and introduced two new notes to the profit and loss account. Larger, diverse companies may also need to comply with the requirements of SSAP 25, Segmental Reporting, which are also covered in outline in this chapter. Finally brief mention of FRS 14, Earnings per Share, is made at the end of this chapter although this area will be covered again in the chapter on Interpretation of Financial Statements.

At the end of this chapter you should have learned the following topics.

- FRS 3 Reporting financial performance.
- SSAP 25 Segmental reporting.
- FRS 14 Earnings per share.

1 FRS 3 - REPORTING FINANCIAL PERFORMANCE

1.1 Introduction

FRS 3 was issued in 1992 and slightly amended in 1993. There were many aims of FRS 3 but the main one was to provide users of the financial statements with more useful information on the components of financial performance.

The main areas of profit and loss account presentation that need to be considered are:

- exceptional items;
- continuing and discontinued activities;
- prior period items;
- the statement of total recognised gains and losses;
- the note of historical cost profits and losses;
- the reconciliation of movements in shareholders' funds.

1.2 Concepts of profit

FRS 3 is based on the view that, as well as the usual profit on ordinary activities, the profit and loss account for the year should include and show separately all profits and losses including all unusual items which are recognised in that year and all prior period items other than prior period adjustments (the 'all-inclusive' concept of profit). Adoption of the all-inclusive concept recognises that the profit on ordinary activities alone is not appropriate for all the uses to which financial statements are put.

> **Definition**   Ordinary activities are any activities which are undertaken by a reporting entity as part of its business and such related activities in which the reporting entity engages in furtherance of, incidental to, or arising from, these activities. Ordinary activities include the effects on the reporting entity of any event in the various environments in which it operates, including the political, regulatory, economic and geographical environments, irrespective of the frequency or unusual nature of the events.

FRS 3 attempts to standardise the treatment of unusual and prior year items and to put a stop to 'reserve accounting', the practice of dealing with unusual and prior year items through reserves, thus having no effect on the reported profit for the year.

1.3   Exceptional items

> **Definition**   Exceptional items are material items which derive from events or transactions that fall within the ordinary activities of the company, and which individually or, if of a similar type, in aggregate, need to be disclosed by virtue of their size or incidence if the financial statements are to give a true and fair view.

Examples of items which may be exceptional where they are material include:

(a)   redundancy costs relating to continuing business segments;

(b)   reorganisation costs unrelated to the discontinuance of a business segment;

(c)   previously capitalised expenditure on intangible fixed assets written off other than as part of a process of amortisation;

(d)   amounts transferred to employee share schemes;

(e)   profits or losses on the disposal of fixed assets;

(f)   abnormal charges for bad debts and write-offs of stock and work-in-progress;

(g)   abnormal provisions for losses on long-term contracts;

(h)   surpluses arising on the settlement of insurance claims;

(i)   amounts received in settlement of insurance claims for consequential loss of profits.

1.4   Accounting treatment of exceptional items

Exceptional items are reflected in the ascertainment of profit or loss on ordinary activities but, because of their exceptional size or incidence, require separate disclosure for the financial statements to give a true and fair view. They should either be disclosed in a note to the accounts or on the face of the profit and loss account if that is required to give a true and fair view.

1.5   Exceptional items shown on the face of the profit and loss account

The following items, including provisions in respect of such items, should be shown separately as exceptional items on the face of the profit and loss account after operating profit and before interest:

●   profits or losses on the sale or termination of an operation;

●   costs of a fundamental reorganisation or restructuring having a material effect on the nature and focus of the company's operations; and

●   profits or losses on the disposal of fixed assets.

This accounting treatment recognises that both restructuring and terminations of operations are an inherent part of financial performance and so profits and losses arising should be treated as part of a company's ordinary activities.

Conclusion   Information about exceptional items must be shown as part of the financial statements. For most exceptional items this will consist of a note to the profit and loss account. However the three types of exceptional items specified in FRS 3 (and noted above) must be shown on the face of the profit and loss account.

1.6   Extraordinary items

Definition   Extraordinary items are material items possessing a high degree of abnormality which arise from events or transactions that fall outside the ordinary activities of the company and which are not expected to recur. They do not include exceptional items nor do they include prior period items merely because they relate to a prior period.

Current practice is now to have no extraordinary items in the accounts. Despite giving a definition of extraordinary items and despite their inclusion within the statutory formats of the CA85, no company is expected to show extraordinary items any more in their profit and loss account. As Professor Tweedie, the ASB chairman, has memorably said 'Martians walking down the street will be extraordinary, everything else exceptional'. No examples of extraordinary items are given in FRS 3 and the ASB hope that extraordinary items have been killed off and will never be seen again.

1.7   Discontinued operations

FRS 3 requires that the results of each of continuing operations, acquisitions (as a component of continuing operations) and discontinued operations should be disclosed separately. The illustrative examples later in this chapter show two methods by which this presentation could be achieved.

Definition   Discontinued operations are those operations of the reporting entity that are sold or terminated and that satisfy all of the following conditions.

(a)   The sale or termination is completed either in the period or before the earlier of three months after the commencement of the subsequent period and the date on which the financial statements are approved.

(b)   If a termination, the former activities have ceased permanently.

(c)   The sale or termination has a material effect on the nature and focus of the reporting entity's operations and represents a material reduction in its operating facilities resulting either from its withdrawal from a particular market (whether class of business or geographical) or from a material reduction in turnover in the reporting entity's continuing markets.

(d)   The assets, liabilities, results of operations and activities are clearly distinguishable, physically, operationally and for financial reporting purposes.

Operations not satisfying all these conditions are classified as continuing.

Note the timing restriction. If the termination is not completed within the time stated, the turnover and costs of the operations remain in continuing operations.

This does not mean, however, that an exceptional item should not be shown in respect of the actual profit/loss or anticipated loss on disposal.

Note also part (c) of the definition. The nature and focus of a reporting entity's operations refers to the positioning of its products or services in their markets including the aspects of both quality and location. For example, if a hotel company which had traditionally served the lower end of the hotel market sold its existing chain and bought luxury hotels then, while remaining in the business of managing hotels, the group would be changing the nature and focus of its operations. A similar situation would arise if the same company were to sell its hotels in (say) the United States of America and buy hotels in Europe.

The regular sales and replacements of material assets which are undertaken by a company as part of the routine maintenance of its portfolio of assets should not be classified as discontinuances and acquisitions. In the example the sale of hotels and the purchase of others within the same market sector and similar locations would be treated as wholly within continuing operations.

1.8   Disposal of fixed assets

The profit or loss on the disposal of an asset should be calculated as the difference between the net sales proceeds and the net carrying amount of the asset in the books. This is also stated in FRS 15 *Tangible fixed assets*.

1.9   Prior period items

 Prior period adjustments are those material adjustments applicable to prior periods arising from changes in accounting policies or from the correction of fundamental errors.   They do not include normal recurring adjustments or corrections of accounting estimates made in prior periods.

The majority of items relating to prior years arise mainly from the corrections and adjustments which are the natural result of estimates inherent in accounting and more particularly in the periodic preparation of financial statements. They are therefore dealt with in the profit and loss account of the year in which they are identified and their effect stated where material.

Prior period adjustments, that is prior period items which should be adjusted against the opening balance of retained profits or reserves, are rare and limited to items arising from changes in accounting policies and from the correction of fundamental errors.

1.10   Changes in accounting policies

It is a fundamental accounting concept that there should be consistency of accounting treatment within each accounting period and from one period to the next. A change in accounting policy may therefore be made only if it can be justified on the grounds that the new policy is preferable to the one it replaces because it will give a fairer presentation of the results and of the financial position of the business.

Following a change in accounting policy, the amounts for the current and corresponding periods are restated on the basis of the new policies. The cumulative adjustments applicable to prior years have no bearing on the results of the current year and they are therefore not included in arriving at the profit or loss for the current year. They are accounted for by restating prior years with the result that the opening balance of retained profits will be adjusted accordingly.

1.11   Corrections of fundamental errors

In exceptional circumstances financial statements may have been issued containing errors which are of such significance as to destroy the true and fair view and hence the validity of those financial statements and which would have led to their withdrawal had the errors been recognised at the time. The corrections of such fundamental errors are accounted for not by inclusion in the profit and loss account of the current year but by restating the prior year(s) with the result that the opening balance of retained profits will be adjusted accordingly.

Conclusion Prior period adjustments are only made for changes of accounting policy and correction of fundamental errors. The adjustment is made by restating the opening balance on retained reserves.

1.12 Profit and loss account presentation

FRS 3 contains two illustrative examples of the correct profit and loss account presentation and these are shown below:

Example 1

	19X3 £m	19X3 £m	19X2 £m
Turnover			
Continuing operations	550		500
Acquisitions	50		
	600		
Discontinued operations	175		190
		775	690
Cost of sales		(620)	(555)
Gross profit		155	135
Administrative expenses		(104)	(83)
Operating profit			
Continuing operations	50		40
Acquisitions	6		
	56		
Discontinued operations	(5)		12
		51	52
Profit on sale of properties in continuing operations		19	6
Loss on disposal of discontinued operations		(7)	(30)
Profit on ordinary activities before interest		63	28
Interest payable		(18)	(15)
Profit on ordinary activities before taxation		45	13
Tax on profit on ordinary activities		(16)	(6)
Profit for the financial year		29	7
Dividends		(8)	(1)
Retained profit for the financial year		21	6

Example 2

	Continuing operations 19X3 £m	Acquisitions 19X3 £m	Discontinued operations 19X3 £m	Total 19X3 £m	Total 19X2 as restated £m
Turnover	550	50	175	775	690
Cost of sales	(415)	(40)	(165)	(620)	(555)
Gross profit	135	10	10	155	135

Net operating expenses	(85)	(4)	(25)	(114)	(83)
Less: 19X2 provision			10	10	
Operating profit	50	6	(5)	51	52
Profit on sale of properties	9			9	6
Provision for loss on operations to be discontinued					(30)
Loss on disposal of discontinued operations			(17)	(17)	
Less: 19X2 provision			20	20	
Profit on ordinary activities before interest	59	6	(2)	63	28
Interest payable				(18)	(15)
Profit on ordinary activities before taxation				45	13
Tax on profit on ordinary activities				(14)	(4)
Profit on ordinary activities after taxation				31	9
Minority interests				(2)	(2)
Extraordinary items (included only to show positioning)				-	-
Profit for the financial year				29	7
Dividends				(8)	(1)
Retained profit for the financial year				21	6

The analysis between continuing operations, acquisitions (as a component of continuing operations) and discontinued operations should be disclosed to the level of operating profit. The analysis of turnover and operating profit is the **minimum** disclosure required in this respect on the **face** of the profit and loss account.

1.13   Statement of total recognised gains and losses

FRS 3 introduced a new primary statement, the statement of total recognised gains and losses.

 The statement of total recognised gains and losses brings together all the gains and losses for the period, including items which do not pass through the profit and loss account.

The most common example of an item which does not pass through the profit and loss account is a gain on the revaluation of a fixed asset. Revaluation gains cannot be taken to the profit and loss account because they are unrealised, but nevertheless, they may form an important part of a company's overall performance. Before the introduction of FRS 3, revaluation gains and losses were required to be disclosed as a movement on reserves and within the tangible fixed asset note. However, it was often difficult for users of the financial statements to appreciate their impact upon the company's overall financial performance. The statement of total recognised gains and losses highlights the effect of revaluations and other items such as prior period adjustments.

A pro-forma statement is shown below.

Statement of total recognised gains and losses

	19X3	19X2 as restated
	£m	£m
Profit for the financial year	29	7
Unrealised surplus on revaluation of properties	4	6
Unrealised (loss)/gain on trade investments	(3)	7
Total recognised gains and losses relating to the year	30	20
Prior year adjustment (as explained in Note X)	10	
Total gains and losses recognised since last annual report	20	

The statement should appear directly after the profit and loss account. If there are no recognised gains or losses other than the profit or loss for the year a statement to this effect should appear immediately below the profit and loss account.

1.14 Note of historical cost profits and losses

Where assets are stated at a valuation, rather than on a historical cost basis, FRS 3 requires the presentation of a note of historical cost profits and losses.

Definition The note of historical cost profits and losses reconciles reported profit on ordinary activities before taxation with the equivalent historical cost amount. It also states the historical cost profit for the year after taxation and dividends.

Some companies carry fixed assets at historical cost while others include them at a valuation. Valuation is subjective and companies may use different bases and revalue at different intervals. The note of historical cost profits and losses is designed to enable users of the financial statements to make fair comparisons between the results of different entities.

An example of the note is shown below:

Note of historical cost profits and losses

	19X3	19X2
	£m	£m
Reported profit on ordinary activities before taxation	45	13
Realisation of property revaluation gains of previous years	9	10
Difference between a historical cost depreciation charge and the actual depreciation charge of the year calculated on the revalued amount	5	4
Historical cost profit on ordinary activities before taxation	59	27
Historical cost profit for the year retained after taxation, extraordinary items and dividends	35	20

The note should appear immediately after the profit and loss account or statement of total recognised gains and losses.

1.15   Reconciliation of movements in shareholders' funds

FRS 3 requires financial statements to include a note reconciling the opening and closing shareholders' funds (share capital and reserves). This can be presented either as a primary statement or as a note to the accounts.

The profit and loss account and the statement of total recognised gains and losses together reflect the performance of an entity in a period. However, there may be other items which affect shareholders' funds, such as issues of share capital or the payment of dividends. The reconciliation highlights these items and brings them together into one statement.

An example of the note required is given below:

Reconciliation of movements in shareholders' funds

	19X3 £m	19X2 £m
Profit for the financial year	29	7
Dividends	(8)	(1)
	21	6
Other recognised gains and losses relating to the year	1	13
New share capital subscribed	20	1
Net addition to shareholders' funds	42	20
Opening shareholders' funds (originally £375m before deducting prior year adjustment of £10m)	365	345
Closing shareholders' funds	407	365

1.16   Example

Strathdon Ltd had the following share capital and reserves at 1 January 19X3:

	£'000
Share capital (£1 ordinary shares)	100
Share premium	50
Revaluation reserve	225
Profit and loss account	200
	575

During the year ended 31 December 19X3, the company issued a further 50,000 £1 ordinary shares at a market price of £1.60.

On 31 December 19X3 it disposed of a property for £450,000. The property had originally cost £300,000 and was revalued to £500,000 on 1 January 19X1, when it was four years old and its net book value was £250,000. From that date depreciation was charged on a straight line basis over its estimated remaining useful economic life of 20 years.

On 31 December 19X3 another property was revalued at £400,000 and this valuation was incorporated into the financial statements. This property had previously been stated at historic cost of £250,000 less accumulated depreciation of £50,000.

All other fixed assets were included in the financial statements at historic cost less accumulated depreciation.

An extract from the profit and loss account of Strathdon Ltd for the year ended 31 December 19X3 is shown below:

	£'000
Profit on ordinary activities before taxation	100
Tax on profit on ordinary activities	(40)
Profit on ordinary activities after taxation	60
Dividends	(10)
Retained profit for the financial year	50

You are required to prepare:

(a)   the statement of total recognised gains and losses;
(b)   the note of historical cost profits and losses;
(c)   the reconciliation of movements in shareholders' funds; and
(d)   the reserves note

for the year ended 31 December 19X3.

1.17   Solution

(a)   **Statement of total recognised gains and losses for the year ended 31 December 19X3**

	£'000
Profit for the financial year (Note 1)	60
Unrealised surplus on revaluation of properties (Note 2) (400 – 200)	200
Total recognised gains and losses relating to the year	260

(b)   **Note of historical cost profits and losses**

	£'000
Reported profit on ordinary activities before taxation	100.0
Realisation of property revaluation gains of previous years (Note 3) (W1)	212.5
Difference between a historical cost depreciation charge and the actual depreciation charge of the year calculated on the revalued amount (W2)	12.5
Historical cost profit on ordinary activities before taxation	325.0
Historical cost profit for the year retained after taxation and dividends (50 + 212.5 + 12.5)	275.0

(c)   **Reconciliation of movements in shareholders' funds**

	£'000
Profit for the financial year (Note 1)	60
Dividends	(10)
	50

Other recognised gains and losses relating to the year (revaluation)			200
New share capital subscribed (50,000 × £1.60)			80
Net addition to shareholders' funds			330
Opening shareholders' funds			575
Closing shareholders' funds			905

(d)   **Reserves**

	Share premium account	Revaluation reserve	Profit and loss account	Total
	£'000	£'000	£'000	£'000
At the beginning of the year	50	225	200	475
Premium on issue of shares (50,000 × 60p)	30			30
Transfer from profit and loss account of the year			50	50
Transfer of realised profit (Notes 3 and 4)		(225)	225	
Surplus on property revaluation (Note 2)		200		200
At end of year	80	200	475	755

Notes

1   Both the statement of total recognised gains and losses and the reconciliation of movements in shareholders' funds start with profit **before** dividends. This is the amount which is available for distribution to shareholders. Dividends are an appropriation of profit, rather than an expense.

2   The surplus on revaluation appears in the statement of total recognised gains and losses for the accounting period in which the revaluation takes place. Because it is unrealised, it does not pass through the profit and loss account, but the gain is recognised in the financial statements and taken to the revaluation reserve.

3   Where a fixed asset has been revalued, FRS 3 requires the profit or loss on disposal of a fixed asset to be calculated as the difference between the sales proceeds and the net book value based on the revalued amount. The disposal realises the surplus that was recognised at the time the revaluation took place. This accounting treatment is confirmed by FRS 15 *Tangible fixed assets*.

4   The disposal of the revalued property causes the unrealised revaluation surplus to become realised. The surplus is transferred from the revaluation reserve to the profit and loss account reserve; only amounts relating to assets that the company still holds should remain in the revaluation reserve.

At its simplest level, this transfer would be equal to the original surplus on revaluation, in this case, £250,000. The actual amount transferred is £225,000, which is made up of the two reconciling items in the note of historical cost profits and losses. These are the difference between the profit based on the revalued amount and the profit based on the original cost (W1) and the difference between the annual depreciation charge based on the revalued amount and that based on the historic cost (W2). (The disposal took place on the final day of the accounting period). In previous accounting periods, the company has made an annual transfer of £12,500 from revaluation reserve to profit and loss account reserve. This is the figure which would have been disclosed in the note of historical cost profits and losses for 19X1 and 19X2 and represents the additional depreciation charged on the revalued amount.

Where assets are carried at a valuation, FRS 15 states that depreciation must be based on the revalued amount and that the whole charge must pass through the profit and loss account. It is not acceptable to split the charge between the reserves so that only depreciation charged on historic cost passes directly through the profit and loss account while the additional depreciation on the revalued amount is set against the revaluation reserve. However, it has become normal practice to make an annual reserve transfer equal to the difference between depreciation on the revalued amount and depreciation on the original cost. The illustrative examples included in FRS 3 adopt this treatment, thereby legitimising it.

WORKINGS

(W1) Realisation of property revaluation gains

Profit on disposal (included in profit on ordinary activities before taxation):

	£'000	£'000
Sale proceeds		450
Valuation at 1 January 19X1	500	
Less: Accumulated depreciation (500/20 × 3)	(75)	
		425
		25

Profit on disposal (based on historic cost):

	£'000	£'000
Sale proceeds		450.0
Cost	300.0	
Less: Accumulated depreciation to 31 December 19X0		
(300/24 × 4)	(50.0)	
Accumulated depreciation from 1 January 19X1		
(300/24 × 3)	(37.5)	
		212.5
		237.5

Difference between historical cost profit and profit based on the revalued amount (realised gain) (237.5 – 25)	212.5

(W2) Difference between historical cost depreciation and depreciation based on the revalued amount

	£'000
Annual depreciation based on revalued amount (500/20)	25.0
Annual depreciation based on historic cost (300/24)	12.5
Difference	12.5

(W3)   Revaluation reserve

	£'000	£'000
Revalued amount		500
Historic cost	300	
Less: Accumulated depreciation	(50)	
		(250)
Unrealised surplus at 1 January 19X1		250
Less: Additional depreciation (3 × 12.5)		(37.5)
		212.5

1.18   Activity

The following figures have been calculated for Phibbs plc for the year ended 31 December 19X9, together with comparatives for the previous year.

	19X9	19X8
	£m	£m
Profit before tax	50	35
Tax	(12)	(7)
Profit for the financial year	38	28
Dividends	(18)	(15)
Retained profit	20	13
Unrealised surplus on revaluation of property	2	1
Opening shareholders' funds	222	204
Share capital issued during the year		
Par value	10	3
Premium	2	1
Additional depreciation charged on property revaluations (ie, over and above what would have been charged on their historical cost)	3	2

You are required to draft the following statements for Phibbs plc for inclusion in the 19X9 accounts:

(a)   statement of total recognised gains and losses;
(b)   reconciliation of movements in shareholders' funds;
(c)   note of historical cost profits and losses.

1.19 Activity solution

(a)

Phibbs plc
Statement of total recognised gains and losses
for the year ended 31 December 19X9

	19X9 £m	19X8 £m
Profit for the financial year	38	28
Unrealised surplus on revaluation of property	2	1
Total recognised gains and losses relating to the year	40	29

(b)

Reconciliation of movements in shareholders' funds
for the year ended 31 December 19X9

	19X9 £m	19X8 £m
Profit for the financial year	38	28
Dividends	(18)	(15)
	20	13
Other recognised gains and losses relating to the year (net)	2	1
New share capital subscribed	12	4
Net addition to shareholders' funds	34	18
Opening shareholders' funds	222	204
Closing shareholders' funds	256	222

(c)

Note of historical cost profits and losses
for the year ended 31 December 19X9

	19X9 £m	19X8 £m
Reported profit before taxation	50	35
Difference between a historical cost depreciation charge and the actual depreciation charge for the year calculated on the revalued amount	3	2
	53	37
Historical cost profit for the year retained after taxation and dividends	23	15

Conclusion FRS 3 introduces what it calls a layered format for the profit and loss account, highlighting separately:

(a) results of continuing operations (including the results of acquisitions);

(b)   results of discontinued operations;

(c)   profits or losses on the sale or termination of an operation, costs of a fundamental reorganisation or restructuring, and profits or losses on the disposal of fixed assets;

(d)   extraordinary items.

It also requires the presentation of a statement of total recognised gains and losses, a note of historical cost profits and losses and the reconciliation of movements in shareholders' funds. The ASB hopes that by requiring this new layered format and by discouraging companies from using extraordinary items users of accounts will better be able to assess the performance achieved by a company during an accounting period.

2   SSAP 25 – SEGMENTAL REPORTING

2.1   Introduction

Many enterprises carry on several classes of business or operate in several geographical areas, with different rates of profitability, different opportunities for growth and different degrees of risk. It is usually not possible for the reader of the financial statements of such enterprises to make judgements about the nature of different activities carried on by the enterprise or of their contribution to the overall financial results of the enterprise unless some segmental analysis of the financial statements is given. The purpose of segmental information is, therefore, to provide information to assist the readers of financial statements:

(a)   to appreciate more thoroughly the results and financial position of the enterprise by permitting a better understanding of the enterprise's past performance and thus a better assessment of its future prospects; and

(b)   to be aware of the impact that changes in significant components of a business may have on the business as a whole.

2.2   Determining reportable segments

The directors identify the **reportable segments** having regard to differences in:

(a)   return on capital employed;
(b)   risk;
(c)   rate of growth;
(d)   potential for future development for both classes of business and geographical areas.

All **significant** segments should be identified as reportable segments.

Definition   A segment is significant if:

(a)   third party turnover is 10% or more of the total third party turnover;

(b)   its segment result is 10% or more of the combined result of all segments in profit, or in loss (whichever is greater ie, do not net off profits and losses to a net profit figure of say £20,000 and use £2,000 as a significance test when total profits might be £5.02m and losses total £5.00m);

(c)   its net assets are 10% or more of the total net assets.

The directors should review the identified segments annually and redefine them when appropriate.

2.3   Classes of business

Definition   A **class of business** is defined as a distinguishable component of an entity that provides a separate product or service or a separate group of related products or services.

To identify reportable classes of business, directors should consider the following factors:

(a)   nature of products or services;

(b)   nature of production processes;

(c)   markets in which products or services are sold;

(d)   the distribution channels for the products (eg, are the items sold by retail or mail order?);

(e)   the manner in which the entity's activities are organised;

(f)   any separate legislative framework relating to part of the business (eg, a bank or insurance company).

2.4   Geographical segments

Definition   A **geographical segment** is a geographical area comprising an individual country or group of countries in which an entity operates or to which it supplies products or services.

The analysis should help the users to assess the extent to which the operations are subject to factors such as:

(a)   expansionist or restrictive economic climates;
(b)   stable or unstable political regimes;
(c)   exchange control regulations;
(d)   exchange rate fluctuations.

2.5   Standard disclosures

If an entity has two or more classes of business or operates in two or more geographical segments it should:

- define its classes of business and geographical segments in its financial statements; and

- for each class of business and geographical segment, disclose;

  (i)   turnover, distinguishing;

    - turnover derived from external customers; and
    - turnover derived from other segments;

  (ii)   result before tax, minority interests and extraordinary items;

  (iii)   net assets.

- The geographical segmentation of turnover should be done by origin and also by destination where the latter is different.

Definition   **origin** of turnover – the geographical segment from which products or services are supplied;

Definition   **destination** of turnover – the geographical segment to which products or services are supplied.

2.6   Reconciliation

The total of the amounts disclosed by segment should agree with the total in the financial statements. If it does not, the reporting entity should provide a reconciliation between the two figures. Reconciling items should be properly identified and explained.

2.7   Scope

The standard applies to any entity that:

(a)   is a plc or has a plc subsidiary; or
(b)   is a banking or insurance company; or
(c)   exceeds the criteria multiplied by 10 for defining a medium-sized company.

All other entities are encouraged to apply the provisions of the accounting standard.

2.8   Pro forma

An appendix to SSAP 25 provides an illustrative example for guidance only. Part of this is shown below:

	Classes of business							
	Industry A		*Industry B*		*Other*		*Group*	
	19X1	*19X0*	*19X1*	*19X0*	*19X1*	*19X0*	*19X1*	*19X0*
	£'000	*£'000*	*£'000*	*£'000*	*£'000*	*£'000*	*£'000*	*£'000*
Turnover								
Total sales	33,000	30,000	42,000	38,000	26,000	23,000	101,000	91,000
Inter-segment sales	(4,000)	-	-	-	(12,000)	(14,000)	(16,000)	(14,000)
Sales to third parties	29,000	30,000	42,000	38,000	14,000	9,000	85,000	77,000
Profit before taxation								
Segment profit	3,000	2,500	4,500	4,000	1,800	1,500	9,300	8,000
Common costs							300	300
Operating profit							9,000	7,700
Net interest							(400)	(500)
							8,600	7,200
Group share of the profits before taxation of associated undertakings	1,000	1,000	1,400	1,200	-	-	2,400	2,200
Group profit before taxation							11,000	9,400
Net assets								
Segment net assets	17,600	15,000	24,000	25,000	19,400	19,000	61,000	59,000
Unallocated assets							3,000	3,000
							64,000	62,000
Group share of the net assets of associated undertakings	10,200	8,000	8,800	9,000	-	-	19,000	17,000
Total net assets							83,000	79,000

Common costs refer to costs where allocation between segments could mislead. Likewise, the segmental disclosure of net assets might include unallocated assets.

The geographical analysis would contain two analyses of turnover (by origin and destination)

Geographical segments	United Kingdom		North America		Far East		Other		Group	
	19X1	*19X0*	*19X1*	*19X0*	*19X1*	*19X0*	*19X1*	*19X0*	*19X1*	*19X0*
	£'000	£'000	£'000	£'000	£'000	£'000	£'000	£'000	£'000	£'000
Turnover										
Turnover by destination										
Sales to third parties	34,000	31,000	16,000	14,500	25,000	23,000	10,000	8,500	85,000	77,000
Turnover by origin										
Total sales	38,000	34,000	29,000	27,500	23,000	23,000	12,000	10,500	102,000	95,000
Inter-segment sales	-	-	(8,000)	(9,000)	(9,000)	(9,000)	-	-	(17,000)	(18,000)
Sales to third parties	38,000	34,000	21,000	18,500	14,000	14,000	12,000	10,500	85,000	77,000

Conclusion Large companies must provide an analysis of their results both by classes of business and by geographical segments.

3 FRS 14 - EARNINGS PER SHARE

3.1 Introduction

Earnings per share (EPS) is a widely used measure of a company's performance, particularly over a number of years, and is a component of the very important Stock Exchange yardstick – the price/earnings (P/E) ratio.

FRS 14 *Earnings per share* was issued in October 1998 and supersedes the previous SSAP on EPS, SSAP 3. The objective of the FRS is to ensure comparability of the performance of entities. This is both in the same entity over time and between different entities. It does this by prescribing methods for determining the number of shares to be included in the calculation and by specifying the presentation of the results.

Definition

$$EPS = \frac{\text{Net profit or loss for the period attributable to ordinary shareholders}}{\text{Weighted average number of ordinary shares outstanding during the period}}$$

Definition Net profit or loss for the period is the profit or loss after deducting dividends and other appropriations in respect of non-equity shares.

3.2 Activity

From the information below calculate the earnings per share figure for 19X7.

	19X7
Ordinary profit attributable to the ordinary shareholders for the year ending 31 Dec.	£460,000
Number of ordinary shares in issue during the year	800,000

3.3   Activity solution

Calculation of earnings per share

$$19X7 \quad EPS = \frac{£460,000}{800,000} = 57.5p$$

3.4   Presentation of EPS

The earnings per share figure for the year (and the comparative for the previous year) should be shown on the face of the profit and loss account, at the bottom of the profit and loss account. A note to the accounts should disclose the earnings figure and number of shares used in the calculation.

| Conclusion | The earnings per share figure is an important financial indicator for a company and as such is disclosed on the face of the profit and loss account. |

4   SELF TEST QUESTIONS

1   What are the ordinary activities of a business according to FRS 3? (1.2)

2   What is the FRS 3 definition of an exceptional item? (1.3)

3   What are the three exceptional items that must be shown on the face of the profit and loss account? (1.5)

4   What is the FRS 3 definition of discontinued operations? (1.7)

5   How is the profit or loss on the disposal of a fixed asset to be determined? (1.8)

6   What are the two valid reasons for a prior period adjustment? (1.9)

7   What does the statement of total recognised gains and losses show? (1.13)

8   What is the aim of the FRS 3 note of historical cost profits and losses? (1.14)

9   How would the different classes of business of a company be determined for SSAP 25 purposes? (2.3)

10   What items should be disclosed for each segment of a business under SSAP 25? (2.5)

16 MISCELLANEOUS STANDARDS

PATHFINDER INTRODUCTION

This chapter covers the following performance criteria and knowledge and understanding.

- Draft accounts comply with domestic standards and legislation (performance criteria 10.2)
- Main requirements of relevant SSAPs, FRSs and other relevant pronouncements and their application to this element (knowledge and understanding 10.2)

Putting the chapter in context – learning objectives.

There are three remaining accounting standards that have not been covered elsewhere in the study text which will now be briefly considered in this chapter. Firstly FRS 4, issued by the ASB in December 1993, which deals with accounting for capital instruments, therefore loan and share capital. Secondly SSAP 24 on pension costs and finally SSAP 20 on foreign currency translation. In all three cases the accounting standards are dealing with fairly complex situations and for the purposes of this syllabus only a brief overview of the problems and requirements is necessary.

At the end of this chapter you should have learned the following topics.

- FRS 4 Capital instruments.
- SSAP 24 Accounting for pension costs.
- SSAP 20 Foreign currency translation.

1 FRS 4: CAPITAL INSTRUMENTS

1.1 Introduction

Definition Capital instruments are all instruments that are issued by reporting entities as a means of raising finance, including shares, debentures, loans and debt instruments, options and warrants that give the holder the right to subscribe for or obtain capital instruments.

Capital instruments will therefore include bank loans, corporate debentures, convertible debt, ordinary shares and preference shares.

1.2 Purpose of FRS 4

The ASB had two main aims in mind when issuing FRS 4:

- to ensure that all capital instruments were correctly categorised on the balance sheet as either debt or shareholders' funds;

- to ensure that the full cost of all capital instruments was charged to the profit and loss account over the life of the capital instrument.

For the purposes of this syllabus only a brief overview of the requirements of the FRS is necessary.

1.3   Balance sheet presentation

All capital instruments are to be shown on the balance sheet either as liabilities or as part of shareholders' funds. For most capital instruments it will be quite clear whether they are debt instruments or part of shareholders' funds. However for some, such as convertible debt, it may not be quite so clear.

FRS 4 states that if any capital instrument is a liability then it must be shown as such on the balance sheet.

Definition   A liability is where there is an obligation to transfer economic benefits.

1.4   Convertible debentures

Convertible debentures are currently debt, loan creditors of the company, but they may be converted into ordinary shares at some stage in the future.

Therefore convertible debentures, because they carry an obligation to transfer economic benefits, must be shown as liabilities on the face of the balance sheet. However as convertible debentures are slightly different in nature from other forms of debentures they will be shown as a separate category of debt.

1.5   Shareholders' funds

Any capital instruments that are not classified as liabilities must be shown as part of shareholders' funds. These will normally consist of ordinary shares and preference shares.

Shareholders' funds are now to be split, according to FRS 4, into equity and non-equity.

Definition   If shares contain any debt type characteristics then they should be classified as non-equity shares. All other shares should be classified as equity shares.

Debt type characteristics will include terms such as a fixed rate of dividend or limited rights upon the liquidation of a company.

1.6   Ordinary shares and preference shares

Preference shares will normally have debt type characteristics. For example 5% £1 preference shares have a fixed dividend of 5 pence per share each year. Therefore preference shares will be classified on the balance sheet as non-equity within the heading of shareholders' funds.

Ordinary shares will be classified as equity on the face of the balance sheet as they will generally contain no debt type characteristics.

Conclusion   Within the balance sheet heading of shareholders' funds preference shares will be classified as non-equity and ordinary shares and reserves will be classified as equity.

1.7   Cost of capital instruments

The second concern of the ASB was that the full cost each year or finance charge for the capital instrument should be charged to the profit and loss account. Due to the complexity of the types of capital instruments that have been issued in recent years it has been possible for companies to delay charging the cost of capital instruments or even to avoid charging the cost to the profit and loss account altogether. However FRS 4 details the methods by which the full finance charge for all capital instruments must be charged to the profit and loss account in order to give a constant charge each year based on the outstanding amount. These calculations are beyond the scope of this syllabus.

[Conclusion] FRS 4 is a standard that deals largely with fairly complex types of capital instrument. However its basic principles apply to all capital instruments, ie, to all instruments issued by a company in order to raise finance. If a capital instrument can be classified as a liability due to the obligation to transfer economic benefits then it must be shown as a liability on the face of the balance sheet. This includes convertible debentures although they are now shown as a separate classification within liabilities.

Within the balance sheet heading of shareholders' funds ordinary shares and reserves are classified as equity whilst preference shares are classified as non-equity.

2   SSAP 24: ACCOUNTING FOR PENSION COSTS

2.1   Introduction

The provision of a pension is part of the remuneration package of many employees. Pension costs form a significant proportion of total payroll costs and they give rise to special problems of estimation and of allocation between accounting periods. For this syllabus only a very brief overview of the problem and accounting solutions is required.

2.2   Types of pension schemes

Pension schemes may be divided into **defined contribution** schemes and **defined benefit** schemes.

[Definition] In a defined contribution scheme the employer will normally discharge his obligation by making agreed contributions to a pension scheme and the benefits paid will depend upon the funds available from these contributions and investment earnings thereon.

The cost to the employer can, therefore, be measured with reasonable certainty as to the amount of contribution. A number of pension schemes in the United Kingdom and Ireland, including many smaller ones, are defined contribution schemes.

[Definition] A defined benefit scheme is one in which the final pension is determined now and the employer must make appropriate contributions in order to meet those future benefits.

In a defined benefit scheme, the benefits to be paid will usually depend upon either the average pay of the employee during his or her career, or more typically, the final pay of the employee. In these circumstances, it is impossible to be certain in advance that the contributions to the pension scheme, together with the investment return thereon, will equal the benefits to be paid.

The employer may have a legal obligation to provide any unforeseen shortfalls in funds or, if not, may find it necessary to meet the shortfall in the interests of maintaining good employee relations.

Conversely, if a surplus arises the employer may be entitled to a refund of, or reduction in, contributions paid into the pension scheme.

Thus, in this type of scheme the employer's commitment is generally more open than with defined contribution schemes and the final cost is subject to considerable uncertainty. The larger UK schemes are generally of the defined benefit kind and these cover the great majority of members of schemes.

2.3 **Actuarial considerations**

In view of the very long-term nature of the pensions commitment it is necessary to make use of actuarial calculations in determining the pension cost charge in respect of defined benefit schemes. In the case of defined contribution schemes there is no need for actuarial advice in order to establish the pension cost although such advice may be required for other purposes in connection with the operation of the scheme.

In defined benefit schemes the choice of assumptions and the choice of valuation method can each have a major effect on the contribution rate calculated at each valuation. The choice of assumptions can be as significant as the choice of method.

The assumptions which the actuary must make in carrying out his valuation will be about matters such as future rates of inflation and pay increases, increases to pensions in payment, earnings on investments, the number of employees joining the scheme, the age profile of employees and the probability that employees will die or leave the company's employment before they reach retiring age. The actuary will view the assumptions as a whole; he will make assumptions which are mutually compatible, in the knowledge that, if experience departs from the assumptions made, the effects of such departures may well be offsetting, notably in the case of investment yields and increases in prices and earnings.

2.4 **The accounting objective and how it is achieved**

The accounting objective of *SSAP 24* is that the employer should recognise the expected cost of providing pensions on a systematic and rational basis over the period during which he derives benefit from the employee's services.

For defined contribution schemes this objective is achieved by charging against profits the amount of contributions payable to the pension scheme in respect of the accounting period.

For defined benefit schemes this objective is achieved by the actuary calculating a 'regular' pension cost which is a substantially level percentage of the current and expected future pensionable payroll (on the basis of the current actuarial assumptions).

2.5 **Surpluses and deficits in defined benefit schemes**

As a result of actual events not coinciding with actuarial assumptions, 'experience' surpluses and deficits will inevitably arise in defined benefit schemes between actuarial valuations (which are normally carried out every three years).

The standard requires that these surpluses and deficits are normally eliminated over the expected remaining service lives of current employees in the pension scheme, using the matching concept. The pension cost charge in the profit and loss account is then said to comprise a regular cost and a variation from regular cost.

Conclusion | The annual cost to a company of a defined contribution pension scheme will normally be determined simply as the annual contribution made by the employer.

The annual cost of a defined benefit pension scheme is more complex to determine and will normally require an actuarial valuation. The eventual cost to the company each year that is determined by the actuary will be made up of the regular cost and any variations from regular cost. The regular cost is usually a percentage of the payroll total whilst variations are made up of any surplus or deficiency which is then normally spread over the average remaining service lives of the employees.

3   SSAP 20: FOREIGN CURRENCY TRANSLATION

3.1   Foreign currency conversion

> **Definition**   Foreign currency conversion is the process of physically exchanging one currency for another currency.

An individual converts currency when he buys, say, Spanish pesetas for sterling at the start of a holiday. If he has any money left at the end of the holiday, he reconverts the pesetas to sterling. If the exchange rate has changed in the meantime he will make a gain or loss on the transaction less the costs of commission and the buy/sell price spread.

A business will also convert currencies when it has to pay for an item which it has purchased which is denominated in another currency. For example a UK business may purchase goods from a French supplier and agree to pay a certain number of francs. When it comes to pay for the goods, it is likely to have to convert sterling into francs to pay for the goods.

3.2   Foreign currency translation

From a business viewpoint however, the need to **translate** items denominated in a foreign currency is more important.

> **Definition**   Foreign currency translation is the statement of an item denominated in a foreign currency in terms of the domestic reporting currency.

SSAP 20 identifies two sets of circumstances in which a business must consider how to deal with foreign currency amounts within its accounts

(a)   direct business transactions
(b)   operations conducted through a foreign entity.

3.3   Direct business transactions

Whenever a UK business enters into a contract where the consideration is expressed in a foreign currency, it will be necessary to translate that foreign currency amount at some stage into sterling for inclusion into its own accounts. Examples include

(i)   imports of raw materials (purchases)
(ii)   exports of finished goods (sales)
(iii)   importation of foreign-manufactured fixed assets (purchases of fixed assets)
(iv)   raising an overseas loan (loan finance).

Translation may be necessary at more than one time. For example, the import of raw materials creates a foreign currency liability when the goods are supplied and for which a sterling value must be incorporated in the books. Where settlement is delayed due to normal credit terms, the actual sterling cost of settlement may differ from the liability initially recorded.

Similarly, the sterling value of a long-term loan is likely to fluctuate from one period to another.

3.4   Exchange rates

The reason for the value of these foreign currency items possibly fluctuating over time is that the exchange rates between various currencies will alter over time.

> **Definition**   An exchange rate is a rate at which two currencies may be exchanged for each other at a particular point in time.

3.5   Operations conducted through a foreign entity

Companies frequently establish local subsidiaries in foreign countries through which to conduct their operations.   These subsidiaries will maintain full accounts in the local currency and these accounts must clearly be translated into the currency of the parent before they can be consolidated.

> **Conclusion**   Foreign currency translation will become necessary where a company buys/sells items of foreign currency or when a company invests in an overseas subsidiary company.

3.6   Methods of translation

There are two exchange rates which can generally be used to translate any foreign currency balance. These are

(a)   **The historic rate**

This is simply the exchange rate which applied at the date of the transaction.

(b)   **The closing rate**

This is the rate of exchange ruling at the balance sheet date.

Thus a fixed asset might have been acquired for Fr 100,000.   At that date the exchange rate was Fr 12 = £1 and now the exchange rate has moved to Fr 10 = £1.   The asset could either be shown at

(a)   Historic rate – £8,333 or
(b)   Closing rate – £10,000

It should be clear that selection of an appropriate translation rate will have a significant impact on balance sheet values and on reported profits.   Where the historic rate is employed, the value of the asset is unchanging.   However, if the closing rate is applied, the book value is increased by £1,667 and this exchange difference must be reflected either in reported profits or as a movement in reserves.

> **Definition**   An exchange difference will appear if an item is originally translated at one rate in the financial statements and then retranslated at a different rate.

For this syllabus only an appreciation of the need for foreign currency translation is required rather than an understanding of detailed requirements of SSAP 20.   Therefore the section is completed with a brief illustration of the problem.

3.7   Sales and debtors

Where goods are sold to overseas customers and payment is to be received in a currency other than the functional currency, the following transactions may need to be recorded

- the sale – at the rate of exchange applicable at the time of sale;
- the debtor - at the rate of exchange at the balance sheet date;
- the receipt of cash – the actual proceeds.

Any exchange differences will be reported as part of the profit for the period from normal operations.

3.8   Activity

On 7 May 19X6 a UK company sells goods to a German company for DM 48,000 when the rate of exchange was £1 = DM 3.2.

By 30 June, the UK company's year end, the exchange rate has gone up to £1 = DM 3.3.

On 20 July 19X6 the customer remits a draft for DM 48,000 which realises £15,150 when the DM are converted with a bank.

Prepare the journal entries for this transaction and write up the debtor account.

3.9   Activity solution

7 May 19X6 - original sale

		£	£
Dr	Debtors (DM 48,000 @ 3.2)	15,000	
	Cr Sales		15,000

30 June 19X6 - year end - retranslate closing debtor

DM 48,000 @ 3.3 = £14,545

		£	£
Dr	Profit and loss account (exchange difference 15,000 − 14,545)	455	
	Cr Debtor		455

20 July 19X6 - eventual receipt

		£	£
Dr	Bank	15,150	
	Cr Debtor		14,545
	Cr Profit and loss account (exchange difference)		605

Debtor's account

19X6		*DM*	£	19X6		*DM*	£
May 7	Sales a/c	48,000	15,000	Jun 30	Balance c/d (@ 3.3)	48,000	14,545
				June 30	P&L a/c (exchange difference - gain)		455
		48,000	15,000			48,000	15,000
Jul 1	Balance b/d	48,000	14,545	Jul 20	Bank a/c (proceeds)	48,000	15,150
Jul 20	P&L a/c (exchange difference - gain)		605				
		48,000	15,150			48,000	15,150

| Conclusion | If a company buys/sells goods abroad in a foreign currency it will need to translate the original currency amount into sterling. At the year end any debtor/creditor in the balance sheet must also be retranslated to reflect the closing rate of exchange. |

Finally when settlement is eventually made this may be at yet a further exchange rate. Each retranslation will lead to an exchange difference.

4   SELF TEST QUESTIONS

1   What is a capital instrument? (1.1)

2   What were the two main aims of the ASB on issuing FRS 4? (1.2)

3   What is the ASB's definition of a liability? (1.3)

4   What are the two categories of shareholders' funds to be shown on the balance sheet? (1.5)

5   How will preference shares normally be categorised on the balance sheet? (1.6)

6   Why is accounting for pension costs important for a company? (2.1)

7   What is SSAP 24's aim in accounting for pension costs? (2.4)

8   What are the two elements that may make up the annual pension cost for a defined benefit scheme in the profit and loss account? (2.5)

9   Distinguish between currency conversion and currency translation. (3.1/3.2)

10   What are the two circumstances when a company may be required to account for currency translation? (3.2)

17 CASH FLOW STATEMENTS

PATHFINDER INTRODUCTION

This chapter covers the following performance criteria and knowledge and understanding.

- A cash flow statement is correctly prepared and interpreted where required (performance criteria 10.2)
- Draft accounts comply with domestic standards (performance criteria 10.2)
- Main requirements of relevant SSAPs and FRSs (knowledge and understanding 10.2)

Putting the chapter in context – learning objectives.

This chapter concerns the preparation of a cash flow statement for a company per FRS 1. It will be necessary firstly to learn the pro-forma of the cash flow statement and its related notes and then to learn how to find the correct figures to put into the statement itself.

Large companies are required by FRS 1 to include a cash flow statement as a primary statement in their financial statements alongside the balance sheet, profit and loss account and statement of total recognised gains and losses. Smaller companies are encouraged to produce cash flow statements as they provide useful additional information to the users of other accounts.

At the end of this chapter you should have learned the following topics.

- Background information to the need for cash flow statements.
- Calculations for the net cash flow from operating activities.
- Calculations for the remaining items in a cash flow statement.
- Question approach for preparing a cash flow statement.
- Interpretation of the cash flow statement.

1 CASH FLOW STATEMENTS

1.1 Cash and profit

In the preparation of financial statements we have covered so far, we have stressed the importance of accounting concepts of accruals and matching in order to compute a profit figure which shows the additional wealth created for the owners of the business during an accounting period. However, it is important for a business to generate cash as well as make profits. The two do not necessarily go hand in hand.

Profit represents the increase in net assets in a business during an accounting period.

This increase can be in cash or it may be 'tied up' in other assets, for example:

- Fixed assets may have been purchased

- There may be an increased amount of debtors

- There may be increased investment in stock

- The liabilities of the business may have decreased ie, more cash has been spent this year in paying off creditors more quickly than was the case last year.

We can reconcile profit to cash in an accounting period by taking into account these and other factors. This reconciliation is examined in detail later in the chapter.

1.2   The need for a cash flow statement

A cash flow statement is needed as a consequence of the above differences between profits and cash. In particular, there is a need for a further statement to be presented as part of the financial statements which will help to achieve the following.

- Provide additional information on business activities.

- Help to assess the current liquidity of the business

- Allow the user to see the major types of cash flows into and out of the business

- Help the user to estimate future cash flows

- Determine cash flows generated from trading transactions as opposed to other sources of cash flows.

- Cash flow statements remove accrual accounting from financial information.

1.3   FRS 1: Cash flow statements

In 1991 the ASB issued FRS 1: **Cash flow statements** requiring large companies to include a cash flow statement in their accounts. Smaller entities are encouraged to produce the statement as well. FRS 1 was revised in 1996.

A cash flow statement can be presented in a number of ways. A cash flow statement is simply a summary of the cash receipts and payments of a business. Thus a summarised cash book would be a cash flow statement.

FRS 1, however, requires a cash flow statement to be presented using standard headings. The objective of the standard headings is to ensure that cash flows are reported in a form that highlights the significant components of cash flow and facilitates comparison of the cash flow performance of different businesses.

The standard headings shown in the statement are

(a)   operating activities
(b)   dividends received from associates (unlikely to appear in your examination)
(c)   returns on investments and servicing of finance
(d)   taxation
(e)   capital expenditure and financial investment
(f)   acquisitions and disposals (unlikely to appear in your examination)
(g)   equity dividends paid
(h)   management of liquid resources
(i)   financing

The figure at the bottom is the resultant increase or decrease in cash during the accounting period.

Definition   Cash includes deposits in the bank which are repayable on demand.

Overdrafts also come within the definition of cash as they are repayable on demand.

1.4   Proforma cash flow statement

The illustrative cash flow statement from FRS 1 (revised) is shown below, with some minor changes to try to ease understanding.

Study the items in conjunction with the explanatory notes which follow the statement. The numbers to the left refer to the explanatory notes.

Cash Flow Statement for the year ended 31 December 1996

(1)   **Reconciliation of operating profit to net cash inflow from operating activities**

		£'000	£'000
	Operating profit		6,022
	Depreciation charges		899
	Increase in stocks		(194)
	Increase in debtors		(72)
	Increase in creditors		234
	Net cash inflow from operating activities		6,889

Cash Flow Statement

(2)	Net cash inflow from operating activities		6,889
(3)	Returns on investments and servicing of finance		
	Interest received	2,911	
	Dividends received	100	
	Interest paid	(12)	
			2,999
(4)	Taxation		(2,922)
(5)	Capital expenditure		
	Payments to acquire:		
	intangible fixed assets	(71)	
	tangible fixed assets	(1,496)	
	Proceeds from sale of tangible fixed assets		42
			(1,525)
			5,441
(6)	Equity dividends paid		(2,417)
			3,024
(7)	Management of liquid resources		
	Purchase of current asset investment		(450)
(8)	Financing		
	Issue of ordinary share capital	206	
	Redemption of debentures	(149)	
			57
(9)	Increase in cash		2,631

Explanatory notes

(1)   Reconciliation of operating profit to net cash inflow from operating activities.

Before the cash flow statement itself, we show how the operating cash flow of £6,889 can be reconciled with the operating profit.

The reconciliation opens with the operating profit of £6,022. We have to add on the depreciation because this is a non-cash expense - the cash goes out when the asset is bought, and the depreciation charges the cost against profit over the useful life of the asset.

We then adjust for the movements during the year in the operating assets and liabilities - stock, debtors and creditors. The reconciliation shows that stock and debtors have both increased. That means that some of the cash generated by the operations has gone into financing these increases. We must therefore show these movements as negatives - reducing cash inflow.

Finally we have the movement in creditors. These have also increased during the year. If we owe more, we have more cash as a result, so an increase in creditors is added in the reconciliation.

Notice the use of brackets here and throughout the cash flow statement. Inflows or pluses are shown without brackets, while outflows or minuses are in brackets.

(2)   The cash flow statement opens with the cash inflow from operations calculated in the reconciliation with operating profit.

(3)   Returns on investments and servicing of finance

The main item here is likely to be interest paid on borrowings. Dividends and interest received are included here with non-equity dividends paid, but equity dividends paid appear later in the statement.

(4)   Taxation

The cash flow statement deals with cash received and paid, so this item is likely to be mainly the corporation tax liability for the previous year, paid in the current year.

(5)   Capital expenditure

This is obviously the cash paid out during the year to buy tangible and intangible assets. The cash inflow from the **proceeds of sale** of assets sold also appears here.

(6)   Equity dividends paid

The equity dividends **paid** in the year appear here. Note that these are likely to be last year's final dividend plus this year's interim dividend.

(7)   Management of liquid resources

Under this heading we show movement in 'current asset investments held as readily disposable stores of value'. To qualify, the investments must be readily disposable without curtailing or disrupting the company's business and readily convertible into known amounts of cash at or close to its carrying amount. Movements in any investments not meeting both these conditions will have to appear under Capital Expenditure.

(8)   Financing

Typical items appearing here are the proceeds of the issue of shares or new long-term borrowings (inflows) and also any repayments of loans or redemptions of shares or debentures (outflows).

(9)   Increase (or decrease) in cash

This is the final balance of the cash flow statement and shows the increase or decrease in cash during the period covered by the cash flow statement.   Only cash balances and overdrafts repayable on demand may be included.

Study the format and the notes explaining the items until it becomes familiar to you.

Conclusion   FRS 1 requires that cash flows are reported under the following headings:

- operating activities
- returns on investments and servicing of finance
- taxation
- capital expenditure and financial investment
- equity dividends paid
- management of liquid resources
- financing.

1.5   Reconciliation of net cash flow to net debt

FRS 1 requires two notes to the cash flow statement.   The first is a reconciliation of net cash flow to 'net debt'.

Definition   Net debt means borrowings minus cash and liquid resources.

If cash and liquid resources exceed borrowings we refer to the balance as 'net funds'.

Here is the reconciliation from the specimen format in an appendix to FRS 1:

Reconciliation of net cash flow to movement in net debt

	£'000	£'000
Increase in cash for the period	2,631	
Cash to repurchase debentures	149	
Cash needed to increase liquid resources	450	
Change in net debt		3,230
Net debt at 1 January 1996		(2,903)
Net funds at 31 December 1996		327

1.6   Analysis of changes in net debt

The second note is an analysis of changes in net debt

The analysis is presented in the form of a table which picks up relevant figures from the cash flow statement and balance sheet:

- opening and closing cash or overdrafts and the movements in them
- borrowings and the movements in borrowings
- current asset investments and the movements in them.

Here is the example illustrating the note in FRS 1 (revised). Numbers to the left again refer to the explanatory notes which follow:

		At 1 Jan 1996 £'000	Cash flows £'000	Other changes £'000	At 31 Dec 1996 £'000
(1)	Cash in hand, at bank	42	847		889
(2)	Overdrafts	(1,784)	1,784		
			2,631		
(3)	Debt due within 1 year	(149)	149	(230)	(230)
(4)	Debt due after 1 year	(1,262)		230	(1,032)
(5)	Current asset investments	250	450		700
(6)	Total	(2,903)	3,230	-	327

Notes:

(1) + (2) We can see that the cash flow of the year (£2,631,000) has eliminated the overdraft and converted the opening cash balance of £42,000 into a closing one of £889,000.

(3) + (4) The borrowings are analysed into those due for repayment within one year and those due after more than one year, an analysis which would, of course also be made in the balance sheet.

The analysis shows that the opening borrowings due for repayment within one year were duly repaid (£149,000) and that £230,000 of the opening longer-term debt has become short-term by the end of the year and is therefore transferred in the column headed 'Other changes'.

The £149,000 is in the cash flow statement; the other figures would be picked up from the opening and closing balance sheets.

(5) As the cash flow statement shows, current asset investments have increased by £450,000, from £250,000 to £700,000. This was an outflow of cash in the cash flow statement but into a short-term investment which can be counted as reducing net debt.

(6) The overall effect of the changes is that an opening net debt position of (£2,903,000) has been converted into a closing net funds balance of £327,000 by the cash flows of the year.

That analysis too needs careful study to ensure that you understand what it is trying to show and what figures go into it. However, it is unlikely that this syllabus would require such a complex analysis.

2   CASH FLOW FROM OPERATING ACTIVITIES

2.1   Introduction

The item requiring most work in a cash flow statement will often be the first line of the statement - net cash flow from operating activities. The two alternative methods of calculation are shown below.

Direct method	£'000	*Indirect method*	£'000
Cash received from customers	15,424	Operating profit	6,022
Cash payments to suppliers	(5,824)	Depreciation charges	899
Cash paid to and on behalf of employees	(2,200)		
Other cash payments	(511)	Increase in stocks	(194)
		Increase in debtors	(72)
		Increase in creditors	234
Net cash inflow from operating activities	6,889		6,889

Definition The direct method records the gross trading cash flows. The net cash flow from operating activities is determined directly from the operating cash inflows and outflows.

Definition The indirect method starts with operating profit and then adjusts this for non-cash items in order to return to cash flow from operating activities.

2.2 Which method to use?

As can be seen from the illustration above the direct and indirect methods give the same figure for cash flow from operating activities. Therefore the method used will depend upon the information given in a question. It is most common to use the indirect method.

FRS 1 allows either method to be used. However FRS 1 does state that the reconciliation of operating profit to operating cash flow (the indirect method) must be shown as a note to the cash flow statement even if the direct method is used. Therefore wherever possible the indirect method should be used in a central assessment as this will save time.

2.3 Indirect method

Using the indirect method to find the cash flow from operating activities, operating profit is taken and then adjusted for the following non-cash items.

- **Depreciation**

    Depreciation is a book write off of capital expenditure. Capital expenditure will be recorded under 'capital expenditure and financial investment' at the time of the cash outflow. Depreciation has been written off in the profit and loss account and must be added back to operating profit in deriving cash flow.

- **Profit/loss on disposal of fixed asset**

    The cash inflow from a sale needs to be recorded under 'capital expenditure'. As a consequence any profit or loss on disposal included within operating profit needs to be removed as this is not a cash flow. An alternative name for loss on sale is 'depreciation under provided on disposal'; thus, like depreciation, a loss is added to operating profit. A profit on sale is a deduction from operating profit. (Following the issue of FRS 3 **Reporting Financial performance**, profits and losses on disposal are unlikely to be included in operating profit, but are normally disclosed as exceptional items on the face of the profit and loss account.)

- **Balance sheet change in debtors**

  A sale once made creates income irrespective of the date of cash receipt. If the cash has not been received by the balance sheet date however there is no cash inflow from operating activities for the current accounting period. Similarly opening debtors represent sales of a previous accounting period most of which will be cash receipts in the current period.

  The change between opening and closing debtors will thus represent the adjustment required to move from operating profit to net cash inflow.

  (i)   An increase in debtors is a deduction from operating profit. The company is owed more and thus has less cash.

  (ii)   A decrease in debtors is an addition to operating profit.

- **Balance sheet change in stocks**

  Stock at the balance sheet date represents a purchase which has not actually been charged against current operating profits. As, however, cash was spent on its purchase or a creditor incurred, it does represent an actual or potential cash outflow.

  (i)   An increase in stock is a deduction from operating profit
  (ii)   A decrease in stock is an addition to operating profit.

- **Balance sheet change in creditors**

  If creditors are greater at the end of the year than at the beginning, the company must have more cash.

  (i)   An increase in creditors between two balance sheet dates is an addition to operating profit in calculating cash flow

  (ii)   A decrease in creditors is a deduction from operating profit.

2.4   Direct method

It also allowable under FRS 1 to determine the net cash flow from operating activities using the direct method. As the name implies, under this method the net cash flow is determined directly from the operating cash flows themselves:

	£'000
Cash received from customers	15,424
Cash payments to suppliers	(5,824)
Cash paid to and on behalf of employees	(2,200)
Other cash payments	(511)
Net cash inflow from operating activities	6,889

These figures are effectively a summary of the company's cash book and can be taken directly from the accounting records. Alternatively the relevant figures could be derived from the financial statements. For example if sales and opening and closing debtors are known then the debtors ledger control account could be reconstructed in order to determine the "cash received from customers".

Conclusion   The direct method shows the actual operating cash flows. The indirect method reconciles operating profit with net cash flow from operating activities. FRS 1 requires the indirect method information to be disclosed, but entities may choose to use the direct method in addition to the indirect method.

3   PREPARATION OF A CASH FLOW STATEMENT

3.1   Introduction

It is common for central assessments to present the opening and closing balance sheets of a company together with a summarised profit and loss account for the year. From this information the figures needed for the cash flow statement can then be derived. There will also often be a variety of additional information given which may give clues as to some of the figures required.

The best approach is to set out a proforma of the cash flow statement headings and then use a workings sheet to calculate the cash flows that have take place. Each of the cash flows relevant to this syllabus will now be considered.

3.2   Returns on investments and servicing of finance

The figures likely to be needed under this heading are:

- interest received
- interest paid
- dividends received.

Some of this information may be given to you in the extra information provided but other figures may need to be derived from the financial statements.

3.3   Activity

Balance sheet - extracts

	19X4	19X3
	£	£
Debtors:		
Interest receivable	600	800
Creditors: amounts falling due within one year		
Interest payable	2,100	1,400
Profit and loss account for 19X4 - extract		
Interest receivable	1,200	
Interest payable	4,000	

What are the cash flows for interest received and paid in the year?

3.4   Activity solution

Step 1 Reconstruct the ledger accounts for interest receivable and payable from the balance sheet and profit and loss account figures.

Step 2 Enter the cash received as interest or cash paid as interest as the balancing figure.

Interest receivable

	£		£
Opening balance	800	Cash received (bal fig)	1,400
P&L A/c	1,200	Closing balance	600
	2,000		2,000

Interest payable

	£		£
Cash paid (bal fig)	3,300	Opening balance	1,400
Closing balance	2,100	P&L A/c	4,000
	5,400		5,400

(Tutorial Note: Dividends received could be derived in exactly the same way as interest received using the relevant balance sheet and profit and loss account figures).

3.5   Taxation

The cash payment for taxation again may be given in the additional information or may need to be derived from the balance sheets and profit and loss accounts. The amount for tax paid in a year will normally be the tax liability for the previous year but this can also be derived from the Corporation Tax creditors and profit and loss account charge.

3.6   Activity

Balance sheet - extract

	19X4 £	19X3 £
Creditors: amounts falling due within one year		
Corporation tax	7,000	6,000

The charge for Corporation Tax in the profit and loss account for 19X4 was £25,000.

How much Corporation Tax was paid in 19X4?

3.7   Activity solution

Step 1   Reconstruct the Corporation Tax creditor ledger account.

Step 2   Enter the cash movement as the balancing figure.

Corporation Tax

	£		£
Cash paid (Bal fig)	24,000	Opening balance	6,000
Closing balance	7,000	P&L A/c	25,000
	31,000		31,000

The cash payment for Corporation Tax for the year was £24,000.

3.8   Capital expenditure

Under the heading of capital expenditure the following figures might be required:

- Payments to acquire fixed assets;
- Proceeds from sale of fixed assets.

The information can again be given in a variety of different ways but normally it will be necessary to reconstruct the various fixed asset accounts in order to find all of the relevant figures for the cash flow statement.

3.9   Activity

Balance sheet - extract

	19X4	19X3
	£	£
Fixed assets - cost	64,000	58,000
depreciation	(24,000)	(20,000)

During the year a fixed asset that had originally cost £10,000 was sold for £6,000. The net book value of the asset at the date of sale was £7,000.

Determine the figures required for the cash flow statement for fixed assets.

3.10   Activity solution

Step 1   Reconstruct the fixed asset ledger accounts.

Step 2   Enter the cash paid to acquire fixed assets and the depreciation charge as balancing figures.

Fixed assets - cost

	£		£
Opening balance	58,000	Disposal at cost	10,000
Cash paid to acquire		Closing balance	64,000
fixed assets (bal fig)	16,000		
	74,000		74,000

Fixed assets - depreciation

	£		£
Disposal (10,000 - 7,000)	3,000	Opening balance	20,000
Closing balance	24,000	P&L A/c charge (bal fig)	7,000
	27,000		27,000

The depreciation charge for the year of £7,000 should be added back to operating profit in the reconciliation of operating profit to operating cash flow.

The cash payment to acquire fixed assets appears under the heading of capital expenditure as £16,000. The proceeds from the sale of fixed assets of £6,000 also appears as a cash inflow under the heading of capital expenditure.

3.11   Equity dividends paid

[Definition]   Equity dividends paid are the dividends paid on the ordinary shares of the company in the year.

The dividend paid in any year will normally be made up of:

- the previous year's final proposed dividend;
- the current year's interim dividend.

If the figure cannot be determined from the additional information given then it may be necessary to derive the cash flow for dividend payments from the financial statements.

3.12   Activity

Balance sheet - extract

	19X4 £	19X3 £
Creditors: amounts falling due within one year		
Proposed dividend	3,000	2,000

Profit and loss account - extract for 19X4

	£
Profit after tax	26,000
Dividends - paid	(5,000)
proposed	(3,000)
Retained profit for the year	18,000

What is the amount of cash dividend paid during 19X4 to appear in the cash flow statement?

3.13   Activity solution

[Step 1]   Reconstruct the dividend payable ledger account.

[Step 2]   Put in the cash payment for dividend as the balancing figure.

Dividend payable			
	£		£
Cash paid (bal fig)	7,000	Opening balance	2,000
Closing balance	3,000	P&L A/c charge	
		(5,000 + 3,000)	8,000
	10,000		10,000

The figure to appear under the cash flow statement heading of Equity Dividends Paid is £7,000. This is made up of the previous year's final proposed dividend of £2,000 (from the opening balance sheet) and the current year's interim paid dividend of £5,000 (from the P&L account).

3.14   Other cash payments/receipts

It is also possible for there to be some other cash payments or receipts such as:

- purchase or sale of investments (if these are short term they will normally be classified as Management of liquid resources)

- issue of ordinary shares;

- issue or redemption of debentures.

Most of these figures can be easily found by comparing the opening and closing balance sheets. However some care should be taken with the issue of ordinary shares.

3.15   Activity

Balance sheet - extract

	19X4	19X3
	£	£
Ordinary share capital	20,000	15,000
Share premium	8,000	5,000

What is the cash reciept from issue of ordinary shares during the year?

3.16   Activity solution

The nominal value of the ordinary shares has increased by £5,000 (£20,000 - £15,000). The share premium account has also increased by £3,000 (£8,000 - £5,000). Therefore the total amount of cash received from the issue of the shares was £8,000 (£5,000 + £3,000).

Conclusion   The figures required for the cash flow statement will either be effectively given in the additional information to a question or can be derived from the opening and closing balance sheets and profit and loss account by reconstructing the relevant ledger account and putting the cash flow in as the balancing figure.

3.17   Example

The balance sheets of Fox Limited as at 31 December were as follows:

	19X8		19X7	
	£'000	£'000	£'000	£'000
Fixed assets				
Freehold property (as revalued)		22,000		12,000
Plant and machinery				
Cost	10,000		5,000	
Aggregate depreciation	2,250	7,750	2,000	3,000
		29,750		15,000
Trade investment at cost		-		7,000
		29,750		22,000
Current assets				
Stock	16,000		11,000	
Debtors	9,950		2,700	
Cash	-		1,300	
	25,950		15,000	

Less:
Creditors: amounts falling due within one year				
Trade creditors	(8,000)		(11,000)	
Bank overdraft	(11,700)	6,250	-	4,000
		36,000		26,000

Less:
Creditors: amounts falling due after more than one year		
10% debentures	(6,000)	(10,000)
	30,000	16,000
Called up share capital	16,000	14,000
Revaluation reserve	4,000	-
Profit and loss account	10,000	2,000
	30,000	16,000

Notes:

(1)   At the beginning of the year machinery which had cost £1,000,000 and which had a book value of £250,000, was sold for £350,000.

(2)   In addition to the interest on the debentures, interest paid on the overdraft amounted to £800,000.

(3)   £4,000,000 of debentures were redeemed on 31 December 19X8.

(4)   The trade investment was sold for £10,000,000 during the year. No dividends were received from it.

(5)   The operating profit for the year before interest but after profits/losses on sale of fixed assets was £9,800,000.

You are required to prepare a cash flow statement for the company for the year ended 31 December 19X8 complying with the requirements of FRS 1 (revised).

3.18   Solution

Fox Ltd

Cash flow statement for the year ended 31 December 19X8

Reconciliation of operating profit to net cash inflow from operating activities

	£'000
Operating profit (given in note 5)	9,800
Depreciation charges (W2)	1,000
Profit on sale of plant (W3)	(100)
Profit on sale of investment (10,000 – 7,000)	(3,000)
Increase in stocks (16,000 – 11,000)	(5,000)
Increase in debtors (9,950 – 2,700)	(7,250)
Decrease in creditors (8,000 – 11,000)	(3,000)
Net cash outflow from operating activities	(7,550)

Cash flow statement

	£'000	£'000
Net cash outflow from operating activities		(7,550)
Returns on investments and servicing of finance		
Interest paid (W4)		(1,800)
Capital expenditure		
Payments to acquire tangible fixed assets:		
plant and machinery (W1)	(6,000)	
freehold property (10,000 – 4,000) (revaluation)	(6,000)	
Receipts from sale of investments	10,000	
Receipts from sale of plant	350	(1,650)
		(11,000)
Financing		
Issue of ordinary share capital (16,000 – 14,000)	2,000	
Redemption of debentures (6,000 – 10,000)	(4,000)	(2,000)
Reduction in cash (1,300 + 11,700)		(13,000)

WORKINGS

(W1)

Plant and machinery - cost

	£'000		£'000
Balance b/d	5,000	Transfer - disposal	1,000
Additions during		Balance c/d	10,000
year (balancing figure)	6,000		
	11,000		11,000

(W2)

Plant and machinery - aggregate depreciation

	£'000		£'000
Depreciation: disposals during		Balance b/d	2,000
year £(1,000 – 250)	750	Depreciation provided	
		for year (bal fig)	1,000
Balance c/d	2,250		
	3,000		3,000

(W3)

Plant and machinery - disposal

	£'000		£'000
Cost of disposals	1,000	Depreciation on disposals	750
Profit on sale	100	Sale proceeds	350
	1,100		1,100

(W4)   The fact that the debentures were redeemed at the end of the year means that debenture interest at 10% must have been paid on the whole £10,000,000. Therefore debenture interest paid was £1,000,000 plus overdraft interest (note 2) of £800,000.

Note 1   Reconciliation of net cash flow to movement in net debt.

	£'000	£'000
Decrease in cash for the period	(13,000)	
Cash to redeem debentures	4,000	
Change in net debt		(9,000)
Net debt at 1 January 19X8 (10,000 – 1,300)		(8,700)
Net debt at 31 December 19X8 (11,700 + 6,000)		(17,700)

Note 2   Analysis of changes in net debt

	At 1 Jan 19X8 £'000	Cash flows £'000	At 31 Dec 19X8 £'000
Cash at bank	1,300	(1,300)	-
Overdraft	-	(11,700)	(11,700)
Debt	(10,000)	4,000	(6,000)
Total	(8,700)	(9,000)	(17,700)

(Tutorial note: The debt was all shown in the opening balance sheet as falling due after more than one year. Nevertheless, £4,000,000 was repaid during the year. This is perfectly possible, but we may find questions in which some of the debentures are shown as current liabilities.*)*

4   QUESTION APPROACH

4.1   Introduction

Cash flow statement questions are not particularly difficult but a sensible, logical approach to them is all important.

4.2   Activity

The summarised financial statements of Charlton Ltd are as follows

(a)   Balance sheets at 31 December

	19X5 £	19X6 £
Fixed assets (net book value)	40,406	47,759
Stock	27,200	30,918
Debtors	15,132	18,363
Bank	4,016	2,124
	86,754	99,164
Share capital	40,000	50,000
Share premium	8,000	10,000

Profit and loss account	13,533	16,748
Debenture stock	10,000	-
Creditors	3,621	10,416
Taxation	5,200	6,000
Proposed dividend	6,400	6,000
	86,754	99,164

(b)   Profit and loss account for the year ended 31 December 19X6

	£	£
Trading profit (after charging depreciation of £2,363 and interest of £900)		17,215
Taxation		6,000
Profit after tax		11,215
Dividends		
Paid	2,000	
Proposed	6,000	
		8,000
Retained profit		3,215
Balance b/d		13,533
Balance c/d		16,748

An item of machinery with a net book value of £1,195 was sold for £1,614. The depreciation charge of £2,363 does not include the profit/loss on the sale of the fixed asset.

You are required to prepare a cash flow statement for the year ended 31 December 19X6.

4.3   Activity solution

Step 1   Allocate a page to the cash flow statement so that easily identifiable cash flows can be inserted. Allocate a further page to workings.

Step 2   Go through the balance sheets and take the balance sheet movements to the cash flow statement, the reconciliation note or to workings as appropriate. Tick off the information in the balance sheets once it has been used.

Step 3   Go through the additional information provided and deal with as per Step 2.

Step 4   The amounts transferred to workings can now be reconciled so that the remaining cash flows can be inserted on the statement or in the profit reconciliation note.

Step 5   The profit reconciliation note can now be totalled, the operating cash flow transferred to the cash flow statement and the cash flow statement completed.

Step 6   Prepare the analysis of net debt if required in the question.

Reconciliation of operating profit to net cash inflow from operating activities

	£
Operating profit (17,215 + 900)	18,115
Depreciation charge	2,363
Profit on sale of fixed asset (W1)	(419)
Increase in stocks (30,918 – 27,200)	(3,718)
Increase in debtors (18,363 – 15,132)	(3,231)
Increase in creditors (10,416 – 3,621)	6,795
Net cash inflow from operating activities	19,905

Cash flow statement for the year ended 31 December 19X6

	£	£
Net cash inflow from operating activities		19,905
Returns on investments and servicing of finance		
Interest paid (given in P&L a/c)	(900)	
Net cash outflow from servicing of finance		(900)
Tax paid (W2)		(5,200)
Capital expenditure		
Payments to acquire tangible fixed assets (W1)	(10,911)	
Receipts from sales of tangible fixed assets (given in question)	1,614	
Net cash outflow from capital expenditure		(9,297)
		4,508
Equity dividends paid (W3)		(8,400)
Net cash outflow before financing		(3,892)
Financing		
Issue of shares (10,000 + 2,000)	12,000	
Redemption of debentures	(10,000)	
Net cash inflow from financing		2,000
Decrease in cash		(1,892)

Reconciliation of net cash flow to movement in net debt

	£
Decrease in cash for the period	(1,892)
Cash to redeem debentures	10,000
Change in net debt	8,108
Net debt at 1 January 19X6 (10,000 – 4,016)	(5,984)
Net funds at 31 December 19X6 (bank)	2,124

Note: Analysis of changes in net debt

	At 1 Jan 19X6 £	Cash flows £	At 31 Dec 19X6 £
Cash at bank	4,016	(1,892)	2,124
Debt due within 1 year	(10,000)	10,000	-
	(5,984)	8,108	2,124

WORKINGS

(W1)

Fixed assets - NBV

	£		£
Balance b/d	40,406	Fixed assets disposal	1,195
Bank (bal fig)	10,911	Depreciation (profit and loss)	2,363
		Balance c/d	47,759
	51,317		51,317

(Tutorial note: the above account summarises the balances and transactions relating to fixed assets during the year. It was necessary to combine fixed asset cost and fixed asset depreciation in one account because only the net book values were given).

The account is required in order to derive the expenditure on fixed assets for the year.

Fixed assets disposal

	£		£
Fixed assets - NBV	1,195	Bank	1,614
Profit on sale (profit and loss)	419		
	1,614		1,614

(W2)

Taxation

	£		£
Bank (bal fig)	5,200	Balance b/d	5,200
Balance c/d	6,000	Profit and loss	6,000
	11,200		11,200

(Tutorial note: the taxation paid in the year has been last year's charge. Often there will be a change from last year's estimate and thus a ledger account will derive the correct figure paid.)

(W3)

Dividends

	£		£
Bank (bal fig)	8,400	Balance b/d	6,400
Balance c/d	6,000	Profit and loss	8,000
	14,400		14,400

(*Tutorial note:* the dividends paid this year will be

	£
Last year's proposed	6,400
This year's interim	2,000
	8,400

5   SCOPE OF FRS 1

FRS 1 applies to all financial statements intended to give a true and fair view of the financial position and profit or loss (or income and expenditure) except those of:

(a)   subsidiary undertakings where 90 per cent or more of the voting rights are controlled within the group, provided that consolidated financial statements in which the subsidiary undertakings are included are publicly available.

(b)   companies incorporated under companies legislation and entitled to the exemptions available in the legislation for small companies when filing accounts with the Registrar of Companies (see Chapter 9).

(c)   entities that would have been in category (b) above if they were companies incorporated under companies legislation (eg, sole traders and partnerships, which meet the 'small company' criteria).

Conclusion   'Small' companies are exempt from the requirements of FRS 1.

6   USEFULNESS OF THE CASH FLOW STATEMENT

6.1   Advantages of the cash flow statement

A cash flow statement can provide information which is not available from balance sheets and profit and loss accounts.

(a)   It may assist users of financial statements in making judgements on the amount, timing and degree of certainty of future cash flows.

(b)   It gives an indication of the relationship between profitability and cash generating ability, and thus of the quality of the profit earned.

(c)   A cash flow statement in conjunction with a balance sheet provides information on liquidity, viability and adaptability. The balance sheet is often used to obtain information on liquidity, but the information is incomplete for this purpose as the balance sheet is drawn up at a particular point in time.

(d)   Cash flow cannot easily be manipulated and is not affected by judgement or by accounting policies.

6.2   Limitations of the cash flow statement

Cash flow statements should normally be used in conjunction with profit and loss accounts and balance sheets when making an assessment of future cash flows.

(a)   Cash flow statements are based on historical information and therefore do not provide complete information for assessing future cash flows.

(b)   There is some scope for manipulation of cash flows. For example, a business may delay paying creditors until after the year-end, or it may structure transactons so that the cash balance is favourably affected. It can be argued that cash management is an important aspect of stewardship and therefore desirable. However, more deliberate manipulation is possible (eg, assets may be sold and then immediately repurchased). Following the issue of FRS 5 *Reporting the substance of transactions* users of the financial statements will be alerted to the true nature of such arrangements.

(c)   Cash flow is necessary for survival in the short term, but in order to survive in the long term a business must be profitable. It is often necessary to sacrifice cash flow in the short term in order to generate profits in the long term (eg, by investment in fixed assets). A huge cash balance is not a sign of good management if the cash could be invested elsewhere to generate profit.

Neither cash flow nor profit provide a complete picture of a company's performance when looked at in isolation.

6.3   The advantages and disadvantages of the direct and indirect methods

The two methods which can be used to prepare the cash flow statement are the direct (gross) and indirect (net) methods as we have seen.

The advantages of the direct method are as follows:

(a)   Information is shown which is not shown elsewhere in the financial statements. This is therefore of advantage to the user of the information.

(b)   The method does show the true cash flows involved in the trading operations of the entity.

The disadvantage is the significant cost that there may be in preparing the information. Given that the information is not revealed elsewhere in the financial statements, it follows that there must be some cost in obtaining the information.

The advantages of the indirect method are as follows:

(a)   Used in conjunction with a statement which reconciles operating profit to net cash flow from operating activities, the user can easily relate trading profits to cash flow and thus understand the 'quality' of the earnings made by the entity in the accounting period. Earnings are of a good quality if they are represented by real cash flows now or in the near future.

(b)   There is a low cost in preparing the information.

The disadvantage is the lack of information on the significant elements of trading cash flows.

Conclusion   A cash flow statement provides useful informaton but must always be used in conjunction with the profit and loss account and the balance sheet.

7   INTERPRETATION OF CASH FLOW DATA

7.1   Introduction

The estimation of the future cash flows is very important in determining the solvency or otherwise of a business.

The financial accounts are, of course, historical records, but they can give some indication of whether a business will be able to meet future demands for cash. This section summarises the areas to consider.

7.2   Interpretation of the cash flow statement

Points to watch for within the various headings in the cash flow statement include:

(a)   **Cash inflow/outflow from operating activities**

The figure should be compared to the operating profit. The reconciliation note to the cash flow statement is useful in this regard. Overtrading may be indicated by:

(i)   high profits and low cash generation
(ii)   large increases in stock, debtors and creditors

(b)   **Dividend and interest payouts**

These can be compared to cash generated from trading operations to see whether the normal operations can sustain such payments. In most years they should.

(c)   **Capital expenditure and financial investment**

The nature and scale of a company's investment in fixed assets is clearly shown.

(d)   **Management of liquid resources and financing**

The subtotal 'cash inflow/outflow before use of liquid resources and financing' indicates the financing required unless existing cash is available. The changes in financing (in pure cash terms) are clearly shown. There may be a note to the cash flow statement provided which links the inflows/outflows with the balance sheet movement.

(e)   **Cash flow**

The statement clearly shows the end result in cash terms of the company's operations in the year. Do not overstate the importance of this figure alone however. A decrease in cash in the year may be for very sound reasons (eg, there was surplus cash last year) or may be mainly the result of timing (eg, a new loan was raised just after the end of the accounting period).

To help in determining the future cash position other areas of the published accounts should be considered as illustrated below.

7.3   Cash requirements

There are four areas to consider when identifying whether or not the company has sufficient cash.

(a)   **Repayment of existing loans**

All loans to be repaid in the next couple of years should be considered including any convertible loans if the conversion rights are unlikely to be exercised.

(b)   **Increase in working capital**

If the business is expanding (making more sales) working capital will also need to increase. The extra cash needed to finance the expansion can easily be calculated by comparing working capital to sales.

$$\frac{\text{Stocks} + \text{debtors} - \text{creditors}}{\text{Turnover}} \times 100\%$$

Suppose this is 20% and turnover is currently £5m, a 10% increase in turnover requires finance of £0.1m (£5m × 10% × 20%) to increase the working capital.

(c)   **Capital expenditure requirements**

The notes to the financial statements should disclose capital expenditure contracted for.

It is necessary to consider if the company will have sufficient cash to meet this capital expenditure.

(d)   **Other commitments**

(i)   **Contingent liabilities**

Most contingent liabilities do not crystallise, but if the liabilities are very high their crystallisation can cause real problems for the company. In particular any sharp increases in the amounts involved should act as a warning.

(ii)   **Leasing commitments**

If these are material, they should be compared to the cash available. The accounts should disclose both finance lease commitments (for new leases where repayments have not commenced) and also operating lease commitments.

8.4   Cash shortfall

If there appears to be a cash shortfall, the company may have to take one or more of the following steps:

(a)   increase its overdraft (if it is not already at the limit)

(b)   increase its longer term borrowings. Remember that the articles often restrict the borrowings by reference to shareholders' funds, which may need to be artificially increased, for example by revaluing assets.

Alternatively the company may ask the shareholders to pass a resolution changing the borrowing restriction.

(c)   raising money through a share issue

(d)   tightening credit and stock control, paying creditors later

(e)   limiting capital expenditure

(f)   entering into sale and leaseback arrangements

(g)   selling some assets (for example investments, or parts of the business which are less related to the main trade).

The company should consider most measures in preference to

(a)   reducing dividends, or
(b)   reducing its level of activity.

Conclusion   When attempting to interpret a cash flow statement, key areas are:
-     cash inflow/outflow from operating activities
-     dividends and interest payments
-     capital expenditure
-     management of liquid resources and financing
-     total cash flow

8   SELF TEST QUESTIONS

1   Why is cash flow information important to users of financial statements? (1.1)

2   What are the standard headings in a cash flow statement? (1.3)

3   What is net debt? (1.5)

4   What appears in the reconciliation of net cash flow to movement in net debt? (1.5)

5   What are the main categories of items to adjust profit for in order to arrive at net cash flow from operating activities? (2.3)

6   Is an increase in stocks a deduction or addition to operating profit in the reconciliation note? (2.3)

7   Is a decrease in creditors a deduction or addition to operating profit in the reconciliation note? (2.3)

8   How would net cash flow from operating activities be determined using the direct method? (2.4)

9   What figures would appear in a cash flow statement on the sale of a fixed asset? (3.10)

10   What items normally make up the equity dividend paid cash flow for the year? (3.11)

18 INTERPRETATION OF FINANCIAL STATEMENTS

PATHFINDER INTRODUCTION

This chapter covers the following performance criteria and knowledge and understanding.

- Interpret the relationship between elements of limited company financial statements (performance criteria 10.1)
- Unusual features or significant issues are identified within financial statements (performance criteria 10.1)
- Valid conclusions are drawn from the information contained within financial statements (performance criteria 10.1)
- Conclusions and interpretations are clearly presented (performance criteria 10.1)
- Methods of analysing and interpreting the information contained in financial statements (knowledge and understanding 10.1)
- Computing and interpreting accounting ratios (knowledge and understanding 10.1 and 10.2)

Putting the chapter in context – learning objectives.

So far this study text has concentrated on the preparation of sets of financial statements for sole traders, partnerships and companies. It is important that students can not only prepare sets of financial statements but can also use the financial statements once prepared to gain valid information about the organisation concerned. The interpretation process starts with the calculation of a variety of financial ratios that can then be used to draw conclusions about the organisation. The chapter concentrates on the financial statements of companies but the process can also be used for sole traders, partnerships and 'not for profit' organisations.

At the end of this chapter you should have learned the following topics.

- An introduction to analysis of accounting statements and use of ratios.
- A description of the ratio calculations to be performed.
- Profitability ratios.
- Working capital ratios.
- Solvency ratios.
- Investor ratios.
- An approach to interpreting financial statements.

1 ANALYSIS OF ACCOUNTING STATEMENTS AND USE OF RATIOS

1.1 The internal and external users of accounting information

Users of accounting information have been discussed in an earlier chapter. The main users we will normally be concerned with are management, lenders and shareholders (including potential shareholders).

1.2 Relevant information

The various users of financial statements require information for quite different purposes. There are a large number of ratios, not all of which will be relevant to a particular situation. It is therefore important to determine the precise information needs of the user, and the decisions he has to take after analysing the relevant information.

The needs of the three particular users may be summarised:

User	Required for
Management	Control of costs, improved profitability
Lenders	Borrowing and credit purposes

Shareholders and investment analysts   Investment decisions – buying and selling shares

Ask yourself the questions 'What decision is being made?' and 'What information is relevant to that decision?'

1.3   The shortcomings of interpretation

The main function for many users is to estimate the future. However an estimation can only be made by interpretation of the past. There is thus a significant shortcoming in any interpretation as to its effectiveness in estimating the future.

Even if the needs of the user are more concerned with historical stewardship of the business, there are limitations of interpretation as the information presented to the user is of necessity summarised in some form. The summarisation process may have the effect of distorting the nature of some of the information. For example, creditors will be classified into those payable within one year and those payable beyond one year. Two loans which have two days difference in their payment date may well as a consequence be classified under separate headings. The user, unless he is provided with further information will tend to take the two resultant totals at face value.

Finally, it should be noted that the emphasis on information produced by an undertaking is financial. In many cases, non-financial data would be useful in order to see a complete picture of the state of the organisation. Non-financial data includes for example the number of employees in the organisation and the type of skills they possess or indicators of efficiency with which the organisation addresses complaints from customers.

1.4   Techniques of interpretation

The syllabus at this level of accounting emphasises the use of ratios to interpret information but this is only one stage in the interpretation process. A most important first step is to understand the environment in which the business operates.

Factors that need to be considered include:

- Markets in which the business operates
- General economic conditions
- Size of business in relation to competitors

1.5   Ratio calculation

In the context of examination questions much of this information is not available and thus we start at the calculation of ratios stage.

When calculating ratios, the two main points to bear in mind are:

- calculate only those ratios which are relevant to the needs of the user
- state the definitions used.

Some ratios can be calculated in alternative ways and therefore it is important to define the terms used.

1.6   Ratio analysis

Having calculated the ratios, the results must be analysed. Consideration needs to be given to such matters as:

- If a ratio has been computed over a number of time periods does it show a worsening or an improving situation?

- Can the ratio be compared to an objective standard? That is can it be compared with an 'ideal' ratio?

- Do all the ratios when taken together support the conclusions drawn from each individual ratio?

The final stage of interpretation is the critical review.

The limitations of the data used to calculate the ratios need to be considered so that a prudent overall conclusion can be reached.

The information gathered by calculating ratios will allow comparisons with:

(a)   the performance of the business in previous years;
(b)   the budgeted or planned performance in the current year;
(c)   the performance of similar businesses.

The ratios themselves do not tell one what to do, but they do help to point one in the right direction. Ratios should, therefore, make it easier to make better decisions.

1.7   Shortcomings of ratio analysis

It must be emphasised that accounting ratios are only a means to an end; they are not an end in themselves. By comparing the relationship between figures, they merely highlight significant features or trends in the accounts. Indeed, they may well create more problems than they solve. The real art of interpreting accounts lies in defining the reasons for the features and fluctuations disclosed. To do this effectively, the interested party may need more information and a deeper insight into the affairs of the business. He should also bear in mind the following:

(a)   The date at which the accounts are drawn up. Accurate information can only be obtained with any degree of certainty from up-to-date figures. Furthermore, seasonal variations in the particular trade should be taken into account. Final accounts tend to be drawn up at the end of seasonal trade when the picture they present is of the business at its strongest point financially.

(b)   The accuracy of the position shown in the balance sheet. The arrangement of certain matters can be misleading and present a more favourable picture eg, such 'window-dressing' operations as:

(i)   making a special effort to collect debts just before the year-end in order to show a larger cash balance and lower debtors than is normal;

(ii)   ordering goods to be delivered just after the year-end so that stocks and creditors can be kept as low as possible.

(c)   Interim accounts. Whenever possible interested parties should examine accounts prepared on a monthly basis, as a clearer picture of the trends and fluctuations will emerge from these than from the annual financial statements.

(d)   Accounting ratios are based on accounting information and are, therefore, only as accurate as the underlying accounting information. At a time, as at present, when traditional accounting procedures are coming in for heavy criticism, students should remember that ratios based on those procedures can be easily criticised.

(e)   The accounting ratios of one company must be compared with those of another similar company in order to draw meaningful conclusions. These conclusions will only be so if that other company's trade is similar.

1.8   Interpretation and 'Not-for-Profit' organisations

Most public sector bodies now prepare commercial style accounts and may be required to comply with generally accepted accounting principles and applicable accounting standards. These accounts can be interpreted using ratio analysis and observation in exactly the same way as the accounts of a commercial organisation.

When interpreting the accounts of a public sector body you should bear in mind the following major differences between private sector and public sector organisations.

	Private sector	*Public sector*
Primary objective	To make profits	To provide a service (economy, effectiveness, efficiency).
Stewardship responsibilities	To investors (shareholders)	To the general public

The main users of the accounts of private sector organisations are investors and potential investors, lenders and potential lenders and management. The main users of the accounts of public sector organisations are:

(a)   taxpayers;
(b)   those who benefit from their activities; and
(c)   electors.

Other users may include:

(a)   central government;
(b)   employees;
(c)   lenders of funds; and
(d)   pressure groups.

As always, you should interpret the accounts in the light of the objective of the organisation and the needs of those who are interested in its accounts (these should normally be stated or implied in the question).

Conclusion   When calculating ratios:

- be aware of the needs of the users of the accounts
- calculate only those ratios relevant to those needs
- always state the definitions used.

Remember that ratios cannot be used in isolation. They must always be interpreted in relation to other information, e.g.

- comparative figures
- budgeted figures
- performance of similar businesses.

2   RATIO CALCULATION AND ANALYSIS

2.1   Types of ratios

Ratios fall into several groups, the relevance of particular ratios depending on the purpose for which they are required. The groups to be considered here are:

- profitability ratios;
- working capital ratios;
- medium and long term solvency ratios;
- investor ratios.

2.2   Illustration

Each of the above ratios will be illustrated by reference to the following example. In each case the ratio will be defined and explained, calculated and then interpreted.

Summarised balance sheets at 30 June

	19X7		*19X6*	
	£'000	£'000	£'000	£'000
Fixed assets (net book value)		130		139
Current assets:				
Stock	42		37	
Debtors	29		23	
Bank	3		5	
	74		65	
Creditors: Amounts falling due within one year:				
Trade creditors	36		55	
Taxation	10		10	
	46		65	
Net current assets		28		-
Total assets less current liabilities		158		139
Creditors: Amounts falling due beyond one year:				
5% secured loan stock		40		40
		118		99

Ordinary share capital (50p shares)	35	35
8% Preference shares (£1 shares)	25	25
Share premium account	17	17
Revaluation reserve	10	-
Profit and loss account	31	22
	118	99

Summarised profit and loss account for the year ended 30 June

	19X7		*19X6*	
	£'000	£'000	£'000	£'000
Sales		209		196
Opening stock	37		29	
Purchases	162		159	
	199		188	
Closing stock	42		37	
		157		151
Gross profit		52		45
Interest	2		2	
Depreciation	9		9	
Sundry expenses	14		11	
		25		22
Net profit		27		23
Taxation		10		10
Net profit after taxation		17		13
Dividends:				
Ordinary shares	6		5	
Preference shares	2		2	
		8		7
Retained profit		9		6

3   PROFITABILITY RATIOS

3.1   Introduction

There are several ratios which attempt to assess the profitability of a business. These are more conveniently expressed in percentage form and look at various aspects of a business's operations.

3.2   Gross profit percentage

Definition   Gross profit is expressed as a percentage of sales. It is also known as the gross profit margin.

This is a very popular ratio and is used by even the smallest of businesses. In the illustration the ratios for the two years are as follows:

19X7   *19X6*

$$\frac{52}{209} \times 100 = 24.9\% \qquad\qquad \frac{45}{196} \times 100 = 23.0\%$$

What can be learned from these figures? Clearly, the gross profit percentage has improved but it is not known why. Nor is it obvious whether these figures are better or worse than those which would be expected in a similar type of business. Before coming to definite conclusions one would need further information. For example, most businesses sell a wide range of products, usually with different gross profit percentages (or profit margins). It may be that in 19X7 the **sales mix** changed and that a larger proportion of items with a high profit percentage were sold, thus increasing the overall gross profit percentage of the business.

3.3   Percentage change in sales

Definition   Increase or decrease in sales/turnover expressed as a percentage of the earliest years turnover.

It is relevant to consider the change in sales at this point. The percentage growth in sales is:

$$\frac{209 - 196}{196} \times 100 = 6.6\%$$

This may not be a significant increase. A larger increase might have given some evidence of the type of changes in trading conditions that have occurred.

3.4   Net profit percentage

Definition $\dfrac{\text{Net profit}}{\text{Sales}} \times 100$. This is also known as the net profit margin.

19X7   *19X6*

$$\frac{27}{209} \times 100 = 12.9\% \qquad\qquad \frac{23}{196} \times 100 = 11.7\%$$

What conclusions can be drawn from this apparent improvement? Very few! Since net profit equals gross profit less expenses, it would be useful to tabulate, for each of the two years, the various expenses and express them as a percentage of sales. A suitable tabulation might be:

	19X7		19X6	
	£'000	%	£'000	%
Sales	209	100.0	196	100.0
Cost of sales	157	75.1	151	77.0
Gross profit	52	24.9	45	23.0
Interest	(2)	(1.0)	(2)	(1.1)
Depreciation	(9)	(4.3)	(9)	(4.6)
Sundry expenses	(14)	(6.7)	(11)	(5.6)
Net profit	27	12.9	23	11.7

Given a detailed trading and profit and loss account, the above type of summary could be very useful. Care must be taken in interpreting the results, particularly since sales (£) are used as the denominator. An increase in sales (£) could be due to a combination of price and quantity effects.

3.5   Return on capital employed (ROCE)

[Definition]   Profit is expressed as a percentage of the capital invested in the business. Due to its importance the ROCE is sometimes referred to as the **primary ratio**.

This is an important ratio as it relates profit to the capital invested in a business. Finance for a business is only available at a cost – loan stock finance requires interest payments and further finance from shareholders requires either the immediate payment of dividends or the expectation of higher dividends in the future. Therefore a business needs to maximise the profits per £ of capital employed.

There are several ways of measuring ROCE, but the essential point is to relate the profit figure used to its capital base. The profit figure used must match with the capital employed figure.

[Definition]   **Total capital employed in the business**

$$\frac{\text{Profit before interest and tax}}{\text{Share capital + Reserves + Long term liabilities}} \times 100$$

The denominator could alternatively be calculated as total assets less current liabilities. This is the profit available for all of the providers of finance as a percentage of all of the sources of finance.

[Definition]   **Equity shareholders' capital employed**

$$\frac{\text{Profit after interest and preference dividend but before tax}}{\text{Ordinary share capital + Reserves}} \times 100$$

This is the profit available to the ordinary shareholder (before tax) as a percentage of the ordinary shareholder's capital.

3.6   Activity

Using the figures in the illustration in Section 2.2, calculate ROCE for 19X6 and 19X7 using each of these alternatives.

3.7   Activity solution

Total capital employed

19X7	*19X6*

$$\frac{(27 + 2)}{158} \times 100 = 18.4\% \qquad\qquad \frac{(23 + 2)}{139} \times 100 = 18.0\%$$

Equity capital employed

19X7	*19X6*

$$\frac{27 - 2}{118 - 25} \times 100 = 26.9\% \qquad\qquad \frac{23 - 2}{99 - 25} \times 100 = 28.4\%$$

(The ordinary shareholders' funds is the capital and reserves total minus the preference shares.)

There is a slight improvement in total ROCE and a falling off in equity ROCE.

A reason for the variation is the revaluation of fixed assets during the year. This has the effect of increasing the denominator in 19X7 relative to 19X6 and creates an unfair comparison as it is likely that the fixed assets were worth more than their book value last year as well. It is not common, however, for UK companies to revalue their assets every year so that comparisons from year to year can be difficult.

The differences in returns for equity compared to total capital employed are large. It means that equity shareholders have had a significant increase in their return because of the company's using fixed interest finance to enlarge the capital employed in the business.

3.8   Structure of operating ratios

ROCE can be broken down into a further pattern of operating ratios as shown in the diagram below.

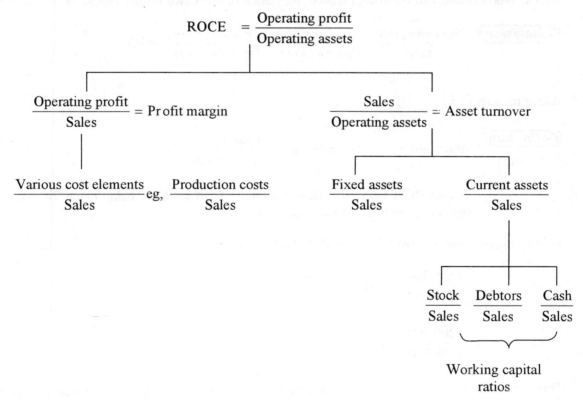

3.9   Analysis of ROCE

As can be seen from the diagram the initial breakdown of ROCE is into two further ratios:

- Profit margin
- Rate of asset utilisation or asset turnover

Note: that the product of these two gives the return on capital employed:

$$\frac{\text{Operating profit}}{\text{Sales}} \times \frac{\text{Sales}}{\text{Operating assets}} = \frac{\text{Operating profit}}{\text{Operating assets}} = \text{ROCE}$$

In the example for 19X7 using total capital employed:

$$ROCE = \frac{£29,000}{£158,000} = 18.3\%$$

$$Profit\ margin = \frac{Operating\ profit}{Sales} = \frac{£29,000}{£209,000} = 13.9\%$$

$$Asset\ turnover = \frac{Sales}{Operating\ assets} = \frac{£209,000}{£158,000} = 1.32$$

$$13.9\% \times 1.32 \times 100 = 18.3\%$$

As ROCE is made up of the product of profit margin and asset turnover then any initial analysis of ROCE over a period will normally involve calculation of these two further ratios.

Conclusion $$\frac{Operating\ profit}{Sales} \times \frac{Sales}{Operating\ assets} = \frac{Operating\ profit}{Operating\ assets} = ROCE$$

3.10   Asset turnover

Definition   Asset turnover is calculated as $\dfrac{Sales}{Operating\ assets}$

The resultant figure indicates how many £s of sales are being made for every £1 of operating assets or capital employed.

In our example asset turnover for each of the two years is:

$$19X6 = \frac{£196,000}{£139,000} = 1.41$$

$$19X7 = \frac{£209,000}{£158,000} = 1.32$$

This shows that for every £1 invested in the business in 19X6 £1.41 of sales were being made whilst this has fallen to £1.32 of sales for every £1 invested in 19X7.

The profit margin can also be considered for each of the two years:

$$19X6 = \frac{£25,000}{£196,000} = 12.8\%$$

$$19X7 = \frac{£29,000}{£209,000} = 13.9\%$$

The initial analysis of ROCE (using total capital employed) might therefore be that it has increased over the two year period due to an increase in profit margin and indeed despite of a reduction in the efficient use of the assets as measured by asset turnover.

(Tutorial note: If this analysis of ROCE is to be carried out it is important that the same profit figure and capital employed figure is used in all three ratios otherwise the result will be meaningless.)

3.11 Fixed asset turnover

Definition $\dfrac{\text{Sales}}{\text{Fixed assets}}$

The resultant figure indicates the amount of £ sales being made for every £1 investment in fixed assets.

This measures the efficiency of just the fixed asset utilisation rather than all of the assets in total.

In our example the fixed asset turnover is:

$$19X6 \quad = \quad \frac{£196,000}{£139,000} = 1.41$$

$$19X7 \quad = \quad \frac{£209,000}{£130,000} = 1.61$$

This indicates that there has been a substantial increase in the efficiency of the utilisation of the fixed assets although not of the overall assets over the two year period. This is also despite the fact that there has been a revaluation of the fixed assets in 19X7.

Conclusion   From the analysis it becomes clear that the subdivision of the key ratio, return on capital employed, is limited only by the detail in the data available. The important point to remember is that if ROCE is to be subanalysed care must be taken with the profit and capital employed figures used.

4   WORKING CAPITAL RATIOS

4.1   Introduction

The working capital (net current assets) of a business can be considered in total and also broken down into their component elements.

4.2   The current ratio

Definition   The ratio of current assets to current liabilities

19X7	*19X6*
$\dfrac{74}{46} = 1.61$	$\dfrac{65}{65} = 1.0$

The current ratio is sometimes referred to as the working capital ratio.

4.3   The liquidity (or quick) ratio

Definition   The ratio of current assets excluding stock to current liabilities

19X7   *19X6*

$$\frac{32}{46} = 0.7$$ $$\frac{28}{65} = 0.43$$

Stock is excluded from this ratio as it is much less liquid than cash and even debtors.

4.4   Analysis

Both of these ratios show a strengthening.

The extent of the change between the two years seems surprising and would require further investigation.

It would also be useful to know how these ratios compare with those of a similar business, since typical ratios for supermarkets are quite different from those for heavy engineering firms.

What can be said is that in 19X7 the current liabilities were well covered by current assets. Liabilities payable in the near future (creditors), however, are only half covered by cash and debtors (a liquid asset, close to cash).

Conventional wisdom has it that an ideal current ratio is 2 and an ideal quick ratio is 1. It is very tempting to draw definite conclusions from limited information or to say that the current ratio **should** be 2, or that the liquidity ratio **should** be 1. However, this is not very meaningful without taking into account the type of ratio expected in a similar business.

It should also be noted that a high current or liquidity ratio is not necessarily a good thing. It may indicate that working capital is not being used efficiently. This in itself can be investigated by calculation of ratios for each individual element of working capital.

4.5   Stock turnover ratio

Companies have to strike a balance between being able to satisfy customers' requirements out of stock and the cost of having too much capital tied up in stock.

Definition   The stock turnover ratio is the cost of sales divided by the average level of stock during the year. Using the example:

19X7   *19X6*

$$\frac{157}{\frac{1}{2}(37 + 42)} = 4.0 \text{ times pa}$$ $$\frac{151}{\frac{1}{2}(29 + 37)} = 4.6 \text{ times pa}$$

The stock turnover ratio has fallen.

Note: the average of opening and closing stocks is used here, but examination questions frequently do not provide the opening stock figure and the **closing** stock has to be taken instead of the average stock. In any case, the average of opening and closing stock will not necessarily give the true average level of stock during the year if the stock fluctuates a lot from month to month.

Unless the nature of the business is known, it is not possible to say whether either 4.6 or 4.0 is satisfactory or unsatisfactory. A jeweller will have a low stock turnover ratio, but it is hoped that a fishmonger selling fresh fish has a very high turnover ratio.

An alternative calculation of the stock turnover ratio is to show the result in days. The calculation is:

$$\frac{\text{Average stock during the accounting period}}{\text{Cost of sales}} \times 365 \text{ (ie, length of accounting period)}$$

| *19X7* | *19X6* |

$$\frac{\frac{1}{2}(37 + 42)}{157} \times 365 = 92 \text{ days} \qquad\qquad \frac{\frac{1}{2}(29 + 37)}{151} \times 365 = 80 \text{ days}$$

4.6   Debt collection period (or average period of credit allowed to customers)

Businesses which sell goods on credit terms specify a credit period. Failure to send out invoices on time or to follow up late payers will have an adverse effect on the cash flow of the business.

Definition   The debt collection period relates closing trade debts to the average daily credit sales. It shows the number of days that debtors are outstanding on average.

In the example:

	19X7		*19X6*	
Credit sales per day	$\dfrac{£209,000}{365} = £573$		$\dfrac{£196,000}{365} = £537$	
Closing trade debtors	£29,000		£23,000	
Debt collection period	$\dfrac{£29,000}{£573} = 50.6$ days		$\dfrac{£23,000}{£537} = 42.8$ days	

Compared with 19X6 the debt collection period has worsened in 19X7.

If the average credit allowed to customers was, say, thirty days, then something is clearly wrong. Further investigation might reveal delays in sending out invoices or failure to 'screen' new customers.

The quickest way to compute the debt collection period is to use the formula:

$$\frac{\text{Closing trade debtors}}{\text{Credit sales for year}} \times 365$$

| *19X7* | *19X6* |

$$\frac{29,000}{209,000} \times 365 = 50.6 \text{ days} \qquad\qquad \frac{23,000}{196,000} \times 365 = 42.8 \text{ days}$$

(Tutorial note: In this example it has been assumed that all sales are on credit.)

4.7   Average period of credit allowed by suppliers

Definition   This relates closing creditors to average daily credit purchases. It shows the number of days it takes the business to pay its creditors.

	19X7	19X6
Credit purchases per day	$\dfrac{£162,000}{365} = £444$	$\dfrac{£159,000}{365} = £436$
Closing trade creditors	£36,000	£55,000
Average period of credit allowed by suppliers	81.1 days	126.3 days

(Tutorial note: Again it has been assumed here that all purchases are on credit.)

The average period of credit allowed has fallen substantially from last year. It is however, in absolute terms still a high figure.

Often, suppliers request payment within thirty days. The company is taking nearly three months. Trade creditors are thus financing much of the working capital requirements of the business which is beneficial to the company.

However, there are three potential disadvantages of extending the credit period.

(i)   Future supplies may be endangered.

(ii)   Possibility of cash discounts is lost.

(iii)   Suppliers may quote a higher price for the goods knowing the extended credit taken by the company.

The quick calculation is:

$$\frac{\text{Closing trade creditors}}{\text{Credit purchases for year}} \times 365$$

19X7	19X6
$\dfrac{36,000}{162,000} \times 365 = 81.1$ days	$\dfrac{55,000}{159,000} \times 365 = 126.3$ days

4.8   The working capital cycle

The investment made in working capital is largely a function of sales and, therefore, it is useful to consider the problem in terms of a firm's working capital (or **cash operating**) cycle.

The cash operating cycle

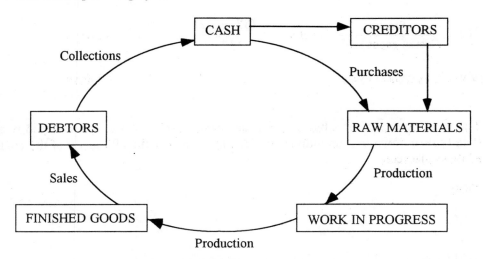

The cycle reflects a firm's investment in working capital as it moves through the production process towards sales. The investment in working capital gradually increases, firstly being only in raw materials, but then in labour and overhead as production progresses. This investment must be maintained throughout the production process, the finished goods holding period and up to the final collection of cash from trade debtors. Note that the net investment can be reduced by taking trade credit from suppliers.

The faster a firm can 'push' items around the operating cycle the lower its investment in working capital will be. However, too little investment in working capital can lose sales since customers will generally prefer to buy from suppliers who are prepared to extend trade credit, and if items are not held in stock when required by customers, sales may be lost.

With some fairly basic financial information it is possible to measure the length of the working capital cycle for a given firm.

4.9   Activity

Using the example in section 2.2 determine the working capital cycle for 19X7.

4.10   Activity solution

(1)   Creditors:

Average payment collection period

$$= \quad \left(365 \times \frac{\text{Creditors}}{\text{Purchases}}\right) \qquad 365 \times \frac{36}{162} = \qquad (81 \text{ days})$$

(2)   Debtors:

Average collection period

$$= \quad \left(365 \times \frac{\text{Debtors}}{\text{Sales}}\right) \qquad 365 \times \frac{29}{209} = \qquad 51 \text{ days}$$

(3)   Stock turnover:

$$= \quad 365 \times \frac{\text{Stock}}{\text{Cost of goods sold}} \qquad 365 \times \frac{\frac{1}{2}(37 + 42)}{157} \qquad \text{92 days}$$

Length of working capital cycle   62 days

Conclusion   The working capital of a business can be considered in total to assess liquidity and then broken down into its individual elements to assess the efficiency of the control of these elements.

5   SOLVENCY RATIOS

5.1   Introduction

Most companies will be financed by a variety of sources of finance, some by share capital and some by loan finance. Typical examples of sources of finance are given below:

Source of finance	Priority in relation to profit	Priority on liquidation
Secured loan stock (debentures)	Interest must be paid whether or not the company makes a profit	Secured by a fixed or floating charge – first claim on assets
Unsecured loan stock	Interest must be paid whether or not the company makes a profit.	Ranks as unsecured creditor
Preference share capital (assumed non-participating)	If the company makes a profit, the preference dividend has a priority over the ordinary dividend	Cannot be repaid until all liabilities have been met. Has priority over ordinary shareholders
Ordinary share capital	Dividends paid after debenture interest and fixed preference dividends have been paid	Ranks behind all the above but usually entitled to surplus assets in a liquidation

The aim of solvency ratios is to assess how much a business is financed by loan capital rather than owners' capital.

5.2   Capital gearing

Gearing is one of the most widely-used terms in accounting. Unfortunately it can be defined and calculated in several different ways. It is essential to state the definition used.

Gearing is relevant to the long term financial stability of a business. Two possible definitions will be considered, both based on book values of assets. Both of these consider the relationship between:

(a)   ordinary shareholders' funds (or equity interest);
(b)   fixed return capital – comprising loans and preference share capital.

5.3   Equity gearing

Definition   Preference share capital plus loans

Ordinary share capital and reserves

<table>
<tr><td align="center">*19X7*</td><td align="center">*19X6*</td></tr>
</table>

$$\frac{25+40}{118-25} \times 100 = 69.9\%$$ $$\frac{25+40}{99-25} \times 100 = 87.8\%$$

5.4   Total gearing

Definition   Preference share capital plus loans
                 Total long term capital

19X7

$$\frac{65}{158} \times 100 = 41.1\%$$

19X6

$$\frac{65}{139} \times 100 = 46.8\%$$

There is no real difference between the two types of calculation as the components of the numerator remain the same. Some prefer to use the equity gearing as it shows a more pronounced change if either fixed return capital or equity capital changes. Most use the second calculation as it is perhaps clearer to note the relationship of fixed interest finance to **total** finance.

There is no immediate cut-off between a low-geared company and a highly-geared company. Gearing is a matter of degree.

In our example there has been no increase or decrease in the amount of fixed interest finance. The only reason for the change in ratio is due to retained profit and revaluation for 19X7.

5.5   The advantages and disadvantages of raising finance by issuing debentures

Gearing may have an important effect on the distribution of profits. For example, consider two companies with the same profit record but different capital structures. The return of the ordinary shareholders can vary considerably.

	A Ltd £	*B Ltd* £
Capital structure:		
10% Loan stock	20,000	-
Ordinary share capital and reserves	10,000	30,000
	30,000	30,000
	Highly geared	*No gearing*
Year 1 – Profits £4,000 before interest		
∴ Returns:		
10% Interest	2,000	-
Ordinary shares – balance	2,000	4,000
	4,000	4,000
Year 2 – Profits double to £8,000 before interest		
∴ Returns:		
10% Interest	2,000	-
Ordinary shares – balance	6,000	8,000
	8,000	8,000

Therefore, increase in return to ordinary shareholders	3 times	2 times

Thus, the doubling of the profits in year 2 has the effect of tripling the return to the equity shareholders in the highly-geared company. The effect would be even more dramatic if the profits fell below £2,000 because then there would be no return at all to the ordinary shareholders in A Ltd. Thus an investment in ordinary shares in a highly-geared company is a far more speculative investment than a purchase of ordinary shares in a low-geared company.

5.6 Interest cover

Definition $\dfrac{\text{Profit before interest and tax}}{\text{Interest}}$

Interest on loan stock (debenture stock) must be paid whether or not the company makes a profit. The ratio emphasises the cover (or security) for the interest by relating profit before interest and tax to interest paid.

19X7	*19X6*
$\dfrac{52-9-14}{2} = \dfrac{29}{2}$ ie, 14.5 times	$\dfrac{45-9-11}{2} = \dfrac{25}{2}$ ie, 12.5 times

From the point of view of medium and long term solvency, the company is in a strong position as regards the payment of interest. Profit would have to drop considerably before any problem of paying interest arose.

Conclusion   The medium to long term solvency of a business will be of concern to most users of the financial statements. Therefore gearing ratios will be very important but to avoid confusion any calculation must be defined.

6 INVESTOR RATIOS

6.1 Information required by investors

An investor is interested in the income earned by the company for him and the return on his investment (the income earned related to the market price of the investment).

An investor in ordinary shares can look to the earnings of the company available to pay the ordinary dividend or to the actual ordinary dividend paid as a measure of the income earned by the company for him. The ratios he would compute in each case would be:

Dividends	*Earnings*
Dividends per share Dividend cover Dividend yield	Earnings per share Price earnings ratio

Suppose that the company in the Activity is quoted on the Stock Exchange and that the market value of each ordinary share is 204 pence.

6.2   **Dividend per share**

Definition
$$\frac{\text{Total ordinary dividend}}{\text{Total number of ordinary shares}}$$

19X7	19X6
$\dfrac{£6,000}{70,000} = 8.6$ pence per share	$\dfrac{£5,000}{70,000} = 7.1$ pence per share

(*Tutorial note:* The ordinary share capital of the company is made up of £35,000 of 50p shares. Therefore a total of 70,000 shares.)

6.3   **Dividend cover**

Definition   A measure of how many times the profit covers the ordinary dividend payment.

This is calculated by dividing profit available for ordinary shareholders (ie after preference dividend) by the dividend for the year (ie, interim plus final):

19X7	19X6
$\dfrac{£17,000 - £2,000}{£6,000} = 2.5$ times	$\dfrac{£13,000 - £2,000}{£5,000} = 2.2$ times

Note: that the profits available for ordinary shareholders are after the deduction of the preference dividend. The cover represents the 'security' for the ordinary dividend – in this company the cover is reasonable.

6.4   **Dividend yield**

Definition   This expresses dividend per share as a percentage of the current share price.

The net yield at today's date is:

$$\frac{8.6p}{204p} \times 100 = 4.2\%$$

6.5   **Earnings per share (EPS)**

When a company pays a dividend, the directors take many factors into account, including the need to retain profits for future expansion. Earnings per share looks at the profits which could in theory be paid to each ordinary shareholder.

Definition $$EPS = \frac{\text{Net profit or loss attributable to ordinary shareholders}}{\text{Weighted average number of ordinary shares outstanding during the period}}$$

FRS 14 requires earnings per share to be disclosed on the face of the profit and loss account of quoted companies.

19X7	*19X6*
$\dfrac{£17,000 - £2,000}{70,000} = 21.4\text{p per share}$	$\dfrac{£13,000 - £2,000}{70,000} = 15.7\text{p per share}$

6.6   Price earnings ratio (P/E ratio)

Definition $\text{P/E ratio} = \dfrac{\text{Current share price per share}}{\text{EPS}}$

This is often regarded as the most important ratio. It expresses the current share price (market value) as a multiple of the earnings per share. For 19X7, the price earnings ratio is:

$$\frac{204\text{p}}{21.4\text{p}} = 9.5$$

The ratio of 9.5 implies that if the current rate of EPS is maintained it will take nine and a half years to repay the cost of investing. The higher the PE ratio the longer the payback period. Thus we could conclude that the lower the PE ratio, the better investment it is. However, this is not generally the case. **High** PE ratios are generally viewed as better than low ones.

The apparent paradox is resolved if the forward looking nature of stock exchange investments is considered. The PE ratio is based on **current** EPS but the stock market is pricing the share on expectations of **future** EPS. If the market considers that a company has significant growth prospects, the market price of the share will rise giving a higher P/E ratio.

6.7   Earnings yield

Definition $\dfrac{\text{EPS}}{\text{Current share price per share}} \times 100$

This term is not often referred to these days. It expresses the earnings per share as a percentage of the current share price, ie:

Earnings yield $=$ $\dfrac{21.4\text{p}}{204\text{p}} \times 100$

$=$ 10.5%

It is merely the reciprocal of the PE ratio:

$\dfrac{1}{\text{PE ratio}}$ $=$ Earnings yield

$\dfrac{1}{9.5}$ $=$ 0.105 ie, 10.5%

Conclusion   An investor or potential investor in a company will be concerned with the return that he is receiving or is likely to receive on that investment. This may be measured in terms of the actual return, dividend paid, or the potential return, earnings for the year.

7   INTERPRETATION OF FINANCIAL STATEMENTS

7.1   Introduction

So far this chapter has concentrated on the calculation of a variety of ratios for different purposes and provision of information. It is now important to consider using these ratios in order to interpret a set of financial statements and to draw valid conclusions from the information contained in a set of financial statements.

7.2   Example

A Ltd has been trading steadily for many years as ski shoe manufacturers. In 19X4 a surge in skiing increased the level of A Ltd's turnover significantly. The summarised balance sheets of the last two years are given below:

	19X4		19X3	
	£'000	£'000	£'000	£'000
Fixed assets:				
Intangible assets		30		40
Tangible assets:				
Property		640		216
Plant		174		142
		844		398
Current assets:				
Stock	540		140	
Debtors	440		170	
Investments	-		120	
Cash at bank	4		150	
	984		580	
Creditors – Amounts falling due within one year:				
Trade creditors	520		250	
Taxation	70		80	
Dividend proposed	60		20	
	650		350	
Net current assets		334		230
Total assets less current liabilities		1,178		628
Creditors – Amounts falling due after more than one year:				
10% debentures		120		-
		1,058		628
Capital and reserves:				
Called up share capital:				
Ordinary 50p shares		300		250
Revaluation reserve		270		-
Capital redemption reserve		-		50
Profit and loss account		488		328
		1,058		628

Sales for 19X4 and 19X3 respectively were £1,600,000 and £1,150,000. Cost of goods sold for 19X4 and 19X3 respectively were £1,196,000 and £880,000.

Given that this is the only information available, you are required to comment as fully as you can on A Ltd's financial position.

7.3   Solution

Comments on A Ltd – Financial position

Profitability and growth

Profit and loss accounts have not been given but laying these out as far as they are available:

	19X4 £	19X3 £
Sales	1,600,000	1,150,000
Cost of sales	1,196,000	880,000
Gross profit	404,000	270,000

Profit margin:

$$\frac{\text{Gross profit}}{\text{Sales}} \times 100 \qquad\qquad 25.25\% \qquad\qquad 23.48\%$$

Return on capital employed:

$$\frac{\text{Gross profit}}{\text{Share capital} + \text{Reserves} + \text{Debt}} \times 100 \qquad \frac{404,000}{1,178,000} \quad \frac{270,000}{628,000+270,000}$$

(see note below)

$$= 34.30\% \qquad = 30.07\%$$

(Average capital employed should be used but year-end figures have been taken so that a figure for 19X3 can be computed. It is assumed that property was worth £270,000 more than its book value in 19X3 also.)

Asset turnover:

$$\frac{\text{Sales}}{\text{Share capital} + \text{Reserves} + \text{Debt}} \times 100 \qquad \frac{1,600,000}{1,178,000} \quad \frac{1,150,000}{898,000}$$

$$= 1.36 \qquad = 1.28$$

The ROCE figures have been computed in a rough and ready fashion but they indicate an improvement in 19X4 compared with 19X3. The gross profit/sales shows a (slight) improvement as does the efficiency measure of asset turnover. This would appear to be encouraging as the sales have grown considerably.

19X4 Sales	£1,600,000
19X3 Sales	£1,150,000
Percentage increase	39.13%

Solvency: long term

Gearing

There was no debt in 19X3. The 10% debentures issued in 19X4 were to enable the investment to be made to finance growth.

The year-end gearing is:

$$\frac{\text{Debt}}{\text{Capital employed (as above)}} \times 100 \quad = \quad \frac{120,000}{1,178,000} \times 100$$

$$= \quad 10.19\%$$

In absolute terms this is a low figure.

Solvency: short term

	19X4	*19X3*
Current ratio		

$$\frac{\text{Current assets}}{\text{Current liabilities}} \qquad \frac{984,000}{650,000} = 1.5 \qquad \frac{580,000}{350,000} = 1.7$$

Quick ratio

$$\frac{\text{Current assets - Stock}}{\text{Current liabilities}} \qquad \frac{444,000}{650,000} = 0.7 \qquad \frac{440,000}{350,000} = 1.3$$

Both ratios have shown a decline – particularly the quick ratio. Conventional opinion states that for many businesses an ideal current ratio is 2 and an ideal quick ratio is 1. However, the ideal ratio will depend on the type of business of a company. More important is the constancy of the ratio over time (assuming that the ratios reflect the efficient use of working capital).

The decline should not be viewed with alarm, particularly as the 19X3 figures include current assets which were surplus to the working capital requirements of the business at that time, ie, the investments and cash. Both these items have been spent in purchasing new fixed assets. The quick ratio is, however, now low and should be watched carefully.

Working capital efficiency

	19X4	*19X3*
Stock turnover		

$$\frac{\text{Cost of sales}}{\text{Year - end stocks}} \qquad \frac{1,196,000}{540,000} = 2.2 \text{ times pa} \qquad \frac{880,000}{140,000} = 6.3 \text{ times pa}$$

Year-end stock has been taken so that the 19X3 figure can be computed.

A very significant fall in stock turnover. This may indicate that:

(a)   the growth in sales has been made by offering many more types of shoes, some of which are not selling quickly; or

(b)   further growth in sales is expected so that the company has stepped up production to anticipate this.

A closer look at this area is required.

	19X4	*19X3*

Debtor collection period

$$\frac{\text{Year - end trade debtors}}{\text{Sales}} \times 365 \qquad \frac{440,000}{1,600,000} = 100.4 \text{ days} \qquad \frac{170,000}{1,150,000} = 54.0 \text{ days}$$

54 days to collect debts is not very impressive – 100 days is potentially disastrous. Immediate action is required to ensure prompter payment although the situation may not be as bad as it appears if it is the case that the growth in sales took place shortly before the year end rather than throughout the year. Debtors at the year end would then not be typical of the sales throughout the whole year.

Creditor collection period

(Cost of sales will have to be used in this example in the absence of purchases figures).

	19X4	*19X3*

$$\frac{\text{Year - end trade creditors}}{\text{Cost of sales}} \times 365 \qquad \frac{520,000}{1,196,000} \times 365 = 159 \text{ days} \qquad \frac{250,000}{880,000} \times 365 = 104 \text{ days}$$

The creditor collection period was high in 19X3 but is now even higher. Clearly one of the ways in which the company's considerable growth has been financed has been through taking long periods of credit from its suppliers. This area may need further investigation as this policy may backfire at some point in the future.

Working capital cycle

	19X4	*19X3*
Stock turnover in days		
$\dfrac{540,000}{1,196,000} \times 365$	165 days	
$\dfrac{140,000}{880,000} \times 365$		58 days
Debtors turnover in days	100 days	54 days
Creditors turnover in days	(159 days)	(104 days)
	106 days	8 days

Overall analysis

The company has quite clearly had considerable growth over the past year. This has been financed by a small amount of loan capital but largely by a reduction in overall short term liquidity and in particular an increase in time taken to pay creditors. This can be further seen from the drastic increase in the working capital cycle.

The growth appears to be worthwhile as the company continues to be profitable, indeed the ROCE has increased as has the profit margin.

The major concern for this company would therefore appear to be regarding its working capital control.

8   SELF TEST QUESTIONS

1   Name three different user groups of financial statements and state the particular interests of each group. (1.2)

2   Distinguish between the gross profit margin and the net profit margin (3.2/3.4)

3   How do you calculate the return on capital employed for a company? (3.5)

4   Which two ratios can be multiplied together to give the return on capital employed? (3.7)

5   What does fixed asset turnover represent? (3.9)

6   What are the two key ratios to assess a company's liquidity? (4.2/4.3)

7   How would you assess whether a company's debt collection procedures were improving or deteriorating? (4.6)

8   How is capital gearing determined? (5.3/5.4)

9   What is the formula to calculate the dividend yield? (6.4)

10   How is the P/E ratio of a company calculated? (6.6)

19 | CONSOLIDATED BALANCE SHEET

1 INTRODUCTION TO CONSOLIDATED ACCOUNTS

1.1 What is a 'group'?

Although every company is a separate entity from the legal point of view, from the economic point of view several companies may not be separate at all. In particular, when one company owns enough shares in another company to have a majority of votes at that company's annual general meeting, the first company may appoint all the directors of, and decide what dividends should be paid by, the second company. This degree of control enables the first company to manage the trading activities and future plans of the second company as if it were merely a department of the first company.

The first company referred to above is called a 'parent company' or 'holding company', and the second is called a 'subsidiary'.

Definition   The essential feature of a group is that one company controls all the others **absolutely**.

Company law recognises that this state of affairs often arises and includes a requirement that the parent company must produce 'group accounts', showing the results of the whole group, in addition to its usual accounts: s229 CA85.

1.2   Normal form of group accounts

Group accounts could consist of a variety of things, but in normal circumstances much the best way of showing the results of a group is to imagine that all the transactions of the group had been carried out by a single equivalent company and to prepare a balance sheet, a profit and loss account, and (if required) a cash flow statement for that company. These accounts are called 'consolidated accounts'.

Two different methods of accounting have been developed to deal with the preparation of consolidated accounts. These are 'acquisition accounting' and 'merger accounting'. The most commonly required method is acquisition accounting and this is the method of preparing consolidated accounts required for this syllabus.

1.3   General procedure

Each company in a group prepares its accounting records and annual financial statements in the usual way. From the individual companies' balance sheets, the holding company prepares a consolidated balance sheet for the group, and likewise a consolidated profit and loss account from the individual companies' profit and loss accounts.

2   BALANCE SHEET CONSOLIDATION

2.1   Introduction

Definition   A consolidated balance sheet is a joint balance sheet for all of the companies in the group prepared as though they were a single entity.

2.2   Example

Balance sheets at 31 December 19X4

	P Ltd £'000	P Ltd £'000	S Ltd £'000	S Ltd £'000
Fixed assets		60		40
Investment in S Ltd at cost		50		
Current assets	40		40	
Less: Current liabilities	(20)		(30)	
Net current assets		20		10
		130		50
Ordinary share capital (£1 shares)		100		50
Profit and loss account		30		-
		130		50

P Ltd acquired all the shares in S Ltd on 31 December 19X4 for a cost of £50,000. Prepare a consolidated balance sheet.

2.3   Solution

Step 1   The consolidated balance sheet will differ from that of P Ltd's (the holding company's) balance sheet, in that the balance on 'investment in subsidiary account' will be replaced by the underlying net assets which the investment represents.   The cost of the investment in the subsidiary is effectively cancelled with the ordinary share capital and reserves of the subsidiary.   In this simple case, it can be seen that the relevant figures are equal and opposite, and therefore cancel directly, the cost of the investment in S Ltd is £50,000 and the share capital of S Ltd acquired is £50,000.

Step 2   This then leaves a balance sheet showing:

- the net assets of the whole group **(P + S)**;

- the share capital of the group which is always solely the share capital of the holding company **(P only)**; and

- the profit and loss account comprising profits made by the group: in this case we have profits made by the parent company but none made by the subsidiary to bring in to the calculations.

P Ltd

Consolidated balance sheet at 31 December 19X4

	£'000	£'000
Fixed assets £(60 + 40)		100
Current assets £(40 + 40)	80	
Creditors: amounts falling due within one year £(20 + 30)	50	
Net current assets		30
Total assets less current liabilities		130
Called up share capital (£1 ordinary shares)		100
Profit and loss account		30
		130

Conclusion   Under no circumstances will any share capital of any subsidiary company ever be included in the figure of share capital on the consolidated balance sheet.

2.4   Goodwill on consolidation

When the investment in the subsidiary costs more or less than the net assets acquired in the subsidiary, there will be a difference between the cost of the investment in the subsidiary and the share capital and reserves of the subsidiary.

Definition   Goodwill on consolidation is the difference between the cost of the investment in the subsidiary and the fair value of the net assets acquired in the subsidiary.

2.5 Accounting treatment of goodwill

Under FRS 10 any goodwill on consolidation will normally be capitalised in the consolidated balance sheet and then written off over its useful economic life.

2.6 Activity

Balance sheets at 31 December 19X4

	P Ltd £'000	P Ltd £'000	S Ltd £'000	S Ltd £'000
Fixed assets		60		40
Investment in S Ltd at cost		60		
Current assets	30		40	
Less: Current liabilities	20		30	
Net current assets		10		10
		130		50
Ordinary share capital (£1 shares)		100		50
Profit and loss account		30		-
		130		50

P Ltd acquired all the shares in S Ltd on 31 December 19X4 for a cost of £60,000. Prepare the consolidated balance sheet for P Ltd. Any goodwill has a useful economic life of 5 years.

2.7 Activity solution

Step 1 Deal with any goodwill.

In this case the cost of the shares in S Ltd exceeds S Ltd's share capital by £10,000. This is the goodwill on consolidation or premium on acquisition. It represents the excess of the purchase consideration over the fair value of the net assets acquired. The calculation may be set out as a consolidation schedule as follows:

	£'000	£'000	Notes
Cost of investment		60	1
Less: Share of net assets acquired (at fair value)			
Ordinary share capital	50		2
Profit and loss account	-		3
	50		
Group share	× 100%	(50)	4
		10	

Notes to the calculation.

1   The cost of the investment will appear in the balance sheet of P Ltd (the individual company). If there is more than one investment details will be given of the cost of individual investments in the question.

2   We are actually comparing the cost of the investment with the net assets of the subsidiary acquired, as represented by the share capital and reserves of the subsidiary at the date of acquisition. Remember **Net assets = Capital + Reserves.**

3   In this case there are no reserves of the subsidiary to consider. However, it is important to note here that the reserves which are taken into consideration in the calculation of goodwill are those at the **date of acquisition** of the subsidiary. Whilst the share capital of the subsidiary is unlikely to have altered since that date, the profit and loss account will have changed.

4   As 100% of the shares in S Ltd were acquired, we compare the cost of the shares with 100% of the net assets of S Ltd. If only a proportion of the shares are acquired, say 90%, we compare the cost of those shares with the appropriate share (90%) of the net assets acquired. This is further illustrated later on in the chapter.

[Step 2]   Prepare the consolidated balance sheet.

P Ltd

Consolidated balance sheet at 31 December 19X4

	£'000	£'000
Goodwill		10
Fixed assets £(60 + 40)		100
Current assets £(30 + 40)	70	
Creditors: amounts falling due within one year £(20 + 30)	50	
Net current assets		20
Total assets less current liabilities		130
Called up share capital (£1 ordinary shares)		100
Profit and loss account		30
		130

The goodwill is capitalised and shown on the face of the consolidated balance sheet. Over the next 5 years £2,000 will be amortised to the profit and loss account each year.

2.8   Negative goodwill

Where the cost of the investment is less than the net assets purchased, a credit balance will arise ie, a profit. This is known as **negative goodwill** or **discount on acquisition**. It is shown directly beneath the goodwill heading on the balance sheet according to FRS 10.

[Conclusion]   Goodwill represents the difference between the amount paid to acquire the net assets of a subsidiary and the fair value of those net assets. It will normally be capitalised and amortised over its useful economic life.

3   PRE AND POST ACQUISITION RESERVES

3.1   Introduction

In the examples so far, the unrealistic case of a company (S Ltd), where the shareholders' interest consisted solely of ordinary share capital, was considered. Usually, of course, shareholders' interest includes also the profit and loss account reserve. An additional point is that P Ltd may have acquired the controlling interest in S Ltd part way through the year. When looking at the revenue reserves of S Ltd at the year end, a distinction must be made between pre-acquisition reserves and post-acquisition reserves.

Definition   Pre-acquisition reserves are those reserves of S Ltd which existed at the date of acquisition by P Ltd.

Definition   Post-acquisition reserves are the increase in the reserves of S Ltd which arose after acquisition by P Ltd.

3.2   Example

Balance sheets at 31 December 19X4

	P Ltd £'000	P Ltd £'000	S Ltd £'000	S Ltd £'000
Fixed assets		50		40
Investment in S Ltd at cost		70		-
Current assets	30		40	
Less: Current liabilities	20		10	
		10		30
		130		70
Ordinary share capital (£1 shares)		100		50
Profit and loss account		30		20
		130		70

You are further informed that P Ltd acquired **all** the shares in S Ltd at 1 January 19X4 when the profit and loss account reserves of S Ltd amounted to £15,000. Goodwill has a useful economic life of 5 years.

3.3   Solution

Step 1   First, deal with the goodwill which is effectively computed at the date of take-over. The cost of the investment (£70,000) is compared with the net assets of S Ltd at 1 January 19X4 as represented by ordinary share capital (£50,000) and profit and loss account reserves (£15,000). Note that what are concerned are the reserves at the date of acquisition (£15,000) as opposed to reserves at the date of consolidation (£20,000). The calculation becomes:

Goodwill on consolidation

	£'000	£'000
Cost of investment		70
Less: Share of net assets acquired		
Ordinary share capital	50	
Profit and loss account	15	
	65 × 100%	65
		5

This goodwill of £5,000 will be capitalised in the consolidated balance sheet and then £1,000 will be written off to the profit and loss account each year.

Step 2 In addition, a new consolidation schedule, a **consolidated profit and loss account reserve**, is required. Profits made by S Ltd prior to acquisition by P Ltd (pre-acquisition profits) are not regarded as those of the group whereas profits of S Ltd arising **after** acquisition (post-acquisition profits) **are** regarded as group profits. Allocate the reserves of S Ltd at the balance sheet date (31 December 19X4) between pre-acquisition and post-acquisition. Pre-acquisition reserves are effectively capitalised, being dealt with in the goodwill consolidation schedule (shown above), whereas post-acquisition reserves, together with the present balance on P Ltd reserves, are transferred to consolidated profit and loss account reserves.

The consolidated revenue reserves or profit and loss account reserves schedule is set out as follows:

	£'000
P Ltd: (all)	30
S Ltd: (only post acquisition ie, reserves now, less on acquisition)	
(20 – 15)	5
Less: Goodwill amortised for 19X4	(1)
	34

Step 3 The consolidated balance sheet now appears as follows:

P Ltd

Group balance sheet at 31 December 19X4

	£'000	£'000
Goodwill (5 – 1)		4
Fixed assets £(50 + 40)		90
Current assets £(30 + 40)	70	
Creditors: amounts falling due within one year £(20 + 10)	30	
		40
Total assets less current liabilities		134

Called up share capital (£1 ordinary shares)	100
Consolidated profit and loss account	34
	134

Conclusion   Pre-acquisition profits of S Ltd are treated as part of the net assets acquired and dealt with in the goodwill calculation. Post acquisition profits of S Ltd have been earned by the group and are included in the consolidated reserves.

4   MINORITY INTEREST

4.1   Introduction

What happens if P Ltd owns only 80% of the ordinary shares of S Ltd? In this case there is said to be minority interests of 20%. What problems does this present?

4.2   Concept of control

The main decision to make on accounting principles is whether to consolidate all the net assets of S Ltd, or merely to consolidate the proportion of the net assets represented by the shares held and the proportion of the reserves which apply to those shares ie, consolidate only 80% of the net assets of S Ltd.

The dominant principle is that the directors are preparing accounts of their custody of all the assets under their control, even though there are owners other than the parent company.

Therefore, the generally accepted solution is to consolidate all the subsidiary's net assets and then bring in a counterbalancing liability on the consolidated balance sheet to represent that part of the assets controlled but not owned, the minority interest.

Definition   The minority interest credit balance in the consolidated balance sheet represents the assets of S Ltd that are owned by a third party, the minority.

4.3   Example

Balance sheets at 31 December 19X4

	P Ltd		S Ltd	
	£'000	£'000	£'000	£'000
Fixed assets		50		40
Investment in S Ltd at cost		70		-
Current assets	30		40	
Less: Current liabilities	20		10	
		10		30
		130		70
Ordinary share capital (£1 shares)		100		50
Profit and loss account		30		20
		130		70

P Ltd acquired 40,000 £1 shares in S Ltd on 1 January 19X4 for £70,000, when the profit and loss account reserves of S Ltd amounted to £15,000. Goodwill has a useful economic life of 6 years. Prepare the consolidated balance sheet at 31 December 19X4.

4.4   Solution

Step 1   Goodwill

	£'000	£'000
Cost of investment		70
Less: Share of net assets acquired		
Share capital	50	
Profit and loss account	15	
	65	
Group share	× 80%	
		(52)
		18

This is to be capitalised and written off over a period of 6 years.

Step 2   Profit and loss account

	£'000
P Ltd: all	30
S Ltd: P Ltd's share of S Ltd's post acquisition profits	
80% (20 − 15)	4
Less: Goodwill written off (18/6)	(3)
	31

Step 3   A third consolidation schedule is required to calculate the minority interest in the net assets of the subsidiary

Minority interest

Net assets of S at the balance sheet date

	£'000
Share capital	50
Profit and loss account	20
	70
Minority %	× 20%
	14

Conclusion   The minority interest balance is the minority share of the net assets of S Ltd at the balance sheet date.

Note how the reserves of S Ltd are allocated during the consolidation process:

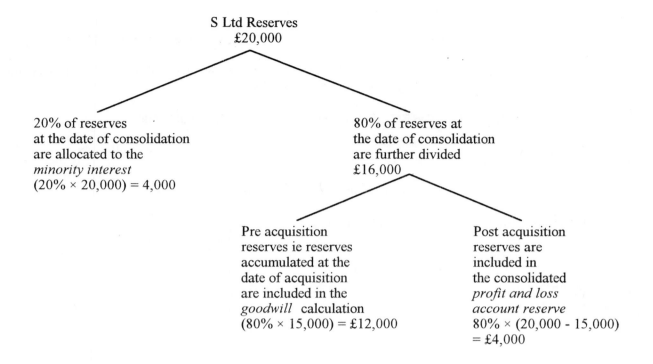

S Ltd Reserves
£20,000

20% of reserves
at the date of consolidation
are allocated to the
minority interest
(20% × 20,000) = 4,000

80% of reserves at
the date of consolidation
are further divided
£16,000

Pre acquisition
reserves ie reserves
accumulated at the
date of acquisition
are included in the
goodwill calculation
(80% × 15,000) = £12,000

Post acquisition
reserves are
included in
the consolidated
*profit and loss
account reserve*
80% × (20,000 - 15,000)
= £4,000

Similarly, the share capital of S Ltd is allocated to the goodwill calculation (the group's share, 80%) and to the minority interest calculation (the minority's share, 20%).

Step 4   Taking the balances from the consolidation schedules and then adding the other balance sheet items together, the consolidated balance sheet can be constructed:

	£'000	£'000
Goodwill (18 − 3)		15
Fixed assets £(50 + 40)		90
Current assets £(30 + 40)	70	
Creditors: amounts falling due within one year £(20 + 10)	30	
		40
Total assets less current liabilities		145
Called up share capital (£1 ordinary shares)		100
Profit and loss account		31
Minority interests		14
		145

Conclusion   This last example includes all the three basic elements of a balance sheet consolidation:

(a)   reserves in subsidiary company;

(b)   acquisition of less than 100% of S Ltd's shares (minority interest);

(c)   acquisition earlier than balance sheet date (pre- and post-acquisition reserves and write off of goodwill).

5   STEP-BY-STEP PROCEDURE FOR BALANCE SHEET CONSOLIDATION

5.1   Introduction

You should memorise the following step-by-step procedure.

Step 1   Analyse the shareholdings in S Ltd

	%
Group	P
Minority	M
	100

Step 2   Goodwill consolidation schedule

Goodwill

	£	£
Cost of investment		X
Less: Share of net assets of S Ltd at acquisition date		
Share capital	X	
Profit and loss account	X	
	X	
Group share	× P%	(X)
Goodwill - capitalise and then amortise through the consolidated reserves		X

Step 3   Reserves consolidation schedule

Profit and loss account reserve

	£
P Ltd:	X
S Ltd: Group share of S's post acquisition profits	
P% (S now − S at acquisition)	X
Less: Goodwill amortised (from step 2)	(X)
	X

Step 4   Minority interest consolidation schedule

Minority interest

	£
Net assets of S Ltd at the balance sheet date	
Share capital	X
Profit and loss account	X
	X
Minority share	× M%
	X

Step 5   Prepare the consolidated balance sheet, comprising:

(i)   balances on consolidation schedules (steps 2 to 4 above); **plus**
(ii)   items in original balance sheets not transferred to consolidation schedules.

5.2   Activity

The summarised draft balance sheets of a group at 31 December 19X4 were:

	P Ltd £	S Ltd £		P Ltd £	S Ltd £
Sundry assets	106,000	34,500	Share capital (£1 ord.)	100,000	20,000
Investment in S Ltd			Profit and loss account	22,000	6,500
(shares at cost)	27,000	-	Creditors	11,000	8,000
	133,000	34,500		133,000	34,500

P Ltd acquired 16,000 shares in S Ltd on 1 January 19X3, when S Ltd had profit and loss account reserves of £6,000. Goodwill has a useful economic life of 8 years.

Prepare the consolidated balance sheet at 31 December 19X4.

5.3   Activity solution

Note: your balance sheets should be prepared in vertical format. The examiner will occasionally give you 'draft' horizontal balance sheets as above, but your solution should always accord with best practice.

Step 1   Shareholdings in S Ltd

		%
Group	(16,000/20,000)	80
Minority	(4,000/20,000)	20
		100

Step 2   Goodwill

	£	£
Cost of investment		27,000
Less: Share of net assets of S Ltd at the acquisition date		
Share capital	20,000	
Profit and loss account	6,000	
	26,000	
Group share	× 80%	
		(20,800)
Goodwill - write off to consolidated profit and loss account reserve over 8 years ie £775 each year		6,200

Step 3   Reserves

Consolidated profit and loss account reserve

	£
P Ltd:	22,000
S Ltd: 80% (6,500 – 6,000)	400
Less: Goodwill amortised for 19X3 and 19X4 (2 × £775)	(1,550)
	20,850

The goodwill has been owned for 2 years therefore 2 years' amortisation charge must be deducted from consolidated reserves.

Step 4   Minority interest

Net assets of S Ltd at the balance sheet date

	£
Share capital	20,000
Profit and loss account	6,500
	26,500
Minority share	× 20%
	5,300

Step 5   P Ltd Group

Consolidated balance sheet at 31 December 19X4

	£
Goodwill (6,200 – 1,550)	4,650
Sundry assets (106,000 + 34,500)	140,500

Creditors (11,000 + 8,000)	(19,000)
Total assets less current liabilities	126,150
Called up share capital	100,000
Profit and loss account	20,850
Minority interest	5,300
	126,150

Conclusion   The steps to preparing a basic consolidated balance sheet are:

1. Establish the group structure.
2. Calculate goodwill arising on the acquisition.
3. Calculate consolidated reserves.
4. Calculate minority interest.
5. Prepare the consolidated balance sheet.

6   INTER-COMPANY ITEMS

6.1   Introduction

The individual balance sheets of the holding company and subsidiary companies are likely to include inter-company items ie, amounts owing between the group companies.   These inter-company items must be eliminated when the consolidated balance sheet is prepared, in order to show the proper position of the economic unit, the group as a single entity.

6.2   Current accounts

Definition   Current accounts are debtor/creditor balances between group companies.

They normally exist due to intra group trading where one group company sells goods to another group company.

6.3   Consolidation treatment

If the debtor current account in one company's books agrees with the creditor current account balance in the other company's books then the debtor and creditor balances can be cancelled against each other for consolidation purposes.

However the current accounts may not agree owing to either goods or cash in transit.

6.4   Goods/cash in transit

- If the goods or cash are in transit between the parent company and the subsidiary, make the adjusting entry to the balance sheet of the holding company, irrespective of the direction of transfer ie,

  Dr   Goods/Cash in transit
     Cr   Current account with subsidiary

  Note that this is for the purpose of consolidation only.

- Once in agreement, the current accounts may be contra'd and cancelled as part of the process of cross casting the upper half of the balance sheet.

6.5   Activity

Balance sheets at 31 December 19X4

	P Ltd £	S Ltd £
Investment in S Ltd (at cost)	19,000	
S Ltd current account	10,000	
P Ltd current account		(9,000)
Cash at bank	10,000	23,000
Sundry net assets	41,000	16,000
	80,000	30,000
Share capital (£1 ord)	50,000	10,000
Profit and loss account	30,000	20,000
	80,000	30,000

P Ltd bought 7,500 shares in S Ltd on 1 January 19X4 when the balance on the profit and loss account reserve of S Ltd was £12,000. The current account difference has arisen as a cheque sent by S Ltd to P Ltd on 30 December 19X4 was not received by P Ltd until 3 January 19X5. Goodwill has a useful life of 5 years.

Prepare the consolidated balance sheet at 31 December 19X4.

6.6   Activity solution

An adjustment for cash in transit has to be made before the consolidation can be completed. An extra step is therefore required in the consolidation procedure; it is a good idea to make this sort of adjustment early on so that it is not forgotten.

Step 1   Shareholdings in S Ltd

	%
Group (7,500/10,000)	75
Minority	25
	100

Step 2   Adjustments

Cash in transit

Dr:	Cash in transit		£1,000
	Cr:	S Ltd current account	
		(P's balance sheet)	£1,000

Cancel the current accounts which are now in agreement.

A working schedule could be produced as below:

		P Ltd	S Ltd	Group
		£	£	£
Investment in S Ltd (at cost)		19,000		
S Ltd current account	(1,000)	10,000		
P Ltd current account			(2,000)	
Cash at bank		10,000	23,000	**33,000**
Cash in transit	**1,000**	-		**1,000**
Sundry net assets		41,000	16,000	**57,000**
		80,000	30,000	**91,000**

However to save time these adjustments could be made on the question paper itself.

Step 3 Goodwill

	£	£
Cost of investment		19,000
Less: Share of net assets of S Ltd at the acquisition date		
Share capital	10,000	
Profit and loss account	12,000	
	22,000	
Group share	× 75%	
		16,500
Goodwill - capitalise and amortise over 5 years		2,500

Step 4 Reserves

Consolidated profit and loss account

	£
P Ltd:	30,000
S Ltd: 75% (20,000 − 12,000)	6,000
Less: Goodwill written off	(500)
	35,500

Step 5 Minority interest

Net assets of S Ltd at the balance sheet date

	£
Share capital	10,000
Profit and loss account	20,000
	30,000
Minority share	× 25%
	7,500

Step 6   P Ltd

Consolidated balance sheet at 31 December 19X4

	£
Goodwill (2,500 − 500)	2,000
Cash at bank (10,000 + 23,000)	33,000
Cash in transit	1,000
Sundry net assets	57,000
	93,000
Called up share capital	50,000
Profit and loss account	35,500
Minority interest	7,500
	93,000

Conclusion   When current accounts between members of a group disagree as a result of cash in transit, the balance sheets show the correct position from each individual company's point of view, but adjustment is required before the consolidation can be performed. The two current accounts will then cancel as the balance sheets are cross-cast.

6.7   Intra group profits

Where goods have been sold by one group company to another at a profit and some of these goods are still in the purchaser's stock at the year end, then the profit loading on these goods is **unrealised** from the viewpoint of the group as a whole.

This is because we are treating the group as if it is a single entity. No-one can make a profit by trading with himself. Therefore adjustments are required to remove the unrealised profit from the consolidated profit and loss account and reduce the value of the stock to cost to the group.

6.8   Wholly-owned subsidiary

Where goods are sold by S Ltd (a wholly-owned subsidiary) to P Ltd (its parent company), or by P Ltd to S Ltd, and some of the goods are in stock at the year end, there are two steps:

Step 1   calculate the unrealised profit in closing stock;

Step 2   make the consolidation adjustment for the unrealised profit as a double entry prior to drawing up the consolidated balance sheet:

Dr   Consolidated profit and loss account reserve
   Cr   Consolidated stock

This adjustment reduces stock to cost and removes unrealised profit from the group reserves.

6.9   Partly-owned subsidiary

Suppose P Ltd owns 90% of S Ltd. During the year S Ltd sells goods to P Ltd at cost plus 25%. At the year end the closing stock of P Ltd includes £8,000 of goods, at invoice value, acquired originally from S Ltd. What adjustments are required in the consolidation working papers?

In the past this was an area in which opinions differed. The CA89 requires intra-group profits to be eliminated but where a subsidiary is partly owned it allows the elimination to be either of the whole of the profit or in proportion to the group's shareholding in the subsidiary.

FRS 2 removes the choice as to who should suffer the deduction of intra-group profit.

Profit or losses on any intra-group transactions should be eliminated in full. The elimination should be set against the interests held by the group and the minority interest in proportion to their holdings in the undertaking whose individual financial statements recorded the eliminated profits or losses.

Thus, sales from the parent company to the subsidiary produce profits in the parent company. Any unrealised profits should be charged against the group. Sales from the subsidiary to the holding company produce profits in the subsidiary company. The unrealised profits should be split between the group and the minority.

6.10   Activity

P Ltd owns 90% of S Ltd. S Ltd sells goods to P Ltd at cost plus 25%. At the year end P Ltd's stock includes £8,000 of goods at invoice value from S Ltd.

What is the consolidation adjustment required?

6.11   Activity solution

Step 1   Calculate the unrealised profit

$$\frac{25}{125} \times £8,000 = £1,600$$

Note: the denominator in the fraction. The £8,000 is at **selling** price to S Ltd ie, $100 + 25$.

Step 2   Put through the consolidation adjustment.

Consolidated stock must be reduced (credited) by £1,600, the minority interest will be reduced by its share of this ($10\% \times 1,600$), £160, and the remaining 90%, £1,440, will be borne by the group as a reduction in revenue reserves.

This may be achieved by means of a consolidation adjustment put through prior to drawing up the balance sheet.

		£	£
Dr	Consolidated revenue reserves		
	$90\% \times 1,600$	1,440	
Dr	Minority interests		
	$10\% \times 1,600$	160	
	Cr Consolidated stock		1,600

If the sale of the goods had been from P Ltd to S Ltd then the profit would have been made in the books of P Ltd and there would be no minority interest effect. The consolidation adjustment would simply be:

Dr	Consolidated revenue reserves	£1,600	
	Cr Consolidated stock		£1,600

Conclusion   Profits made by members of a group on transactions with other group members are quite properly recognised in the accounts of the individual companies concerned. But in terms of the group as a whole, such profits are **unrealised** and must be eliminated from the consolidated accounts as a consolidation adjustment. If the profit is made by the subsidiary then there will be an adjustment to the minority interest.

6.12   Activity

Balance sheets at 31 December 19X4

	P Ltd £	S Ltd £
Investment in S Ltd (at cost)	75,000	
Stock	12,000	5,000
Other net assets	83,000	95,000
	170,000	100,000
Share capital (£1 ord)	50,000	40,000
Profit and loss account	120,000	60,000
	170,000	100,000

P Ltd acquired 32,000 shares in S Ltd on 1 January 19X4 when the balance on the profit and loss account of S Ltd was £50,000. During the year S Ltd sold goods to P Ltd for £80,000 making a standard mark up of 25%. At 31 December 19X4, P Ltd included in its stock value £5,000, being the price paid for goods purchased from S Ltd. Goodwill is to be written off over 3 years.

Prepare the consolidated balance sheet at 31 December 19X4.

6.13   Activity solution

Step 1   Shareholdings in S Ltd

	%
Group (32,000/40,000)	80
Minority	20
	100

Step 2   Adjustments

Unrealised profit on stock

$$5,000 \times \frac{25}{125} = £1,000$$

S Ltd sold the goods and made the profit, therefore the consolidation adjustment is:

		£	£
Dr	Consolidated revenue reserves	800	
Dr	Minority interest	200	
Cr	Consolidated stock		1,000

The unrealised profit adjustment is only made for stock remaining in the balance sheet at the year end. Stock not remaining in the balance sheet has been sold outside the group and therefore the profit has been realised.

Step 3   Goodwill

	£	£
Cost of investment		75,000
Less: Share of net assets of S Ltd at the acquisition date		
Share capital	40,000	
Profit and loss account	50,000	
	90,000	
Group share	× 80%	
		72,000
Goodwill - amortise to reserves over 3 years		3,000

Note: this calculation is unaffected by the provision for unrealised profit as the net assets of S Ltd at the date of acquisition are sold.

Step 4   Reserves

Consolidated profit and loss account

	£
P Ltd:	120,000
S Ltd: 80% [(60,000 − 1,000)* − 50,000]	7,200
Less: Goodwill written off	(1,000)
	126,200

Step 5   Minority interest

Net assets of S Ltd at the balance sheet date

	£
Share capital	40,000
Profit and loss account (60,000 − 1,000)*	59,000
	99,000
Minority share	× 20%
	19,800

* the revised reserves figure from step 2, as reduced by the provision for unrealised profit.

Step 6   P Ltd

Consolidated balance sheet at 31 December 19X4

	£
Goodwill (3 − 1)	2,000
Stock (12 + 5 − 1)	16,000
Other net assets (83 + 95)	178,000
	196,000
Called up share capital	50,000
Profit and loss account	126,200
Minority interest	19,800
	196,000

Conclusion   The consolidation adjustment for any unrealised profit on stock sold between group companies has two/three effects on the consolidation procedure:

- the consolidated stock must be reduced by the amount of the provision;

- the consolidated reserves must be reduced by the provision - if the profit was made by S Ltd this will affect S's post acquisition profits;

- if the profit was made by S Ltd there will also be an adjustment to the minority interest in the consolidated balance sheet.

7   PREFERENCE SHARES AND DEBENTURES IN SUBSIDIARIES

7.1   Preference shares in a subsidiary company

As a **general** rule, preference shares held by one company in another are irrelevant in determining whether the parent company/subsidiary company relationship exists.

The treatment of holdings in preference shares reflects the entitlement of preference shareholders to participate in profits on the winding up of a company. Generally, preference shareholders are only entitled to repayment of their share capital, whereas ordinary shareholders are entitled to their share capital and their share of any profits.

7.2   Effect of preference shares on consolidation workings

(a)   Shareholdings in S Ltd

	Ordinary shares %	Preference shares %
Group	A	C
Minority	B	D
	100	100

The % holdings of each type of share is calculated.

(b)   Goodwill on consolidation

	£	£
Cost of investment (ordinary + preference shares)		X
Less: Share of net assets acquired		
Ordinary share capital	X	
Profit and loss account	X	
	X	
Group share	× A%	
		(X)
Preference share capital	X	
Group share	× C%	
		(X)
		X

The group shareholding percentage in ordinary shares is applied to the ordinary share capital and reserves, whilst the group shareholding percentage in preference shares is applied to the preference share capital.

(c)   Reserves

The calculation is performed as usual, taking the ordinary shareholding percentage (A%) of the subsidiary's post acquisition profits.

(d)   Minority interest

	£	£
Net assets of S Ltd attributable to		
ordinary shareholdings:		
Ordinary share capital	X	
Profit and loss account	X	
	X	
Minority share	× B%	
		X
Attributable to preference shareholdings:		
Preference share capital	X	
Minority share	× D%	
		X
		X

Again, share capital and reserves are split between those attributable to ordinary shareholdings and those attributable to preference shareholdings.   The minority interest in each is then found separately.

7.3   Example

The draft balance sheet of S Ltd at 31 January 19X5 is as follows:

	£		£
Net assets	180,000	Ordinary share capital	100,000
		Profit and loss account	30,000
		Preference share capital	50,000
	————		————
	180,000		180,000
	————		————

At 31 January 19X5 P Ltd has reserves of £150,000 on the profit and loss account. During the previous year P Ltd acquired 70% of the ordinary share capital of S Ltd at a cost of £90,000 when the reserves of S Ltd amounted to £10,000 and 40% of the preference share capital at a cost of £22,000 when the reserves of S Ltd amounted to £15,000. Goodwill is to be written off over 5 years.

Show the consolidation schedules and shareholdings in S Ltd workings.

7.4   Solution

Shareholdings in S Ltd

	Ordinary shares %	Preference shares %
Group	70	40
Minority	30	60
	———	———
	100	100
	———	———

Goodwill

	£	£
Cost of investment (90 + 22)		112,000
Less: Share of net assets of S Ltd at the acquisition date		
Ordinary share capital	100,000	
Profit and loss account	10,000	
	————	
	110,000	
Group share	× 70%	
	————	
		(77,000)
Preference share capital	50,000	
Group share	× 40%	
	————	
		(20,000)
		————
Goodwill		15,000
		————

Reserves - consolidated profit and loss account

		£
P:		150,000
S:	70% (30,000 – 10,000)	14,000
Less:	Goodwill written off (15,000/5)	(3,000)
		161,000

Minority interest

	£	£
Net assets of S Ltd		
Attributable to ordinary shareholdings		
Ordinary share capital	100,000	
Profit and loss account	30,000	
	130,000	
Minority share	× 30%	
		39,000
Attributable to preference shareholdings:		
Preference share capital	50,000	
Minority share	× 60%	
		30,000
		69,000

(Tutorial notes:

(1) The revenue reserves of S Ltd at the date of the purchase of the preference shares by P Ltd are irrelevant.

(2) What would happen if P Ltd owned 70% of the ordinary share capital of S Ltd, but none of the preference share capital? In this case all the nominal value of the preference capital would be dealt with in the minority interests account. Hence, it is quite possible to have the apparent contradiction of crediting the minority interests account with the majority of preference share capital.*)

Conclusion   The existence of preference share capital in a subsidiary does not affect the holding company's control of the subsidiary. However it will have an effect on most of the consolidation workings.

7.5   Debentures in a subsidiary company

Debentures are also irrelevant for the purpose of determining the parent company/subsidiary relationship. However if the subsidiary company has debentures then these may appear in the consolidated balance sheet.

7.6   Procedure

The nominal value of debentures held by the parent company is cancelled with that same value of debentures of the subsidiary as the balance sheets are cross cast. This leaves the debentures of the subsidiary, held by outsiders, in the balance sheet as a long term creditor.

Conclusion   Preference shares of the subsidiary company **not** held by the parent company are included in the minority interest on the consolidated balance sheet. Debentures held by outsiders are shown separately on the consolidated balance sheet – they are **not** part of the minority interest.

7.7   Activity

Maximus Ltd acquired 90,000 £1 ordinary shares, 50,000 £1 preference shares and £10,000 debentures in Minimus Ltd on 1 January 19X1.

The balances in the books of Maximus Ltd and Minimus Ltd as at 31 December 19X4 were as follows:

	Maximus Ltd £	*Minimus Ltd* £
Ordinary shares of £1	500,000	120,000
8% non-cumulative preference shares of £1	-	80,000
7% debentures	-	40,000
Profit and loss account	200,000	96,000
Provision for depreciation	70,000	55,000
Creditors	130,000	32,500
	900,000	423,500
Fixed assets, at cost	450,000	280,000
90,000 ordinary shares in Minimus Ltd, at cost	185,000	-
50,000 preference shares in Minimus Ltd, at cost	55,000	-
£10,000 debentures in Minimus Ltd	10,000	-
Current assets	200,000	143,500
	900,000	423,500

You are also given the following information:

(a)   The profit and loss account reserve of Minimus Ltd as at 1 January 19X1 was £42,500.

(b)   The stock of Minimus Ltd at 31 December 19X4 includes £22,800 in respect of goods purchased from Maximus Ltd. Maximus invoices Minimus at cost plus 20%.

(c)   Goodwill has a useful economic life of 5 years.

You are required to prepare the consolidated balance sheet of Maximus Ltd and its subsidiary Minimus Ltd as at 31 December 19X4. Workings should be shown.

7.8   Activity solution

Step 1   Shareholdings in Minimus Ltd

	Ordinary shares	*Preference shares*
Group	3/4 (75%)	5/8 (62.5%)
Minority	1/4 (25%)	3/8 (37.5%)

Step 2   Adjustments

1   Unrealised profit on stock $=$ $\dfrac{20}{120} \times £22,800$

    $=$ £3,800

The profit was made by Maximus Ltd, therefore

Dr Consolidated reserves   £3,800
    Cr   Consolidated stock   £3,800

2   Cancel debentures

Working paper:

The balance sheets given in the question, as adjusted and cross cast to give the upper half of the consolidated balance sheet are as follows at this stage:

	Maximus Ltd		*Minimus Ltd*		*Group*
		£		£	£
Ordinary shares of £1		500,000		120,000	
8% non-cumulative preference shares of £1		-		80,000	
7% debentures		-	30,000	40,000	30,000
Profit and loss account	**(3,800)**	200,000		96,000	
Provision for depreciation		70,000		55,000	**125,000**
Creditors		130,000		32,500	**162,500**
		900,000		423,500	
Fixed assets, at cost		450,000		280,000	**730,000**
90,000 ordinary shares in Minimus Ltd		185,000			
50,000 preference shares in Minimus Ltd, at cost		55,000			
£10,000 debentures in Minimus Ltd	-	10,000			
Current assets	**(3,800)**	200,000		143,500	**339,700**
		900,000		423,500	

Step 3   Goodwill

	£	£
Cost of investment (185 + 55)		240,000
Less: Share of net assets at acquisition		
Ordinary share capital	120,000	
Profit and loss account		42,500
	162,500	
Group share	× 75%	
		(121,875)

Preference share capital

80,000

× 62.5%

(50,000)

Goodwill - write off to profit and loss account reserve
over 5 years

68,125

Step 4

Consolidated profit and loss account

	£
Maximus Ltd: per question	200,000
Unrealised profit on stock	(3,800)
Minimus: 75% (96,000 – 42,500)	40,125
Less: Goodwill written off 4 years - (68,125 × 4/5)	(54,500)
	181,825

Step 5   Minority interest

	£	£
Net assets of Minimus Ltd		
Attributable to ordinary shareholdings		
Ordinary share capital	120,000	
Profit and loss account	96,000	
	216,000	
Minority share	× 25%	
		54,000
Attributable to preference shareholdings		
Preference share capital	80,000	
Minority share	× 37.5%	
		30,000
		84,000

Step 6   Prepare the consolidated balance sheet.

Consolidated balance sheet of Maximus Ltd and its subsidiary, Minimus Ltd at 31 December 19X4

	£	£
Fixed assets:		
Intangible assets		
Goodwill (68,125 × 1/5)		13,625
Tangible assets:		
Cost (Step 2)	730,000	
Depreciation (Step 2)	125,000	
		605,000
Current assets (Step 2)	339,700	

Creditors (amounts falling due within one year) (Step 2)	162,500	
Net current assets		177,200
Total assets less current liabilities		795,825
Creditors (amounts falling due after more than one year) 7% debentures (Step 2)		(30,000)
		765,825

Capital and reserves:	
Called up ordinary share capital, allotted and fully paid	500,000
Profit and loss account	181,825
Minority interest	84,000
	765,825

8   DIVIDENDS AND DEBENTURE INTEREST OF SUBSIDIARIES

8.1   Introduction

In dealing with consolidations which involve one group company paying a dividend or interest instalment to another group company, it is easy to get confused, especially if the information given includes one or more dividends incorrectly or incompletely treated. We need to determine, for each dividend or interest instalment:

(a)   what entries should have been made by each company involved;
(b)   what entries have actually been made;
(c)   the entries to correct or complete the treatment;

and then continue with the consolidation.

8.2   Dividends – The correct treatment

If the dividend is paid by the year-end:

Paying company:	Dr	Profit and loss account ('Dividend paid')	
	Cr	Cash	
Receiving company:	Dr	Cash	
	Cr	Profit and loss account ('Dividend received')	

On consolidating the balance sheet, no adjustment will be required.

If the dividend is outstanding at the year-end:

Paying company:	Dr	Profit and loss account ('Dividend payable/proposed')
	Cr	Proposed dividend/Declared dividend (a creditor)
Receiving company:	Dr	Dividend receivable (a debtor)
	Cr	Profit and loss account ('Dividend receivable')

On consolidating the balance sheet, a cancellation must be made between the current asset, 'dividend receivable' as shown in the receiving company's books and the creditor 'proposed dividend' shown in the paying company's books. If only part of the dividend is payable to the other group company, then that part payable to outsiders must be shown as a current liability in the consolidated balance sheet with the heading 'dividend payable to minority shareholders'.

8.3   Dividends not accrued

Where the correct entries have not been made in the books of the company the general procedure is to make entries in the balance sheet working papers to give effect to the missing entries and, if necessary, to reverse any wrong entries.

8.4   Example

Upminster Ltd acquired 80% of the ordinary share capital of Barking Ltd on 1 January 19X2 when the balance on the profit and loss account of Barking Ltd was £12,000. Their respective draft balance sheets at 31 December 19X4 are as follows:

	Upminster Ltd £	*Barking Ltd* £
Fixed assets	100,000	92,000
Investment in Barking Ltd	55,000	-
Current assets	45,000	31,000
	200,000	123,000
Ordinary share capital	100,000	50,000
Preference share capital	-	10,000
Profit and loss account	80,000	42,000
Proposed dividend	-	10,000
Sundry creditors	20,000	11,000
	200,000	123,000

Upminster has not made any entry for the dividend receivable from Barking for the year. A proposed preference dividend of £2,000 by Barking Ltd has not been accounted for by either company. Upminster Ltd also purchased 30% of the preference shares for £3,500 on 1 January 19X2.

Goodwill is to be written off over 4 years.

Prepare the consolidated balance sheet for Upminster Ltd and its subsidiary company at 31 December 19X4.

8.5   Solution

Step 1   Shareholdings in Barking Ltd

	Ordinary shares %	*Preference shares* %
Group	80	30
Minority	20	70
	100	100

Step 2   Adjustments

1   Proposed preference dividend by Barking Ltd

Dr:	Profit and loss account	£2,000	
	Cr: Proposed dividend		£2,000

2   Dividends receivable by Upminster

    Dr: Dividends receivable
            (ordinary: 80% × 10,000)   £8,000
    Dr: Dividends receivable
            (preference: 30% × 2,000)   £600

        Cr: Profit and loss account   £8,600

3   Cancel dividends receivable/payable when the upper half of the balance sheet is cross cast.

Working paper:

	Upminster Ltd		Barking Ltd			Group
		£	£			£
Fixed assets		100,000	92,000			**192,000**
Investment in Barking Ltd		55,000	-			
Current assets		45,000	31,000			**76,000**
	(2) ~~8,000~~					
Dividends receivable	(2) ~~600~~	200,000	123,000			
Ordinary share capital		100,000	50,000			
Preference share capital		-	10,000			
Profit and loss account	(2) + 8,600	80,000	42,000	(2,000)	(1)	
(Proposed dividend)						
becomes:						
Dividend payable to minority						
shareholders		-	2,000	~~10,000~~ +~~2,000~~ 1,400	(1)	**3,400**
Sundry creditors		20,000	11,000			**31,000**
		200,000	123,000			

Tutorial note: these amendments may be made to the balance sheets given in the question as this ensures they are not forgotten. However, it is also important that your **answer** also shows these amendments, hence the figures bracketed in the schedules and balance sheet following.

⟦Step 3⟧   Goodwill

	£	£
Cost of investment		55,000
Less: Share of net assets at acquisition		
Ordinary share capital	50,000	
Profit and loss account	12,000	
	62,000	
Group share	× 80%	
		(49,600)
Preference share capital	10,000	
Group share	× 30%	
		(3,000)
Goodwill - write off to profit and loss account reserve over 4 years		2,400

Step 4   Reserves

Consolidated profit and loss account

	£
Upminster Ltd: (80,000 + 8,600)	88,600
Barking Ltd: 80% (42,000 − 2,000 − 12,000)	22,400
Less: Goodwill written off (2,400 × 3/4)	(1,800)
	109,200

Step 5   Minority interest

Net assets

	£	£
Attributable to ordinary shareholdings		
Ordinary share capital	50,000	
Profit and loss account (42,000 − 2,000)	40,000	
	90,000	
Minority share	× 20%	
		18,000
Attributable to preference shareholdings		
Preference share capital	10,000	
	× 70%	
		7,000
		25,000

Consolidated balance sheet of Upminster Ltd and its subsidiary, Barking Ltd as at 31 December 19X4

	£	£
Fixed assets:		
Intangible assets (2,400 × 1/4)		600
Tangible assets (100 + 92)		192,000
Current assets (45 + 31)	76,000	
Creditors (amounts falling due within one year):		
Sundry creditors (20 + 11)	31,000	
Dividend payable to minority shareholders	3,400	
	34,400	
Net current assets		41,600
Total assets less current liabilities		234,200
Capital and reserves:		
Called up ordinary share capital allotted and fully paid	100,000	
Reserves – profit and loss account	109,200	

	209,200
Minority interests	25,000
	234,200

> **Conclusion** The only amount to appear in the consolidated balance sheet for the subsidiary company's dividend payable is the amount payable to the minority interest. Any dividends payable by the holding company appear in full in the consolidated balance sheet as a creditor.

8.6 Debenture interest payable by a subsidiary

The procedure for dealing with debenture interest payable is exactly the same as for ordinary or preference dividends payable by a subsidiary. The **only** difference is in the description of the group liability to pay debenture interest. This liability has nothing to do with minority shareholders – it is simply a creditor like any other.

9 FAIR VALUE ADJUSTMENTS

9.1 Introduction

Goodwill is the difference between the cost of an investment and the fair value of the net assets acquired. In acquisition accounting, the assets and liabilities of the subsidiary must be brought into the consolidated accounts at their fair values and goodwill must be based on these fair values.

The fair values of the assets and liabilities of a subsidiary may not be the same as their book values and it may be necessary to adjust the accounts of the subsidiary to reflect this.

9.2 Activity

X plc acquired 80% of the ordinary share capital of Y Ltd on 30 September 19X4 for £320,000.

The net assets of Y Ltd at that date had a book value of £350,000.

The following information is relevant:

(a)   Y Ltd's freehold factory is included in the accounts at £100,000 and no adjustment has been made to recognise the valuation of £120,000 put on the property when it was professionally revalued on 15 September 19X4.

(b)   The fair value of Y Ltd's stock at 30 September 19X4 is estimated to be £4,000 less than its book value at that date.

Calculate:

(i)   Goodwill arising on the acquisition of Y Ltd
(ii)   Minority interest at 30 September 19X4.

9.3   Activity solution

[Step 1]   Adjust the value of Y Ltd's net assets as at 30 September 19X4 to fair value.

	£
Net assets per question	350,000
Revaluation of property	20,000
Write-off of stock	(4,000)
	366,000

[Step 2]   Calculate goodwill.

	£
Fair value of consideration	320,000
Net assets acquired 80% × £366,000	292,800
	27,200

[Step 3]   Calculate minority interest

MI share of fair value of net assets (20% × £366,000) **£73,200**

[Conclusion]   In acquisition accounting, the subsidiary's assets and liabilities must be brought into the consolidated accounts at their fair values at the date of acquisition, rather than their book values.

10   SELF TEST QUESTIONS

1   What is the normal form of group accounts? (1.2)

2   What is represented by the excess of the price paid for a business over the fair value of the net assets acquired? (2.4)

3   How should goodwill on consolidation be treated according to FRS 10? (2.5)

4   Why must a distinction be drawn between a subsidiary's pre-acquisition and post-acquisition reserves? (3.1)

5   How are pre-acquisition reserves treated? (3.3)

6   How are current account balances between the parent company and the subsidiary accounted for in drawing up a consolidated balance sheet? (6.3)

7   How are current account balances made to balance for consolidation purposes? (6.4)

8   How does FRS 2 require that unrealised profits in year-end stocks should be accounted for? (6.9)

9   If P holds 100% of S's ordinary shares but only 10% of S's preference shares, is S still a subsidiary of P? (7.1)

10   What is the correct accounting treatment for intra-group dividends during an accounting period? (8.2)

20 CONSOLIDATED PROFIT AND LOSS ACCOUNT

PATHFINDER INTRODUCTION

This chapter covers the following performance criteria and knowledge and understanding.

- Application of the general principles of consolidation (knowledge and understanding 10.2)

Putting the chapter in context – learning objectives.

This chapter now applies the basic consolidated techniques covered in the previous chapter to the consolidated profit and loss account. The basic technique for a consolidated profit and loss account is introduced first of all and then a variety of complications are added to this.

At the end of this chapter you should have learned the following topics.

- The basic approach to the consolidated profit and loss account.
- Acquisition of a subsidiary during the year.
- Some further complications.

---

1 APPROACH TO CONSOLIDATED PROFIT AND LOSS ACCOUNT

1.1 Introduction

The consolidated profit and loss account for a holding company and its subsidiaries is prepared under exactly the same principles as the consolidated balance sheet. These are:

- that the holding company and subsidiaries are treated as a single entity for accounting purposes;

- any intra-group items in the profit and loss account are cancelled with each other and only income and expenses from/to third parties are shown;

- the group only takes into its profit and loss account post acquisition profits and losses;

- the consolidated profit and loss account shows all of the profits of subsidiaries and then the element of profit that is not owned by the group, the minority interest, is deducted.

1.2 Preparation of consolidated profit and loss account

Many of the figures that go into a consolidated profit and loss account are simply cross casting of the individual items for each of the companies in the group. However there will then tend to be a number of adjustments that require to be made in order to reach the correct consolidation figures. This cross-casting and subsequent adjustments tend to be carried out in a consolidation schedule.

1.3 Example

The draft profit and loss accounts for the year ended 31 March 19X7 of the companies in a group are as follows:

	T Ltd £	W Ltd £
Turnover	216,300	24,400
Cost of sales	136,269	15,372
Gross profit	80,031	9,028
Distribution costs	(21,630)	(2,440)
Income from shares in group companies	1,464	-
Net profit before taxation	59,865	6,588
Taxation	28,119	3,172
Net profit after taxation	31,746	3,416
Dividends	20,000	1,952
Transfer to reserves	11,746	1,464
Reserves brought forward	36,728	7,076
Reserves carried forward	48,474	8,540

The history of the group is as follows:

T Ltd bought 75% of the ordinary shares (the only type) in W Ltd several years ago for £48,000 when that company's reserves amounted to £5,124. The issued share capital of W Ltd is 50,000 £1 shares. The goodwill on acquisition has already been written off through the profit and loss account.

Prepare the consolidated profit and loss account for the year ended 31 March 19X7.

1.4   Solution

Step 1   The master schedule is drafted first, with a column for each company and a 'consolidated' column. The group structure is then summarised at the head of each column. There is also a column for consolidation adjustments. It is not required in this activity but will be later in the chapter.

T is the parent company; W is a 75% owned subsidiary and has been for the entire year.

Step 2   In any example with intra-group dividends, begin by reconciling the amounts receivable by the entire company with the amounts payable by the subsidiaries. This may reveal errors or omissions in accounting for the dividends and, if so, they should be corrected before beginning the consolidation.

Under no circumstances whatever do dividends of subsidiaries ever appear in the consolidated profit and loss account. The dividend income in the holding company's books cancels with the dividend paid/proposed in the subsidiary's books. Any remaining amount of the subsidiary's dividend is automatically included in the minority interest line.

Step 3   For items from 'turnover' to 'net profit after tax' (from ordinary activities), we enter:

For parent company	the full amount
For subsidiary owned throughout the year	the full amount

Step 4   The figure of £33,698 net profit on ordinary activities after tax completes one section of the consolidated profit and loss account, and it represents the total profit from ordinary activities that the directors have obtained by using the assets that they control.

However, not all of this will accrue to the shareholders of T Ltd and the amount that accrues to the minority shareholders in the subsidiaries will be deducted.

In this case, because the companies have only ordinary shares, it is easy to calculate the minority share. It is simply the minority shareholders' fraction of the ordinary shares, multiplied by the last figure, net profit after tax, in the column for the relevant subsidiary.

The resulting sub-total is the amount of profit from ordinary activities that accrues to the parent company shareholders.

Step 5   After minority interest there is a dividend adjustment which does not appear in the consolidated figures. This simply cancels the dividend receivable by T Ltd against the dividend payable by W Ltd.

Step 6   Group reserves brought forward consists of:

(i)   all the parent company's profit;
(ii)   the group share of the subsidiaries' post acquisition profits; and
(iii)   less goodwill amortised up to the beginning of the current accounting period.

The goodwill has not been deducted from the reserves of any particular company in the group as it represents an adjustment purely taking effect in the consolidation working papers.

Step 7   Once the master schedule has been filled in, the actual consolidated profit and loss account can be written out, using the figures from the 'consolidated' column. The account should follow the statutory formats. Minority interests are required to be shown immediately after profit on ordinary activities after taxation.

Master schedule	*T Ltd*	*W Ltd*	*Cons. Adjs.*	*Consolidated*
Group details		*75%*		
		12 months		
	£	£	£	£
Turnover	216,300	24,400		240,700
Cost of sales	(136,269)	(15,372)		(151,641)
Distribution costs	(21,630)	(2,440)		(24,070)
Investment income (W1)	-	-		-
Taxation	(28,119)	(3,172)		(31,291)
Net profit after taxation	30,282	3,416		33,698
Minority interest	-	(854) (W2)		(854)
Dividends – Internal:				
W (W1)	1,464	(1,464)		
Profit before dividend	31,746			
Dividend	(20,000)			(20,000)
Transfers to reserves	11,746	1,098		12,844
Brought forward	36,728	1,464 (W3)		
Less: Goodwill written off			(6,657) (W4)	31,535
Carried forward	48,474	2,562	(6,657)	44,379

WORKINGS

(W1)   Reconciliation of intra-group dividends

	£
Per T, received	1,464
Should agree with:	
W, paid £1,952 × 75%	1,464

This is an amount due/received from a group company therefore it will not appear in the consolidated profit and loss account.

(W2)   25% × £3,416 = £854

(W3)   75% × £(7,076 – 5,124) = £1,464

(W4)   Goodwill on acquisition

	W Ltd £
Share capital	50,000
Reserves at acquisition	5,124
Net assets at acquisition	55,124
Group share	75%
	41,343
Cost of investment	48,000
	6,657

T Ltd and its subsidiary
Consolidated profit and loss account for the year ended 31 March 19X7

	£
Turnover	240,700
Cost of sales	(151,641)
Gross profit	89,059
Distribution costs	(24,070)
Profit on ordinary activities before taxation	64,989
Tax on profit on ordinary activities	(31,291)
Profit on ordinary activities after taxation	33,698
Minority interest	(854)
Net profit after taxation attributable to shareholders of T Ltd	32,844
Dividends	(20,000)
	12,844

Statement of reserves

	£
At 31 March 19X6	31,535
Retained profits	12,844
At 31 March 19X7	44,379

Conclusion   For a basic consolidated profit and loss account the full amounts for the subsidiary are brought in from turnover down to profit after tax (provided that it has been owned all year). At that point the minority share of the subsidiary's profit after tax is deducted on the minority interest line. The dividends that appear in a consolidated profit and loss account are only ever the holding company dividends paid and payable.

2   ACQUISITION OF A SUBSIDIARY DURING THE YEAR

2.1   Introduction

If a subsidiary is acquired during the year complications will arise in the production of consolidated profit and loss accounts.

(a)   The sales and costs of the subsidiary are consolidated into the group figures for the post-acquisition period only. In the absence of any detailed information time apportionment of the annual figures will apply.

(b)   These items may require separate disclosure on the face of the profit and loss account or in the notes to the accounts under the provisions of FRS 3 on acquisition.

(c)   Goodwill may require calculation and partial amortisation through the profit and loss account.

2.2   Example

The draft profit and loss account of a group for the year ended 30 April 19X4 is:

	B Ltd £	G Ltd £	Y Ltd £
Turnover	4,418	2,726	2,256
Cost of sales	1,974	1,218	1,008
Gross profit	2,444	1,508	1,248
Administrative expenses	752	464	384
Net profit before taxation	1,692	1,044	864
Taxation	799	493	408
Net profit after taxation	893	551	456
Dividends	470	290	150
Transfer to reserves	423	261	306
Reserves brought forward	1,070	420	72
Reserves carried forward	1,493	681	378

Further information

(a)   B Ltd acquired all the shares of G Ltd several years ago when G Ltd had reserves of £270. Goodwill of £100 on this acquisition has been written off in full against group reserves.

(b)   B Ltd acquired 80% of the ordinary shares of Y Ltd, which has no other type of share, on 1 December 19X3. Goodwill of £240 is to be written off through the profit and loss account over 4 years.

(c)   B Ltd has accounted for the dividends receivable from G Ltd and Y Ltd by including in turnover the whole amount receivable. All the dividends were outstanding at 30 April 19X4.

Prepare the consolidated profit and loss account for the year ended 30 April 19X4.

2.3   Solution

Step 1   Set up master schedule. Make a clear note that Y Ltd is 80% owned and has been owned for only 5 months of the current year.

Step 2   Deal with the intra-group dividends (W1/W2).

Step 3   Enter figures for turnover down to profit after tax. Remember to include only 5/12 of each of Y Ltd's figures. There is also an additional expense of goodwill in Y Ltd to be amortised.

Step 4   Enter minority interest.

Step 5   Put through internal adjustment for dividends.

Step 6   Calculate reserves b/f. Remember to write off goodwill in G Ltd against brought forward reserves.

Step 7   Complete consolidated profit and loss account.

Master schedule

Group details	B Ltd	G Ltd 100% 12 months	Y Ltd 80% 5 months	Adjustments	Consolidated
	£	£	£	£	£
Turnover	4,008 (W1)	2,726	940 (W3)		7,674
Cost of sales	(1,974)	(1,218)	(420)		(3,612)
Administrative expenses	(752)	(464)	(160)		(1,376)
Goodwill	-	-	25		(25) (W4)
Taxation	(799)	(493)	(170)		(1,462)
Net profit after taxation	483	551	190		1,199
Minority interest	-	-	(38) (W5)		(38)
Dividends – Internal:					
G	290 (W6)	(290)			-
Y	120 (W7)		(120)		-
Profit before dividend	893				
Dividend – B	(470)				(470)
Retained profit	423	261	32		691
Brought forward (W8)	1,070	150	-	(100)	1,120
Carried forward	1,493	411	32	(125)	1,811

WORKINGS

		£
(W1)	Per draft accounts	4,418
	Less: Dividends wrongly included (W2)	410
		4,008

(W2)	B will receive:	
	G 100% × £290	290
	Y 80% × £150	120
	Amount to be removed from turnover	410

(W3)   5/12 × £2,256 = £940. Likewise the next three items in Y's column.

(W4)   Goodwill. £240 × 1/4 × 5/12 = £25 - the amount of goodwill on acquisition of Y Ltd to be written off this year.

(W5)   20% × £190 = £38.

(W6)   B's share of G's dividend = 100% × £290 = £290.

(W7)   B's share of Y's dividend = 80% × £150 = £120.

(W8)   Post acquisition profits:

	£
B Ltd	1,070
G Ltd	
100% × £(420 – 270)	150
Less: Goodwill	(100)
	1,120

No part of Y's reserves formed part of consolidated reserves at the beginning of the year as Y was only purchased during the year.

(Tutorial note: The dividend received from Y Ltd partly relates to the period before that company became a subsidiary. This means that it was paid partly out of pre-acquisition profits. Under current accounting practice, pre-acquisition dividends are credited to the parent company profit and loss account in *full* provided that the value of the investment in the parent's own financial statements is not permanently diminished by the payment of the dividend.)

B Ltd and its subsidiaries
Consolidated profit and loss account for the year ended 30 April 19X4

	£
Turnover:	
Continuing operations	6,734
Acquisitions	940
	7,674

Cost of sales	3,612
Gross profit	4,062
Administrative expenses (1,376 + 25)	1,401

Operating profit:

Continuing operations	2,301	
Acquisitions (190 + 170)	360	

Profit on ordinary activities before taxation	2,661
Tax on profit on ordinary activities	1,462
Profit on ordinary activities after taxation	1,199
Minority interest	38
Net profit after taxation attributable to shareholders of B Ltd	1,161
Dividends proposed	470
Transferred to reserves	691

Statement of reserves

	£
At 30 April 19X3	1,120
Retained profits	691
At 30 April 19X4	1,811

Notes to the accounts

The total figures for continuing operations in 19X4 include the following amounts relating to the acquisition: cost of sales £420 and administrative expenses £160.

(Note: The split of turnover and operating profit in the profit and loss account is the minimum required disclosure of FRS 3. The note above is also an FRS 3 requirement.)

Conclusion   Where a subsidiary is acquired part way through the year, the results of the subsidiary are included in the consolidated profit and loss account for the post-acquisition period only.

3   FURTHER COMPLICATIONS

3.1   Cancellation of intra-group transactions

The previous chapter dealt with the treatment of unrealised profits on stock arising from intra-group trading in the consolidated balance sheet. In consolidating the profit and loss accounts a rather more involved adjustment is required.

3.2   Activity

If in a certain year:

A Ltd buys a stock item for £60, and sells it to its subsidiary B Ltd for £80.

B Ltd has sold the stock by the balance sheet date for £95.

What amounts would be shown in the consolidated profit and loss account?

3.3 **Activity solution**

The profit and loss accounts for the two individual companies to reflect these transactions would be as follows:

	A Ltd £	B Ltd £
Turnover	80	95
Cost of sales	60	80
Gross profit	20	15

However if the two companies are treated as a single entity for consolidation purposes then the only figures to be recorded should be any sales to third parties, purchases from third parties and profits made with third parties. Therefore the profit and loss account for consolidation purposes as a single entity should be:

	A and B Ltd - consolidated £
Turnover	95
Cost of sales	60
Gross profit	35

In order to get to this position a consolidation adjustment is required in the master schedule to remove the £80 of intra-group sale and £80 of intra-group purchase:

	A Ltd £	B Ltd £	Consolidation adjustment £	Consolidated figures £
Turnover	80	95	(80)	95
Cost of sales	60	80	(80)	60
Gross profit	20	15	-	35

Conclusion If any items that have been sold within the group have been sold onto third parties before the year end the consolidated profit and loss account adjustment required is to remove the amount of the intra group sale from both turnover and cost of sales.

3.4 **Items in stock at the year end**

In the previous activity the intra group sale items were not included as part of closing stock as they had already been sold onto a third party and the profit had been realised.

However if the items have not been sold on and are still in stock there are two further problems:

- the profit made by the selling company is an unrealised profit as far as the group is concerned;

- the closing stock figure will be over-valued, it will not represent cost to the group.

3.5   Activity

A Ltd buys stock for £60 and sells it to its subsidiary B Ltd for £80. B Ltd still holds the items in stock at the end of the year.

What adjustments are required for consolidated profit and loss account purposes?

3.6   Activity solution

The profit and loss accounts for the individual companies will be as follows:

	A Ltd		B Ltd	
	£	£	£	£
Turnover		80		-
Purchases	60		80	
Less: closing stock	-		80	
Cost of sales		60		-
Gross profit		20		-

As far as the two companies as a single entity, the group, are concerned the £20 is an unrealised profit and the consolidated profit and loss account should look like this:

	A and B Ltd - consolidated	
	£	£
Turnover		-
Purchases	60	
Less: closing stock	60	
Cost of sales		-
Gross profit		-

This can be achieved by three consolidation adjustments:

- remove intra group sale of £80 from turnover;

- remove intra group purchase of £80 from cost of sales;

- write down closing stock value to £60 by increasing cost of sales by £20, the amount of the unrealised profit.

Again this is achieved using the consolidation adjustment column in the master schedule:

	A Ltd		B Ltd		Consolidation adjustments		Consolidated figures
	£	£	£	£	£	£	£
Turnover		80		-	(80)		-
Purchases	60		80		(80)	60	
Less: closing stock	-		(80)		20	(60)	
Cost of sales		60		-			-
Gross profit		20		-			-

Conclusion When the goods that have been sold from one group company to another are still in stock at the year end then the amount of the intra-group sale must be deducted from both turnover and cost of sales in the consolidated profit and loss account. However a further adjustment is required to cost of sales by adding in to cost of sales the amount of the unrealised profit on the closing stock. This has the effect of writing the closing stock down to cost to the group.

3.7 Effect on minority interests

If the unrealised profit originally arose in the subsidiary company's books, the minority interest must be adjusted for their share in the unrealised profit. However this is an adjustment made in calculating their share of post tax profits; in the first instance all the unrealised profit must be eliminated to determine the correct amount of gross profit earned by the group trading as if it were a single entity.

3.8 Example

The profit and loss accounts of E Ltd and F Ltd for the year ended 31 July 19X7 are as follows:

	E Ltd £	F Ltd £
Turnover	6,956	3,290
Cost of sales	3,108	1,470
Gross profit	3,848	1,820
Administrative expenses	(1,184)	(560)
Net profit on ordinary activities before taxation	2,664	1,260
Tax on profit on ordinary activities	1,258	595
Net profit after taxation	1,406	665
Dividends	800	-
Profit transferred to reserves	606	665

Statement of reserves

	E Ltd £	F Ltd £
As at 31 July 19X6	797	3,955
Retained profit	606	665
As at 31 July 19X7	1,403	4,620

Further information

(a)   E Ltd acquired 6,000 of the issued 10,000 ordinary shares in F Ltd several years ago when the reserves of F Ltd were £980. There was no goodwill on acquisition.

(b)   In the year ended 31 July 19X7 F Ltd sold to E Ltd goods costing £500 for £625 (25% profit margin on cost).

(c)   At 31 July 19X7 E Ltd had sold 40% of these goods for £300.

Prepare the consolidated profit and loss account of E Ltd and its subsidiary for the year ended 31 July 19X7.

3.9   Solution

Step 1   **Dealing with inter-company trading**

- Eliminate from sales **all** inter-company sales at the selling price.

   Therefore deduct £625.

- Eliminate inter company sales, £625, from cost of sales.

- Compute unrealised profit in goods not sold, ie, the same calculation as for the consolidated balance sheet.

   Closing stock re goods sold from F to E

   $60\% \times £625 = £375$

   Unrealised profit

   $$\frac{25}{125} \times £375 = £75$$

   Add this unrealised profit to cost of sales.

- The reduction in cost of sales is **the net figure** (£625 – £75) = £550.

Thus if there are no unrealised profits, cost of sales is reduced by the same amount as sales.

The figures shown/computed above can now be transferred to the consolidation schedule.

Step 2   **Calculation of minority interests**

	£
Minority interest:	
Profit after tax of F Ltd	665
Less: Unrealised profit on intra group sale	(75)
	590

Minority interest $40\% \times 590 = £236$

Step 3   **Group reserves brought forward**

	£
E	797
F: 60% × £(3,955 − 980)	1,785
	2,582

Master schedule

Group details	E Ltd	F Ltd 60% 12 months	Adjustments	Consolidated
	£	£	£	£
Turnover	6,956	3,290	(625)	9,621
Cost of sales	(3,108)	(1,470)	550	(4,028)
Gross profit	3,848	1,820	(75)	5,593
Administrative expenses	(1,184)	(560)	-	(1,744)
Taxation	(1,258)	(595)	-	(1,853)
Profit after taxation	1,406	665	(75)	1,996

Step 4   **E Ltd and its subsidiary**

	£
Turnover	9,621
Cost of sales	4,028
Gross profit	5,593
Administrative expenses	1,744
Profit on ordinary activities before taxation	3,849
Tax on profit on ordinary activities	1,853
Profit on ordinary activities after taxation	1,996
Minority interest	236
Profit attributable to shareholders in E Ltd	1,760
Dividends	800
Profit transferred to reserves	960

Statement of reserves

	£
As at 31 July 19X6	2,582
Retained profit	960
As at 31 July 19X7	3,542

Conclusion   When an intra group sale is made by the subsidiary company then any unrealised profit arising is made by the subsidiary. When this is eliminated on consolidation this will also affect the minority interest calculation.

3.10   Preference shares in the subsidiary company

If the subsidiary company has preference shares in issue then this will affect the minority interest calculation in the consolidated profit and loss account. The reason for this is that some of the profits of the subsidiary will belong to the preference shareholders, the total of their annual dividend, and the remainder of profit belongs to the ordinary shareholders. This means that there is a slightly more complicated calculation in order to determine the amount of profit relating to the minority interest.

3.11   Activity

A Ltd owns 75% of the ordinary £1 shares of B Ltd and 40,000 of the 100,000 £1 6% preference shares of B Ltd. The profit after tax for B Ltd for the year is £50,000.

What is the figure that will appear in the consolidated profit and loss account for minority interest?

3.12   Activity solution

	£	Minority %	Minority interest £
Profit after tax	50,000		
Preference dividend	(6,000)	60%	3,600
Profit available for ordinary shareholders	44,000	25%	11,000
Total minority interest			14,600

Conclusion   When the subsidiary company has preference shares then the minority interest calculation requires a little more thought. Firstly the preference dividend that will not be paid to the holding company belongs to the minority. The remaining profit after the total preference dividend has been deducted is then allocated to the minority interest on the basis of the ordinary shareholding.

4   SELF TEST QUESTIONS

1   How is a dividend received during the year from a subsidiary company treated in the consolidated profit and loss account? (1.4)

2   If a subsidiary has been 80% owned all year how much of its taxation charge should appear in the consolidated profit and loss account? (1.4)

3   What figures make up the group reserves brought forward in the consolidated profit and loss account? (1.4)

4   If a subsidiary is acquired part of the way through the year what effect will this have on the amount of turnover for that subsidiary that is included in the consolidated profit and loss account? (2.1)

5   If a subsidiary is acquired part of the way through the year how is the minority interest figure to appear in the consolidated profit and loss account calculated? (2.3)

6   If a subsidiary is acquired part of the way through the year how are the brought forward reserves for that subsidiary calculated for inclusion in the consolidated profit and loss account? (2.3)

7   If a sale of goods is made between a holding company and subsidiary during a year but the goods do not remain in stock at the year end, what is the consolidation adjustment required? (3.3)

8   If a sale of goods is made between a holding company and a subsidiary during a year and the goods are still in stock at the year end, what is the consolidation adjustment? (3.6)

9   Is it an intra group sale from holding company to subsidiary or subsidiary to holding company that affects the minority interest calculation if the goods are still in stock at the year end? (3.7)

10   How is the minority interest figure for the consolidated profit and loss account calculated if the subsidiary company has preference shares in issue? (3.12)

21 ASSOCIATED UNDERTAKINGS

PATHFINDER INTRODUCTION

This chapter covers the following performance criteria and knowledge and understanding.

- Draft accounts comply with domestic standards and legislation (performance criteria 10.2)
- Application of the general principles of consolidation (knowledge and understanding 10.2)

Putting the chapter in context – learning objectives

The previous chapters have considered in detail the techniques required for consolidation of subsidiary companies. A subsidiary company is a company that is controlled by its parent (holding) company. In this chapter a lesser degree of control will be considered where one company has significant influence over another. This type of investment is known as an associate of the holding company and the required method of accounting is not to consolidate the associate but to use equity accounting.

At the end of this chapter you should have learned the following topics.

- Control and significant influence.
- Equity accounting.

---

1 CONTROL AND SIGNIFICANT INFLUENCE

1.1 Introduction

Where a company controls another company, the CA85 and FRS 2 require group accounts. The law in effect recognises the control which a parent company may exert over a subsidiary company and the existence of an economic unit, the **group**. If a parent company's accounts were to show only dividends received or receivable from subsidiaries, the shareholders of the parent company would not be given sufficient information regarding the underlying profitability of the unit, the group. Consequently, group accounts normally include the parent company's share of the post-acquisition profits of subsidiaries in the consolidated financial statements.

However, if a company, H Ltd, which has subsidiaries, owns (say) 40% of the ordinary share capital of another company, A Ltd, then A Ltd may not come within the legal definition of subsidiary company as it may not be controlled. H Ltd **may** nevertheless be able to exert considerable influence over A Ltd. It would thus seem sensible to allow H Ltd to show information in its accounts about its share of the profits of A Ltd.

1.2 FRS 9: Associates and joint ventures

FRS 9 provides rules for accounting for associated companies, ie, companies which fall into the position described above.

The CA89 introduced into law the requirement for associated **undertakings** to be included in group accounts under the **equity** method. The equity method is the method detailed by FRS 9.

The term **undertakings** includes companies and unincorporated businesses. As the CA89 requires the word 'undertaking' to be used in the published accounts, the rest of this section will follow the CA89 terminology, where it is sensible to do so.

1.3   **What is an 'associated undertaking'? - company law**

An associated undertaking will come within the definition of a **participating interest** in the investing company's **individual** accounts.

> **Definition**   A participating interest is an interest held in the shares of another undertaking, held for the long term, with a view to exercising control or influence to secure a benefit to the investor's own activities. Where an investor holds 20% or more of the shares there is a presumption that this is a participating interest.

In the group accounts participating interests are split into **interests in associated undertakings** and **other participating interests**.

> **Definition**   An associated undertaking means an undertaking in which an undertaking included in the consolidation has a **participating interest** and over whose operating and financial policy it exercises a significant influence, and which is not –
>
> (i)   a subsidiary undertaking, or
>
> (ii)   a joint venture dealt with in the group accounts by proportional consolidation (NB Only **unincorporated** undertakings can be dealt with using proportional consolidation).

Where an undertaking holds 20 per cent or more of the voting rights in another undertaking, it shall be presumed to exercise such an influence over it unless the contrary is shown.

To summarise, most participating interests are associated undertakings. The difference between the two terms mainly relates to the type of share capital held. A participating interest arises when 20% of **any** type of share capital is held. An associated undertaking requires a 20% or more **equity** voting shareholding.

1.4   **What is an associated undertaking? - FRS 9**

The FRS 9 definition is quite complex, but is essentially similar to the company law definition.

> **Definition**   An **associate** is an entity (other than a subsidiary) in which another entity (the investor) has a **participating interest** and over whose operating and financial policies the investor exercises a **significant influence**.

> **Definition**   A **participating interest** is an interest held in the shares of another entity on a long term basis for the purpose of securing a contribution to the investor's activities by the exercise of control or influence arising from or related to that interest.

> **Definition**   The exercise of **significant influence** means that the investor is actively involved and is influential in the direction of its investee through its participation in policy decisions covering aspects of policy relevant to the investor, including decisions on strategic issues such as:
>
> (a)   the expansion or contraction of the business, participation in other entities or changes in products, markets and activities of its investee;
> and
>
> (b)   determining the balance between dividend and reinvestment.

The main thing to note is that the emphasis of the FRS 9 definition is different to that in the Companies Act. Under the Companies Act, a holding of 20% or more is presumed to be an associate unless it can clearly be demonstrated otherwise. The FRS 9 definition centres on the actual substance of the relationship between the parties (ie, whether significant influence is exercised in practice) rather than its strict legal form (the size of the shareholding).

In practice, an investing company's ability to exercise significant influence depends on the other shareholdings as well as its own. For example, if A Ltd holds 30% of the shares in B Ltd, but the remaining 70% of the shares in B Ltd are held by C plc, then A Ltd is extremely unlikely to be able to exercise significant influence over B Ltd.

However, in questions you should assume that a shareholding of between 20% and 50% should be treated as an associate unless you are given information which suggests otherwise.

> **Conclusion**   A company is an associated undertaking if the investing company is able to exercise significant influence over it. A shareholding of between 20% and 50% normally gives significant influence.

2   EQUITY ACCOUNTING

2.1   Introduction

If one company is deemed to be an associate of another company then in the other company's consolidated accounts the associate should be included using the equity method of accounting.

2.2   Equity accounting in the consolidated balance sheet

> **Conclusion**   **Equity accounting** is a method of accounting that brings an investment into its investor's financial statements initially at its cost, identifying any goodwill arising. The carrying amount of the investment is adjusted in each period by the investor's share of the results of its investee less any amortisation or write-off for goodwill, the investor's share of any relevant gains or losses, and any other changes in the investee's net assets including distributions to its owners, for example, by dividend.

This means that in the consolidated balance sheet the investment in the associate is stated as a fixed asset "interest in associated undertaking" or 'investment in associate' at the following value:

	(i)	cost
plus	(ii)	group share of retained post-acquisition profits
less	(iii)	amounts written off.

Assuming goodwill, or premium on acquisition, has been fully written off, this will be equal to the investing company's share of net assets in the associate.

Note that this method of accounting is only used in the consolidated accounts.

2.3   Activity

E plc acquired 25% of the ordinary share capital of A plc for £640,000 when the reserves of A plc stood at £720,000. The premium on acquisition has all been written off to the profit and loss account. E plc appointed two directors to the board of A plc and the investment is regarded as long term. Both companies prepare accounts to 31 December each year. The summarised balance sheet of A plc on 31 December 19X4 is as follows

	£'000
Sundry net assets	2,390

Capital and reserves

Called up share capital	800
Share premium	450
Profit and loss account	1,140
	2,390

A plc has made no new issues of shares nor has there been any movement in the share premium account since E plc acquired its holding.

Show at what amount the investment in A plc will be shown in the consolidated balance sheet of E plc as on 31 December 19X4.

2.4   Activity solution

The final amount can be shown in a ledger account:

Investment in associated undertaking

	£		£
Cost	640,000	Goodwill (W1)	147,500
Group share of post acquisition reserves			
25% × £(1,140 − 720)	105,000	Balance c/d	597,500
	745,000		745,000

or in vertical form:

	£
Cost	640,000
Group share of post acquisition shares 25% × (1,140 − 720)	105,000
Less: Goodwill (W1)	(147,500)
	597,500

WORKINGS

(1)   Goodwill

	£	£
Cost		640,000
Less: Share of net assets at acquisition		
Share capital	800,000	
Share premium	450,000	
Reserves	720,000	
25% ×	1,970,000	(492,500)
Goodwill		147,500

Alternatively the same figure can be calculated as the group share of the associate's net assets at the balance sheet date:

25% × £2,390,000	597,500

Conclusion   In the consolidated balance sheet of a group any associated undertakings will appear as fixed assets 'interest in associated undertakings' at cost, plus group share of retained post-acquisition profits, less goodwill amortised.

In the holding company's individual balance sheet they will appear simply at cost.

2.5   Equity accounting in the consolidated profit and loss account

In the consolidated profit and loss account the group share of the following are brought in under equity accounting:

(i)   operating profit
(ii)   interest receivable and payable (disclosed separately)
(iii)   exceptional items
(iv)   taxation.

2.6   Activity

Continuing with the two companies used in the previous activity the consolidated profit and loss account of E plc (before including any amounts for A plc) and the profit and loss account of A plc for the year ended 31 December 19X4 are as follows

	E plc £'000	A plc £'000
Turnover	11,000	4,000
Cost of sales	(6,500)	(3,000)
Gross profit	4,500	1,000
Distribution costs	(1,000)	(400)
Administrative expenses	(700)	(300)
Profit on ordinary activities before taxation	2,800	300
Taxation	(1,200)	(60)
Profit on ordinary activities after taxation	1,600	240
Minority interests	(300)	-
Profit attributable	1,300	240
Dividends proposed	(300)	(50)
Retained	1,000	190
Retained b/d	6,300	950
Retained c/d	7,300	1,140

Show the amounts to be included in the consolidated profit and loss account of E plc for the year ended 31 December 19X4.

2.7   Activity solution

	£'000	£'000
Turnover		11,000
Cost of sales		(6,500)
Gross profit		4,500
Distribution costs		(1,000)

Administrative expenses	(700)
Group operating profit	2,800
Share of operating profit in associate (25% × £300)	75
Profit on ordinary activities before taxation	2,875

Taxation – group	(1,200)	
– associate (25% × £60)	(15)	(1,215)

Profit on ordinary activities after taxation	1,660
Minority interests	(300)
Profit attributable to the members of E plc	1,360
Dividends	(300)
Retained	1,060
Retained at 1 January 19X4 (W1)	6,210
Retained at 31 December 19X4	7,270

WORKINGS

(1)   Retained profit b/d

	£'000
E plc	6,300
A plc group share of post acquisition profit b/d	
25% × (950 – 720)	58
Less: Goodwill written off (per previous activity)	(148)
	6,210

Conclusion   In the consolidated profit and loss account there are four main entries for an associated undertaking.

- group share of operating profit
- group share of interest receivable/payable (if any)
- group share of exceptional items (if any)
- group share of tax.

This will mean that the group share of the associate's profit after tax is effectively brought in. All that needs to be added is the group share of the associate's reserves brought forward.

3   SELF TEST QUESTIONS

1   Which FRS deals with associated companies? (1.2)

2   How does the CA89 define a participating interest? (1.3)

3   How does the CA89 define an associated undertaking? (1.3)

4   How does FRS 9 define an associated undertaking? (1.4)

5   How does FRS 9 define significant influence? (1.4)

6   How is an associated undertaking included in a consolidated balance sheet? (2.2)

7   How is an associated undertaking included in the holding company's individual balance sheet? (2.4)

8   How is an associated undertaking included in the consolidated profit and loss account? (2.5)

22 CONSOLIDATION PRINCIPLES

PATHFINDER INTRODUCTION

This chapter covers the following performance criteria and knowledge and understanding.

- •   Draft accounts comply with domestic standards and legislation (performance criteria 10.2)
- •   Application of the general principles of consolidation (knowledge and understanding 10.2)

Putting the chapter in context – learning objectives.

In this final chapter some of the theory and principles behind the consolidation techniques covered in the previous chapters is considered. In particular although this text has concentrated on consolidation techniques and equity accounting an awareness of other methods of producing group accounts is also required. However the required form of group accounts in the UK is consolidated accounts and this chapter briefly covers the definitions and requirements of FRS 2 and CA89, the accounting and legal framework for group accounts. The type of consolidation technique that has been learnt in this text is acquisition accounting. There is a lesser used alternative form of consolidation known as merger accounting. An awareness of the existence and use of merger accounting is all that is required for this syllabus.

At the end of this chapter you should have learned the following topics.

-     Different methods which could be used to prepare group accounts.
-     Consolidated accounts – FRS 2 and CA 1989.
-     Exemptions and exclusions from consolidated accounts.
-     Business combinations.

1   THE DIFFERENT METHODS WHICH COULD BE USED TO PREPARE GROUP ACCOUNTS

1.1   Meaning of group accounts

The *CA85* (as amended by the *CA89*), *FRS 2* and *FRS 6* require a parent company to prepare **group** accounts, which must normally be **consolidated** accounts comprising a consolidated balance sheet and a consolidated profit and loss account. The group accounts shall give a true and fair view of the companies included in the consolidation as a whole.

The use of the two terms above – group accounts and consolidated accounts – implies the terms are not the same. Group accounts can be defined as any set of information which gives information about the financial affairs of the group. Consolidated accounts are thus one form of group accounts.

In most circumstances consolidation presents group accounts in the most informative way. There are circumstances where consolidation may not be appropriate and the *CA85* and *FRS 2* allow/require non-consolidation. These situations are dealt with later in this chapter.

At this point we briefly consider the alternative forms in which group accounts could, **theoretically**, be prepared.

1.2   Consolidated financial statements under the entity concept

This is by far the most common form of group accounts. Consolidated financial statements are prepared by replacing the cost of investments with the individual assets and liabilities underlying that investment. If the subsidiary is only partly owned this does not affect the amount of assets and liabilities of the subsidiary which are consolidated, but results in the need to show the minority shareholders' interest in those net assets.

> [Definition]   The entity concept focuses on the existence of the group as an **economic** unit rather than looking at it only through the eyes of the dominant shareholder group. It concentrates on the resources controlled by the entity.

The two forms of consolidation under this concept are **acquisition** accounting (the usual method you have seen in the previous chapters) and **merger** accounting (suitable in rare circumstances as explained later in this chapter).

1.3   Accounting for subsidiaries under the equity method

Under the equity method group accounts record the share of profits attributable to the parent company from the subsidiary and the parent company's **share** in the net assets of the subsidiary. Thus, minority shareholders' interest in the net assets are not shown.

The equity method is required to be used in certain circumstances by *FRS 2* where consolidation would give a misleading view. The equity method is **not** a method of consolidation but a different form of presenting group accounts.

1.4   Consolidated financial statements under the proprietary concept

This is different from the entity concept only where there are minority interests.

The proprietary concept emphasises ownership through the controlling shareholding and produces accounts primarily for the shareholders of the parent company.

There are two main variants:

(i)   the **parent company** concept which in terms of the mechanics of consolidation is similar to the entity concept except that minority interests are shown as quasi-liabilities;

(ii)   the **proportional consolidation** method in which only the group share of individual assets and liabilities are included in the relevant group totals. Thus minority shareholders' interest in the net assets is not shown.

1.5   Separate accounts for the parent company and its subsidiary/ies

It has been argued that in complex groups consolidated accounts are too all-embracing to be of any value and can, by setting off and consolidating unlike items, produce a misleading impression of the group's activities. In such a situation, the disclosure of the separate accounts of the companies within the group may give a more meaningful picture of the group.

Conclusion   **Chart of possible alternative methods of presenting group accounts**

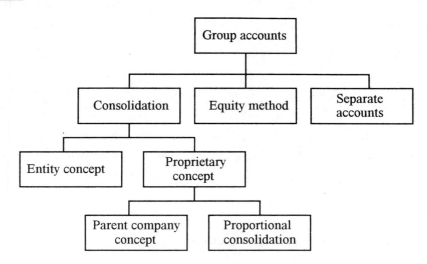

1.6   Comparison of consolidation and equity methods

The two main techniques that have been studied are acquisition accounting (consolidation) and equity accounting. These can now be compared:

1.7   Activity

The separate summarised accounts for the year to 31 December 19X2 of P and S are:

Balance sheets as at 31 December 19X2

	P £	S £
Share capital	2,000	1,000
Reserves	3,000	2,000
Long-term debt	-	8,000
	5,000	11,000
Fixed assets	2,200	10,000
Cost of investment	1,800	-
Net current assets	1,000	1,000
	5,000	11,000

Profit and loss accounts for year ended 31 December 19X2

	P £	S £
Sales	4,000	20,000
Cost of sales	3,500	18,900
Operating profit	500	1,100

Interest payable	-	800
	500	300
Tax	270	160
Retained profit for year	230	140

P acquired an 80% interest in S four years ago when the reserves of S were £500.

Show the group balance sheets and profit and loss accounts under the consolidation method, the equity method, and the proportional consolidation methods. Assume that goodwill is written off in equal instalments over six years.

1.8   Activity solution

Step 1   **Goodwill** - This will be the same under each method,

	£
Share capital and reserves of S at acquisition	1,500
P Ltd share 80% × £1,500	1,200
Cost of investment	1,800
Goodwill	600
Less: Written off after four years	400
	200

Step 2   **Minority interest at 31 December 19X2** - only included under the consolidation method.

	£
Net assets of S Ltd at 31 December 19X2 (11,000 – 8,000)	3,000
Minority share	20%
	600

Step 3   **Group reserves** - The same amount of profit is dealt with under any of the methods.

	£
P Ltd	3,000
S Ltd 80% £(2,000 – 500)	1,200
	4,200
Less: Goodwill written-off	400
	3,800

Group balance sheet of P Ltd and subsidiary as at 31 December 19X2

	Consolidation £	Equity £	Proportional consolidation £
Net assets			(80%)
Fixed assets	12,200	2,200	10,200
Goodwill arising on acquisition of investment in subsidiary	200	200	200
Share of net assets in subsidiary (80% × £3,000) (equity only)	-	2,400	-
Net current assets	2,000	1,000	1,800
	14,400	5,800	12,200
Capital employed			
Share capital	2,000	2,000	2,000
Reserves	3,800	3,800	3,800
	5,800	5,800	5,800
Minority interests (consolidation only)	600	-	-
Long-term debt	8,000	-	6,400
	14,400	5,800	12,200

Group profit and loss accounts of P Ltd for the year ended 31 December 19X2

	Consolidation £	Equity £	Proportional consolidation £ (80%)
Sales	24,000	4,000	20,000
Cost of sales	22,400	3,500	18,620
Operating profit	1,600	500	1,380
Share of profit of subsidiary (80% × £300)		240	
Interest payable	800		640
Goodwill written off	100	100	100
	700	640	640
Tax £(270 + 160)	430		
£(270 + (80% × 160))		398	398
	270	242	242
Minority interest 20% × £140	28		
Profit attributable to H Ltd Group	242	242	242

The group balance sheets are completely different in form, and give contrasting images of the financial stability of the group. The equity group balance sheet appears to show a safe state of affairs. The consolidated balance sheets, however, reveal the considerable long-term debt incurred by the subsidiary.

It is because the equity method fails to reveal the underlying assets and liabilities that its use is not regarded as a valid method of showing group accounts in the majority of situations, and it is therefore only used when, for some reason, consolidation is regarded as inappropriate. The equity method is, however, used in accounting for **associates**.

The proportional method of consolidation has not found favour in the UK as, although it does reveal the underlying assets and liabilities of the subsidiary, it implies that all the assets of the subsidiary are not under the control of the parent company.

2   CONSOLIDATED ACCOUNTS – FRS 2 AND CA 1989

2.1   Purpose of consolidated accounts

The CA85 requires group accounts to be in the form of consolidated accounts which give a 'true and fair' view.

FRS 2: **Accounting for subsidiary undertakings** states the purpose of consolidated accounts is to

'present financial information about a parent undertaking and its subsidiary undertakings as a single economic entity to show the economic resources controlled by the group, the obligations of the group and the results the group achieves with its resources.'

The first step, however, is to decide what constitutes a group.

2.2   Subsidiary undertaking definition

The CA89 extended the definition of a subsidiary beyond the previous (CA85) definition to implement the *EC Seventh Directive*. FRS 2 assists in interpreting the legal definition.

The definitions of a subsidiary under the old CA85 applied when either:

(a)   more than 50% of the equity shares were held; or
(b)   there was control over the composition of the board of directors.

These definitions caused difficulties mainly due to the possibilities of creating a dependent company which was not legally a subsidiary and which could then be used for various 'off balance sheet' activities.

The CA89 fundamentally changed the definitions and brought most of these dependent companies into the group accounts. It is important to note that the new definitions for accounting purposes refer to a subsidiary **undertaking** rather than a subsidiary company. A subsidiary undertaking may include a partnership or an unincorporated business.

[Definition]   An undertaking is the subsidiary of another undertaking where:

(a)   The parent holds a majority of the rights to vote at general meetings of the undertaking/company on all or substantially all matters; or

(b)   The parent is a member and has a right to appoint or remove directors having a majority of the rights to vote at board meetings of the undertaking/company on all or substantially all matters; or

(c)   The parent is a member and has the right to control alone a majority of the rights to vote at general meetings of the undertaking/company pursuant to an agreement with other shareholders; or

(d)   The parent has a right to exercise a **dominant influence** over the undertaking by virtue of provisions in the memorandum or articles or by a lawful contract; or

(e)   The parent has a **participating interest** and **actually exercises** a **dominant influence** or the parent and subsidiary undertaking **are managed on a unified basis**.

For definition (d) above the existence of a **dominant influence** is only deemed to apply if the parent has a right to give directions on operating or financial policies and the subsidiary directors are obliged to comply with those directions whether or not they are for the benefit of the subsidiary.

Definition   A **participating interest** means an interest in shares, held for the long term, to secure a contribution to its activities by the exercise of control or influence. A holding of 20% or more is presumed to be a participating interest unless the contrary can be shown.

FRS 2 gives guidance on the meaning of the CA89 definitions.

(i)   For definition (e) the result of the **actual exercise of dominant influence** is that major decisions will be taken in accordance with the wishes of the dominant party whether these are expressed or perceived. Two or more undertakings **are managed on a unified basis** if the whole of the operations are integrated and managed as a single unit. An interest should be considered as **held on a long-term basis** where it is held other than exclusively with a view to subsequent resale.

(ii)   For definition (d) the phrase **dominant influence** is defined in the Act and is a more restrictive definition than the interpretation given for **the actual exercise of dominant influence** in definition (e). FRS 2 makes it clear that they are two separate definitions.

2.3   Exemptions from consolidation

Exemptions from consolidation are allowed/required in various circumstances by CA89 and FRS 2. These are dealt with later.

2.4   Date of acquisition of subsidiary

The date for accounting for an undertaking becoming a subsidiary undertaking is the date on which **control** passes to its new parent. This ties in with the control concept being the dominant factor in defining a subsidiary.

2.5   Consolidation techniques

The CA89 introduced into the law various rules on consolidation accounting. FRS 2 confirms the rules or reduces the choice in some instances. There are three main areas:

(a)   **Accounting policies**

Uniform group accounting policies should be used for determining the amounts to be included in the consolidated financial statements. In exceptional cases different policies may be used with disclosure. Clearly if the aggregate figures are to make sense they should have been derived using common policies.

(b)   **Accounting periods and dates**

The accounts of all subsidiaries to be used in preparing consolidated financial statements should have the same financial year-end and be for the same accounting period as those of the parent company. Where the financial year of a subsidiary differs from that of the parent company, interim financial statements for that subsidiary prepared to the parent company's accounting date should be used. If this is impracticable, earlier financial statements of the subsidiary undertaking may be used, provided they are prepared for a financial year that ended not more than three months earlier.

(c)   Intra-group transactions

In the past there has been a variety of methods adjusting for the effect of intra-group transactions. Such transactions may result in profits or losses being included in the book value of assets in the consolidation. This has been dealt with in full in the consolidated balance sheet and profit and loss account chapter.

Conclusion   The parent/subsidiary relationship is defined by the Companies Act 1985 and by FRS 2 and exists where the parent controls the subsidiary.

The Companies Act and FRS 2 also require the preparation of group accounts in the form of consolidated accounts.

3   EXEMPTIONS AND EXCLUSIONS FROM CONSOLIDATION

3.1   Introduction

The CA89 and FRS 2 recognise certain situations in which either:

(a)   a parent company is exempted from preparing group accounts; or

(b)   a subsidiary should or may be excluded from consolidation with the rest of the group.

3.2   Exemptions for intermediate parent companies

An intermediate parent company is a company which has a subsidiary but is also itself a subsidiary of another company.

For example:

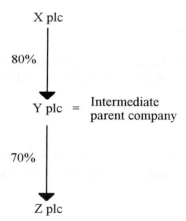

An intermediate parent company is exempt from the requirement to prepare group accounts if:

(a)   none of its securities is listed anywhere in the EC; and

(b)   its immediate parent company is incorporated in the EC;

providing that:

(a)   it is wholly owned by that immediate parent; or

(b)   its immediate parent holds more than 50% and notice for the preparation of group accounts has not been served from shareholders owning either more than one half of the remaining shares or 5% of the total shares.

Various detailed conditions apply for this exemption including the need for the intermediate parent company to be included in the group accounts of an EC parent. A copy of these accounts must be filed with the Registrar of Companies together with an English translation.

3.3   Exemptions for small and medium-sized groups

A parent company need not prepare group accounts if the group headed by that parent satisfies at least two of the following conditions:

Annual turnover	£13.44m gross or £11.2m net
Balance sheet assets	£6.72m gross or £5.6m net
Average employees	250

The 'gross' figures are those calculated prior to any consolidation adjustments whereas the 'net' figures are those after the consolidation adjustments, such as the elimination of intra-group balances, have been made. A company may satisfy the relevant limits on either a net or a gross basis or by a mixture of the two.

The purpose of allowing the calculations to be made using the higher gross figures is to prevent a parent company from having to prepare group accounts in order to discover that it does not need to prepare group accounts.

Surprisingly, if the accounting period is more or less than one year the turnover limit specified is **not** adjusted on a pro-rata basis as it is for individual company abbreviated accounts limits.

The right to the exemption from preparing group accounts does not apply if any company in the group is:

(a)   a public company; or
(b)   a banking or insurance company; or
(c)   a company authorised under the *Financial Services Act*.

3.4   Excluded subsidiaries

Under CA85 there are cases where subsidiary undertakings **need not** or **must not** be included in the consolidation. Where all of the subsidiaries fall within the exclusions, group accounts are not required.

FRS 2 is based on the premise that the value of the information provided by the consolidated accounts depends on the extent to which the information about the group is complete, ie, all undertakings are consolidated. Thus a subsidiary should only be excluded in **exceptional** circumstances. Where such exceptional circumstances are identified FRS 2 makes exclusions mandatory rather than optional.

(a)   Different activities

Subsidiaries **must be** excluded from consolidation where their activities are so different from other undertakings in the consolidation that their inclusion would be incompatible with the obligation to give a true and fair view. The exclusion does not apply merely because some of the undertakings are industrial, some commercial and some provide services or because they carry on industrial or commercial activities involving different products or providing different services.

This is the only mandatory exclusion under the *Companies Act*. However FRS 2 envisages this situation only in exceptional circumstances.

Where a subsidiary is excluded because of dissimilar activities, the group accounts should include separate financial statements for that subsidiary. They may be combined with the financial statements of other subsidiaries with similar operations if appropriate.

In the group accounts the investment in the subsidiary should be stated using the **equity method** of accounting.

(b)   **Materiality**

The Companies Act states that a subsidiary undertaking **may** be excluded from the consolidation where its inclusion is not material for the purpose of giving a true and fair view.

Two or more undertakings may be excluded on these grounds only if they are not material when taken together.

FRS 2 (like any Accounting Standard) does not deal with immaterial items and therefore does not cover this exclusion.

(c)   **Severe long-term restrictions**

A subsidiary **should** be excluded from the consolidation where severe long-term restrictions substantially hinder the exercise of the rights of the parent company over the assets or management of that undertaking.

Subsidiaries excluded from consolidation are to be treated as fixed asset investments. They are to be included at their carrying amount when the restrictions came into force, subject to any write down for impairment in value, and no further accruals are to be made for profits or losses of those subsidiary undertakings, unless the parent undertaking still exercises significant influence. In the latter case they are to be treated as associates.

(d)   **Disproportionate expense or undue delay**

In the CA85 a subsidiary **may** be excluded from the consolidation where the information necessary for the preparation of group accounts cannot be obtained without disproportionate expense or undue delay. Whether the expense is disproportionate or the delay undue should be judged in the context of that information to the group accounts.

FRS 2, however, states that neither reason can justify excluding a subsidiary.

(e)   **Temporary investment**

A subsidiary **should** be excluded from the consolidation where the interest of the parent company is held exclusively with a view to subsequent resale and the undertaking has not previously been included in consolidated group accounts prepared by the parent company.

The investment in the subsidiary will be shown as a **current asset** at the lower of cost and net realisable value.

3.5   Summary of exclusion rules

Reason	CA85	FRS 2	Treatment
Different activities	Mandatory	Mandatory (in exceptional circumstances only)	Equity accounting
Severe long-term restrictions	Optional	Mandatory	If restrictions in force at date of acquisition carry initially at cost. If restrictions came into force at a later date equity account at date when restrictions came into force. Consider need for provisions for impairment in value.
Immaterial	Optional	Not applicable	-
Disproportionate expense or undue delay	Optional	Not permissible	-
Temporary investment	Optional	Mandatory	Current asset at the lower of cost and NRV

Conclusion   The Companies Act 1985 and FRS 2 set out the instances in which a subsidiary may be excluded from consolidation:

- different activities
- severe long term restrictions
- temporary investment

A parent company may be exempt from preparing consolidated accounts. The most important exemption concerns 'small' groups.

4   BUSINESS COMBINATIONS

4.1   Acquisition and merger methods

Business combinations arise when one or more companies become subsidiaries of another company. Two different methods have been developed to account for business combinations – acquisition accounting and merger accounting.

The main criterion employed to determine the appropriate method or methods of accounting is whether or not the combination is based principally on a share for share exchange. Merger accounting is considered to be an appropriate method of accounting when two groups of shareholders continue, or are in a position to continue, their shareholdings as before but on a combined basis. Acquisition accounting is, therefore, required when there is a transfer of the ownership of at least one of the combining companies, and substantial resources leave the group as consideration for that transfer. Conversely, when only limited resources leave the group, merger accounting must be used.

> **Definition**   A **merger** is a business combination that results in the creation of a new reporting entity formed from the combining parties, in which the shareholders of the combining entities come together in a partnership for the mutual sharing of the risks and benefits of the combined entity and in which no party to the combination in substance obtains control over any other, or is otherwise seen to be dominant, whether by virtue of the proportion of the shareholders' rights in the combined entity, the influence of its directors or otherwise.

> **Definition**   An **acquisition** is a business combination that is not a merger.

FRS 6 *Acquisitions and mergers* deals only with accounting in the consolidated accounts and not with accounting in the individual company accounts (although some guidance is provided in an appendix to the standard). For this syllabus no details of the FRS 6 accounting treatment is required, only a basic understanding of when a combination is an acquisition or a merger.

4.2   Conditions necessary to apply merger accounting methods

Both the CA89 and FRS 6 allow merger accounting to be used only in specified circumstances. The CA89 rules were deliberately framed loosely anticipating that the ASB would issue a mandatory accounting standard to provide the detail. This has now been achieved by the issue of FRS 6.

4.3   CA89 conditions

(i)   The subsidiary was acquired by an arrangement providing for the issue of equity shares by the parent company or its subsidiaries;

(ii)   The group has obtained at least 90% of the 'relevant shares' (being shares with unrestricted rights to participate in distributions).

(iii)   The fair value of consideration given other than equity shares does not exceed 10% of the nominal value of the equity shares issued.

(iv)   The adoption of merger accounting complies with generally accepted accounting principles or practice.

It can be seen that condition (iv) anticipates the issue of FRS 6. Generally accepted accounting principles (GAAP) are enshrined in the accounting standards in issue at the time.

4.4   FRS 6 criteria

(i)   No party to the combination is portrayed as either acquirer or acquired, either by its own board or management or by that of another party to the combination.

(ii)   All parties to the combination participate in establishing the management structure for the combined entity and in selecting the management personnel, such decisions being made by consensus.

(iii)   The relative sizes of the combining entities are not so disparate that one party dominates the combined activity by virtue of its relative size.

(iv)   The consideration received by equity shareholders comprises primarily equity shares in the combined entity; any non-equity consideration must represent an immaterial proportion of the fair value of the consideration received by equity shareholders. Where one of the combining entities has, within the period of two years before the combination, acquired shares in another of the combining entities, the consideration for this acquisition should be taken into account in determining whether this criteria has been met.

(v)   No equity shareholders of any of the combining entities retain any material interest in the future performance of only part of the combined entity.

If a combination satisfies all five criteria, it is a merger and FRS 6 requires merger accounting to be used for the combination as long as this is not prohibited by companies legislation.

FRS 6 requires that all other business combinations must be accounted for using acquisition accounting.

4.5   Activity

P is a parent company about to make an offer to acquire another company S.

The initial proposal is to issue 1,000 ordinary shares of £1 each worth £3 per share together with £200 cash.

Demonstrate whether these proposals

(i)   meet the CA89 requirements for merger accounting

(ii)   meet the FRS 6 requirements for merger accounting

4.6   Activity solution

(i)   The proposals would not meet the requirements of CA89 as the cash element is more than 10% of the nominal value of the equity shares.

	Nominal value £	%
Equity shares 1,000 @ £1	1,000	100
Cash	200	20

(This problem could be overcome by P making a bonus issue of 1 for 1 held and then offering to issue 2,000 equity shares worth £1.50 each to the shareholders of S.

	Nominal value £	%
Equity shares 2,000 @ £1	2,000	100
Cash	200	10

However, the current proposals do not meet the CA89 requirements).

(ii)   As the proposals do not satisfy the statutory requirements, immediately it can be stated that they do not satisfy the FRS 6 requirements.

4.7   Consolidated accounts – acquisition accounting

Where a business combination is accounted for as an acquisition, the fair value of the purchase consideration should, for the purpose of consolidated financial statements, be allocated between the underlying net tangible and intangible assets other than goodwill, on the basis of the fair value to the acquiring company in accordance with the requirements of FRS 10.

Any difference between the fair value of the consideration and the aggregate of the fair values of the separable net assets including identifiable intangibles such as patents, licences and trade marks will represent goodwill, which should be accounted for in accordance with the provisions of FRS 10.

In an acquisition the results of the acquired company should be brought into the group accounts from the date of acquisition only.

Acquisition accounting is the form of consolidation studied in this text.

4.8   Consolidated accounts – merger accounting

In merger accounting it is not necessary to adjust the carrying values of the assets and liabilities of the subsidiary to fair value either in its own books or on consolidation. However, appropriate adjustments should be made to achieve uniformity of accounting policies between the combining companies.

In the group accounts for the period in which the merger takes place, the profits or losses of subsidiaries brought in for the first time should be included for the entire period without any adjustment in respect of that part of the period prior to the merger. Corresponding amounts should be presented as if the companies had been combined throughout the previous period and at the previous balance sheet date.

A difference may arise on consolidation between the carrying value of the investment in the subsidiary (which will normally be the nominal value of the shares issued as consideration plus the fair value of any additional consideration) and the nominal value of the shares transferred to the issuing company.

(a)   Where the carrying value of the investment is less than the nominal value of the shares transferred, the difference should be treated as a reserve arising on consolidation.

(b)   Where the carrying value of the investment is greater than the nominal value of the shares transferred, the difference is the extent to which reserves have been in effect capitalised as a result of the merger and it should therefore be treated on consolidation as a reduction of reserves.

Conclusion   Acquisition accounting is the most common form of accounting for consolidated financial statements. It is based upon the principle that the holding company has acquired the subsidiary and therefore any pre-acquisition profits are capitalised and there may be goodwill on the acquisition.

Inn contrast a merger is fairly rare as it must meet both the CA89 and FRS 6 criteria and these criteria are based upon the premise that the two companies have merged as equal partners. Therefore in terms of the accounting there is no distinction between pre and post acquisition profits, no need to revalue the subsidiary's assets and no goodwill on consolidation.

5   SELF TEST QUESTIONS

1   Distinguish between the entity concept of consolidation and the proprietary concept. (1.2/1.4)

2   How does proportional consolidation work? (1.4)

3   How does equity accounting differ from consolidation? (1.2/1.3)

4   What are the five CA89 definitions of a subsidiary undertaking? (2.2)

5   What is meant by dominant influence when determining subsidiary status? (2.2)

6   What are the two reasons why a parent company may be exempted from preparing group accounts although it has subsidiary undertakings? (3.2/3.3)

7   If a subsidiary is excluded from consolidation on the grounds of severe long term restrictions what is the appropriate accounting treatment for this subsidiary? (3.4)

8   If a subsidiary is excluded from consolidation on the grounds of it being only a temporary investment what is the appropriate accounting treatment for this subsidiary? (3.4)

9   What is the definition of a merger for accounting purposes? (4.1)

10   What are the CA89 and FRS 6 criteria for merger accounting to be adopted? (4.3/4.4)

AAT

HOTLINES
Telephone: 0181 844 0667
Enquiries: 0181 831 9990
Fax: 0181 831 9991

AT FOULKS LYNCH LTD
Number 4, The Griffin Centre
Staines Road, Feltham
Middlesex TW14 0HS

Intended Examination Date: Dec 99 ☐ June 2000 ☐		Textbooks	Workbooks	Distance Learning UK MAINLAND ONLY
Foundation		*Combined textbook and workbook*		
Unit 1	Cash Transactions	£9.95 ☐	£9.95 ☐	£85 ☐
Unit 2	Credit Transactions	£9.95 ☐	£9.95 ☐	£85 ☐
Unit 3	Payroll	£9.95 ☐	£9.95 ☐	£85 ☐
Unit 19	Data Processing	£9.95 ☐ *		£85 ☐
Units 21 - 25	The Business Background	£9.95 ☐ *		£40 ☐
Foundation Level Distance Learning Course				£360 ☐
Intermediate				
Unit 4	Financial Records & Preparing Accounts	£9.95 ☐	£9.95 ☐	£95 ☐
Unit 5	Recording Cost Information	£9.95 ☐	£9.95 ☐	£95 ☐
Unit 6	Preparing Reports and Returns	£9.95 ☐	£9.95 ☐	£95 ☐
Unit 20	Using Information Technology	£9.95 ☐ *		£95 ☐
Unit 22	Health and Safety	£3.95 ☐ *		Option-FOC** ☐
Intermediate Level Distance Learning Course			** When any other AAT DLC is purchased	£380 ☐

Technician *Notes:* Units 7, 8 and 9 are compulsory
Students choose 1 out of Units 10, 11, 12, 13 (only 10 available)   Students choose 3 out of Units 14, 15, 16, 17, 18

		Textbooks	Workbooks	Distance Learning
Units 7, 8 & 15	Cost Management, Resource Allocation and Evaluating Activities	£9.95 ☐	£9.95 ☐	
Unit 9	Managing Accounting Systems	£9.95 ☐	£9.95 ☐	Please contact us regarding availability
Unit 10	Drafting Financial Statements	£9.95 ☐	£9.95 ☐	
Unit 14	Cash Management and Credit Control	£9.95 ☐	£9.95 ☐	
Unit 16	Implementing Auditing Procedures	£9.95 ☐	£9.95 ☐	
Units 17 & 18	Business and Personal Taxation	£9.95 ☐	£9.95 ☐	

Technician Level Distance Learning Course (See notes above)				
P & P + Delivery	UK Mainland	£2.00/book	£2.00/book	Post Free
	NI, ROI & EU Countries	£5.00/book	£5.00/book	UK Mainland Only
	Rest of world standard air service	£10.00/book	£10.00/book	
	Rest of world courier service (tel number essential)	£22.00/book	£22.00/book	

SINGLE ITEM SUPPLEMENT: If you only order 1 item, INCREASE postage costs by £2.50 for UK, NI & EU Countries or by £15.00 for Rest of World Service

TOTAL	Sub Total £			
Less 23% tax relief for Distance Learning paid for by student only	£			
	Post & Packing £			
	Total £			

Payments in Sterling in London	Order Total £	

DELIVERY DETAILS
☐ Mr ☐ Miss ☐ Mrs ☐ Ms Other
Initials   Surname
Address

Postcode
Telephone   Deliver to home ☐

Company name
Address

Postcode
Telephone   Fax
Monthly report to go to employer ☐   Deliver to work ☐

PAYMENT
1 I enclose Cheque/PO/Bankers Draft for £_____
Please make cheques payable to AT Foulks Lynch Ltd.

2 Charge Mastercard/Visa/Switch A/C No:

Valid from: ☐☐☐☐   Expiry Date: ☐☐☐☐
Issue No: (Switch only) ☐☐
Signature   Date

DECLARATION
I agree to pay as indicated on this form and understand that AT Foulks Lynch Terms and Conditions apply (available on request). I understand that AT Foulks Lynch Ltd are not liable for non-delivery if the rest of world standard air service is used.

Signature   Date

Please Allow:	UK mainland	- 5-10 w/days	**Notes:**	All delivery times subject to stock availability. Signature required on receipt (except rest of world standard air service). Please give both addresses for Distance Learning students where possible.
	NI, ROI & EU Countries	- 1-3 weeks		
	Rest of world standard air service	- 6 weeks		
	Rest of world courier service	- 10 w/days		